1994

# THE NEW LITERARY CRITICISM
# AND THE NEW TESTAMENT

# THE NEW LITERARY CRITICISM
# AND THE NEW TESTAMENT

Edited by

Edgar V. McKnight

Elizabeth Struthers Malbon

Trinity Press International
Valley Forge, Pennsylvania

Trinity Press International
P.O. Box 851
Valley Forge, PA 19482-0851

Originally published by JSOT Press,
Sheffield, England
Typeset by Sheffield Academic Press
Cover art: St. Peter and St. John at the Beautiful Gate, Dürer
Cover design: Jim Gerhard

Library of Congress Cataloging-in-Publication Data
The new literary criticism and the New Testament / edited by Edgar V. McKnight,
Elizabeth Struthers Malbon.
        p.     cm.
Includes bibliographical references and indexes.
ISBN 1-56338-107-9 (alk. paper)
1. Bible. N.T.—Hermeneutics. 2. Bible as literature. 3. New Criticism.
I. McKnight, Edgar. II. Malbon, Elizabeth Struthers.
BS2331.N47   1994
225.6'6—dc20                                                      94-41734

Printed in the United States of America

94 95 96 97 98 99   6 5 4 3 2 1

In the beginning
(of all our work
as biblical literary critics)
were the words
of Amos Niven Wilder
(1895–1993):

'If the naming of things
is equivalent to
their being called into being,
we find ourselves
on the same ground
with the Genesis account
of the creation.
God spoke and it was done.
Such is the power
of the word...
In the idea
of the creative word
not only is reason implicit
but mutuality and dialogue'
(1964: 14).

Thus to the memory
of this man
and in honor
of his work,
in mutuality and dialogue,
we dedicate
this work,
our words.

## CONTENTS

ACKNOWLEDGMENTS

The publishers are grateful to the following for permission to reproduce copyright material: Mauritshuis, The Hague, for *The Anatomy Lesson of Dr Nicolas Tulp* by Rembrandt; Lea & Febiger, Malvern, PA, for the diagram of the eyeball from Gray's *Anatomy of the Human Body* (ed. C.M. Goss; 29th edn, 1973), p. 1045; Augsburg Fortress, Minneapolis, MN, for the 'eye-agram' from *Anatomy of the Fourth Gospel* by R. Alan Culpepper (Fortress Press, 1983); Cornell University Press, Ithaca, NY, for the diagram from *Story and Discourse: Narrative Structure in Fiction and Film* by Seymour Chatman (Cornell University Press, 1978).

# ABBREVIATIONS

| | |
|---|---|
| AB | Anchor Bible |
| *AJT* | *American Journal of Theology* |
| AnBib | Analecta biblica |
| *ANRW* | *Aufstieg und Niedergang der römischen Welt* |
| BDF | F. Blass, A. Debrunner and R.W. Funk, *A Greek Grammar of the New Testament* |
| BETL | Bibliotheca ephemeridum theologicarum lovaniensium |
| BEvT | Beiträge zur evangelischen Theologie |
| BHT | Beiträge zur historischen Theologie |
| *Bib* | *Biblica* |
| *BTB* | *Biblical Theology Bulletin* |
| BZNW | Beihefte zur *ZNW* |
| *CBQ* | *Catholic Biblical Quarterly* |
| *CH* | *Church History* |
| *CR* | *Critical Review of Books in Religion* |
| EKKNT | Evangelisch-Katholischer Kommentar zum Neuen Testament |
| *ETL* | *Ephemerides theologicae lovanienses* |
| HTKNT | Herders theologischer Kommentar zum Neuen Testament |
| *HTR* | *Harvard Theological Review* |
| ICC | International Critical Commentary |
| *IDB* | G.A. Buttrick (ed.), *Interpreter's Dictionary of the Bible* |
| *IDBSup* | *IDB*, Supplementary Volume |
| *Int* | *Interpretation* |
| *JAAR* | *Journal of the American Academy of Religion* |
| *JBL* | *Journal of Biblical Literature* |
| *JR* | *Journal of Religion* |
| *JSNT* | *Journal for the Study of the New Testament* |
| JSNTSup | *Journal for the Study of the New Testament*, Supplement Series |
| *JSOT* | *Journal for the Study of the Old Testament* |
| JSOTSup | *Journal for the Study of the Old Testament*, Supplement Series |
| *LB* | *Linguistica Biblica* |
| LCL | Loeb Classical Library |
| NCB | New Century Bible |
| *Neot* | *Neotestamentica* |
| *NovT* | *Novum Testamentum* |
| NovTSup | *Novum Testamentum* Supplements |
| NTAbh | Neutestamentliche Abhandlungen |
| *NTS* | *New Testament Studies* |
| PTMS | Pittsburgh Theological Monograph Series |

| | |
|---|---|
| *RB* | *Revue biblique* |
| *RelSRev* | *Religious Studies Review* |
| *RHPR* | *Revue d'historie et de philosophie religieuses* |
| *RSR* | *Recherches de science religieuse* |
| SANT | Studien zum Alten und Neuen Testament |
| SBB | Stuttgarter biblische Beiträge |
| SBL | Society of Biblical Literature |
| SBLDS | SBL Dissertation Series |
| SBLMS | SBL Monograph Series |
| SBLSP | SBL Seminar Papers |
| SBS | Stuttgarter Bibelstudien |
| SNTSMS | Society of New Testament Studies Monograph Series |
| *TDNT* | G. Kittel and G. Friedrich (eds.), *Theological Dictionary of the New Testament* |
| THKNT | Theologischer Handkommentar zum Neuen Testament |
| *TLZ* | *Theologischer Literaturzeitung* |
| *TRev* | *Theologische Revue* |
| *TRu* | *Theologische Rundschau* |
| *TZ* | *Theologische Zeitschrift* |
| WBC | Word Biblical Commentary |
| WMANT | Wissenschaftliche Monographien zum Alten und Neuen Testament |
| *ZNW* | *Zeitschrift für die neutestamentliche Wissenschaft* |

## Contributors to this Volume

Janice Capel Anderson
Department of Philosophy
University of Idaho
Moscow, Idaho

William A. Beardslee
Emeritus, Department of Religion
Emory University
Atlanta, Georgia

Elizabeth A. Castelli
Department of Religious Studies
Occidental College
Los Angeles, California

John A. Darr
Department of Theology
Boston College
Chestnut Hill, Massachusetts

Joanna Dewey
Episcopal Divinity School
Cambridge, Massachusetts

John R. Donahue, SJ
The Jesuit School of Theology at Berkeley
Berkeley, California

Elizabeth Struthers Malbon
Religious Studies Program
Virginia Polytechnic Institute and State University
Blacksburg, Virginia

Edgar V. McKnight
Department of Religion
Furman University
Greenville, South Carolina

Stephen D. Moore
Department of Religion
Wichita State University
Wichita, Kansas

Gary A. Phillips
Religion Department
College of the Holy Cross
Worcester, Massachusetts

Tina Pippin
Department of Bible and Religion
Agnes Scott College
Decatur, Georgia

Vernon K. Robbins
Department of Religion
Emory University
Atlanta, Georgia

Dan O. Via
Emeritus, The Divinity School
Duke University
Durham, North Carolina

Antoinette Clark Wire
San Francisco Theological Seminary
San Anselmo, California

INTRODUCTION

Elizabeth Struthers Malbon and Edgar V. McKnight

*The New Literary Criticism and the New Testament* presents a sampling
of the rich variety of critical methodologies employed in contemporary
literary study of the New Testament. Current New Testament study is
the heir of the historical-critical tradition in biblical study, giving attention to such factors as the history recounted in the texts and the historical contexts out of which the texts grew. But contemporary New
Testament criticism is also heir to the new-critical literary tradition, giving
attention to the literary text as an autonomous object to be judged in
terms of intrinsic criteria, and heir as well to the plethora of post-new-
critical approaches that revive attention to 'extrinsic' factors such as
history, biography, ideology and politics—not as isolated phenomena but
as a part of the literary field. This diverse heritage contributes to the
current multiplicity of literary approaches to the New Testament.

Ideas and approaches that are relegated to the periphery of literary
criticism in one epoch become the dominant concern in another. But in
time, these concerns move to the periphery and other concerns become
dominant. In 1958 M.H. Abrams could illuminate the history and
practice of criticism in terms of the dominance of one of the four
elements in the comprehensive situation of a work of art: the work, the
artist, the universe imitated in the work, and the audience. In the classical
period the focus was on *the universe* imitated in the work, following
primarily the mimetic theories of Plato and Aristotle. Horace's dictum
that 'the poet's aim is either to profit or to please, or to blend in one the
delightful and the useful' united the classical theory of rhetoric with
literary criticism, and pragmatic theories (focused on the effect on *the
audience*) became dominant up through most of the eighteenth century.
With romanticism, expressive theories developed, and the literary work
of art was seen as the expression of the thought and feeling of the poet
(*the artist*) or it was defined in terms of the process of imagination that
utilizes the images, thoughts and feelings of the poet. Objective theories

(focused on *the work*) became dominant in the mid-twentieth century.
New Criticism, for example, approached the literary work in terms of
the work itself as an autonomous object, to be judged in terms of
'intrinsic criteria', such as coherence, integrity, equilibrium, complexity
and the relationships of the parts of the work to each other and to the
work as a whole.

The earliest phase of contemporary literary study of New Testament
texts took place against the background of the alliance in the mid-
twentieth century of older historicists and New Critics. This alliance
supported graduate and undergraduate programs that combined training
in close reading with historical 'coverage'. Although specialties existed
in literary study, general familiarity with the material of the entire field
was expected. Early attempts to correlate biblical study with these
formalist/historical literary studies were less problematic than today's
attempts (although perhaps less interesting).

Amos N. Wilder was a pioneer whose early literary approaches to
New Testament texts continue to inform students of the New Testament,
and for this reason this collection of essays is dedicated to his memory.
In his 1964 publication, *The Language of the Gospel*, Wilder approached
the New Testament as 'language event', an expression used by the New
Hermeneutic to reflect the idea that language and reality are inseparably
connected, that reality comes into being through language. He expounded
this New Testament 'language event' in terms of literary genre,
convinced that 'behind the particular New Testament forms [genres] lies
a particular life-experience and a language-shaping faith' (1964: 17).
Wilder explicitly criticized restriction of meaning to existential concepts
and/or to the structures and conventions of literature. There is reference
in the text, he argued, but the reference is not the same as that in
conventional study of the Gospels. Students of the New Testament can
learn about its literary language and reference from students of poetry:
'This kind of report of reality—as in a work of art—is more subtle and
complex and concrete than in the case of a discursive statement, and
therefore more adequate to the matter in hand and to things of
importance' (1964: 133). The work of Wilder was not immediately
accessible to Anglo-American New Testament scholarship because that
scholarship had not been powerfully influenced by Rudolf Bultmann's
existential hermeneutics and the New Hermeneutic. The exhaustion of
New Testament historical criticism in general in the late 1960s and
1970s, however, brought New Testament scholars to examine literary

resources, including European structuralist models of study akin to American New Criticism.

With the waning of Formalist-New Critical approaches in literary study, emphasis on the text in terms of language and discourse as the 'free play of signifiers' became an important factor in literary study in general and in New Testament literary study. Today changing patterns of reading in English and American literary studies are accompanied by changes in the organization of knowledge that defines the discipline of literary study. According to Steven Greenblatt and Giles Gunn,

> What confronts us at the present time...is not a unified field at all but diverse historical projects and critical idioms that are not organized around a single center but originate from a variety of sources, some of which lie outside the realm of literary study altogether and intersect one another often at strange angles (Greenblatt and Gunn 1992: 3).

Although no one critical ideology has achieved the dominance of New Criticism, many of the major critical schools share a 'hermeneutics of suspicion' that seems entirely natural and inevitable today, as did the New Criticism in its day. Just as New Criticism did not establish complete hegemony, the critical orientations associated with poststructuralism or postmodernism have not placed all things in doubt. Greenblatt and Gunn applaud the dialectical relationship between the old and the new: 'For the goal in literary studies is not to seal off the frontier completely but to keep it conceptually alive; what is sought are not closed boundaries but regulated thresholds, controlled passageways' (1992: 8).

The literary critic Brian McHale sees a modernism–postmodernism dialectic at work in literature in general, which has issued in a turn to ontological questions—albeit from a chastened epistemological perspective. This turn in literary criticism is the move from a dominance of epistemological concerns (modern) to a dominance of ontological concerns (postmodern). Modern questions have to do with knowledge: the object of knowledge, the subject of knowledge, the limits and certainty of knowledge, the transmission of knowledge, and so on. Postmodern questions concern the worlds projected by literary texts: What is a world? What kinds of worlds exist? How do they exist? What is a text? What is the mode of existence of worlds projected by texts? and so on (McHale 1987: 9-10).

The postmodern ontological turn, of course, is not a return to the attempt to ground this world in a foundational way. Rather, it acknowledges epistemological doubt, metalingual skepticism, indefiniteness, incompleteness...But it does not concentrate on these epistemological questions (as literary modernism—for example, New Criticism—did); it concentrates on the construction of worlds in the face of an understanding of language and discourse as the 'free play of signifiers'.

Literary approaches to the New Testament developed just at the time that literary criticism was moving beyond New Criticism and modernism. There has been a catch-up period during which New Testament literary criticism has recapitulated not only the classical approaches of literary study but also New Criticism's move away from an earlier historical or biographical explanation of texts and its attempt to deal with the text in terms of the work itself as an autonomous object. Literary criticism of the New Testament is now moving beyond the exclusion of 'extrinsic' concerns to the inclusion of such concerns as the reader (or audience), history, biography, sociology, theology and so on as part of literature. Contemporary literary criticism of the New Testament, then, does not ignore history and theology, but it does not treat history and theology (ideology) as did earlier New Testament studies. In an earlier period there was a sharp distinction between biblical studies and theology. Theology dealt with the questions of revelation and the sacred and constructed theological systems in conformity with philosophical assumptions and procedures. Biblical study, however, dealt with theological questions second-hand, distancing the text and the text's treatment of theological issues for 'objective' study and dealing with matters amenable to critical and historical analysis. Today history continues to be dealt with in literary studies of the New Testament, but not as the originating cause of the literary text. History itself is seen in literary terms. Theology also is dealt with in literary study, but in terms of literature and literary worlds and in light of the move from modernism to postmodernism.

Most of the essays in this volume are not radically postmodern or deconstructive, but they do share, in one way or another, a hermeneutics of suspicion. And even the most postmodern or deconstructive essays here utilize deconstruction not for nihilistic puposes but for making sense that is appropriate in a post-Enlightenment or postmodern epoch. Clearly the tradition of study represented in the essays in this volume lies beyond the mid-twentieth-century alliance of older historicists and New Critics at the conjunction of dynamic developments in biblical study and literary criticism that preclude simple correlation. The new literary criticism of the New Testament has proceeded and will proceed in fits and starts along many thoroughfares, follow many different by-ways, and run down numerous valleys, cul-de-sacs and indeed dead-ends. Like the ongoing approaches it seeks to present, this 'sampler' is incomplete. It is an open-ended invitation to challenge and affirm, to explore and extend work in progress.

The essay by John R. Donahue opens the collection of fourteen essays by chronicling the move from historical-critical (especially redaction-critical) and new-critical biblical and literary studies to contemporary literary study of the New Testament. Donahue asks whether the main street of redaction criticism has become a blind alley ('Redaction Criticism: Has the *Hauptstrasse* Become a *Sackgasse*?'), playing off the vocabulary of Norman Perrin, who in 1966 said that the *Wredestrasse* (concern with the theological nature of the evangelist in the style of Wrede) had become the *Hauptstrasse*. The important contribution of this essay is its finely nuanced tracing of the origin, development and transformation of redaction criticism. Donahue concludes that redaction criticism has become genuine literary criticism (as predicted by Perrin) but that the fundamental concern of redaction criticism for the historical contexts of the Gospels remains a part of most contemporary biblical criticism. In his opinion, the *Hauptstrasse* did not become a *Sackgasse* but a *Querstrasse* (a crossroad) where different methods continue to intersect.

Among the essays situated at that crossroad beyond redaction criticism, and illustrating especially the influence of New Criticism, is that of Elizabeth Struthers Malbon. With New Criticism, close reading and attention to the characters in the narrative became important. Cleanth Brooks and Robert Penn Warren specify that questions such as the following be asked in reading:

> What are the characters like?... What do they want?... Why do they do what they do?... What do their actions tell about their characters?... How are the characters related to each other?... How are the characters...related to the theme? (1943: 28).

In her essay on 'The Major Importance of the Minor Characters in Mark', Malbon makes a two-fold contribution: she examines characters in themselves and in relation to each other (not reducing them in the first instance to plot), and she examines minor characters with the attention normally reserved for major characters. But Malbon's concern for the implied audience moves beyond New Criticism's focus on 'the text' as an autonomous object. She argues that the minor characters, extending the continuum of potential responses to Jesus established by the major characters, provide a bridge from the text to the implied audience, and that stories of minor characters serve as 'narrative punctuation' (parentheses, exclamation points and colons), marking where the implied audience is to pause, reflect and connect.

A concern for the audience, as well as the influence of New Criticism's close reading of the text, also marks the contribution of John A. Darr. In his essay on '"Watch How You Listen" (Lk. 8.18): Jesus and the Rhetoric of Perception in Luke–Acts', Darr, a reader-response critic, argues that 'readers' of the Gospel of Luke (the general readers the author of Luke had in mind while writing the Gospel) are influenced in their own reading process by what Jesus says to his audience in the narrative. Darr's essay concentrates on Lk. 4.16-30 and 8.4-21, passages that are seen not only as programmatic for the plot and ideology of Luke–Acts but also as paradigmatic of the Lukan Jesus' repertoire on issues related to perception. Jesus' sayings about the immediacy of the revelation draw the reader into the story world and break down resistance and disbelief; his reference to Scripture helps control intertextual reading; and other sayings help link perception and the complex web of ethical values woven by Luke. Jesus' injunction to 'watch how you listen' is a challenge to examine how we live before God as well as a warning to monitor how we read the text.

The audience with which Janice Capel Anderson's essay is concerned is not 'implied' but 'real'—a significant sampling of real readers (interpreters) of Acts 9.36-42. Anderson's essay, 'Reading Tabitha', presents 'A Feminist Reception History'. She consciously writes in the tradition of feminist reader-response criticism. Following a brief review of feminist reader-response criticism, Anderson presents in her reception history representative readings from modern male biblical scholarship, male readings from church history, three late nineteenth-century/early twentieth-century women's readings, and several modern feminist scholars' readings. Among the insights Anderson draws from this reception history from the perspective of a feminist critic are that feminist biblical critics now have 'a tradition of our own', that this tradition oscillates between affirming 'equality' and affirming 'difference', and that it emphasizes the multiplicity of texts and readers.

Joanna Dewey also takes notice of a multiplicity of 'texts' and audiences, but her concern is with the first-century 'Gospels of Mark' and their first-century audiences. She sees the audiences of Mark as groups taking part in an oral performance of the Gospel narrative.

Dewey's essay on 'The Gospel of Mark as an Oral–Aural Event: Implications for Interpretation' shows how a recognition of the characteristics of narrative performed orally for and with nonliterate audiences helps us interpret aspects of Mark that have puzzled and divided biblical scholars. The essay both challenges and extends the work of literary scholars who read Mark as print narrative with the internal consistency and linear plot development characteristic of such narrative.

Vernon K. Robbins's essay on 'Socio-Rhetorical Criticism: Mary, Elizabeth and the Magnificat as a Test Case' seeks to incorporate with a close reading of a narrative segment (in the heritage of New Criticism) attention to historical, social and cultural information as an integral part of the text. Robbins presents socio-rhetorical criticism as an exegetically-oriented approach that gathers current practices of interpretation together in a new interpretative paradigm. Instead of seeing historical, social and cultural information as referring to data outside the text, such information is seen in intertextual relation to the signs in the text. And the text is seen as social, cultural, historical, theological and ideological discourse. Robbins traces the development of socio-rhetorical criticism from its beginnings with Amos N. Wilder's questioning of the basic nature of religious symbol and of symbolic discourse to its more developed form in the work of such scholars as John H. Elliott and Jerome H. Neyrey. Then he illustrates his own 'four texture' socio-rhetorical approach in a treatment of the account of Mary's encounter with the angel Gabriel and Elizabeth in the Gospel of Luke.

Rhetoric is also central to the analysis of Antoinette Clark Wire. Wire's essay, entitled '"Since God is One": Rhetoric as Theology and History in Paul's Romans', shows how the discipline of rhetoric allows attention to the text of Romans not only as literature but also as theology and history. Paul's announcement that the gospel is God's righteousness revealed from faith to faith is not seen by Wire as the programmatic theme of Romans, but as a part of the explanation of Paul's eagerness to tell the Romans the gospel. From a rhetorical perspective, Rom. 1.16–11.36 is a digression in an 'argument of explanation'. To understand Paul's argument of God's justice as an explanation of his Gentile gospel is at once a literary, historical and theological task. In Romans Paul used theological commitments that the Jews could not deny and remain recognizable as Jews to explain his Gentile gospel as integral to but distinct from Judaism. Historical and theological data are taken into account, then, without losing sight of the fact that the issue is the right reading of Paul's persuasion in the argument.

Multiple readings of Paul's allegory of Hagar are the concern of Elizabeth A. Castelli's essay, 'Allegories of Hagar: Reading Galatians 4.21-31 with Postmodern Feminist Eyes'. Working in the complex matrix formed by postmodernism, feminism and liberal biblical studies, Castelli seeks to understand Paul's allegorical rendering of the Hagar–Sarah–Abraham narrative of Genesis in light of both the persistence of the figure of Hagar in the collective imagination of the West and the interpretative character of allegory. In her work on this topic, Castelli's focus has shifted away from a post-Romantic indictment of allegorical readings as doing violence to innocent original texts, and towards reading allegory itself as undermining the fixed character of meaning—even as it insists upon it. She understands her postmodern feminist reading of allegory, and specifically the allegory of Hagar, as embedded in the paradox that is allegory—a rendering of truth that asserts that truth is always somewhere else, something other than where or what appears.

A postmodern feminist perspective is also manifest in the essay of Tina Pippin, 'Peering into the Abyss: A Postmodern Reading of the Biblical Bottomless Pit'. Pippin notes that the subject and method of her essay coincide: the abyss is an entry point into a strange and fragmented reading of the Apocalypse, a reading that is postmodern because it is not rooted in any historical-critical starting point. Traditional readings of the book of Revelation assert the final order of the end of time and God's victory over the forces of evil, but she argues that the text is unbound in its own disorder—that the New Jerusalem as an ordered space is decentered by the well of chaos, which is seen as the abyss, and the whole area outside the holy city where the evil powers still dwell (though in different states of punishment and tortured existence), making order tenuous at best. Pippin understands that the interpreter too stands in the abyss, that to say that in the Apocalypse of John the abyss means such-and-such is ultimately to say nothing. And yet...leaving the void intact creates the possibility of change.

New Criticism focused attention on the text as an autonomous verbal object with public meaning accessible to competent readers. Post-new-critical moves have questioned the autonomy of the text, emphasizing intertextuality, that is, the multiple ways in which a particular text is linked to other texts—by citation, allusion and participation in a common stock of literary conventions. The reading involved with such a view of a literary text allows the reader a large measure of creativity. Stephen D. Moore's essay is an intertextual 'performance' showing 'How Jesus' Risen Body Became a Cadaver'. His resources are the history of biblical and medical scholarship in general, and in particular R. Alan Culpepper's *Anatomy of the Fourth Gospel*, Henry Gray's *Anatomy of the Human Body* and Michel Foucault's *The Birth of the Clinic: An Archaeology of Medical Perception*. The reader who expects conventional historical-critical and/or literary analysis privileging the overt intention of authors has such expectations transformed as texts hook up across space and time independently of the intentions of their producers. Moore's essay, however, must not be viewed as a random, meaningless collection of texts. It is a collage in which dissimilar materials are combined to produce surprising and bizarre coincidences of overlapping in terms of the history and texts of biblical and medical scholarship.

Deconstruction, as intertextuality, questions new-critical assumptions about textual autonomy and public meaning accessible to competent readers. According to the theory of deconstruction no text is capable of representing in a determinate way (much less demonstrating) the 'truth' about its subject. Gary A. Phillips offers an understanding of deconstruction at odds with its conventional interpretation as unethical, irresponsible, self-serving and nihilistic in his essay on 'The Ethics of Reading Deconstructively, or Speaking Face-to-Face: The Samaritan Woman Meets Derrida at the Well'. To be sure, deconstruction aims not simply at disclosing what the biblical text says (its reference to the world and its common-sense nature as a sign signal), it also aims at disclosing a secondarity or otherness about the Bible. It is this aim that makes deconstruction ethical. This Other is not something reducible by means of an instrumental concept and use of language and text. The Other, in fact, names the event that escapes such human control. It is in a reader's active engagement with the text that response to the Other takes place. Phillips performs a reading of John 4 against the dominant tradition that regards the Samaritan woman as culturally and religiously other. He sees his responsibility 'to read John's text at face value, which means attending to the face of that woman/other traced within it and to read self-reflectively for my face reflected in the text'.

Edgar V. McKnight also treats the relationship between the conventional ways of discovering meaning in biblical texts and postmodern and deconstructive ways of making sense. McKnight's essay on 'A

Sheep in Wolf's Clothing: An Option in Contemporary New Testament Hermeneutics' examines the promise of literary criticism as a movement related to the hermeneutical tradition of Schleiermacher and Bultmann that may be used for the prolongation of the text in the life of contemporary readers. The meaning in the constructive moment is local, ad hoc and provisional and may be deconstructed in its turn; but the meaning is real. The goal and strategies of the radical reformers and modern-day feminist critics are paralleled with a literary-hermeneutical approach. Feminist literary study of New Testament texts is employed by McKnight to illustrate one way of extending the meaning and significance of New Testament texts hermeneutically.

Concern for hermeneutics and the influence of the Bultmannian tradition are also evident in Dan O. Via's essay on 'Matthew's Dark Light and the Human Condition'. Via's essay is generated by the question raised in the statement, 'The eye is the lamp of the body', the question about human being in principle (the ontological) and about the actual human condition (the ontic). He examines Mt. 6.22-23 as a grammatical-logical-philosophical structure, as a metaphorical structure and as a narrative structure, and concludes that human beings in principle have the capacity for a true vision of reality, the reality that in actual fact the light is darkness. Via's essay combines a close reading that gives attention to linguistic and literary rules and conventions, awareness and appreciation of the narrative structures emphasized by French structuralists, and a keen theological sensitivity.

William A. Beardslee's essay brings the collection to an appropriate close by returning to an old question from new perspectives. Beardslee's essay on 'What is it About? Reference in New Testament Literary Criticism' revisits the question of the 'aboutness' of the New Testament text. The assumption that the values of the world represented in the text are totally dependent upon the world created by the text or upon the point of view of the reader is challenged, and, therefore, also challenged is the present-day lack of concern with reference on the part of scholars who are nevertheless providing rich and varied studies of the New Testament from poetic and rhetorical perspectives. Beardslee claims that a literary approach to the question of non-literal language leads to the referential question if it is to do justice to the text. Beardslee sees the affirmations of the tradition, including the eschatological and apocalyptic forms of 1 Corinthians 15, as testimonies to experiences of value that are also at work in a wide range of experience. The soaring images of resurrection are all transformations of a more general structure of 'being remembered'. The text with its specific images can be interpreted in light of this wide range of possible expressions of the theme and the confidence that these transformations in their various ways all express a response to something real.

The new literary context for New Testament study authorizes and sustains a rich variety of methods and approaches—as evidenced in the essays in this volume. Awareness of the traditions of literary and New Testament study at work in the new context allows us to see ourselves as recipients of the gift of a rich heritage. As faithful heirs, however, we do not simply attempt to pass on intact one particular approach, one particular strand of the tradition. Even when we concentrate upon one critical methodology, we are aware of the interpenetration of methodologies, the interpenetration of world-views supporting those methodologies, and the socio-political contexts influencing those world-views. We are also aware of the local, ad hoc and provisional nature of our own contributions. Consciousness of the dialectic between the old and the new and between the different strands of the new makes us humble and proud, experimental and experienced. We recapitulate in ourselves the modern and the postmodern.

The essays in this volume are offered not only as a sample of contemporary methodologies but also as an example and model of goodwill and cooperation. The editors and writers have experienced this goodwill and cooperation in a variety of associations, in seminars in the Society of Biblical Literature and the Society for New Testament Studies, for example. What the editors of the companion volume, *The New Literary Criticism and the Hebrew Bible*, said about the spirit of goodwill in their endeavor has also been true of ours:

> [T]here appears a spirit of goodwill, cooperation even…Whatever the reason, the message these essays convey, however subliminally, is that there are no holds barred, and no automatically inappropriate angles of vision upon our texts—and that even in centres of institutional power there are no longer any arbiters of what may and may not be legitimately and fruitfully said about our texts (Exum and Clines 1993: 13).[1]

---

1. The 'Select Bibliography' in *The New Literary Criticism and the Hebrew Bible* (Exum and Clines 1993: 20-25) contains entries that are also pertinent for New Testament literary criticism. Bibliographies on the various approaches followed in the present volume are found at the conclusions of the essays.

The editors would emphasize the goodwill and cooperation of the authors of the essays in this volume. Our own perspectives and horizons have been challenged and expanded as we have entered into conversation with our colleagues about their essays. Our hope is that this conversation will continue to be productive as it moves through these essays into the wider world of New Testament study.

## BIBLIOGRAPHY

Abrams, M.H.
   1958        *The Mirror and the Lamp: Romantic Theory and the Critical Tradition*
               (New York: W.W. Norton).
Brooks, Cleanth, Jr and Robert Penn Warren
   1943        *Understanding Fiction* (New York: F.S. Crofts).
Exum, J. Cheryl and David J.A. Clines (eds.)
   1993        *The New Literary Criticism and the Hebrew Bible* (Sheffield: JSOT
               Press).
Greenblatt, Steven and Giles Gunn (eds.)
   1992        *Redrawing the Boundaries: The Transformation of English and
               American Literary Studies* (New York: The Modern Language
               Association of America).
McHale, Brian
   1987        *Postmodernist Fiction* (New York: Methuen).
Wilder, Amos N.
   1964        *The Language of the Gospel: Early Christian Rhetoric* (New York:
               Harper & Row).

REDACTION CRITICISM:
HAS THE *HAUPTSTRASSE* BECOME A *SACKGASSE*?

John R. Donahue, SJ

## The Journey of a Method

In 1966 Norman Perrin in an article with the intriguing title 'The *Wredestrasse* [Wrede Street] Becomes the *Hauptstrasse* [main street]' described *Redaktionsgeschichte* as the 'lusty infant' of form criticism (Perrin 1966: 298). For the next decade, until his early death in 1976, Perrin was a major mentor for this infant as it grew on American soil. In 1969 he offered a comprehensive definition of redaction criticism as an approach 'concerned with the theological motivation of an author as this is revealed in the collection, arrangement, editing, and modification of traditional material, and in the composition of new material or the creation of new forms within the traditions of early Christianity' (Perrin 1969: 1). Shortly before his death he commented that redaction criticism had developed in its own special way in the United States: '...it was necessary for redaction criticism to mutate into a genuine literary criticism, which it has done here in America' (1976: 120). Twenty years after he welcomed this lusty infant, Mary Ann Tolbert, a former student of Perrin, characterized redaction criticism as a 'transitional discipline [that] has led directly to the beginnings of more broadly conceived literary examinations of the Gospels on the one hand and to more sophisticated sociological analysis of the Gospels' communities on the other' (Tolbert 1989: 23).

The present essay will follow the journey of redaction criticism by commenting on its origin, development and contributions, by addressing some of its limitations, and by sketching some of its transformations as predicted by Perrin. Readers following this journey may wish to judge whether the 'main street' has become a blind alley (*Sackgasse*). Since a thorough survey of the results of redaction criticism is beyond the scope of the present essay, I will center on works that exemplify important aspects of *the method* (broadly conceived to include composition criticism). Initial attention will be given to the Gospel of Mark—which has been the subject of a disproportionate number of redaction-critical studies, and where conflict and reservations about the method have been most forcefully expressed. I will also mention significant directions in the study of Matthew and Luke and highlight the extension of redaction criticism in studies of Q and the Gospel of John.

Though a lusty infant in the United States in 1966, redaction criticism had developed earlier in Germany as both heir and successor to form criticism. As far as I can ascertain, the term 'Redaktionsgeschichte' (literally, the history of the editing), in reference to a new movement in New Testament studies, was coined by Willi Marxsen (1954) in a review of the work of Hans Conzelmann. Shortly thereafter Marxsen published his own study, *Der Evangelist Markus—Studien zur Redaktionsge-schichte des Evangeliums* (1956). The works of Conzelmann and Marxsen, along with the studies of Günther Bornkamm and his students Gerhard Barth and Heinz-Joachim Held (1960), and the overview of the method and its principal exemplars by Joachim Rohde (1966) provided an unofficial canon of works through which US graduate students in the late 60s and early 70s were introduced to redaction criticism. Though seen as a new direction in the late 1950s, redaction criticism has roots in earlier research. As the method emerges, its two principal features are stress on the Evangelist as author (not merely collector of traditions) and awareness that the Evangelist's literary activity is a key to his theology. Norman Perrin, as the title of his article suggests, viewed William Wrede as a precursor of redaction criticism, principally because Wrede broke with the 'Markan hypothesis' of nineteenth-century criticism, which viewed the Gospel as a collection of early reminiscences of Jesus. By analyzing the 'Messianic Secret' texts in Mark (e.g. 1.25, 34, 43-45; 3.12; 5.43; 7.36; 8.26, 30; 9.9), Wrede claimed that, though the motif came from Mark's inherited tradition, his use of these traditions is strongly theological. Wrede wrote: '...Mark too is already far removed from the actual life of Jesus and is dominated by views of a dogmatic kind. If we look at Mark through a large magnifying-glass, it may well be that we find a type of authorship such as is exhibited in John' (1971: 145).

Often overlooked in histories of the method is the work of B.W. Bacon (1860–1932), who taught at Yale from 1896 to 1928 (Harrisville 1976: 1-4). As early as 1909 Bacon spoke of 'the redactional treatment of

Mark by Matthew and Luke respectively', and noted that we must pay attention to 'their actual process of redaction' (1909b: 614). In his study of the Synoptic apocalypses (Mk 13, Mt. 24, Lk. 21) Bacon stated, 'we must distinguish between the intrinsic bearing of the parables themselves and the selection, order and adaptation made by Mark' (1909a: 5). Though Bacon recognized the editorial activity of the Evangelists and correlated this with their theological concerns, he was criticized both for the complexity of his reconstruction of the sources of the Gospels and for his often idiosyncratic proposals (Harrisville 1971: 88-91). During the 1930s Ernst Lohmeyer in Germany and R.H. Lightfoot in England called attention to the 'theological geography' of Mark, again undercutting the notion that geographical references are simply residues of historical reminiscence. Equally influential was the final major section of Bultmann's *History of the Synoptic Tradition*, 'The Editing (*Redaktion*) of the Traditional Material', where he noted the ways in which the Evangelists edited and incorporated the sayings and narrative material into their Gospels (1963: 347-400).

## Strict Editorial Criticism

As Perrin's description indicates, redaction criticism describes a complex of approaches to the text rather than a single unified method. The term is subsequently used in a double, and often confusing, sense. Narrowly conceived it means 'editorial criticism'. The more widely-used sense comprises composition criticism in which other activities, such as the arrangement of material and the creation of new material, are attributed to the Evangelists. As heir to form criticism in Germany it developed with a strong stress on the history of the traditions that lay behind a given work, Mark and Q in the case of Matthew and Luke, and reconstructed traditions in the case of Mark. (The vast majority of redaction critics have held the two-source theory.) In Germany the emphasis was predominantly on the separation of tradition and redaction. For the sake of convenience we can describe this as 'strict editorial criticism'. Marxsen states that 'we depend on literary-critical analysis for separating tradition from redaction' (1969: 26), and Rudolf Pesch in his influential study of Mark 13 writes,

> The division of tradition from redaction must be undertaken on a verse-by-verse basis, and occasionally word by word. Only in this fashion does one attain a foundation for a complete understanding of the tradition and of the redaction by the Evangelist (1968: 47, my translation).

Robert Fortna comments that 'the redaction critic pays closest attention to what distinguishes the work before him from the earlier material on which it is based' (1976: 733).

An internal tension characterized many important early 'editorial-critical' studies. On the one hand the Gospel of Mark became an area of intensive investigation. On the other there was no agreed-upon received tradition (*Vorlage*) for Mark. Yet, during the first decades of redaction criticism, in particular studies (Quesnell 1969: 39-57; Dormeyer 1974: 24-33; Pesch 1968) and in more explicit methodological statements such as those by Robert Stein (1969, 1970, 1971) a number of procedures and implicit criteria developed for distinguishing tradition and redaction.

A brief summary of these would include: (1) Use of form criticism and tradition history to uncover possible oral traditions or blocks of tradition behind the Markan text, for example, an earlier apocalyptic pamphlet (*Flugblatt*) at the basis of Mark 13. (2) Study of characteristic Markan vocabulary and stylistic features (Pryke 1978; Neirynck 1981; Zerwick 1937), and compositional devices such as intercalation (or sandwiching) of one pericope within another, for example, Mk 14.3-9 within 14.1-2, 10-11 (Donahue 1973: 58-59, 240-43), or fondness for duplication (Neirynck 1972). Crucial to this aspect of the method was study of the Markan seams and introductions to pericopes, which were thought most to reveal the hand of the author (Grobel 1940). (3) Determination of the extent of given pericope and analysis of 'tensions' that would suggest the joining of sections not originally joined (e.g. Mk 2.1-12, which seems to combine a miracle story and a controversy story), as well as the study of duplicates within the same Gospel, which might suggest different traditions (Achtemeier 1970, 1972). Quentin Quesnell describes one of the ways in which study of tensions discloses redaction: redactional by nature is that which shows signs of having been written in the light of a larger whole than the pericope or speech in which it stands, or at least from a different viewpoint and/or giving form to the pericope in which it stands' (1969: 51). (4) Examination of parallel material in Matthew and Luke to speculate whether the ways in which Matthew and Luke edited Mark might reveal the distinctive characteristics of Mark. (5) Study of the postulated literary activity of 'Mark' in a given pericope in comparison with 'Markan' editing of other places in the Gospel to find if a consistent pattern emerges, for example, the tendency of Mark to universalize scenes by the frequent addition of 'all' or 'very many' (Donahue 1973: 66-67). From examination of the editorial activity of Mark, hypotheses were then formed about the intention—most often described as the 'theological intention'—of the author. As redaction criticism has evolved, three elements have come to characterize it: (1) study of the editorial or composition activity of an 'author', (2) as a key to theological intention (or in more neutral literary terms, ideology), (3) which is in response to questions or issues alive in a particular community within the last decades of the first century CE.

The separation of tradition from redaction results in a view of the Evangelist either in dialogic or dialectical relationship with the tradition. For example, in his study of the Markan miracle tradition Karl Kertelge (1970) concludes that miracles traditionally functioned primarily as divine epiphanies. Mark, according to Kertelge, does not deny this primary focus but subsumes the miracles into his Gospel as epiphanies of the crucified and risen one. Ludger Schenke (1974b), conversely, states that in the pre-Markan tradition the miracles functioned as props for an incorrect *theios anēr* (divine man) Christology. Mark is thought to oppose the proponents of this Christology and by his redaction to refute their use of miracles. By inserting them into a temporal and geographical structure Mark deprives the miracles of their power as isolated epiphanies and reduces them to episodes of the life of Jesus. They are subordinated to teaching, and the motif of secrecy deprives them of their revelatory power. This dialectical relation of Mark to the tradition has been postulated in respect to Mark 13 (Pesch 1968), the picture of discipleship (Tagawa 1966; Weeden 1971) and the passion narrative (Schenk 1974; Schenke 1974a).

*Composition Criticism*
In addition to 'strict editorial criticism', redaction criticism (as a generic term) developed into 'composition criticism'. In his commentary on Mark (1968) Ernst Haenchen stresses that he is interested in the Markan material in its *Sitz im Leben der Evangelist selbst*, that is, primarily in the location of a given block of material in the Gospel in relation to its immediate and larger context as an index of the intention of the author (pp. 23-24). In his published dissertation from the Pontifical Biblical Institute, William Thompson distinguishes a 'vertical' from a 'horizontal' reading of Matthew (1970: 12-13). In a vertical reading Matthew is read (as on a scroll) in terms of his own sequential text. In a 'horizontal' reading one looks across the page (as in a synoptic edition) to see the changes Matthew makes in Mark. Composition criticism, which directed

attention to the setting of a given pericope in the larger context of a particular Gospel, quickly gave birth to a great number of studies on the themes or motifs of each Gospel.

The term 'composition criticism' conveys a certain ambiguity since it can be used for the *creation* or composing of new material or the *putting together* in a new arrangement of pre-existing material. Thus composition criticism came to describe a method employed by two major groups of scholars with distinct views of the relation of Mark to tradition. One group views virtually everything in the Gospel as tradition and sees Mark at work as 'author' only in brief introductory sentences and occasional editorial additions. Ernest Best suggests that rather than referring to Mark as author, one should think of him as an artist creating a collage (1974). Another group of scholars who practice composition criticism are willing to admit that Mark may be the actual author (composer) of large parts of the text and are ready to abandon the attempt to distinguish tradition from redaction.

The shift from 'editorial criticism' to 'composition criticism' can be seen most dramatically in the career of Rudolf Pesch. His first work, *Naherwartungen* (1968), was a model of careful attention to the text of Mark 13 in order to distinguish the extent of Markan editing of an earlier reconstructed tradition. Mark's purpose in this was to deflect attention of the Markan community shortly after the destruction of Jerusalem away from an expectation that the tragic events of 70 CE were the immediate prelude to the return of Jesus. Rather, Mark substitutes a 'near expectation', which does not identify the parousia with any particular event and redacts the apocalyptic tradition in the direction of parenesis by warning the community against false messianic claimants (especially Mk 13.21-22). By the time Pesch publishes his two-volume commentary on Mark in 1976–77, he holds that the bulk of Mark's text is tradition and that Mark is a 'conservative redactor' whose creativity is manifest primarily in his *arrangement* of material.

Two things explain Pesch's radical shift in abandonment of strict editorial criticism in favor of composition criticism and his refusal to attribute literary creativity to Mark. First, in a series of reviews he manifests growing disenchantment with dissection of Markan narratives into different strata of tradition and redaction. Particularly biting was his description of Ludger Schenke's *Der gekreuzigte Christus* as a 'Summe von literarkritischen Fehlurteilen' (a collection of literary-critical errors in judgment) and his further remark that the often contradictory conclusions of studies of the redaction of the passion narrative called into question the very scientific character of the discipline of New Testament studies (1976b: 102), a perspective that he reiterated in additional reviews a year later (1977b). The second and major reason for Pesch's change was the influence of Gerd Theissen's *The Miracle Stories of the Early Christian Tradition* (1974), which was initially described by Ulrich Luz as a work that would be important twenty years after its publication (Luz 1976: 173-74). Two aspects of Theissen's work are particularly influential on Pesch: (1) Theissen's positing a connection between the microtext, the miracle story, and the macrotext, the Gospel, and (2) Theissen's description of the kind of composition that takes place when a 'reproduced text' is incorporated within the framework of a Gospel. Theissen argues that when narratives such as miracle stories move from oral tradition to written text there exists strong continuity between the structure and meaning of the smaller units and the final, larger composition. Theissen also calls attention to four modes of composition in Mark, which Pesch adopts completely: (1) connecting or linking composition, through temporal and spatial references; (2) typifying composition, elevation of a motif from one pericope to characterize a whole narrative; (3) classifying composition, linking by common point of view; and (4) overlapping or overarching composition, which creates throughout the Gospel a series of 'overarching motifs' (*Spannungsbögen*) that provide creative tension between different motifs in the Gospel, for example, the early intimations of the coming death of Jesus, culminating in the arrest and crucifixion (1976a: 19-21).

For Pesch the principal body of material that Mark incorporates virtually untouched from 8.27 to 16.8 is a pre-Markan passion narrative originating in Jerusalem c. 37 CE (1977a: 1-27). This passion tradition thus gives shape to the whole of Mark's narrative. By drawing on Theissen's hypothesis of how ancient miracle cycles were composed and by applying it to Mark, Pesch is able to conclude with the seeming paradox that Mark is a conservative redactor who rarely alters the wording of traditions and a very creative composer and theologian who by arranging received tradition in a definite form adapts this tradition to the missionary needs of his community in Rome shortly after the destruction of Jerusalem. Pesch thus claims to avoid the arbitrary reconstruction of tradition, while at the same time moving beyond the older view of Mark as an unsophisticated collector of undigested traditions.

Though Pesch hoped to re-introduce some scientific rigor into the discussion of redaction criticism, by the time his commentary was known and used in the United States, most scholars had already abandoned the attempt to separate tradition from redaction and a distinctive composition criticism was developing, with more stress on the theological themes of Mark in relation to the overall content and structure of the Gospel. Partly this is because, almost from its very inception, redaction criticism was understood differently in Germany and in the United States. In Germany it was primarily a *historical* discipline where the focus was on origin and settings of traditions, on the conditions of their development and on the historical circumstances that best explained their final editing. Using terminology that became current only later, we can say that in Germany redaction criticism concentrated on 'the world behind the text'. In the United States, redaction criticism developed primarily as an exercise in *literary* criticism, where the emphasis was on the final product as a unitary composition with concern for the overarching themes and motifs and for the structure of the whole and of the individual parts.

### Redaction Criticism and the Gospels of Matthew and Luke

Given the wide acceptance of the priority of Mark and the two-source theory, strict editorial criticism of Matthew and Luke in relation to Mark provided a solid basis for judgments about the theological intention and social settings of Matthew and Luke.[1] The seminal studies of Bornkamm, Barth and Held all employed strict editorial criticism in studying Matthew's editing of Markan tradition, especially the miracle stories. Yet, as in the case of Mark, redaction criticism, broadly conceived, moved from strict editorial criticism to composition criticism and narrative criticism.

In writings on Matthew spanning a quarter century Jack Dean Kingsbury embodied these different shifts in method. In his initial study of Matthew 13, he examined Matthew's alterations of Mark 4, noted the addition of Q and M (that is, special Matthean material), and attended to the location of Matthew 13 in the structure of the Gospel (1969). He then argued that the chapter presented a crucial turning point where Jesus forsakes controversy with opponents and turns to instruction of his disciples. Later (1975) he studied the composition of Matthew by challenging the widely-accepted five-book structure proposed by

---

1.    For representative surveys of the principal results of redaction criticism see Carlson 1975; Fitzmyer 1981: 3-283; Harrington 1985; Kealy 1982; Kee 1978; Kee 1989; McKnight 1989; Richard 1983; Stanton 1984; Talbert 1976; Talbert 1989.

B.W. Bacon (1930). Kingsbury argued that the phrase 'from that time on Jesus began', in Mt. 4.17 and 16.21 constitutes Matthew's indication of structural divisions, which form a christological tableaux: the person of Jesus the Messiah (1.1–4.16); the proclamation of Jesus (4.17–16.20); and the suffering, death and resurrection of Jesus Messiah (16.21–28.20). Kingsbury also devoted considerable attention to Matthew's christological titles, with a primary focus on their use within the total composition of Matthew. In his most recent writings on Matthew, Kingsbury has virtually abandoned editorial and composition criticism in favor of a consistent narrative criticism (1987, 1988).

A particularly strong and important aspect of Matthean redaction criticism was concern for the *Sitz im Leben* of the Gospel as a whole. Though early studies centered mainly on Matthew's ecclesial understanding (McKnight 1989: 158-59), recently the emphasis has shifted strongly to the Gospel's relation to Judaism. Matthew has long presented a paradox as the most Jewish of the Gospels, yet the one with the harshest statements about Jewish groups (e.g. Mt. 23.13-39; 27.24-25). More recent research argues that the bitter conflict between Jesus and the Pharisees does not reflect the *Sitz im Leben Jesu*, but the polemics between emergent Christianity and an emergent rabbinic Judaism, both of which laid claim to a common heritage in the latter decades of the first century—further, it appears that first-century Judaism is itself pluriform (Balch 1991; Levine 1988; Overmann 1990).

None of the original pioneers in redaction criticism determined the agenda of subsequent research as strongly as did Hans Conzelmann in the case of Luke. By use of strict editorial criticism, Conzelmann noted two major changes Luke made in his Markan source. First, Luke modified radically Mark's eschatology by moving away from Mark's expectation of the imminent return of Jesus. The life of Jesus is an event of past history. In his alteration of Mk 9.1, Luke (9.27) omits Mark's realistic reference to the kingdom 'coming with power' and makes of the kingdom a timeless concept (McKnight 1989: 155). Second, in three crucial passages (4.21; 16.16; 22.35-37) Luke signals three stages of salvation history: (a) the period of Israel, from creation to the imprisonment of John the Baptist; (b) the period of Jesus, from his baptism to the ascension; and (c) the period of the *ecclesia pressa* (the persecuted church) from Jesus' ascension to the (delayed) parousia.

Post-Conzelmann research on Luke consisted in large measure in confronting the issues he raised, and therefore employed similar methods.

Joseph Fitzmyer's major commentary (1981, 1985) is a parade example of this since his method is consistently redactional, comprising both strict editorial criticism and composition criticism. As in the case of Mark and Matthew, Lukan redaction criticism stressed distinctive Lukan theological themes: Christology, discipleship and social concerns. Of special interest were a number of studies on the function of the distinctive Lukan passages dealing with the rich and the poor.[2]

### Redaction Criticism of Q and John

The early attempts in Germany to describe the composition and final redaction of Q, by Dieter Lührmann and Athanasius Polag (see Neirynck 1982), have now been supplemented by a spate of recent works published in the United States (Jacobson 1992; Kloppenborg 1987; Kloppenborg 1988; Koester 1990; Mack 1993). John Kloppenborg (1987: 102-70) set the future agenda by arguing for a cluster of traditions in Q united by a theme of judgment (3.7-9, 16-17; 7.1-10, 18-35; 11.14-52; 12.39-59; 17.23-37).[3] Another group of texts classed as 'sapiential speeches' (6.20b-49; 9.57-62 + 10.2-16, 21-24) reflect the radical life-style of the early Q community (pp. 171-245). The temptation story (4.1-13) is a later interpolation into Q, which differs 'in form, style and theological orientation' from the rest of Q (p. 248). Kloppenborg constructs his proposal on the development of the Q source on the basis of this identification of clusters united by similar content. The sapiential strain, which served instructional purposes, is the earliest cluster, to which is joined the judgment strain, used in controversy and parenesis, and the temptation story, which serves as a biographical introduction to the whole collection. In his more popular presentation (1993) Burton Mack divides Q into $Q^1$, $Q^2$ and $Q^3$, which correspond closely to Kloppenborg's three strata of Q.

In addition to presenting the longest analysis of the composition and literary unity of Q, Arland Jacobson (1992: 33-76) gives the clearest articulation of the redactional method at work in Q studies. He writes,

---

2.    The surveys mentioned above (n. 1) touch on issues of wealth and poverty. See also Donahue 1989 and Johnson 1977.

3.    It has become customary in studies of Q to refer simply to the chapter and verses of a reconstructed Q source, which in general corresponds closely to the content and order of Q as found in Luke. The notation '3.7-9' refers to Q as found in Lk. 3.7-9. See Kloppenborg 1988.

> What is needed is a history of the composition of Q. Redaction and composition criticism are the primary tools for such a history, though form-critical analysis of the sayings compositions is also indispensable. It may be that a rhetorical analysis will also prove useful in moving us beyond the present impasse (p. 60).

Jacobson also proposes a 'stratigraphy' of Q. An early layer consists of sayings stressing the radical lifestyle of the followers of Jesus, but with a promise of positive blessings (6.20-21). Deuternomistic-wisdom material characterizes the second major stratum of Q, found especially in the Q portions of Luke 10–12. Like Kloppenborg and others, Jacobson views the temptation story as the latest addition to Q. The final document has a basic literary unity that Jacobson argues follows basically the Lukan order of Q. The deuteronomistic-wisdom perspective of the second stratum shapes the final composition of the whole work and gives it its theological framework. Though Jacobson speaks often of a redactor at work in specific sayings from these strata, he does not identify or locate this redactor in any detail.

An equally impressive array of studies has appeared on the tradition history and redaction of John. As in the case of redaction criticism of the Synoptics, Bultmann determined the parameters of subsequent research. As is well-known, in his magisterial commentary on John he argued that two major bodies of material in John are interwoven in the present text (D.M. Smith 1965, 1989). The first of these is the 'Signs Source', which draws its name from the Johannine description of the miracles of Jesus as 'signs' (e.g. Jn 2.11, 18, 23; 3.2; 7.31; 11.47; 12.18). Though 'he nowhere spelled out the criteria for his separation of a pre-Johannine source from the Johannine Gospel, nor did he precisely or systematically indicate what this source contained' (Fortna 1992: 19), Bultmann's proposal continues to be refined and buttressed by the subsequent work of Fortna (1970, 1998, 1992), Nicol (1972) and von Wahlde (1989). This 'source' was then combined with elaborate revelation discourses in which Jesus the Gnostic-like redeemer from heaven mediates a saving message to his followers. Bultmann recognized the presence of other sources, such as passion and Easter traditions, and argued that the text as we have it was the result of the arrangement and editing of an ecclesiastical redactor.

While Bultmann's reconstruction did not carry the day, especially in regard to the influence of Gnosticism on the revelation discourses, the attempt to determine levels of tradition in John and to describe the theological motifs at work in the traditions and their editing continues, especially in the work of Louis Martyn (1978, 1979) and Raymond E. Brown (1979), who have correlated the history of the Johannine community from its inception to the late first or early second century with stages in the development of tradition.

This long and admittedly inadequate detour through Q and John serves to support the contention that redaction criticism is still *alive*, albeit somewhat transformed. Whether it is also *well* awaits the same kind of critical examinations of the reconstructions of Q and John that were applied to Mark.[4]

### Major Contributions of Redaction Criticism

Before addressing the limitations of redaction criticism as well as its transformation into literary criticism, I would like to highlight some of its major contributions. Research on the Synoptic Gospels received a fresh impetus. Important studies appeared on the distinctive theological perspectives of each Gospel in areas such as Christology, discipleship and eschatology. Major commentaries, such as those of Joachim Gnilka on Mark, Ulrich Luz on Matthew, and Joseph Fitzmyer on Luke, consciously adopted redaction-critical perspectives. Concern for the distinctive theological motifs quickly led to the realization that the Synoptic Evangelists were not mere collectors but theologians in their own right. Interesting proposals arose about the social location of each Gospel.

Redaction criticism also disclosed a significant theological pluralism within the Synoptic tradition. While John's distinctive Christology had long been recognized, the Synoptic Christology was normally homogenized. Redaction criticism disclosed distinctive 'portraits' of Jesus among the Synoptic Evangelists (Kingsbury 1981). Matthew and Luke, for example, consistently omit or refine Markan statements in which Jesus shows violent emotions (e.g. Mk 1.41, 43; 3.5; 8.12; 10.14; see Donahue 1978). By addition of a great deal of wisdom-like material from Q and from his own tradition Matthew creates a magisterial Jesus who delivers five great discourses to his disciples. Luke recasts Mark's Jesus as a healer and a prophet inexorably making his way to Jerusalem to meet his predetermined fate (Moessner 1989). The picture of the disciples in each Gospel is also quite different. Most dramatically, neither Matthew

---

4.    Important qualifications about the stratigraphy of Q and the attempts to determine social location on the basis of reconstructed strata have been expressed by Attridge 1991; Horsley 1991; and Tuckett 1989.

nor Luke (Luz 1983: 98-128; Fitzmyer 1989: 117-45) hand on the negative Markan picture of the disciples as those who consistently misunderstand Jesus and ultimately abandon him (Weeden 1971).

Redaction criticism also spawned noteworthy research in other areas. The careful studies by the Leuven scholar Frans Neirynck (1972, 1981) have provided scholars with a solid basis on which to discuss the literary characteristics and compositional techniques of Mark, comparable in impact to H.J. Cadbury's early studies on Luke. The question of the genre of Mark and of the Gospels in general, which was the subject of one of Marxsen's pioneering studies, has been renewed with ongoing discussion of Jewish and Greco-Roman influences (Burridge 1992; A.Y. Collins 1992; Talbert 1977). Redaction criticism has provided new ways of thinking about tradition. Tradition itself is not a fixed entity or block that is simply 'taken over'. A tradition 'lives' precisely through its reinterpretation and adaptation to new circumstances. Most importantly, as noted, redaction criticism provided an important transition to the new horizons of New Testament research, specifically to the 'literary turn' and to the more sophisticated attempts to determine the social location of the Gospels.

Finally redaction criticism was a method with immediate pedagogical and pastoral yield. By comparing Gospels and by studying the literary techniques and themes of a given Gospel, students learned to do 'close reading' of biblical texts and to experience a certain joy in discovering the distinctive emphases of each Gospel. Redaction criticism also had a strong influence on preaching, since its flowering was coincidental with the introduction into Sunday worship of a triennial cycle of sequential readings of the Gospels by Roman Catholics and major Protestant denominations. With its emphasis on the literary context of a given pericope, and the need to evaluate the religious meaning of individual incidents in terms of the total theology of a Gospel, redaction criticism offered preachers a helpful tool for mediating the results of scholarship in a pastoral situation.

*Limitations of Redaction Criticism*

One of the major defects of redaction criticism has been its reigning model of the relation of tradition and redaction, especially when applied to Mark.[5] It was generally assumed that Mark had before him fairly

5. The most sustained and careful criticisms of redaction criticism are by Black 1988, 1989.

fixed traditions that he edited in the same way that Matthew and Luke dealt with Mark and Q. The standard procedure was to postulate distinct Markan characteristics and then subtract them from a given pericope and assume that what resulted was tradition. This produced at times seemingly absurd hypotheses in which a relatively short section, such as the passion narrative, was broken down into layers of tradition, consisting often of verses or half-verses (Soards 1985), often reminiscent of the earlier deconstruction of the Pentateuch into not only four major sources but a myriad of editions of each source.

The major defect of this perspective is that, excepting the literary relationships within Synoptic Gospels, it does not reflect the manner in which traditions were reinterpreted in antiquity (Downing 1988). In two very important articles, which have been relatively neglected by redaction critics, F. Gerald Downing studies carefully the manner in which Josephus uses his sources (Downing 1980). Downing examines how Josephus treats similar biblical and extra-biblical sources in *The Jewish War* and in the *Antiquities of the Jews* (written almost twenty years apart in different historical circumstances) and makes a careful list of the way Josephus alters tradition in terms of his literary, apologetic and religious interests. Downing then applies these insights to Luke and finds that the Third Evangelist employs similar techniques. Studies by Hebrew Bible scholars on the phenomenon of 'rewritten Bible' (Harrington 1986), understood as the retelling and reinterpretation of traditions within the Bible itself, such as similar incidents in the books of Kings and Chronicles (Fishbane 1985), also reveal that traditions rarely exist in the form postulated by Markan editorial critics, nor does 'editing' involve the kinds of activities often postulated for Markan editing. The Gospel of Mark presents a paradox. Most of it is 'tradition', that is, it was put together by Mark out of pre-existing materials; all of it is composition, that is, Mark retold every story and probably recast every incident in terms of his theological and rhetorical purpose. Though it may be possible to determine in general the shape or thrust of a tradition used by Mark, for example, in the case of parables, the miracle stories, or the passion narrative, the attempt to determine his purpose from a study of minute and hypothetical alterations of a reconstructed tradition has resulted in so many contradictory statements that it is obviously flawed.[6]

6.   H. Conzelmann (1972: 250), in reviewing various studies of Mk 13, described the chapter as a training ground for different hypotheses (*Tummelplatz der Hypothesen*), and U. Luz (1980), in surveying recent Markan studies, has spoken of

To adopt categories used by Joachim Jeremias in the quest for the historical Jesus, one could say the *ipsissima verba* of Markan tradition are forever lost, while strains of the *ipsissima vox* may still echo in the Markan text.

Another reservation alleged about redaction criticism has been whether a first-century author such as Mark could have employed the apparently subtle literary devices found in the text (e.g. intercalation, chiastic structure) or could have 'intended' the theological perspectives found there. Often this betrays a certain sociological bias that Mark was basically an unlettered religious enthusiast who wrote in simple Greek, resonant of the late nineteenth-century view of the Gospels as artless writings (*Kleinliteratur*). Such a view of authorship when applied to literature in general was also severely criticized by earlier proponents of the 'New Criticism' who rejected the 'intentional fallacy', which postulated that the author's intention is the key to literary meaning. It betrays also the 'romantic fallacy' that literature is somehow an expression of the inner life and dispositions of an author. Many of the early redaction critics showed awareness of this objection by noting that when they used the term 'Mark' they were not referring necessarily to the historical person who finally composed the Gospel but were employing the name as a personification of the text. When literary criticism (understood not as detection of sources, but in the sense used in general literary studies) began to be used in earnest in Gospel study, the concept of the 'implied author', understood as a sum of the literary techniques and ideological perspectives of the text, itself offered scholars a proper way to speak of 'Mark', free of the charge of historicizing the text or offering anachronistic readings.

## *The Transformations of Redaction Criticism*

### *Genuine Literary Criticism*
It is somewhat ironic that by the time sustained criticism of redaction criticism had crested, the method had already been largely transformed into 'genuine literary criticism' (Perrin 1976).[7] This too has roots in

delight in hypothetical assumptions (*Hypothesenfreudigkeit*). See also Black 1988, 1989.

7. Two recently published, lengthy bibliographies (Powell 1992; Minor 1992) are evidence for the expansion of the dialogue between biblical studies and modern literary criticism.

previous research. In 1959, Helen Gardner, an Oxford literary critic, spoke of 'The Poetry of St Mark', in the sense that

> reading the Gospel is like reading a poem. It is an imaginative experience. It presents us with a sequence of events and sayings which combine to create in our minds a single complex and powerful symbol, a pattern of meaning. Reading St Mark is quite unlike reading a series of entries made by a compiler of annals, or a collection of separate anecdotes (p. 103).

In 1964 Amos Wilder, whose work in New Testament spanned 70 years of this century, called for renewed attention to the literary quality of New Testament texts. Later, reflecting on the literary turn in biblical studies, Wilder stated that 'both scholars and general readers have failed to do justice to what one can call the operations of the imagination in the Scriptures—to the poetry, the imagery and the symbolism'. He attributes this failure to an 'occupational cramp' due to a philological interest in minutiae that reduced poetry to prose and to a theological tradition that was interested in ideas (1982: 15).

The concerns of Wilder and others came to fruition in the mid-1970s with the flowering of literary critical studies of the Gospels, understood not in the traditional New Testament sense as detection of literary sources, but with the meaning employed in general literary criticism (often prefaced with the misnomer 'secular', as if there is a distinct 'religious' literary criticism). Apropos of Mark, but with implications for the other Gospels, Tolbert sketches the fundamental assumptions of such an approach: 'The first and most important of these assumptions...is that Mark is a self-consciously crafted narrative, a fiction, resulting from literary imagination, not from photographic detail' (1989: 30). After pointing out that its status as fiction does not mean that Mark has no connection with history, but, rather, that the author has 'made' the narrative, Tolbert articulates a second assumption: 'a narrative is unified and coherent' (p. 38, see also Moore 1989: 7-10). Stephen Moore notes another important assumption of the literary turn that distinguishes it from redaction or composition criticism:

> For composition critics, the meaning resides in the text's theological or (ideational) content. The content is separable in principle from the narrative form; narrative is the vehicle of theology. Narrative criticism, in contrast, is a formalist criticism; the meaning of the biblical text is located in the details of its structure (p. 10).

One of the initial directions the literary turn took was 'structural exegesis', or structuralism, which Robert Spivey in 1974 called the 'uninvited guest' of biblical studies. Elizabeth Struthers Malbon describes well the dimensions of structuralism: (1) it stresses that language is communication and focuses *on the text* as a medium of communication between author and reader; (2) it stresses that language is a system of signs, so that no text exists in isolation from the work as a whole, and that a narrative is a system of configurations of different signs; (3) it stresses that language is a cultural code that often covers a deeper system of convictions underlying a particular text (Malbon 1992: 25-26). Heavily in debt to the work of French structuralists, Roland Barthes and Algirdas Greimas (Leitch 1988: 261), in the United States structuralist studies of the New Testament are most identified with the work of Daniel Patte of Vanderbilt University (1976, 1986, 1989). Although New Testament scholars such as Dan O. Via and J. Dominic Crossan tested the waters of structuralism, and, although it has contributed fruitfully to the important studies of Mark's geography and topography by Struthers Malbon, and of the parables by Bernard Brandon Scott, it never elicited wide following in the United States.[8] According to Vincent Leitch structuralism had already begun to fade among literary critics at the time it became the 'guest' of biblical studies (1988: 260-61), and it received the *coup de grâce* with the dissemination in America of the (post-structuralist) work of Jacques Derrida (Leitch 1988: 266). Structuralist exegesis was, however, an important transitional moment in biblical studies. It called attention to the need for a close reading of texts and moved scholars away from an atomizing exegesis that centered on particular pericopes to concern for the total literary and cultural context of any segment of a larger narrative.

Of more lasting impact have been a series of studies employing narrative criticism. Biblical specialists now began reading the Gospels with an eye to character, plot, setting and point of view, heavily influenced by the categories developed in Seymour Chatman's *Story and Discourse: Narrative Structure in Fiction and Film*, which Leitch calls 'the most popular book of American Structuralist Narratology' (1988: 251). Concern for *what* the text meant shifted to questions of *how* meaning occurs (Malbon 1992: 24). Interest in the actual author yielded to a concern for the 'implied author', which owes much to the work of Wayne Booth. At present there are not only a number of important monographs employing literary criticism, but significant introductions to its techniques (e.g. Kingsbury 1988; Moore 1989; Powell 1990; Rhoads and

8.    It is not formally discussed in Anderson and Moore 1992.

Michie 1982; Malbon 1992; Tannehill 1990; Tannehill 1991). Perrin's prediction of 1976 seems fulfilled.

Narrative criticism was soon supplemented by 'reader response' criticism, which focused on the manner in which the text created its own 'internal' reader, rather than on interpreting the text from the standpoint of a supposed or reconstructed historical audience. Drawing on the theoretical work of Wolfgang Iser (1974, 1978), on the extensive writings of Stanley Fish (1972,1980), and on the authors collected in the anthology edited by Jane Tompkins (1980), practitioners of this method shed new light primarily on the Gospels, epitomized in the thorough studies of Mark by Robert Fowler (1991, 1992). What neither Perrin nor anyone could have predicted two decades ago was the many tributaries that would branch out from this new literary current in New Testament studies. The conversation with 'secular' literary critics developed in earnest when, 'in the domain of literary theory and criticism, America witnessed an amazing growth of new schools and movements' (Leitch 1988: 185). In a very short time biblical critics recapitulated the major critical currents of the past half-century—from  variations of New Criticism to post-structuralism and deconstruction. The proliferation continues. In the introduction to their map of the new movements, Stephen Greenblatt and Giles Gunn comment: 'Literary studies in English are in a period of rapid and sometimes disorienting change' (1992: 1), and 'what confronts us at the present time in English and American literary studies is not a unified field at all, but diverse historical projects and critical idioms...' (p. 3; see also Leitch 1992). These new opportunities have created a host of new problems for biblical scholars, not the least of which is balancing the linguistic and historical competencies required for biblical exegesis with the demands of maintaining dialogue with diverse movements in literary criticism—vividly described by a contemporary critic:

> The sights stretch as far as the eye can see—to the immense zoo of Kenneth Burke, the bracing gymnasium of Lionel Trilling, the chaffering marketplace of Clifford Geertz, the broadcasting house of Mikhail Bakhtin with its phone-in programs on the logic of the dialogic; all this and then low on the horizon the bog of deconstruction, swallowing everything in readiness for the final exquisite pleasure of swallowing itself. Milton's vast Serbonian bog where whole armies have sunk (Ricks 1987: 10).

*The Return of Historical Concerns*

Above I called attention to the tension in redaction criticism between its literary orientation and its historical concern. This explains the second major transformation of redaction criticism—into a variety of social scientific studies. Since redaction criticism was interested in the *Sitz im Leben* of the final edition or composition, new methods of social analysis were applied to the quest for the communities addressed by the text (Donahue 1992; Kee 1977; Theissen 1991). 'Social scientific methods' is an umbrella phrase for a host of emergent subdisciplines: study of social facts in early Christian texts; social history involving, 'political history and theology within an informed theoretical framework'; study of social organization, forces and institutions, and probing of the social world— 'what it felt like to live in a world described by the symbols, rituals, and language of early Christianity' (J.Z. Smith 1975: 19). In recent years the methods have been broadened and enriched to include considerations from cultural anthropology (Elliott 1986; Malina 1981; Malina 1986; Neyrey 1991). Social analysis quickly became a congeries of sub-disciplines no less diverse than those evoked by the literary turn.

Since the focus of this present volume is on 'the new literary criticism', I want to call attention to the marriage of historical and literary concerns in recent, important works and movements. The formalism of narrative criticism (that is, its concern with literary technique rather than meaning), and its 'new critical' bias toward inner textual meaning to the exclusion of extra-textual referent, have left many biblical critics uneasy. The biblical books are from a different cultural and historical setting than our own and extra-textual information is indispensable to understanding the text. The New Testament books are also fundamentally rhetorical. Their original purpose was to move people to action or conviction. They were read by communities of believers and addressed concerns alive in communities, and these concerns lie behind the texts of particular books. A pure inner-textual narrative criticism, while necessary to disclose the world of the text, must be supplemented by concerns that treat the historical setting and historical impact of the text.

In her *Sowing the Gospel* Mary Ann Tolbert offers a fine paradigm for joining literary sophistication to historical research. Tolbert treats Mark as a literary unity that demands attention to its literary devices and rhetorical structure. She also situates the Gospel in its own historical and cultural milieu, arguing that Hellenistic romances, especially *An*

*Ephesian Tale*, provide the closest literary counterpart. While similarity between these novels and the Gospels in form (ornate plots and multiple characters versus the relatively short and dramatically simply Gospels) and content (adventure tales of star-crossed lovers versus the *bios* [life] of a martyred leader) may be the most fragile part of her work, in terms of method the most significant element is the way in which Tolbert, by combining knowledge of ancient literary conventions and rhetorical techniques, shows a similarity in narrative style and social function between the novels and the Gospels.

Equally important is the renewed interest in rhetorical criticism of biblical documents. Though allied to reader response criticism, it is more historical in its method and orientation. This approach seeks to uncover the 'rhetorical strategy' and 'rhetorical situation' of a given text. The method proceeds from the world behind the text (the situation out of which it arose) through the world of the text (its internal literary structure and argument) to the world in front of the text (the audience addressed by the text) and seeks to uncover the power of the text to persuade, convince or move its original readers, also painting a tableaux of these readers.

Such rhetorical criticism, as embodied in the work of Vernon Robbins (1992), Norman Petersen (1985) and Elisabeth Schüssler Fiorenza (1985, 1987, 1991), to mention only some examples, integrates literary criticism and social analysis. Literary criticism discloses the narrative structure and symbolic world of the text, and social analysis uncovers the world out of which the text emerges and for which it is produced. Schüssler Fiorenza presents a concise and systematic exposition of the task and method of rhetorical criticism, which involves four operations that interpreters employ as they attempt to assess the rhetorical situation and strategy of a given document: (1) identification of the rhetorical interests and models of contemporary interpretation, (2) delineation of the rhetorical arrangement, interests, and modifications introduced by the author, (3) elucidation and establishment of the rhetorical situation of the document, and (4) reconstruction of the common historical situation and symbolic universe of the writer/speaker and the recipient/audience (1987: 388-89; 1991: 1-37).

Rhetorical criticism integrates study of the symbolic and narrative worlds of the Bible. It is also helpful in examining how a text is the medium of communication in a particular social context. Even the Gospels, which are not as evidently 'rhetorical' as Paul's letters, contain a 'narrative rhetoric' whereby 'the narrator constructs a narrative world which readers are invited to inhabit imaginatively, a world constructed according to certain values and beliefs' (Tannehill 1990: 8). Even granted that reconstructions of ancient rhetorical situations are hypothetical with varying degrees of conviction, rhetorical criticism, as practiced in diverse ways by Tolbert and Schüssler Fiorenza, when combined with narrative criticism, offers, I would suggest, the best promise for a method of reading New Testament texts that does justice to both their literary quality and their historical setting. Finally, this essay cannot conclude without some, albeit inadequate, mention of a major new current in literary studies, which has barely begun to attract the attention of biblical critics. It is variously called 'the new historicism' or 'cultural poetics'. I would claim to be nothing more than an initiate hovering at the gate of the shrine. The movement originated principally in Renaissance studies with Stephen Greenblatt of the University of California at Berkeley. While it is difficult to define precisely, Holman and Harmon (1992) offer a handy description:

> The *New Historicism* tends to be social, economic and political, and it views literary works (particularly Renaissance dramas and Victorian novels) as instruments for the displaying and enforcing of doctrines about conduct, etiquette and law. In a dynamic circle, the literature tells us something about the surrounding ideology...and the study of ideology tells us something about the embedded literary works (p. 318).

One of its early proponents describes it as 'a renewed concern with the historical, social, and political conditions and consequences of literary production and reproduction...'(Montrose 1989: 15).

The 'new' historicism differs from the older historicism associated with nineteenth-century German historiography by its suspicion of literal representation in texts and by its rejection of essentialism. It also breaks with modern literary movements associated with the New Criticism and formalism and consciously adopts post-structuralist perspectives. In arguing for the intersection of political, literary, and economic forces it is also in critical dialogue with Marxist literary criticism, especially that of Frederic Jameson (Thomas 1989: 182-84; Greenblatt 1992: 4-5). It does not give pride of place to any particular literary 'canon' and does not disparage writings of a given period that emanate from people on the margin (such as the Gospels) rather than from the 'elites' or cultural leaders. Less a method than a perspective that integrates historical research, especially research into cultural and social practice, literary methods and philosophical perspectives, it provides a challenge to New Testament studies once again to join historical and literary criticism, but now clothed in a multi-colored cloak of interdisciplinary studies.

## Conclusion

Redaction criticism represents a complex phenomenon. Though it began as a well-defined method ('strict editorial criticism'), it quickly became a network of different approaches to a text. It still survives in its original form, primarily in published German dissertations that employ the model of the separation of tradition and redaction as an entree to the Evangelists' concerns. As noted, in its modified tradition history form, it is still vital in studies of Q and John. Perrin's prediction of its trans-formation into 'genuine literary criticism' has been more than fulfilled. Yet, the fundamental goals of redaction criticism—careful reading of a complete text (rather than form criticism's stress on pre-textual units), attention to the meaning (theology) of the text as a whole, and a search for the world behind and in front of the text (that is, its origin and audience)—remain a significant part of most contemporary biblical criticism. Perrin's main street (*Hauptstrasse*) did not quite become a dead end (*Sackgasse*). To continue the metaphor, it might be called a *Querstrasse* (a crossroad), where different methods continue to intersect.

## BIBLIOGRAPHY

Achtemeier, Paul J.
  1970       'Toward the Isolation of Pre-Markan Miracle Catenae', *JBL* 89: 265-91.
  1972       'The Origin and Function of the Pre-Markan Miracle Catenae', *JBL* 91: 198-221.
Anderson, Janice Capel, and Stephen Moore (eds.)
  1992       *Mark and Method: New Approaches in Biblical Studies* (Minneapolis: Fortress Press).
Attridge, Harold W.
  1991       'Reflections on Research into Q', *Semeia* 55: 223-34.
Bacon, B.W.
  1909a      'The Apocalyptic Character of the Synoptic Gospels', *JBL* 28: 1-25.
  1909b      'The Composition of Mark's Gospel', *AJT* 13: 613-14.
  1930       *Studies in Matthew* (London: Constable).
Balch, David L. (ed.)
  1991       *Social History of the Matthean Community: Cross-Disciplinary Approaches* (Minneapolis: Fortress Press).

Best, Ernest

1974 'Mark's Preservation of the Tradition', in M. Sabbe (ed.), *L'évangile selon Marc* (BETL, 34; Leuven: Leuven University Press): 21-34, repr. in W. Telford (ed.), *The Intepretation of Mark* (Philadelphia: Fortress Press; London: SPCK, 1985): 119-33.

Black, C. Clifton

1988 'The Quest of Mark the Redactor: Why Has it Been Pursued, and What Has it Taught Us?', *JSNT* 33: 19-39.

1989 *The Disciples according to Mark: Markan Redaction in Current Debate* (JSNTSup, 27; Sheffield: JSOT Press).

Booth, Wayne C.

1961 *The Rhetoric of Fiction* (Chicago: University of Chicago Press, 2nd edn, 1983).

Bornkamm, Günther, G. Barth and H.-J. Held

1963 *Tradition and Interpretation in Matthew* (Philadelphia: Westminster Press [1st German edn, 1960]).

Brown, Raymond E.

1979 *The Community of the Beloved Disciple* (New York: Paulist Press).

Bultmann, Rudolf

1963 *History of the Synoptic Tradition* (New York: Harper & Row [1st German edn, 1921]).

1971 *The Gospel of John: A Commentary* (Philadelphia: Westminster Press [1st German edn, 1941]).

Burridge, Richard A.

1992 *What Are the Gospels? A Comparison with Greco-Roman Biography* (SNTSMS, 70; Cambridge: Cambridge University Press).

Cadbury, H.J.

1969 *The Style and Literary Method of Luke* (New York: Klaus Reprint, Orig. 1920).

1927 *The Making of Luke–Acts* (New York: Macmillan).

Carlson, Charles E.

1975 'Interpreting the Gospel of Matthew', *Int* 29: 3-12, repr. in Mays 1981: 55-65.

Chatman, Seymour

1978 *Story and Discourse: Narrative Structure in Fiction and Film* (Ithaca, NY: Cornell University Press).

Collins, Adela Yarbro

1992 'Is Mark's Gospel a Life of Jesus? The Question of Genre', in *The Beginning of the Gospel: Probings of Mark in Context* (Minneapolis: Fortress Press): 1-38.

Conzelmann, Hans

1960 *The Theology of St Luke* (New York: Harper & Row [1st German edn, 1953]).

1972 'Literaturbericht zu den Synoptischen Evangelien', *TRu* 37: 220-72.

Crossan, John Dominic

1975 *The Dark Interval: Towards a Theology of Story* (Niles, IL: Argus Communications).

Donahue, John R.
    1973      *Are You the Christ? The Trial Narrative in the Gospel of Mark* (SBLDS, 10; Missoula: Scholars Press).
    1978      'Jesus as the Parable of God in the Gospel of Mark', *Int* 32: 369-86, repr. in Mays 1981: 148-61.
    1989      'Two Decades of Research on the Rich and the Poor in Luke–Acts', in D.A. Knight and P. Paris (eds.), *Justice and the Holy: Essays in Honor of Walter Harrelson* (Atlanta: Scholars Press): 175-91.
    1992      'The Quest for the Community of Mark's Gospel', in F. Van Segbroeck *et al.* (eds.), *The Four Gospels 1992: Festschrift Frans Neirynck* (3 vols.; Leuven: Leuven University Press): I, 817-38.
Dormeyer, Detlev
    1974      *Die Passion Jesu als Verhaltensmodel* (NTAbh, nf, 11; Münster: Aschendorf).
Downing, F. Gerald
    1980      'Redaction Criticism: Josephus' *Antiquities* and the Synoptic Gospels, (I) Josephus', *JSNT* 8: 46-65; '(II) Luke and the Other Synoptics', *JSNT* 9: 29-48.
    1988      'Compositional Conventions and the Synoptic Problem', *JBL* 107: 69-85.
Elliott, J.H.
    1986      'Social Science Criticism of the New Testament: More on Methods and Models', *Semeia* 35: 1-33.
Epp, E.J. and G.W. MacRae (eds.)
    1989      *The New Testament and its Modern Interpreters* (Atlanta: Scholars Press).
Fish, Stanley
    1972      *Self-Consuming Artifacts* (Berkeley: University of California Press).
    1980      *Is There a Text in This Class? The Authority of Interpretive Communities* (Cambridge, MA: Harvard University Press).
Fishbane, Michael
    1985      *Biblical Interpretation in Ancient Israel* (Oxford: Clarendon Press).
Fitzmyer, Joseph A.
    1981      *The Gospel according to Luke I–IX* (AB, 28; Garden City, NY: Doubleday).
    1985      *The Gospel according to Luke X–XXIV* (AB, 28A; Garden City, NY: Doubleday).
    1989      *Luke the Theologian: Aspects of his Teaching* (New York: Paulist Press).
Fortna, Robert T.
    1970      *The Gospel of Signs: A Reconstruction of the Narrative Source Underlying the Fourth Gospel* (SNTSMS, 11; Cambridge: Cambridge University Press).
    1976      'Redaction Criticism, NT', *IDBSup*, 733-35.
    1988      *The Fourth Gospel and its Predecessors: From Narrative Source to Present Gospel* (Philadelphia: Fortress Press).
    1992      'Signs/Semeia Source', in D.N. Freedman (ed.), *The Anchor Bible Dictionary* (New York: Doubleday): VI, 19.

Fowler, Robert M.
1991        *Let the Reader Understand: Reader Response Criticism and the Gospel of Mark* (Minneapolis: Fortress Press).
1992        'Figuring Mark's Reader: Reader Response Criticism', in Anderson and Moore 1992: 50-83.

Gardner, Helen
1959        'The Poetry of St. Mark', in *The Business of Criticism* (Oxford: Clarendon Press): 110-26.

Gnilka, Joachim
1978–79     *Das Evangelium nach Markus* (EKKNT, II/1-2; Zürich: Benziger Verlag; Neukirchen–Vluyn: Neukirchener Verlag).

Greenblatt, Stephen
1992        'Towards a Poetics of Culture', in Veeser 1989: 1-14.

Greenblatt, Stephen and Giles Gunn (eds.)
1992        *Redrawing the Boundaries: The Transformation of English and American Literary Studies* (New York: Modern Language Association).

Grobel, Kendrick
1940        'Idiosyncrasies of the Synoptists in their Pericope Introductions', *JBL* 59: 405-10.

Haenchen, Ernst
1968        *Der Weg Jesu* (Berlin: de Gruyter, 2nd rev. edn).

Harrington, Daniel J.
1985        'A Map of Books on Mark (1975–1984)', *BTB* 15: 12-16.
1986        'The Bible Rewritten (Narratives)', in R.A. Kraft and G.W. Nickelsburg (eds.), *Early Judaism and its Modern Interpreters* (Atlanta: Scholars Press; Philadelphia: Fortress Press): 230-47.

Harrisville, Roy A.
1976        *Benjamin Wisner Bacon: Pioneer in American Biblical Criticism* (Missoula, MT: Scholars Press).

Havener, Ivan
1987        *Q: The Sayings of Jesus, with a Reconstruction of Q by Athanasius Polag* (Collegeville: Liturgical Press).

Holman, C. Hugh and William Harmon
1992        *A Handbook to Literature: Sixth Edition* (New York: Macmillan).

Horsley, Richard A.
1991        'Q and Jesus: Assumptions, Approaches, and Analyses', *Semeia* 55: 175-209.

Iser, Wolfgang
1974        *The Implied Reader: Patterns of Communication in Prose Fiction from Bunyan to Beckett* (Baltimore: Johns Hopkins University Press).
1978        *The Act of Reading: A Theory of Aesthetic Response* (Baltimore: Johns Hopkins University Press).

Jacobson, Arland D.
1992        *The First Gospel: An Introduction to Q* (Sonoma, CA: Polebridge Press).

Jameson, Frederic
1981        *The Political Unconscious: Narratives as a Socially Symbolic Act* (Ithaca, NY: Cornell University Press).

Jeremias, Joachim
1971    *New Testament Theology*, I (London: SCM Press).
Johnson, Luke T.
1977    *The Literary Function of Possessions in Luke–Acts* (SBLDS, 39; Missoula, MT: Scholars Press).
Kealy, Sean P.
1982    *Mark's Gospel: A History of its Interpretation* (New York: Paulist Press).
Kee, Howard
1977    *Community of the New Age: Studies in Mark's Gospel* (Philadelphia: Westminster Press).
1978    'Mark's Gospel in Recent Research', *Int* 32: 353-68, repr. in Mays 1981: 130-47.
1989    'Synoptic Studies', in Epp and MacRae 1989: 245-69.
Kertelge, Karl
1970    *Die Wunder Jesu im Markusevangelium: Eine redaktionsgeschichtliche Untersuchung* (SANT, 23; Munich: Kösel).
Kingsbury, Jack Dean
1969    *The Parables of Jesus in Matthew 13* (Richmond, VA: John Knox; repr. London: SPCK; St Louis: Clayton Publ. House, 1977).
1975    *Matthew: Structure, Christology, Kingdom* (Philadelphia: Fortress Press).
1981    *Jesus Christ in Matthew, Mark, and Luke* (Philadelphia: Fortress Press.
1987    'The Developing Conflict between Jesus and the Jewish Leaders in Matthew's Gospel: A Literary-Critical Study', *CBQ* 49: 57-73.
1988    *Matthew as Story* (Minneapolis: Fortress Press, 2nd rev. edn).
Kloppenborg, John S.
1987    *The Formation of Q: Trajectories in Ancient Wisdom Collections* (Studies in Antiquity and Christianity; Philadelphia: Fortress Press).
1988    *Q Parallels: Synopsis, Critical Notes and Concordance* (Sonoma, CA: Polebridge Press).
Koester, Helmut
1990    *Ancient Christian Gospels: Their History and Development* (Philadelphia: Trinity Press International; London: SCM Press).
Leitch, Vincent
1988    *American Literary Criticism From the 30s to the 80s* (New York: Columbia University Press).
1992    *Cultural Criticism, Literary Theory, Poststructuralism* (New York: Columbia University Press).
Lightfoot, R.H.
1934    *History and Interpretation in the Gospels* (New York: Harper & Brothers).
1938    *Locality and Doctrine in the Gospels* (New York: Harper & Brothers).
Levine, Amy-Jill
1988    *The Social and Ethnic Dimension of Matthean Social History* (Lewiston, NY: Edwin Mellen).
Lohmeyer, Ernst
1936    *Galiläa und Jerusalem* (Göttingen: Vandenhoeck & Ruprecht).

Lührmann, Dieter
1969 *Die Redaktion der Logienquelle* (WMANT, 33; Neukirchen–Vluyn: Neukirchener Verlag).
Luz, Ulrich
1976 Review of Gerd Theissen, *Urchristliche Wundergeschichten*, in *TZ* 32: 173-74.
1980 'Markusforschung in der Sackgasse?', *TLZ* 105: 653-54.
1983 'The Disciples in the Gospel according to Matthew', in Graham Stanton (ed.), *The Interpretation of Matthew* (Philadelphia: Fortress Press; London: SPCK): 98-122; German orig., *ZNW* 62 (1971): 141-71.
1989 *Matthew 1–7* (Minneapolis: Augsburg; German edn, *Das Evangelium nach Matthäus*, I [EKKNT, I/1; Zürich: Benziger Verlag; Neukirchen–Vluyn: Neukirchener Verlag, 1985). Available only in German is *Das Evangelium nach Matthäus*, II (*ibid.*, 1990).
Mack, Burton
1993 *The Lost Gospel: The Book of Q and Christian Origins* (San Francisco: Harper).
McKnight, Edgar
1989 'Form and Redaction Criticism', in Epp and MacRae 1989: 149-74.
Malbon, Elizabeth Struthers
1986 *Narrative Space and Mythic Meaning in Mark* (New Voices in Biblical Studies; San Francisco: Harper & Row; repr. The Biblical Seminar, 13; Sheffield: JSOT Press, 1991).
1992 'Narrative Criticism: How Does the Story Mean?', in Anderson and Moore 1992: 23-49.
Malina, Bruce
1981 *The New Testament World: Insights from Cultural Anthropology* (Atlanta: John Knox).
1986 *Christian Origins and Cultural Anthropology* (Atlanta: John Knox).
Martyn, J. Louis
1978 *The Gospel of John in Christian History* (New York: Paulist Press).
1979 *History and Theology in the Fourth Gospel* (Nashville: Abingdon Press, rev. and enlarged edn).
Marxsen, Willi
1954 Review of Hans Conzelmann, *Die Mitte der Zeit*, in *Monatsschrift für Pastoraltheologie* 6: 254.
1969 *Mark the Evangelist: Studies on the Redaction History of the Gospel* (Nashville: Abingdon Press; German edn, 1956).
Mays, James L. (ed.)
1981 *Interpreting the Gospels* (Philadelphia: Fortress Press).
Minor, Mark
1992 *Literary-Critical Approaches to the Bible: An Annotated Bibliography* (West Corwall, CT: Locust Hill).
Moessner, David P.
1989 *Lord of the Banquet: The Literary and Theological Significance of the Lukan Travel Narrative* (Minneapolis: Fortress Press).

Montrose, Louis A.
1989          'Professing the Renaissance: The Poetics and Politics of Culture', in
              Veeser 1989: 15-36.
Moore, Stephen
1989          *Literary Criticism and the Gospels: The Theoretical Challenge* (New
              Haven: Yale University Press).
Neirynck, Frans
1972          *Duality in Mark: Contributions to the Study of the Markan Redaction*
              (BETL, 31; Leuven: Leuven University Press).
1981          'The Redactional Text of Mark', *ETL* 57: 144-62; repr. in
              F. van Segbroeck (ed.), *Evangelica I: Gospel Studies: Collected
              Essays by Frans Neirynck* (BETL, 60; Leuven: Leuven University
              Press, 1982): 618-36.
1982          'Recent Developments in the Study of Q', *ETL* 59: 29-75; repr. in
              F. van Segbroeck (ed.), *Evangelica II: 1982–1991: Collected Essays
              by Frans Neirynck* (BETL, 99; Leuven: Leuven University Press,
              1991): 409-64.
Neyrey, Jerome H. (ed.)
1991          *The Social World of Luke–Acts: Models for Interpretation* (Peabody,
              MA: Hendrickson).
Nicol, N.
1972          *The Sēmeia Source in the Fourth Gospel: Tradition and Redaction*
              (NovTSup, 32; Leiden: Brill).
Overmann, J. Andrew
1990          *Matthew's Gospel and Formative Judaism: The Social World of
              Matthew's Community* (Minneapolis: Fortress Press).
Patte, Daniel
1976          *What is Structural Exegesis?* (Philadelphia: Fortress Press).
1986          *The Gospel according to Matthew: A Structural Commentary on
              Matthew's Faith* (Philadelphia: Fortress Press).
1989          *Structural Exegesis for New Testament Critics* (Minneapolis: Fortress
              Press).
Perrin, Norman
1966          'The *Wredestrasse* becomes the *Hauptstrasse*: Reflections on the
              Reprinting of the Dodd Festschrift', *JR* 46: 296-300.
1969          *What is Redaction Criticism?* (Philadelphia: Fortress Press).
1976          'The Interpretation of the Gospel of Mark', *Int* 30: 115-24.
Pesch, Rudolf
1968          *Naherwartungen: Tradition und Redaktion in Mk 13* (Düsseldorf:
              Patmos).
1976a         *Das Markusevangelium* (HTKNT, 2.1; Freiburg: Herder).
1976b         Review of L. Schenke, *Der gekreuzigte Christus*, in *TRev* 72: 101-102.
1977a         *Das Markusevangelium* (HTKNT, 2.2; Freiburg: Herder).
1977b         Review of John R. Donahue, *Are You the Christ?* and Klemens Stock,
              *Die Boten aus dem Mit-Ihm-Sein*, in *TRev* 73: 459-60.
Petersen, Norman
1985          *Rediscovering Paul: Philemon and the Sociology of Paul's Narrative
              World* (Philadelphia: Fortress Press).

Polag, Athanasius
1977 *Die Christologie der Logienquelle* (WMANT, 45; Neukirchen–Vluyn: Neukirchener Verlag). [See Havener 1987 for a summary of his position].
Powell, Mark A.
1990 *What Is Narrative Criticism?* (Minneapolis: Fortress Press).
Powell, Mark A., with Cecile Gray
1992 *The Bible and Modern Literary Criticism: A Critical Assessment and Annotated Bibliography* (Westport, CT: Greenwood Press).
Pryke, Edgar J.
1978 *Redactional Style in the Marcan Gospel: A Study of Syntax and Vocabularly as Guides to Redaction in Mark* (SNTSMS, 33; Cambridge: Cambridge University Press).
Quesnell, Quentin
1969 *The Mind of Mark* (AnBib, 38; Rome: Biblical Institute Press).
Rhoads, David, and Donald Michie
1982 *Mark as Story: An Introduction to the Narrative of a Gospel* (Philadelphia: Fortress Press).
Richard, Earl
1983 'Luke—Writer, Theologian, Historian: Research and Orientation of the 1970s', *BTB* 13: 3-15.
Ricks, Christopher
1987 Review of Giles Gunn, *The Culture of Criticism and the Criticism of Culture* (New York: Oxford University Press, 1987), in *New York Times, Book Review*, May 10, 1987, p. 10.
Robbins, Vernon
1992 *Jesus the Teacher: A Socio-Rhetorical Interpretation of Mark* (Minneapolis: Fortress Press).
Rohde, Joachim
1968 *Rediscovering the Teaching of the Evangelists* (Philadelphia: Westminster Press; German edn, 1966).
Schenk, Wolfgang
1974 *Der Passionsbericht nach Markus: Untersuchungen zur Überlieferungsgeschichte der Passionstraditionen* (Gütersloh: Gerd Mohn).
Schenke, Ludger
1974a *Der gekreuzigte Christus* (SBS, 69; Stuttgart: Katholisches Bibelwerk).
1974b *Die Wundererzählungen des Markusevangeliums* (SBB, 5; Stuttgart: Katholisches Bibelwerk).
Schüssler Fiorenza, Elisabeth
1985 'The Followers of the Lamb: Visionary Rhetoric and Social-Political Situation', in F. Segovia (ed.), *Discipleship in the New Testament* (Philadelphia: Fortress Press): 144-65.
1987 'Rhetorical Situation and Historical Reconstruction in 1 Corinthians', *NTS* 33: 386-403.
1991 *Revelation: Vision of a Just World* (Minneapolis: Fortress Press).
Scott, Bernard B.
1989 *Hear Then the Parable: A Commentary on the Parables of Jesus* (Minneapolis: Fortress Press).

Smith, D. Moody
    1965      *The Composition and Order of the Fourth Gospel: Bultmann's Literary Theory* (New Haven: Yale University Press).
    1989      'Johannine Studies', in Epp and MacRae 1989: 271-96.
Smith, Jonathan Z.
    1975      'The Social Description of Early Christianity', *RelSRev* 1: 19-25.
Soards, Marion
    1985      'The Question of a Pre-Markan Passion Narrative', *Bible Bhashyam* 11: 144-69.
Spivey, R.A.
    1974      'Structuralism and Biblical Studies: The Uninvited Guest', *Int* 28: 133-45.
Stanton, Graham A.
    1984      'The Origin and Purpose of Matthew's Gospel: Matthean Scholarship from 1945–1980', *ANRW* II/25/3: 1889-1951.
Stein, Robert H.
    1969      'What is Redaktionsgeschichte?', *JBL* 88: 45-56.
    1970      'The "Redaktionsgeschichtlich" Investigation of a Markan Seam (Mc 1.21f.)', *ZNW* 61: 70-94.
    1971      'The Proper Methodology for Ascertaining a Markan Redaction History', *NovT* 13: 181-98.
Tagawa, Kenzo
    1966      *Miracles et Evangile: La pensée personnele de l'évangile Marc* (Etudes d'histoire et de philosophie religieuses, 62; Paris: Presses universitaires de France).
Talbert, C.H.
    1976      'Shifting Sands: The Recent Study of the Gospel of Luke', *Int* 30: 381-95, repr. in Mays 1981: 197-213.
    1977      *What Is a Gospel? The Genre of the Canonical Gospels* (Philadelphia: Fortress Press).
    1989      'Luke–Acts', in Epp and MacRae 1989: 297-320.
Tannehill, Robert C.
    1990, 1991  *The Narrative Unity of Luke–Acts: A Literary Interpretation* (2 vols.; Minneapolis: Fortress Press).
Theissen, Gerd
    1983      *The Miracle Stories of the Early Christian Tradition* (Philadelphia: Fortress Press; German edn, 1974).
    1991      *Social and Political History in the Synoptic Tradition* (Minneapolis: Fortress Press).
Thomas, Brook
    1989      'The New Historicism and other Old-Fashioned Topics', in Veeser 1989: 182-203.
Thompson, William
    1970      *Matthew's Advice to a Divided Community: Mt. 17,22–18,35* (AnBib, 44; Rome: Biblical Institute Press).
Tolbert, Mary Ann
    1989      *Sowing the Word: Mark's World in Literary-Historical Perspective* (Minneapolis: Fortress Press).

Tompkins, Jane P.
 1980 Reader-Response Criticism: From Formalism to Post-Structuralism (Baltimore: Johns Hopkins University Press).
Tuckett, Christopher M.
 1989 'A Cynic Q?', *Bib* 70: 349-76.
Veeser, Aram (ed.)
 1989 *The New Historicism* (London: Routledge & Kegan Paul).
Via, Daniel O.
 1975 *Kerygma and Comedy in the New Testament: A Structuralist Approach to Hermeneutic* (Philadelphia: Fortress Press).
Wahlde, Urban von
 1989 *The Earliest Version of John's Gospel: Recovering the Gospel of Signs* (Wilmington, DE: Michael Glazier).
Weeden, Theodore
 1971 *Mark—Traditions in Conflict* (Philadelphia: Fortress Press).
Wilder, Amos N.
 1971 *The Language of the Gospel: Early Christian Rhetoric* (Cambridge, MA: Harvard University Press, rev. edn with new preface; orig. edn, 1964).
 1982 *Jesus' Parables and the War of Myths* (Philadelphia: Fortress Press).
Wrede, William
 1971 *The Messianic Secret* (Cambridge: James Clark; German edn, 1901).
Zerwick, Maximillan
 1937 *Untersuchungen zum Markus-Stil* (Rome: Biblical Institute Press).

# THE MAJOR IMPORTANCE OF THE MINOR CHARACTERS IN MARK[*]

## Elizabeth Struthers Malbon

### Introduction

Not everyone who theorizes about biblical narrative investigates characterization per se. Robert Funk, for example, in his monumental *Poetics of Biblical Narrative* focuses on plot, with detailed attention to segmentation of narrative units and sequences of narrative events. One who looks up 'characters' in Funk's index is referred to 'participants'. Characters are not abstracted from the plot and examined in themselves or in relation to each other but are considered only as participants in narrative events.

Not everyone who investigates characterization in biblical narrative attends to the role and significance of 'minor' characters. Meir Sternberg, for example, in his equally monumental *Poetics of Biblical Narrative*, devotes two chapters (9 and 10) to characterization, and three columns of entries under 'character' and 'characterization' appear in the index. Yet 'minor' characters are not specifically discussed, anonymous characters are considered 'faceless' (Sternberg 1985: 330), 'typal' characters are said to be resisted in the (Hebrew) Bible (e.g. pp. 347-48, 362), and greatest attention is given the relation between 'the truth' (i.e. 'explicit statements made about character') and 'the whole truth' (i.e. 'the

*   I wish to acknowledge the major importance of some minor characters in my life as I began to reduce to writing these thoughts on Markan minor characters: (1) the contributors to *Characterization in Biblical Literature* (*Semeia* 63), which I have edited with Adele Berlin, containing nine essays and four responses dealing with theory and exegesis of characterization in the Hebrew Bible and the New Testament, and especially Adele Berlin, who graciously extended her editorial service to read this essay; (2) Joel F. Williams, who sent me a copy of his dissertation, 'Other Followers of Jesus: The Characterization of the Individuals from the Crowd in Mark's Gospel', now published by JSOT Press (JSNTSup, 102; Sheffield, 1994).

secrets and consequences of character'; p. 321) with regard to such major characters as the patriarchs and Saul, David and Absalom.

Some who do attend to the role and significance of 'minor' characters in biblical narrative misconstrue these on the basis of over-generalization on the one hand or dismissive labeling on the other. David Rhoads and Donald Michie, for example, over-generalize that 'minor characters in the gospel [of Mark] consistently exemplify the values of the rule of God' (Rhoads and Michie 1982: 129) and that the 'narrator consistently introduces the little people favorably' (p. 130). As we shall see below, the Markan depiction of minor characters is more complex than that. Markan redaction critics, at the other extreme, frequently ignore or dismiss the minor characters because they are generally labeled as coming from 'the tradition' rather than from 'the redaction' (see Williams 1992: 28-31). Perhaps twentieth-century readers have a tendency to dismiss minor characters because they are 'flat'—one-dimensional, static, stereotypical—rather than 'round'—multi-dimensional, developing, individual (the terms 'flat' and 'round' are from Forster 1927). However, not only must attention to characterization be integrated with analysis of plot, settings, rhetoric, etc., but also all the characters—'minor' as well as 'major'—must be observed in relation with each other if we are to be competent and sensitive readers of biblical narratives.

What makes a Markan character minor rather than major? It is some lack. Is it the lack of a name? Minor characters frequently are anonymous: the leper, the poor widow, the centurion. But minor characters may also be named: Bartimaeus, Simon of Cyrene, Joseph of Arimathea. Is it a lack of a 'rounded' portrayal? Minor characters are frequently 'flat': trusting suppliants and antagonistic demons. But 'flat' characters are not always minor: the Markan 'Pharisees' are one-dimensional in their opposition to Jesus, but that opposition is critical to the movement of the plot; the 'Pharisees' are not minor characters. Is it the lack of a contribution to the major plot line that makes a character minor? This is much more difficult to judge, since it would require, at least, clear delineation of the major plot line. If the major plot line of Mark were considered the outworking of who Jesus is as 'Christ, Son of God' (1.1), would those who, as recipients of his healing power, bring out his authority and those who bring about his death, and thus enable him to give his life as a ransom for the many (10.45), be minor characters? If the major plot line were considered the outworking of who Jesus is *and* what following him entails, even fewer characters could be labeled 'minor'. It does seem, however, that minor characters tend to present commentary on the plot more than contribute to its movement; yet the role of providing narrative commentary is not unique to minor characters. Neither anonymity nor 'flatness' demarcate 'minor' characters. And 'contribution to the major plot line' is not a clear enough criterion to prove useful.

For my purposes a 'minor' character is one who lacks a continuing or recurrent presence in the story as narrated. For the most part minor characters appear only once: the Gerasene demoniac, the Syrophoenician woman, the anointing woman. Occasionally minor characters appear two or three times.[1] If the appearances of Jesus' family at 3.21 and 3.31-32 are considered two separate scenes rather than (as is more usual) one scene into which a scene with the scribes has been intercalated (3.22-30), then Jesus' family (3.21)—or mother and brothers (3.31)—appears twice. If 'the centurion' whom Pilate summons to confirm Jesus' death (15.44) is the same centurion who commented at his death, 'Truly this man was Son of God' (15.39), and if the death and the confirmation of it are considered two scenes (narrative material does intervene), then this minor character appears twice—in close succession. If the *neaniskos* (young man) who flees naked at Gethsemane (14.51-52) and the *neaniskos* who greets the women at the tomb (16.5) were to be considered the same character—a much more dubious denotative hypothesis, although the two reverberate connotatively—this minor character would be counted as appearing twice. The women characters who appear at the crucifixion (15.40-41), at the burial (15.47) and at the empty tomb (16.1-8) are a more complicated case. Three are named in the first and third instances, and two in the second; and the second Mary

1.    The non-human characters, which will not be discussed in this paper (but see n. 4), appear—or are alluded to—more than three times each: Satan (1.13; 3.23 *bis*, 26; 4.15; 8.33), demons (1.34 *bis*, 39; 3.15, 22 *bis*; 6.13; 7.26, 29, 30; 9.38), unclean spirits (1.23, 26, 27; 3.11, 30; 5.2, 8, 13; 6.7; 7.25; 9.17, 20, 25 *bis*), the (Holy) Spirit (1.8, 10, 12; 3.29; 12.36; 13.11) and God (speaking: 1.11; 9.7; alluded to: numerous references). The crowd (*ochlos*), which appears many times, is a special case, and I have commented on it elsewhere (1986a). Thus neither the non-human characters nor the crowd lack a continuing or recurrent presence in the story as narrated. The Sadducees appear only once (12.18), but because this appearance is part of a series of appearances of religious leaders (11.27–12.27) I have found it more appropriate to discuss them as part of the general category of (Jewish) religious leaders (1989) than as a minor character group.

(not Mary Magdalene) is named in three slightly different ways. These three scenes are consecutive, so by their presence in them these women characters do not really achieve a continuing presence in the story as narrated. What is most complicated, of course, is that the narrator comments at 15.41 that women, including the three named characters, did have a continuing presence in the story in Galilee that was *not narrated*. These named women characters would thus meet my criterion for minor characters—characters who lack a continuing or recurrent presence in the story as narrated—although they also challenge that criterion, as they challenge much else in a reading of Mark's Gospel.

My present goal is to suggest—illustratively, not exhaustively—that the minor characters of Mark do have major importance. (1) They, alongside the major characters, extend the continuum of potential responses to Jesus in an open-ended way, providing implicit narrative comparisons and contrasts with the responses of the continuing or recurrent characters and providing a bridge from the (internal) characters to the (borderline) implied audience. (2) They mark where the implied audience is to pause, reflect, connect; that is, they provide overall narrative punctuation—parentheses, exclamation points and colons especially. As is probably already clear in my way of stating these functions, and as will become increasingly clear in my discussion of them, they are entirely intertwined.

## Extending the Response Continuum

A narrative represents a communication event that involves an author (real and implied), a text (read or heard), an audience (implied and real, listening or reading), and various contexts (historical, literary, social, etc.). All the characters internal to the narrative exist not for their own sakes but for the sake of the communication between author and audience external to the narrative, with the implied author and implied audience marking the boundary between. The implied author and the implied audience are abstract constructions made by external interpreters on the basis of internal clues. It is important to acknowledge the dynamic relationship between external interpreters and internal clues; implied readers mask real people (you and me) who construct them on the basis of their readings of the text (see Thompson 1993: 184). I read Mark's Gospel as not only the story of Jesus as the Christ, the Son of God, but also the story of others' responses to him in that role. For some time I have been investigating the characters around the Markan Jesus, especially the religious leaders and the disciples or followers. Here I wish to show how the minor characters extend the continuum of responses to Jesus that these major characters present.

*Enemies and Fallible Followers*

The Jewish leaders—including scribes; Pharisees (and Herodians); chief priests, scribes, and elders; Sadducees; and the High Priest—respond to Jesus almost overwhelmingly as enemies. Early and continuing conflicts and arguments (see especially 2.1–3.6 and 11.27–12.27) lead to plots to destroy Jesus (see 3.6 and 14.1-2), which lead in turn to a Jewish trial and condemnation as prelude to a Roman crucifixion. Mark's narrative clearly depicts the Jewish *leaders* as a whole and not the Jewish *people* as enemies to Jesus. Nearly all the characters in the Markan narrative are Jewish, and from them come friends and followers as well as foes of Jesus. Thus it makes more sense to refer to the *religious* leaders than to the Jewish leaders. Nor are the religious leaders portrayed unilaterally as enemies; there are significant exceptions. Jairus, 'one of the leaders of the synagogue' (5.22), is exceptional in his faith in comparison with the religious leaders as a whole; he is more like many of the minor characters who exemplify faith in Jesus' healing power; in fact, his story is inter-calated with the story of one such minor character, the hemorrhaging woman. The story of the exceptional scribe who commends and is commended by Jesus (12.28-34) comes as a surprising contrast after a series of conflicts between Jesus and various religious leaders (11.27–12.27). Joseph of Arimathea, 'a respected member of the council [*bouleutēs*]' (15.43), is also an exceptional religious leader, performing the role of a disciple in burying his master (cf. 6.29, John's disciples), rather than the role of the enemy taken on by 'the whole council [*sumboulion*]' (15.1). The anti-clerical or anti-establishment stereotyping of the Markan narrative is very much a part of its early Christian context, but Mark's Gospel challenges rather than absolutizes that stereotyping by narrating the disciple-like and exemplary actions of Jairus, one of the scribes and Joseph of Arimathea. It is not a character's social group that is decisive for the Markan narrative, but the character's response to Jesus.

An enduring debate in contemporary Markan scholarship is whether the disciples in Mark are portrayed negatively or positively, or, better, whether the disciples, with their positive and negative aspects, are portrayed polemically or pastorally (see e.g. Williams 1992: 31-44; Black 1989). I am not at all convinced by the polemical interpretations that the disciples are 'transparent' to some historical enemies of the real author of Mark (cf. Williams 1992: 44-48), and I have argued elsewhere (Malbon 1983, 1986a, 1993b) for the pastoral interpretation. The disciples are fallible followers—strong in their callings, but also misunderstanding of the nature of Jesus' messiahship, and, as they begin to understand, frightened of the implications for their own followership. The implied author encourages in the implied audience both identification with and judgment of the disciples as a way of eliciting self-judgment and offering hope. Because even Jesus' chosen twelve found it difficult to follow Jesus, the latter-day followers (the implied audience) must take care. But if Jesus never gave up on the twelve, then there is hope for the implied audience as well.

Hope and critique, identification and judgment, are not direct opposites. 'Identification with' characters is not simply equivalent to 'admiration of' them, and 'judgment of' a character group does not necessarily mean 'dissociation from' it. I am in firm disagreement with interpreters who assume that the audience identifies only with characters with positive traits or only with one character or character group—or even only one character or character group at a time. The key issue for the implied audience is *not* identification with positive characters versus dissociation from negative characters (as Williams assumes) but developing sympathy, empathy and community particularly with the paradoxical characters within a range of characters and character groups.

The implied audience is encouraged both to identify with and to judge the fallible followers of Jesus, and the category of fallible followers is open-ended in Mark. It can include the women at the cross and tomb (Malbon 1983); it stretches outward from the disciples to the crowd to 'whoever'—'whoever does the will of God' (3.35), ' whoever gives you a cup of water to drink because you bear the name of Christ' (9.41; see Malbon 1986a: 124-26). It provides a bridge from the characters internal to the narrative to the implied audience at the boundary of the narrative and the external world.

Enemies and fallible followers are two general categories of respondents to the Markan Jesus. Religious leaders are generally, but not always, depicted as enemies. The disciples, but not the disciples alone, are portrayed as fallible followers; and 'fallible followers' itself is a paradoxical category. The open-endedness of the categories is crucial to the Markan narrative. An assumed enemy, like council member Joseph of Arimathea, can take on the actions of a disciple, an exemplary follower. And Judas, 'one of the twelve' (14.10, 20, 43), can become such a *fallible* follower that he gives essential aid to Jesus' enemies. What is implied in Mark is more a response continuum—from enemies to fallible followers—than rigid, stereotyped categories of characters. The minor characters extend that response continuum.

### Exemplars

As the religious leaders are *generally* depicted as enemies of Jesus in Mark, and the disciples are *generally* portrayed as fallible followers, so the minor characters are *most often* presented as exemplars. In their brief moments of narrative time they serve as models for attitudes and behaviors appropriate also for the major characters of the narrative and especially for the implied audience. The division of Mark's narrative into two parts, often observed in relation to narrative space (Galilee/Jerusalem; see Malbon 1986b) or the unfolding of Jesus' messiahship (power/suffering), is obvious as well with regard to the minor characters as exemplars.

In the first half of the narrative the minor characters exemplify primarily faith in Jesus' healing power. Healing and exorcism stories tend to be narrated in pairs, and sometimes in triplets, in ways that suggest inclusiveness of males and females, Jews and Gentiles, among those who have faith in the in-breaking power of the kingdom of God manifest in the Markan Jesus. A male with an unclean spirit is healed in the (public) synagogue in Capernaum (1.21-28); a female with a fever is healed in a (private) home in Capernaum (1.29-31). A leper expresses his faith by imploring Jesus, 'If you choose, you can make me clean' (1.40), and the friends of a paralytic express their faith by digging through the roof to present their paralyzed friend to Jesus for healing (2.4-5). Although an attitude of faith may also be implied on behalf of the man with a withered hand (3.1-6), the conflict theme completely overwhelms this healing narrative. The Gerasene demoniac is male and Gentile; Jairus' daughter and the hemorrhaging woman, whose stories are intercalated, are female and Jewish. Since these three healings are especially difficult ones (the Gerasene was so desperately ill that he lived among the tombs, the woman had been hemorrhaging for twelve years, and Jairus' daughter died while Jesus was en route), they serve to exemplify Jesus' mighty power and the certainty that the kingdom of God has come near. The two intercalated healings also serve to exemplify the profound faith of Jairus and the woman (see esp. 5.23, 28). Jesus' words to the woman are not lost on the implied audience: 'Your faith has made you well' (5.34).

The Syrophoenician woman is, obviously, female and Gentile; and her faith—and boldness and cleverness—in pleading for her daughter echoes—and elaborates—that of the male Jew, Jairus, in pleading for his. The healing of the daughter of this most definitely Gentile woman in the region of Tyre (7.24-30) is followed almost immediately by the healing of a very possibly Gentile man in the region of the Decapolis (7.31-37). The response of the crowd, a usual aspect of healing stories, in the case of the deaf mute of the Decapolis is unusually elaborated, serving, it turns out, as the conclusion to a certain kind of healing story in Mark: 'They were astounded beyond measure, saying, "He has done everything well; he even makes the deaf to hear and the mute to speak"' (7.37). From the exorcism of the man with the unclean spirit in the Capernaum synagogue to the healing of the deaf mute in the Decapolis, the Markan Jesus has done all things well. He has exemplified his power and authority as the Christ, the Son of God, the proclaimer and bringer of the kingdom of God. Only minor characters, never major characters such as the disciples or the religious leaders, are healed by Jesus in the Markan narrative, and the minor characters whom he has healed exemplify faith in Jesus' power and authority. Their stories of faith and healing are absolutely essential to Mark's story of Jesus as the Christ. Their responses of exemplary faith extend the Markan response continuum: from enemies to fallible followers to exemplars.

While in the first half of Mark minor characters appear primarily as suppliants, in the second half they appear in that role only three times, and all of these occur in the middle section, 8.22–10.52: the blind man of Bethsaida, the father of the 'epileptic' boy and blind Bartimaeus of Jericho. Commentators generally recognize the symbolic significance of the two stories of giving sight to the blind, made more obvious by their functioning as a frame around the section in which the Markan Jesus is attempting to give his disciples insight into his passion—and theirs. But the symbolic significance of the story of the healing of the epileptic boy, embedded as it is in this same section, generally goes unmentioned. The healing story begins with double manifestations of fallibility: the disciples have failed in their attempt to cast out the unclean spirit (9.17-18), and Jesus expresses his frustration with the faithlessness of the entire generation (9.19). Rather than being a straightforward exemplar of faith, the epileptic's father presents dramatically the image of a fallible follower: 'I believe; help my unbelief!' (9.24).

The sequence of scenes in 8.22–10.52, focused on minor characters but bearing symbolic significance not only for the major characters but also for the implied audience, is impressive. The two-stage healing of the blind man at Bethsaida (8.22-26) prepares the implied audience for a second stage of seeing and understanding, one that the major character Peter has not yet reached (8.27-33). The healing of the epileptic boy (9.14-29) also takes place in two stages: the disciples' attempt at healing fails, Jesus' attempt succeeds. The boy's father is caught between faith and unfaith; he seeks to follow in faith, but he is fallible. However, his request *is* granted by Jesus; the Markan Jesus does not give up on one struggling between faith and unfaith. Fallibility is forgiven. The final healing story in the second half of Mark is that of blind Bartimaeus of Jericho, who is an exemplar not only of faith and perfect sight but also of followership: he 'followed him [Jesus] on the way' (10.52). But before the story of Bartimaeus there occurs one more story of a minor character—not a healing, but the encounter of Jesus and the rich man. After a conversation about eternal life and the commandments, Jesus asks the rich man to give up his possessions and 'come, follow me' (10.21). This is a call—not unlike the call of the four fishermen (1.16-20) or the call of Levi (2.13-17), but the rich man turns away. Interpreters have observed that the so-called healing story of Bartimaeus manifests many aspects of a call story (see Williams 1992: 228-44). Whereas the rich man abandons an explicit call, Bartimaeus follows one that is only implicit. Two minor characters, the blind man and the epileptic boy's father, not unlike the major character Peter, struggle betwixt and between—between sight and no sight, between faith and no faith. One minor character, the rich man, not unlike Judas, turns away from the struggle. And one minor character, Bartimaeus, perhaps as a special invitation to the implied audience,[2] follows on the way, the way of discipleship, the way to Jerusalem.

---

2.   For Williams, Bartimaeus becomes the pivotal 'individual from the crowd' in Mark's Gospel, portrayed as 'both an exemplary figure and a transitional figure' (Williams 1992: 228). According to Williams the Bartimaeus' story marks the place where 'the reader' begins to associate with a series of exemplary individuals from the crowd and to dissociate from the disciples, although still maintaining sympathy for them (p. 253; see pp. 227-54). My view of the idea of association versus disassociation

The implied audience approaches Jerusalem with Bartimaeus (10.52–11.1). For the remainder of the Markan narrative the minor characters are not suppliants who exemplify faith in Jesus' healing power but exemplars who model service, sacrifice and recognition of Jesus' identity as Teacher, Christ (Messiah), Son of God. We have mentioned above the exceptional scribe who says to Jesus, 'You are right, Teacher' (12.32), and to whom Jesus says, 'You are not far from the kingdom of God' (12.34). We will note below the significant, framing (or parenthetical) placement of the stories of the poor widow (12.41-44) and the anointing woman (14.3-9). The poor widow symbolizes Jesus' death by giving her whole life (*holon ton bion autēs*, 12.44); the anointing woman prepares for Jesus' death by anointing his body beforehand for burial (14.8). It is also entirely possible that the implied audience sees in her action of anointing Jesus' head a recognition of Jesus as the Christ (Greek), the Messiah (Hebrew), 'the anointed one'. It is paradoxical, to say the least, for the Messiah to be anointed by an unnamed woman in a leper's house (14.3) rather than by the High Priest in the temple, but Mark's Gospel has nothing against paradox!

The centurion's role as a minor character is certainly paradoxical: he assisted with Jesus' crucifixion, and then, when he saw how Jesus 'breathed his last, he said, "Truly this man was Son of God!"' (15.39). The scene is a dramatization of a central thrust of Mark's Gospel: Jesus is a suffering messiah; Jesus can only be truly seen as Son of God when this reality is experienced. It is paradoxical that one of the executioners expresses this experience. It is paradoxical that a minor character completes the half-way confession of a major character (Peter, 8.27-33). It may even be paradoxical that the centurion, like the chief priests and the scribes who mocked Jesus on the cross as 'the Christ, the King of Israel' (15.32), does not comprehend the significance of his own words within the narrative. But I find it a more natural reading to assume that the centurion is portrayed as knowing what he is saying (cf. Lightfoot 1950: 56-57), just as the anointing woman is depicted as knowing what she is doing. His words and her actions, like the actions of the poor widow, of course, take on for the implied audience a symbolic significance; these

was stated above. I find that Williams inflates the 'unique' position of Bartimaeus, dismissing Levi—who also follows Jesus—as an individual from the crowd (p. 155 n. 36) and underestimating the parallel between the blind man of Bethsaida and Bartimaeus as symbolic characters whose stories of healing become subsidiary to their significance as narrative representations of the nature of followership.

minor characters are exemplars of the paradox of suffering service as a manifestation of the power of the kingdom of God.

With the remaining minor characters in the Markan narrative we continue this major paradox and add the paradoxical application of quite specific names to minor characters we would have expected, on the basis of the preceding narrative, to be anonymous: Simon of Cyrene, the father of Alexander and Rufus; Joseph of Arimathea; Mary Magdalene; Mary the mother of James the younger and of Joses; and Salome. Simon of Cyrene, described simply as 'a passer-by, who was coming in from the country' (15.21), suffers and serves by carrying Jesus' cross to Golgotha (15.21-22). The implied audience can easily be supposed to hear in this action an echo of Jesus' words: 'If any want to become my followers, let them deny themselves and take up their cross and follow me' (8.34). Joseph of Arimathea, described amazingly as 'a respected member of the council'—presumably the council that had turned Jesus over to Pilate (15.1)—'who was also himself waiting expectantly for the kingdom of God' (15.43)—with echoes of the exceptional scribe 'not far from the kingdom of God' (12.34)—suffers and serves by bearing the expense, the labor and the risk of burying Jesus' body (15.42-46). Mary Magdalene and the other Mary watch the burial (15.47), as they, and also Salome, had watched the crucifixion (15.40-41). The three women take action in the following scene. Their suffering is grieving; their offered service is to complete the hurried burial by anointing the body. Of course there is no body in the tomb to anoint, the symbolic anointing having been sufficient for the narrative. The specificity of personal names—as well as place names and times—focuses the attention of the implied audience on the passion of Jesus. Minor characters serve not only as witnesses but also as exemplars of the necessity and possibility of suffering service in the kingdom of God Jesus proclaims as having come near.

The narrative situation—and thus the interpretation—of the three named women at the close of the Markan Gospel is more complex than that of the other minor characters. Not only are the women present at the crucifixion *and* the burial *and* the empty tomb, whereas most minor characters appear but once, but the three named women—and nameless others—are reported, retrospectively, to have followed Jesus (*ēkolouthoun*, 15.41) and to have ministered to him (*diēkonoun*, 15.41; cf. 1.31 and 10.45) in Galilee. They were really major characters in the story behind the narration, although minor characters in the narrative itself. And like another group of major characters, the disciples, they seem sometimes to be exemplars, but are, in the end, fallible followers. The women stay with the Markan Jesus longer than the twelve, but even they look on the crucifixion 'from a distance' (15.40; cf. Peter following 'at a distance' at 14.54). The women come to the tomb as faithful followers, but they depart in stunned silence rather than proclaiming the young man's requested message. They too are fallible followers (Malbon 1983).[3]

Thus the minor characters around Jesus, generally presented as exemplars, occur in three sequential sets in the Markan narrative. From 1.1 through 8.21 the minor characters are generally suppliants who exemplify faith in Jesus' healing power and authority as proclaimer of the kingdom of God. In 8.22 through 10.52, the middle section of Mark, three suppliants appear—all with rich connotative and symbolic significance for understanding the nature of followership, especially fallible followership—as well as the rich man who is a negative exemplar of followership. From 11.1 through 16.8, the passion story, the minor characters are generally exemplars of suffering and service as paradoxical aspects of the messiahship of Jesus and the kingdom of God, although Pilate and the soldiers, of course, act as enemies. Like the disciples as fallible followers and the religious leaders as enemies, the minor characters as exemplars manifest a certain rhythm in their appearance, but the rhythm of each group is distinctive. If the disciples may be said, schematically, to move from their best, to worse, to their worst, and the religious leaders from bad to worse to the worst, then the minor characters as exemplars might be said to move from good to mixed to best. The implied author is concerned to illustrate who Jesus is as the Christ and who can be his followers and how. As the disciples increasingly manifest the difficulty of followership by their fallibility, the minor characters are increasingly called on to manifest the possibility of even difficult followership. The unfolding of the plot demands and

3. In my 1983 article focused on the woman characters of Mark, I discussed all the woman characters under the category of fallible followers. Although I discussed each character separately, the label fallible followers was actually applied to the entire group as a whole. I now find that the characters I described then as 'Bold and Faithful Woman' (hemorrhaging woman, Syrophoenician woman) and 'Self-denying Serving Women' (poor widow, anointing woman)—each of whom initiates action in a striking way, to which Jesus responds (1983: 35)—are better described as exemplars, while the three named women at the cross and the tomb are indeed best described as fallible followers.

depends on changes in the characters and groups of characters. Such changes are particularly evident with the minor characters, who are not in themselves a group, but simply a collection of characters.[4]

*Parallel Characters*

A few minor characters are not clearly enemies, fallible followers or exemplars in relation to the Markan Jesus; these related characters include John the baptizer, Herod and Herodias. Perhaps John could be considered an exemplar of Jesus' proclamation since John, like Jesus, preaches repentance (1.4-5, 14-15), but John is Jesus' precursor more than exemplar. John goes out to preach, is rejected and handed over, and is killed; Jesus goes out to preach, is rejected and handed over, and is killed (Malbon 1993a: 222-23). Thus John is more accurately described as a character parallel to Jesus than as an exemplar (or fallible follower). John appears three times in the narrative, but the second and third times are retrospective (1.2-8; 1.14; 6.14-29). In his final retrospective appearance John is intertwined with Herod and Herodias. Perhaps Herod could be considered an enemy of Jesus since when Herod hears of Jesus' activity he worries that Jesus is John (whom he beheaded) resurrected (6.14-16), and Jesus warns his disciples to 'beware of the yeast of the Pharisees and the yeast of Herod' (8.15), but Herod is really John's enemy more than Jesus' enemy. (The Herodians, however, in concert with the Pharisees, do act as Jesus' enemies at 3.6 and 12.13.) Thus Herod is more accurately described as a character parallel to Pilate, Jesus' political enemy, than as a direct enemy of Jesus. By a similar narrative analogy Herodias and her daughter are parallel to the chief priests, scribes and elders (the council) and the crowd because the former (Herodias; the council) stir up the latter (the daughter; the crowd) to influence another (Herod; Pilate) to bring about a desired death (John's; Jesus'; see Malbon 1983: 46). This parallel story, presented as a narrative flashback, is intercalated between the sending out and the return of Jesus' twelve disciples to preach and heal as he had done. The Markan narrative rhetoric discloses a parallel between the preaching,

---

4.    Because of their distinctive status the non-human characters (see n. 1) are not entirely comparable to human enemies, fallible followers and exemplars of Jesus, but if enemies represent the extreme negative value and exemplars the extreme positive value on the response continuum, the non-human characters might be arrayed as follows: Satan—demons and unclean spirits—enemies—fallible followers—exemplars—Holy Spirit—God.

being rejected, being handed over, and death of John, Jesus and the disciples (see 13.9-13). At ch. 6 John is dead, Jesus is rejected (6.1-6) and the disciples are preaching. What will happen to Jesus next? What will happen to the disciples? (Malbon 1992: 41).

There are other parallels between characters who can be designated enemies, fallible followers or exemplars of Jesus, or between such characters and Jesus. An unnamed woman provides a positive parallel to Jesus by giving 'her whole life' (12.44). An unnamed follower of Jesus provides a negative parallel to Jesus by striking the slave of the high priest and cutting off his ear (14.47) while Jesus is being arrested with no personal resistance in order to be taken to the high priest (Malbon 1989: 269 n. 34). Parallels also exist between Judas who betrays Jesus and the rich man who turns away from him, and between Peter and both the half-healed blind man of Bethsaida and the half-faithful father of the epileptic. Peter also provides a negative parallel to Jesus in the inter-calated scenes of Jesus' trial by the high priest and Peter's 'trial' by one of the servant-girls of the high priest (14.53-72; Malbon 1983: 46). These parallel scenes serve to underscore the movement of Judas from fallible follower to enemy and the movement of Peter from initial exemplar (1.16-18) to most definitely fallible follower.

Thus, overall, the minor characters of the Gospel of Mark extend the response continuum by adding the category of exemplars. The characters around Jesus respond to him as enemies, as fallible followers or as exemplars. Generally the (Jewish) religious leaders respond as enemies, the disciples as fallible followers and the minor characters as exemplars, with the continuum of responses providing the framework for understanding any particular response. But the exceptions are crucial to the narrative. Not all religious leaders exhibit enmity; a few are exemplary (Jairus, the exceptional scribe, Joseph of Arimathea). And not only religious leaders are enemies; so are political leaders (Herod, Pilate) and even one disciple (Judas). Not only disciples are fallible followers; so are some minor characters. Thus not all minor characters are exemplars; while some are fallible followers (the epileptic's father) others are enemies (Pilate, perhaps the rich man).

For the most part, the exceptional characters within a given category appear late in the Markan narrative. The passion story, an exceptional story indeed, is filled with exceptional characters: the exceptional scribe and Joseph of Arimathea are exceptions to the religious leaders as enemies; the centurion is an exception to the political leaders (Pilate and his soldiers) as enemies; Judas is an exception to the eleven disciples who, however fallible as followers, are certainly not enemies actively contributing to Jesus' death; the three named women at the cross and tomb are exceptions to the more usual exemplars because of their suggestive presentation as fallible followers. There are several obvious reasons for the late appearance of exceptional characters: (1) Unless the general expectations of characters were presented first the exceptions would not clearly stand out as such. (2) The entire narrative turns on a reversal of expectations—not only power but suffering is a manifestation of Jesus' messiahship and the kingdom of God. (3) The plot requires certain actions late in the narrative—e.g. a centurion commenting on how Jesus died must appear at the close of the crucifixion scene. The requirements of the plot also explain why the exceptional religious leader Jairus does *not* appear late in the narrative: he is one of the leaders of the synagogue (5.22, 35), and, with Jesus' rejection in the synagogue in his *patris* ('hometown', 6.1-6), the synagogue is left behind as a spatial setting in the Markan narrative (see Malbon 1986b). While the more typical characters contribute to the implied audience's perception of the response continuum of enemies—fallible followers—exemplars, the exceptional characters contribute to the implied audience's sense of the dynamism and open-endedness of the response continuum. Enemies can become exemplary followers, but fallible followers can become enemies. Nothing is static. Nothing is absolute.

### Narrative Punctuation

In addition to their significance in extending the continuum of responses to the Markan Jesus, minor characters often appear at significant points in the narrative. Especially when Mark's Gospel is heard rather than read, certain stories of minor characters serve to 'punctuate' the narrative. Here I wish to apply this evocative metaphor of narrative punctuation to several stories of minor characters that mark where the implied audience is to pause, reflect, connect. Most familiar are paired stories serving as 'parentheses' around a larger narrative unit. Other examples include stories functioning as 'exclamation points' to indicate surprising end points or conclusions, or as 'colons' to direct attention to narrative material that follows as an explanation or spelling out of implications. My examples are not intended to be exhaustive; nor do I intend to construct a systematic 'narrative punctuation', analogous to a 'narrative grammar'. My goal is, rather, to complement the primarily synchronic (or paradigmatic) look (shown above) at the way minor characters extend the response continuum by a more diachronic (or syntagmatic) look at when in the narrative sequence some stories featuring minor characters occur.

### 8.22–10.52

One of the most consistent observations of Markan redaction critics and literary critics has been that the material in 8.22–10.52 is artfully arranged. Three times the Markan Jesus predicts his passion and resurrection; three times the disciples display their misunderstanding (or denial of the implications of Jesus' passion for themselves, his followers); three times Jesus instructs his disciples concerning the nature of his suffering/serving messiahship and the parallel nature of followership. (Of course, as Jesus teaches the disciples, the implied author teaches the implied audience.) These three passion prediction units (passion prediction—misunderstanding —instruction; 8.31–9.1; 9.30–50; 10.32-45) form the well-recognized and substantial framework of 8.22–10.52, the center section of the Gospel.

Less attention has been paid to the overall arrangement of four intervening passages: Peter's confession (8.27-30), Jesus' transfiguration (9.2-13), his healing of the 'epileptic' boy (9.14-29) and his teaching on household themes and/or metaphors: marriage and divorce, children, riches, a new 'family' (10.1-31; see Carmody 1993). But these four passages also appear to be significantly placed. To the question 'Who is Jesus?' the story of Peter's confession gives the answer 'Christ'. To the question 'Who is Jesus?' the story of Jesus' transfiguration gives the answer 'Son of God'. Manifesting Jesus as Christ, Son of God (1.1), is central to chs. 1–3 of Mark. In the midst of a section structured around foreshadowings of Jesus' suffering death, the healing of the 'epileptic' boy and the teaching on household themes and/or metaphors provide a flashback to Jesus' powerful life as healer and teacher, which is central to chs. 4–8. Minor characters come to the fore in these two scenes: the epileptic boy and, especially, his father (9.14-29) and the rich man (10.17-22).

Minor characters also come forward in the two scenes that frame this entire section—the two-stage healing of the blind man of Bethsaida (8.22-26) and the healing of blind Bartimaeus of Jericho (10.46-52), and this framing pair has received much attention from commentators (see e.g. Williams 1992: 9-24, 227-54). Clearly these two stories of the gift of sight, the only two such in Mark's Gospel, lead the implied audience to reflect on the gift of insight. The half-sight/half-blindness of the Bethsaida man as he sees persons as trees walking is immediately paralleled by Peter's half-sight/half-blindness as he sees Jesus as only a powerful Christ and not also a suffering servant. The man from Bethsaida receives a second healing touch directly and immediately; Peter's second healing touch is indirectly indicated (ch. 13, especially v. 9; 14.28; 16.7) for the story's future: the Markan Jesus predicts—and he is a faithful predictor of the future—that Peter 'will see' him in Galilee and that Peter and others 'will stand before governors and kings...as a testimony' to him. Bartimaeus not only receives his sight immediately and completely but also follows Jesus 'on the way'—in narrative context, both the way to Jerusalem and the way of discipleship—bringing to closure 8.22–10.52 with its predominant theme of discipleship and its dominant setting of 'the way'. Thus these two stories of minor characters serve as a pair of parentheses or brackets around the central section of the Gospel, marking it off for audience reflection. In oral presentation such a device would be 'say-able' and 'hear-able as echoing (see Malbon 1993a). In written form it can be presented as a simple diagram:

| | | |
|---|---|---|
| 8.22-26 | D* | healing blindness (man of Bethsaida) |
| 8.27-30 | A | Peter's confession (Who is Jesus? Christ!) |
| 8.31–9.1 | C | first passion prediction unit |
| 9.2-13 | A | Jesus' transfiguration (Who is Jesus? Son of God!) |
| 9.14-29 | B* | healing 'epileptic' boy |
| 9.30-50 | C | second passion prediction unit |
| 10.1-31 | B* | teaching on household themes/metaphors |
| 10.32-45 | C | third passion prediction unit |
| 10.46-52 | D* | healing blindness (Bartimaeus of Jerusalem) |

A = review of chs. 1–3 (now esp. for disciples)
B = review of chs. 4–8 (now esp. for disciples)
C = preview of chs. 11–16 (esp. for disciples)
D = view of proper viewing
* = involvement of minor characters

Although most of the material in 8.22–10.52 involves major characters (especially Jesus and the disciples but also the Pharisees), the crowd is never far in the background, and four minor characters come to the foreground at significant points in the narration. Two stories of renewed seeing (D*) frame the overall unit as appropriate narrative parentheses or brackets around material concerned with seeing something new. Within this frame, or echo, two additional stories of minor characters (B*) surround the middle passion prediction unit. Although many minor characters in the Markan narrative are entirely exemplary in their actions, for example, Bartimaeus, who models not only faith but also followership, the epileptic's father and the rich man are not. However, it is entirely appropriate that, as part of a larger narrative segment in which the disciples struggle with the implications of following Jesus, one minor character struggles with half-belief/half-unbelief (9.24) and another turns away from following Jesus on the way (10.22). As the epileptic's father echoes the man from Bethsaida (both *do* finally receive the healing they request), so the rich man foreshadows the road not taken by Bartimaeus.

### 2.1–3.6

Also consistently observed by Markan interpreters is the concentric arrangement of the five conflict stories in 2.1–3.6 (see Dewey 1980). This is a smaller narrative unit, but, like 8.22–10.52, it is framed, encircled or echoed by a pair of stories focused on minor characters. The opening narrative of the healing of the paralytic is complemented by the closing narrative of the healing of the man's withered hand. Stories of useless legs and a useless hand set off (and are part of) stories in which Jesus' opponents, the established religious leaders, are depicted as more concerned with 'useless' regulations regarding when and with whom to eat and not eat than with the persons to whom the rules are applied. The Markan Jesus, of course, triumphs in these conflicts; the legs and the hand are restored to usefulness. It is not insignificant that minor characters form the parentheses or brackets around this collection of stories that enacts the importance of just such characters in the kingdom of God the Markan Jesus proclaims has come near (1.14-15).

Obviously the echo effect of 3.1-6 (the withered hand) with 2.1-12 (the paralytic) cannot be heard until 3.1-6 has been sounded. 'Framing' is a label that reflects a previously completed hearing or reading; terms such as 'framing' or 'narrative parentheses' are signs of rereading (on rereading see Malbon 1993a). In the immediate process of hearing or reading Mark's Gospel the audience first catches an echo of 1.40-45, the healing of the leper, in 2.1-12, the healing of the paralytic. In each case a person with a serious physical need comes or is brought to Jesus, and the encounter leads to restored health for the individual, a minor character who exemplifies faith in Jesus' power to heal. In the former instance the leper's open proclamation apparently creates such a clamor for Jesus' aid that he can no longer enter a town openly (1.45), a problem already noted in the narrative (1.33, 37). In the latter instance the silent dialogue with some of the scribes about Jesus' words of forgiveness to the paralytic begins to enact a conflict only implied earlier (1.22, 'for he taught them as one having authority, and not as the scribes') and not fully developed until 3.6 (they 'conspired...against him, how to destroy him').[5]

In addition to the two stories of its frame, 2.1–3.6 includes a third story focused on a minor character, who is frequently not recognized as such: Levi (see e.g. Williams 1992: 155 n. 36). Levi does bear a name, of course; and the striking parallels between the narrative of his call (2.13-14) and that of Simon and Andrew and James and John (1.16-20) lead the implied audience to anticipate his name in the list of the twelve (3.13-19); but his name does not appear. Levi lacks a continuing or recurrent presence in the story as narrated. The fact that this apparent 'disciple' is not among the twelve expands for the implied audience the category of Jesus' disciples or followers.

### 12.41-44 and 14.3-9

The eschatological discourse of the Markan Jesus is framed by stories of two exemplary women: the poor widow who gives her last two coins to the temple treasury and the woman who gives an entire jar of ointment in anointing Jesus (Malbon 1983: 39; Malbon 1991: 598-99). The Markan Jesus comments that the poor widow has given 'her whole life' (*holon ton bion autēs*, 12.44) and that what the anointing woman has done will be told 'wherever the good news is proclaimed in the whole world' (14.9). Between these distinctive stories Jesus presents his eschatological discourse or his farewell discourse. This speech, the longest in the Markan narrative, produces a pause in the immediate narrative unfolding of Jesus' passion as it projects parallel trials and suffering for the followers of Jesus in the narrative's future. The passion of the community is to parallel the passion of Jesus (Malbon 1986b:

---

5.     A similar first echo and second echo effect occurs at 8.22-26, the healing of the blind man of Bethsaida. The healing of the blind man has striking parallels with the healing of the deaf man in 7.31-37 (see e.g. Fowler 1981: 105-12); both men suffer communicative disorders; both healings are quite physical. The two stories are not consecutive, as with 1.40-45 and 2.1-12, but in each case the second story becomes the first story in a new echoing—and framing—pair.

151-52); the community is to see and understand its suffering in the context of Jesus' passion. Again a pair of stories focused on minor characters forms a set of parentheses or brackets around a larger narrative unit.

The frame provided by the two giving women is not as obvious as that provided by the two blind men because another small story, that of the chief priests and scribes plotting against the Markan Jesus (14.1-2), intervenes between the close of the eschatological or farewell discourse and the story of the anointing woman. In fact, the story of the exemplary woman is itself framed by two stories of evil men: the religious leaders' plot and Judas' betrayal. The contrast with Judas is especially marked: an unnamed woman gives up money for Jesus; a named man, even 'one of the twelve', gives up Jesus for money (see Malbon 1983: 40; Malbon 1991: 599). The immediately following story narrates the appropriate Passover preparations of Jesus and the disciples (14.12-16), in striking contrast to the inappropriate Passover preparations of the traditional religious leaders (14.1-2). And, of course, the story of the woman who anoints Jesus beforehand for burial (14.8) is echoed in the story of the three women who go to the tomb to anoint Jesus after his burial (16.1-8). The story of the anointing woman is a striking example of how one passage functions in multiple ways: it is a reverse parallel to the Judas story, together with which it is framed by the reverse parallels of the Passover preparations of the chief priests and the scribes and of Jesus and the disciples; it is echoed by the story of the would-be anointing women at the empty tomb (also minor characters); and, along with the story of the poor widow, it sets off a narrative unit (ch. 13) by encircling it by stories focused on minor characters.

The opening parenthesis of this set, the poor widow, also functions in different ways in multiple narrative contexts (see Malbon 1991). In terms of the metaphor of narrative punctuation, it functions as an exclamation point to the extended and final teaching session of Jesus in the temple, 11.27–12.44. The Markan Jesus is challenged by all the major groups of Jewish leaders: chief priests, scribes and elders (11.27–12.12), Pharisees (and Herodians) (12.13-17) and Sadducees (12.18-27); and he beats them all at their own argumentative games. Then Jesus is questioned by one scribe alone, who turns out to be an exceptional scribe, one 'not far from the kingdom of God' (12.34a). This friendly encounter with a scribe ends all questions to Jesus (12.34b), but it is succeeded by two unfavorable comments about scribes made by Jesus, underlining the exceptional attitude of the one scribe. Scribes, of course, are recurrent and continuing characters in the Markan narrative. When the one scribe steps out from that group he functions as a minor character, and his story stands in striking contrast to the immediately preceding stories of Jesus' encounters with religious leaders. The most striking contrast, the final exclamation point in this compound sentence, is then provided by the story of the poor widow. Recurrent and continuing characters, functioning as a group, engage in verbal conflict with the Markan Jesus; one individual separates himself from the group by verbal agreement with Jesus; a total outsider to the group is singled out by Jesus as a model of appropriate *action*!

The story of the poor widow also serves as a narrative colon, a colon being (according to *Webster's New Collegiate Dictionary*) 'a punctuation mark used chiefly to direct attention to matter (as a list, explanation, or quotation) that follows'. What follows is Jesus' eschatological or farewell discourse, illustrating how Jesus' followers will be called upon to give their whole lives, as he will, as the poor widow has done. Willingness to give oneself is called for *and possible* (12.41-44): here are the immediate circumstances in which the disciples within the narrative and the implied audience at its edge will find this to be the case (ch. 13). Thus the poor widow is both the opposite of the religious leaders of ch. 12 ('!') and the model for the disciples (and the implied audience; see esp. 13.14, 37) of ch. 13 (':').

### 12.41-44 and 3.31-35

Mark 3.31-35 is a scene in which Jesus' mother and brothers appear as minor characters; the passage (just as 12.41-44) serves both as an exclamation point, in relation to the material it follows, and as a colon, in relation to the material following it. The parallels between 12.41-44 and 3.31-35 extend not only to their double functions as narrative punctuation but also to the nature of the surrounding narrative material. First, both 2.1–3.6 and 11.27–12.27 narrate controversy stories, the former in Galilee, the latter in the Jerusalem temple (see Dewey 1980). Secondly, both 3.7-19 (3.7-19a in the English text) and 12.28-34 present a break in the pattern of controversy: in the former situation a great crowd follows Jesus; unclean spirits, who certainly are opposed to Jesus, surprisingly fall down before him, saying 'You are the Son of God'; and Jesus chooses twelve of his followers to be disciples (or apostles) in sharing his work of preaching and healing; in the latter situation an exceptional scribe is in surprising agreement with Jesus, who commends him, saying 'You are not far from the kingdom of God'. Thirdly, in 3.20-35 (3.19b-35 in the English text) and 12.35-44 a character or characters juxtaposed with scribes culminates the series of encounters in an exemplary way. Finally, in chs. 4 and 13, a longer discourse of the Markan Jesus follows the example scene, bringing out its implications not only for the characters within the narrative but also for the implied audience at its border. The overarching pattern is controversy—cooperation—example (negative and positive)—implications:

| | | |
|---|---|---|
| 2.1–3.6 | controversy | 11.27–12.27 |
| 3.7-19 | cooperation | 12.28-34 |
| 3.20-35 | example | 12.35-44 |
| | (negative and positive) | |
| 4.1-34 | implications | 13.1-37 |

No doubt it is 3.20-35 that most calls for explanation within this pattern. Commentators often note the intercalation of the coming of Jesus' family at 3.21 and 3.31-32 and the Beelzebub controversy with the scribes at 3.22-30 (see Malbon 1983: 35). The family of Jesus may appear twice as a minor character, yet it all but disappears from the narrative scene under the pressure, first, of the strong negative example provided by the scribes, a continuing character group, and, second, by the strong positive example provided by the metaphorical heirs of Jesus' family, 'whoever does the will of God', a group that includes both characters within the narrative and especially the implied audience at the narrative's edge (see Malbon 1986a: 124-26). Although some interpreters have argued that the family of Jesus is portrayed negatively in Mark (e.g. Crossan 1973; Kelber 1983: 102-104), this assertion strikes me as an overreading of the three verses in which they are mentioned (3.21, 31-32). The family's motive for coming to Jesus is left ambiguous; somebody was saying Jesus is 'outside himself' (3.21), but not necessarily the family. Was the family trying to protect its honor or to protect Jesus? The narrative seems very little interested in the characters constituting the literal family of Jesus; all interest lies in those becoming part of the metaphorical family of Jesus (cf. 10.28-31), the latter, of course, not being limited to the former, and the former not necessarily being excluded from the latter.

Who will be followers of Jesus? Not the established religious leaders (2.1–3.6 and 11.27–12.27) and especially not the scribes (3.22-30 and 12.35-40)—with a notable exception (12.28-34, the one scribe). Not—or not just—the biological family of Jesus (3.31-35). The disciples are indeed especially chosen followers (3.13-19). But 'whoever does the will of God' is kin to Jesus, part of his new metaphorical family! This surprising conclusion—that membership in the family of the Son of God, participation in the community witnessing the in-breaking of the kingdom of God, depends not on the usual high status criteria (roles as established religious leaders or as designated disciples of the new leader or identity as relatives of the new leader) but on doing the will of God— this surprising conclusion comes as a narrative exclamation point at the end of a series of controversy stories and a discipleship story. As the exceptional scribe 'not far from the kingdom of God' (12.28-34) echoes the called and chosen disciples (3.13-19), so the negatively-valued scribes and the positively-valued new family encountered and spoken of by Jesus (3.20-35) is echoed by the negatively-valued scribes and the positively-valued poor widow (12.35-44) observed and commented on by Jesus.

The passage about family (3.31-35) also functions like the passage about the poor widow (12.41-44) as a narrative colon: a mark that directs attention to a list, explanation, or quotation that follows. What follows the poor widow's story of suffering and sacrificial giving is the Markan Jesus' eschatological discourse concerning future suffering for his disciples (ch. 13), a discourse that serves as a narrative interlude in the midst of Jesus' own passion story. What follows the passage about Jesus' family as those who do God's will, while his biological family is waiting 'outside' (3.31-32), is Jesus' parables discourse concerning those inside who have been given the mystery of the kingdom of God and 'those outside' for whom 'everything comes in parables' (4.10-11). The parables discourse serves as a narrative interlude in the midst of Jesus' messianic activity as powerful teacher and healer, decisive proclaimer and bringer of the kingdom of God. Both of Jesus' major discourses have obvious implications for the implied audience. According to R.H. Lightfoot, both are concerned to give assurance: the parables of ch. 4 'give an assurance...of the final, ultimate certain success of His [Jesus'] mission in spite of present, temporary difficulty and hindrance'; and the sayings of ch. 13 provide 'a great divine prophecy of the ultimate salvation of the elect after and indeed through unprecedented and unspeakable suffering, trouble, and disaster' (Lightfoot 1950: 48). Both of Jesus' major discourses are preceded by a story focused on an appropriate minor character or characters.

The above examples should serve to illustrate the point: one aspect of the major importance of the minor characters in Mark is that they provide overall narrative punctuation—especially parentheses, exclamation points and colons—marking where the implied audience is to pause, reflect, connect. Of course, stories focused on minor characters do not provide the only narrative punctuation for Mark's Gospel. Mk 4.35–8.21, for example, is strongly punctuated by three stories involving Jesus and his disciples on the Sea of Galilee, two of which frame the narrative unit. However, stories centered on minor characters do occur at significant points in the narrative: setting off material as parentheses; bringing surprising closure to a series of narrative events as exclamation points; and, as colons, introducing discourses that develop the broader implications of the preceding stories.

Narrative punctuation is an aspect of the syntagmatic or sequential dimension of a narrative. The opening parenthesis occurs prior to the closing parenthesis. The exclamation point follows a series; the colon introduces one. By extending the continuum of responses to Jesus, the minor characters of Mark also make a major contribution to the paradigmatic or schematic dimension of the narrative. When viewed simultaneously, all the characters—major and minor—throughout the narrative form a system based on comparisons and contrasts with each other, and this system enlightens understanding of each character.

## Conclusion: Characters and the Implied Audience

Characters around the Markan Jesus are not to be judged by the implied audience according to their social location in the narrative world (disciples, religious leaders, diseased persons, etc.), nor by the extent of their time on the narrative scene (major or minor), nor by the development of their narrative portrayal (round or flat), but only by their response to the Markan Jesus. This is not to say that the distinctions major or minor and round or flat are without significance for interpreting the Markan narrative.[6] The minor characters, like the religious

6. In actuality I think of major and minor and flat and round as extremes of continua. Along with a number of biblical interpreters I have found the terms flat and round useful heuristic devices for investigating patterns of characterization (see Malbon 1989: 277, 280; Malbon 1991: 601; Malbon 1993b: 93). See especially Berlin's reformulation of Forster's 'flat' and 'round' characters into three types (thought of as points on a continuum): '1) the agent, about whom nothing is known

leaders, are flat in comparison with the more rounded disciples. But the religious leaders are like the disciples in being major characters. The minor characters who are exemplars are positive in value from the point of view of the implied author and implied audience, whereas the religious leaders who are enemies are negative in value and thus the opposite of the exemplars. The disciples and others who are fallible followers manifest both positive and negative values. It is not surprising that the paradoxical fallible followers are generally the rounded disciples, since showing more than one trait is what moves a character from flatness to roundness. Nor is it surprising that there are positive, flat, minor characters (exemplars); negative, flat, major characters (religious leaders as enemies); positive and negative, round, major characters (disciples as fallible followers); but no round, minor characters of whatever value. (The closest would be those minor characters who display in brief encounters the role of fallible followers: the epileptic's father and the three women at the cross and tomb.) Flat and minor, and round and major, are not required linkages; but flat and major seems to be a more feasible category than round and minor.

A close look at these overlapping but not equivalent distinctions helps solve a puzzle encountered by Markan interpreters: Why do some of the minor characters seem to be better models of followership than the disciples? Some interpreters have even thought that these minor characters make the disciples look so bad in comparison that the disciples are to be interpreted as enemies! That designation, of course, washes out the disciples' even greater contrast with the religious leaders as enemies, as well as ignoring all the positive characterization of the disciples. It is not narratively fair (or reasonable) to judge round major characters and flat minor characters over against each other in abstraction, rather than judging both in terms of the entire response continuum and the narrative as a whole. In art as in life (let the reader understand) many could

except what is necessary for the plot; the agent is a function of the plot or part of the setting; 2) the type, who has a limited and stereotyped range of traits, and who represents the class of people with these traits; 3) the character, who has a broader range of traits (not all belonging to the same class of people), and about whom we know more than is necessary for the plot' (p. 32). For discussions of the limits of the flat–round distinction see a number of the essays and responses in Malbon and Berlin 1993. The main significance of the flat–round distinction is not that it allows us to label some characters flat (and possibly dismiss them) and others round (and possibly emphasize them) but that it forces us to consider each character in relation to all other characters. Flat and round are relative—and thus relational—terms.

probably be considered exemplary if only one well-chosen story were recounted! If Levi is exemplary in his response to his call (2.13-14), and he is, then why do we not consider Simon (Peter) exemplary in his parallel response to his call (1.16-18)? Because we know more about Peter, maybe too much about Peter for Peter's sake, but just what the implied author wants us to know for our own sakes as the potential implied audience. The minor characters and the disciples contribute differently to this communication.

In the Markan narrative the exemplars (positive, flat, and minor—and female and male, Gentile and Jew) communicate to the implied audience that anyone can be a follower of Jesus. The disciples (positive and negative, round, and major) communicate that no one finds it easy. Both messages are essential to the Markan Gospel (see Malbon 1983: 46). We see now why the three named women at the cross and the tomb are so distinctive and important in the Markan narrative. As minor characters and exemplars they open up the possibilities of discipleship: anyone can be a follower. As almost-major and almost-round characters they manifest fallibility: no one finds it easy. As the characters who have the final word, or rather the final silence, the women communicate both the inclusivity and the challenge of following Jesus.

The women characters at the cross and the tomb are on the border between flat and round, between minor and major, between exemplars and fallible followers. Perhaps it is for this reason that they form a natural bridge to the implied audience, also on the border, the border between the internal world of the text and the external world of its hearers and readers. Is the women's final silence an exclamation point— marking the surprising turn of events (resurrection) following the surprising turn of events (crucifixion) in the story of Jesus?! Is the women's final silence a colon—directing attention to what will follow:...?

Only by knowing where a minor character is in the unfolding narrative of the Markan Gospel (for example, does her or his story provide narrative punctuation?) and where a minor character is in relation to other characters (how does his or her response to Jesus compare with others' on the response continuum?) do we know who that character is for the implied audience and how that character aids communication from the implied author to the implied audience. Although real (external) interpreters construct the implied audience, we do so on the basis of an understanding of internal evidence. The otherness of the text is a constraint on the interpreter. While it is true, as Paul Armstrong notes, that 'a text is not an independent object which remains the same regardless of how it is construed' (Armstrong 1990: 11), it is also true that an interpretation *of a work* is not independent or autonomous. In fact, the literary work that we interpret is 'heteronomous', that is, 'paradoxically both dependent and independent, capable of taking on different shapes according to opposing hypotheses about how to configure it, but always transcending any particular interpreter's beliefs about it' (Armstrong 1990: x). It is my understanding that, by presenting a response continuum (with some surprises to general expectations about characters) rather than absolutely stereotyped characters, the Markan narrative constrains and shapes not only the implied audience's response to Jesus but also its response to other respondents to Jesus. Perhaps the implied audience is to generalize experiences of non-exclusivity of followership among narrative characters to experiences of inclusivity among other members of the implied audience. Indeed, all the characters internal to the narrative exist not for their own sakes but for the sake of the communication between author and audience external to the narrative, with the implied author and implied audience marking the boundary between. For the implied author of Mark, the minor characters are of major importance, but the implied audience is the most important character of all!

## BIBLIOGRAPHY

Armstrong, Paul B.
  1990      *Conflicting Readings: Variety and Validity in Interpretation* (Chapel Hill: University of North Carolina Press).
Berlin, Adele
  1983      *Poetics and Interpretation of Biblical Narrative* (Sheffield: Almond Press).
Black, C. Clifton
  1989      *The Disciples according to Mark: Markan Redaction in Current Debate* (JSNTSup, 27; Sheffield: Sheffield Academic Press).
Carmody, Timothy R.
  1993      ' "What God Has Joined Together..." ': Mk 10.2-9 as a Metaphor for the Covenant Community' (unpublished paper).
Crossan, John Dominic
  1973      'Mark and the Relatives of Jesus', *NovT* 15: 81-113.
Dewey, Joanna
  1980      *Markan Public Debate: Literary Technique, Concentric Structure, and Theology in Mark 2.1–3.6* (SBLDS, 48; Chico, CA: Scholars Press).

Forster, E.M.
    1927        *Aspects of the Novel* (New York: Harcourt, Brace & World).
Fowler, Robert M.
    1981        *Loaves and Fishes: The Function of the Feeding Stories in the Gospel
                of Mark* (SBLDS, 54; Chico, CA: Scholars Press).
Funk, Robert W.
    1988        *The Poetics of Biblical Narrative* (Sonoma, CA: Polebridge Press).
Kelber, Werner H.
    1983        *The Oral and the Written Gospel: The Hermeneutics of Speaking and
                Writing in the Synoptic Tradition, Mark, Paul, and Q* (Philadelphia:
                Fortress Press).
Lightfoot, R.H.
    1950        'The Connexion of Chapter Thirteen with the Passion Narrative', in
                *The Gospel Message of St Mark* (Oxford: Clarendon Press): 48-59.
Malbon, Elizabeth Struthers
    1983        'Fallible Followers: Women and Men in the Gospel of Mark', *Semeia*
                28: 29-49.
    1986a       'Disciples/Crowds/Whoever: Markan Characters and Readers', *NovT*
                28: 104-30.
    1986b       *Narrative Space and Mythic Meaning in Mark* (New Voices in Biblical
                Studies; San Francisco: Harper & Row; The Biblical Seminar, 13;
                Sheffield: Sheffield Academic Press, 1991).
    1989        'The Jewish Leaders in the Gospel of Mark: A Literary Study of
                Markan Characterization', *JBL* 108: 259-81.
    1991        'The Poor Widow in Mark and her Poor Rich Readers', *CBQ* 53: 589-
                604.
    1992        'Narrative Criticism: How Does the Story Mean?', in Janice Capel
                Anderson and Stephen D. Moore (eds.), *Mark and Method: New
                Approaches in Biblical Studies* (Minneapolis: Fortress Press).
    1993a       'Echoes and Foreshadowings in Mark 4–8: Reading and Rereading',
                *JBL* 112: 211-30.
    1993b       'Texts and Contexts: Interpreting the Disciples in Mark', *Semeia* 62:
                81-102.
Malbon, Elizabeth Struthers and Adele Berlin (eds.)
    1993        *Characterization in Biblical Literature* (*Semeia* 63; Atlanta: Scholars
                Press).
Rhoads, David and Donald Michie
    1982        *Mark as Story: An Introduction to the Narrative of a Gospel*
                (Philadelphia: Fortress Press).
Sternberg, Meir
    1985        *The Poetics of Biblical Narrative: Ideological Literature and the
                Drama of Reading* (Bloomington: Indiana University Press).
Thompson, Marianne Meye
    1993        ' "God's Voice you Have Never Heard, God's Form You Have Never
                Seen": The Characterization of God in the Gospel of John', *Semeia*
                63: 177-204.

Williams, Joel F.
1992          'Other Followers of Jesus: The Characterization of the Individuals
              from the Crowd in Mark's Gospel' (PhD dissertation, Marquette
              University). Now published as *Other Followers of Jesus: Minor
              Characters as Major Figures in Mark's Gospel* (JSNTSup, 102;
              Sheffield: JSOT Press, 1994).

'WATCH HOW YOU LISTEN' (LUKE 8.18):
JESUS AND THE RHETORIC OF PERCEPTION IN LUKE–ACTS

John A. Darr

Religious discourse is largely a matter of 'opening eyes and ears to whatever may be perceived to be sacred' (Chidester 1992: ix). Myth, ritual, symbol and story all utilize rhetorical strategies to condition and control perception, to introduce, inculcate and confirm particular ways of 'seeing and hearing'. This phenomenon is especially apparent in New Testament narratives, the discourse of which focuses repeatedly on recognition and response, knowing and believing, looking and listening. Elsewhere (1992) I have argued at length that the primary purpose of Luke–Acts is to form its readers into *ideal witnesses* of and to sacred history as reported in this two-volume work. In other words, its rhetorical strategies are largely designed to persuade readers to be certain kinds of *hearers* (attentive, receptive, discerning, committed, tenacious) and *retellers* (accurate, bold, effective, persistent) of 'the things that have been fulfilled among us' (Lk. 1.1).[1]

Luke's rhetoric of perception is so ubiquitous, various and nuanced that it cannot be adequately treated in a single study or through a single approach. One is forced, therefore, to get at it bit by bit, topic by topic, passage by passage, as critics have begun to do (e.g. Dillon 1978; Hamm 1986; Hamm 1990; Kelley 1991; Landry 1992). My own work has focused largely on Lukan characterization, and especially on the ways in which secondary characters model perceptional options for the reader. The present study moves beyond that indirect form of rhetoric in which the reader is *shown* correct and incorrect examples of seeing and hearing, to Jesus' speech, a much more direct ploy in which a fully authorized

---

1. By rhetoric I mean the many ways in which narrative texts manipulate and attempt to persuade their readers (cf. Booth 1983; Mailloux 1989), rather than formal principles of rhetorical speech as outlined in the ancient Greek and Roman rhetorical handbooks.

voice *tells* the reader when, where or how to look and listen.[2]

I propose that, when Jesus speaks to his *narrative* audiences (e.g. disciples, crowds, Pharisees) about seeing and hearing, the *authorial* audience infers a direct analogy to the reading process in which they are currently involved, their own seeing/hearing of the story.[3] In other words, Jesus' references to perception guide and condition reading itself. When, for example, Jesus warns his followers to 'watch how you listen' (Lk. 8.18), the reader realizes that he or she also must carefully attend to what is happening in the story world.

'The reader' should probably be envisioned not as an isolated individual reading the narrative silently to him or herself, but rather as part of a group taking in an oral performance of the Gospel narrative. The fact that ancient readers were usually *listeners* buttresses our contention about the rhetorical function of Jesus' references to perception. The group literally hears Jesus' words, even as his narrative audiences hear them, and so is sensitive to instruction about how to listen.[4] Parenthetically, even individual reading would most often have been done out loud (see e.g. Acts 8.30) so that real hearing could take place.

The present study is a reader-response examination of Jesus' sayings about perception in Luke's story. How does Jesus address issues of seeing, hearing, looking, listening, eyes, ears, sight, sound and so forth,

2.   In Luke's story world, Jesus' authority rests on the fact that he is born of, anointed by, filled with and led by the Holy Spirit (Lk. 1.35; 3.22; 4.1, 18), who is the ultimate (and final) validator of persons, actions, speech and Scripture.

3.   By authorial audience I mean the general readers that the author had in mind as he wrote. It is fruitless to try to locate the historical Theophilus, or to reconstruct a 'Lukan community', but we can and should discover much about the knowledge, skills, competence and conventions that Luke expected readers to possess in order to process his text intelligently. Elsewhere (1992: 23-29) I have described in some detail my understanding of Luke's reader. For more on authorial readers, see Tolbert 1989: 52-56.

4.   Although the oral–aural aspect of ancient reading must be taken into account (Kelber 1983), I prefer to continue to refer to the audience as readers, not mere hearers. My choice of terms is based in part on convenience (all of the theoretical literature refers to readers), but also on the need to distinguish this kind of audience from others: they are not simply listening to an extemporaneous speech, for example, but are processing data from a written (fixed) text as it is read aloud. In other words, they are guided by the same textual constraints and draw on the same literary conventions as a person who sight-reads the story. For a sober (perhaps too sober) assessment of levels of literacy in the Roman world of the first century, see Harris 1989: 222-29; very few could read for themselves, even fewer could write.

fulfilled in your ears' (v. 21b)—is succinct, but requires considerable unpacking, for initial oracles are always important signposts for readers.

### *'Fulfilled in your Ears': The Innertext*

Jesus' reference to fulfilment (*peplērōtai*) hearkens back to the prologue, a masterful rhetorical opening that sets up the basic reading dynamics of the entire story.[9] The narrative is to be about 'the things that have been fulfilled (*peplērophorēmenōn*) among (*en*) us', things that eyewitnesses perceived and handed on to others of 'us'. The narrator (also one of 'us') 'followed all these things closely from the beginning', and is now transmitting them to the reader, who, it is hoped, will also be/become one of 'us', that is, one who perceives and transmits accurately the sacred history. In short, the audience is invited to become an *insider*, a fellow witness, not by virtue of having seen and heard the divinely-sanctioned events as they actually took place in the past, but rather through insightful reading and retelling of the ensuing narrative (Darr 1993: 55-57)!

The merging of viewpoints (eyewitnesses–narrator–reader) and the concomitant juxtaposition of the real world and the narrative world ('What the apostles saw and heard is what you, the readers, are about to see and hear [read]') in the prologue is a stratagem designed to help readers 'suspend disbelief' and engage the story with minimal resistance and suspicion. They are being confronted (so the text would have them believe) with the 'real' thing, with the sacred revelation itself. And this tactic of linking present and past (and distant past—Isaiah) in the reading experience is the salient backdrop against which to understand Jesus' reference in Lk. 4.21b to fulfilment 'in the ears'. The reader experiences (or is invited to experience) what the existentialist theologians call a *language event* (Funk 1966: 20-71): the divine is revealed not (just) out there, or back then, but here and now, in the reader's 'ears', in the present act of hearing/reading itself.[10]

9.     Koet (1986: 378-80) realizes that the verb 'to fulfil' is of crucial importance in Lk. 4.21, and he advocates looking at how it and its cognates function in Luke–Acts. Curiously, however, he fails to mention the first, and perhaps most important, occurrence of the term (in the prologue), an occurrence that conditions all following references to fulfilment.

10.     The phrase 'in the ears' is a Semitism found frequently in the LXX. Things are spoken (Deut. 5.1), or told (Exod. 10.2), or read (Deut. 31.11) in (or, into) the ears of an audience. The reference is always to the act of hearing and cognitive appropriation, not just to the presence of someone while something important happens. It is

Later sayings by Jesus reinforce the sense of immediacy first fostered in the prologue and the Nazareth episode. When Jesus sends out the seventy disciples, for example, he tells them that 'the one who hears you hears me, and the one who rejects you rejects me, and the one who rejects me rejects the one who sent me' (Lk. 10.16). The perceptional alignment and its consequences are unmistakable for the authorial reader: hearing the witnesses is the same as hearing Jesus, is equivalent to hearing the divine word (note the Johannine tone of the saying). And, of course, an identical response is required in all cases.

In responding to the Pharisees' question concerning the time of the kingdom's advent, Jesus shifts the focus from externals to the internal realm of perception:

> The kingdom of God does not come *meta paratēreseōs*, nor will they exclaim, 'Look, here it is!' or 'There!' For, in fact, the kingdom of God is *entos humōn* (Lk. 17.20-21).

We need not enter the thorny thickets of controversy over whether these verses indicate that Luke viewed the kingdom as immanent or not. Involvement in such theological issues has sidetracked many critics from the task of determining how this saying functions in its narrative context. This is clearly another ironic situation in which Luke has Jesus criticize his interlocutors' behavior and spiritual shortcomings. That is, *meta paratēreseōs* is understood by the reader as referring to what the Pharisees have been doing: scrutinizing Jesus (see Lk. 6.7; 14.1) but never recognizing what he is all about. This ironic reading, based on what the audience knows about the Pharisees and the discourse of perception to this point in the narrative, helps to unlock the enigmatic final words of the saying as well: the kingdom is *entos humōn* insofar as the sovereign activity of God is well within the *perceptive ranges* of all who encounter Jesus and the other divinely-ordained agents of the story (Darr 1992: 112-14). To substitute a synonymous phrase from Lk. 4.21, the kingdom is happening 'in their ears', but they do not recognize or respond correctly to it. The kingdom 'comes' (is realized) only for those who truly 'see and hear' it, not for those who merely look on or listen in with unreceptive, resistant hearts. And all of this rhetoric is, of course, directed toward the reader. It reinforces the notion that true perception

---

therefore inadequate to translate Lk. 4.21b as 'this writing has been fulfilled in your presence'. Parenthetically, this is the only instance I can find of 'in your ears' being used with the verb 'to fulfil'.

of the story is of utmost importance, but also that authentic perception is not a given: one can, in fact, audit the entire story and not actually 'hear' it. Thus one must always watch how one listens.

To summarize, some of Jesus' sayings about seeing and hearing are designed to draw readers into the story world with a minimum of disbelief, resistance or suspicion. Such sayings encourage a reader to view the events of the story with a sense of *immediacy*; realization of the sacred takes place in the very act of hearing/reading, in the 'innertext' of readers reading, where the 'word' either takes root or dies: *today* the sacred story is 'fulfilled' in hearers' ears (4.21); *already* the kingdom 'comes' to those who are prepared to see and hear (17.21); *in the present* a reader may actually hear the Lord, for whoever listens to his witnesses also listens to him (10.16).

*Sacred Story within Sacred Story: Reading Luke–Acts Intertextually*
Jesus' reference to 'fulfilment' in Lk. 4.21 not only grounds the narrative in the reader's present (in the *inner*text of the reader reading) but also links it *inter*textually to the earlier and much larger sacred epic recounted in Jewish Scripture. By this point in Luke's story, of course, the reader already has been coaxed in numerous ways to process this story in terms of that one. Direct and indirect allusions, citations, the narrator's observations on various 'fulfilments' of prophecy and so forth repeatedly remind the reader that Luke–Acts is not to be read in isolation from the broader horizon of salvation history rehearsed in the Septuagint. On one level, therefore, Jesus' synagogue performance in Lk. 4.16-30 simply concretizes an intertextual relationship that has been developing in the reader's mind since the opening sentence of the narrative.

But Jesus' quotations of and references to Scripture in Lk. 4.16-30 go beyond a mere confirmation of intertextual linkage and the notion of promise and fulfilment. The very structure of this passage *complicates* intertextual reading. In essence, it sets up and springs a hermeneutical trap, forcing the reader to ask, 'How then should I read this narrative with reference to that previous one?' That is, the Nazareth scene sensitizes readers to the fact that the relationship between these sacred narratives is nuanced, intricate and—if misconstrued—potentially hazardous; one must, therefore, tread carefully as one learns to negotiate the complex interface that both divides and connects them. And the discourse in much of what follows is designed to introduce and teach Luke's intertextual hermeneutic. In particular, the Lukan Jesus' use of and references to Scripture will educate readers in the 'proper' appropriation of the Septuagint.

Luke's account of Jesus in his home town may be divided into two major sections that contain significant parallels. Lk. 4.16-22 consists of Jesus' reading of Isaiah, his application of it to his mission, and the people's response. Verses 23-30 include Jesus' comments foreshadowing his rejection as a prophet, his references to the Elijah and Elisha narratives, and the people's response to his words. Central to both sections, therefore, is Jesus' use of Scripture and his audience's reaction to it. What is striking is the *contrast* between how the synagogue-goers respond to the first Scripture-based 'sermon' and how they react to the second lecture of this sort.[11] In the initial case the people embrace Jesus and his words, but in the second case they become so filled with rage that they attempt to kill him. Why the sudden reversal? And how does the reader process all of this?

As we noted above, the reader *identifies* with the synagogue-goers of 4.16-22, for they match the profile for ideal witnesses as developed in the narrative. They are, after all, Jesus' town-folk; and they appear to be attentive, insightful, perceptive and receptive. They see and hear correctly what is read to them, and then they testify (or 'witness') to it.[12] Readers are encouraged to emulate the congregation in applying these Isaianic prophecies to Jesus and his mission, and to follow the crowds' lead as other scriptural oracles are tapped. Almost immediately, however, readers are obliged to *distance* themselves from the congregation because of the latter's refusal to apply the Elijah and Elisha stories to Jesus' ministry (v. 28). The lesson is straightforward and all the more effective because of the reader's earlier identification with the congregation: it is unacceptable to access and apply to the present revelation *only part* of the pertinent Scripture; and the criteria for selecting and applying Scripture are determined not by the audience, but by the narrative's authoritative voices, which, in turn, represent

11. Siker notes (1992: 76) that most commentators (including himself) divide the episode into two parts as follows: 4.16-21, Jesus' sermon; and 4.22-30, the people's responses and further interpretive comments by Jesus. But this division fails to represent the parallelism of Scripture // response in both parts, and to capture the flow of the narrative: upward in the first section (the protagonist is embraced by his homefolk); downward, or tragic, in the second section (the protagonist predicts his rejection [vv. 23-24] by his people and then is indeed rejected).

12. For a strong argument that the crowd's testimony is meant to be understood positively, rather than negatively (as some have argued), see Tannehill 1972: 53.

and articulate the ideological norms of the story.

In more theoretical terms, Luke's discourse is designed in part to control the reader's intertextual moves. When, why and how one is to access and employ *other* texts in order to process *this* text is indicated and strongly advocated through rhetorical strategies of the narrative. One such strategy involves having a fully validated character (in this case, Jesus) speak directly to the issue. The comparative statuses of the present narrative (Luke and Acts) and the prior text (the Septuagint), the selection of relevant passages from that earlier text, and the manner in which those passages are to be applied, are communicated to readers by a fully-authorized spokesperson.

The very language of 'fulfilment' of Scripture (Lk. 4.21), for instance, indicates that the present revelation, the present story, supersedes the earlier one. There is a directionality to be observed here: *that* text points forward to *this* one, and thus the earlier writing is shown to be in service to the current one. This narrative represents the culmination of God's plan, a climax for which those texts prepared. From the Lukan perspective, the ultimate value of Scripture is quite clearly to be found in its ability to illuminate, prepare for and buttress the claims of the sacred story at hand. The Jewish Scripture thus stands in relation to Luke–Acts much as John the Baptist stands in relation to Jesus, that is, as fore-runner and readier of hearts to see the 'salvation of the Lord' when it/he arrives. Luke's narrative now determines what is (and what is not) to be valued in and derived from those earlier sacred texts. Jesus' words to the seventy-two disciples as they return from their mission, for example, confirm the superiority of the present revelation over sacred disclosures of the biblical past.

> Blessed are the eyes that see what you see. I tell you that many prophets and kings wished to see what you see, but they did not see, and to hear what you hear, but they did not hear (Lk. 10.23-24).

The reference to 'prophets and kings' is a thinly-veiled allusion to sacred history as recorded in the Scripture, for the deeds and highly-charged interactions of these two character-types dominate Israel's holy writ (Buber 1946: 63). What happened in those days of divine disclosure, Jesus tells his witnesses, is not nearly as significant as what is taking place now. And, as I have argued, the 'witnesses' include not only the original disciples, but also (it is hoped) the readers. The indefiniteness of Jesus' reference to eyes supports this reading: he does not say 'your eyes', which might connote an exclusivity for the disciples' seeing, but rather, 'the eyes that see what you see', which seems to point to viewers beyond Jesus' band of disciples, to all who will 'see and hear' the wonderful 'things fulfilled among us'.

As we noted above, however, the intertextual rhetoric of the Lukan writings extends beyond a mere subordination of the earlier sacred texts; it also sets hermeneutical guidelines for selecting and appropriating elements of those writings. These interpretative controls are in line with the values and theological norms of the narrative. Jesus' appeal to Elijah and Elisha (Lk. 4.25-27) is an example of how this kind of rhetoric functions. The congregation has no problem with Jesus' application of the Isaiah passage to himself and his ministry, but they balk violently when he reminds them that Elijah and Elisha both ministered to Gentiles. The implication of the latter scriptural allusions is that Jesus' own movement also will extend beyond Israel's (Judaism's) boundaries. The Gentile mission of the church (in Acts) is thus authorized by Jesus in his very first public pronouncement.[13] Universalism, a value that has been urged on the reader in various ways since the birth narratives, is here reinforced intertextually by Jesus; the intertextual repertoire of any legitimate interpretation of Jesus and his mission must include—so readers are being informed—not just 'comfortable' (from a Jewish perspective) texts like Isaiah 61, but also troubling passages like 1 Kings 17–18 and 2 Kings 5, texts that undermine the notion of particularity.

Through texts such as the temptation episode (in which Satan quotes Scripture, Lk. 4.10-11) and the Nazareth scene, readers are learning about the potential hazards of 'uninformed' intertextual moves. Simply knowing the Scripture is not enough; one must also understand Luke's theological agenda and norms, for they function as a kind of intertextual filter, determining what is or is not a valid interface between these texts. Luke's view of Scripture is thus *utilitarian*: 'It is authoritative where it is useful...and when it is correctly interpreted. It is irrelevant at those points where God has provided subsequent alteration or annulment' (Tyson 1987: 630; also 1992: 548). As I have argued, part of the discourse of Luke–Acts is meant to teach 'correct' interpretation and to indicate where new revelation supersedes old. A number of rhetorical strategies are used in this endeavor, but Jesus' voice is perhaps primary

13.  Siker (1992: 74) is right to emphasize the importance of this passage for grounding the Gentile mission of the church, although he goes beyond the literary evidence in arguing that this passage supports the conclusion 'that for Luke the Gentile mission has a functional priority over the Jewish mission'.

in this regard. Following his dramatic sermon in Nazareth, Jesus addresses the issue of Scripture and spiritual perception in several other passages that develop Luke's specific intertextual hermeneutic even further.

In the parable of the Rich Man and Lazarus, for example, Jesus quotes Abraham as saying, 'If they do not *listen* to Moses and the prophets, they will not be convinced even if someone were to rise from the dead' (Lk. 16.31). The reference to rising from the dead is, of course, an ironic allusion to Jesus' resurrection, which, in Luke's view, constitutes one prism for intertextuality: the Scripture points to it, and, in turn, it illumines Scripture (Sanders 1987: 193). Luke's other major intertextual lens is also christological: the necessity of Jesus' suffering. On the road to Emmaus Jesus asks his spiritually-blinded disciples, 'Was it not necessary for the Christ to suffer these things and to enter his glory? And beginning from Moses and all the prophets, he explained to them the things concerning himself in all the Scriptures' (Lk. 24.26-27). This makes their 'hearts burn within them' (24.32), but their eyes are not opened until the Scripture lesson is combined with Jesus' breaking of bread (24.30-31), a clear reference to the ritual act of remembrance Jesus instituted prior to his passion (Lk. 22.19). The latter is part of the new revelation that supersedes the old without replacing it. Both are essential factors in the 'hermeneutical spiral' Luke would have his readers embrace, but each must be understood and employed in the proper (Lukan) manner. The main lesson of the Emmaus episode is that spiritual insight happens only when sacred Scripture and the divine disclosure in Jesus are properly coordinated. And God's revelation in Jesus still can be experienced immediately by later generations who will hear/read the word and break the bread (see Dillon 1978: 155).

Jesus' final characterization of his disciples assembled in Jerusalem is as 'witnesses of these things' (Lk. 24.48). 'These things' are aspects of his experience that were prophesied in the Law of Moses, the Prophets, and the Psalms (24.44). The two most important of these things are specified by Jesus when he proceeds to 'open their mind to understand the Scriptures': that [1] 'the Christ should suffer and [2] rise again from the dead the third day' (24.46). Although the entire narrative ('all the things') about Jesus is to be read in terms of Scripture, his passion and resurrection form the christological core of Luke's intertextual hermeneutic.[14]

14. See also Lk. 18.31-34, a passion prediction that grounds both suffering and resurrection in Scripture.

Continuing his farewell address to the disciples, Jesus adds a missiological lens to the more familiar christological prism of passion and resurrection; it is also written 'that repentance for forgiveness of sins should be proclaimed in [Jesus'] name to all nations (*panta ta ethnē*)— beginning from Jerusalem' (v. 47). The mention of the nations, or *Gentiles*, brings us full circle to Lk. 4.16-30 and Jesus' appropriation of the Elijah and Elisha stories to justify the spread of his movement beyond Israel. But it also prepares the authorial audience to read the upcoming narrative of the church's dispersion and growth throughout the Roman Empire as another fulfilment of the Law and the Prophets. That is, Acts is to be read intertextually with the Scripture even as is the story of Jesus.

*Summary*
The Nazareth episode showcases several rhetorical strategies involving Jesus' sayings on perception. First, it serves to draw the reader into the narrative world with a minimum of resistance; as a reading scene, it enhances reader identification with Jesus' original hearers and encourages a sense of immediacy. The sacred revelation occurs today, in your ears, as you hear/read. Second, by depicting the ultimate failure of the Nazareth congregation to recognize and respond correctly, it causes readers to re-examine their own reading. What constitutes normative reading? How can one hear but not hear, and see but not see, as does the synagogue congregation? What is wrong with their ears (that could be wrong with my [the reader's] ears also)? Third, Jesus' appropriations of Scripture establish guidelines for and controls on intertextual reading. Previous revelations in written form are seen to serve the current revelation (there is a ranking and ordering of texts), and a particular value system and theological agenda condition the selection and application of authoritative texts. All of this is filled out and buttressed in other passages and by other means in the remainder of the narrative.

*Sower, Seed, Soil and Fruit (Luke 8.4-21):*
*The Ethics of Hearing/Reading the Gospel*

The parable of the Sower, its allegorical interpretation and the related material that immediately follows (Jesus' saying about the lamp, vv. 16-18; a visit by his mother and brothers, vv. 19-21) constitute the longest Lukan passage in which Jesus directly and continuously addresses the issue of perception. Here he focuses not on the immediacy of revelation or on intertextual hearing and seeing, as in the Nazareth episode, but rather on the audience's *attention* to and *retention* of the word—perceptional values that produce spiritual fruit. At this point Jesus adds another aspect to the rhetoric of perception by explicitly linking one's ability to hear, retain and produce the word to the condition of one's 'heart'. The discourse of the passage is thus largely *ethical* in nature; in processing it, the reader is confronted with both the *external* (doing the word) and the *internal* (attitudes and values) exigencies involved in recognizing and responding to the sacred.

### Hearing and Doing the Word

The parable itself (vv. 4-8a) is familiar: a sower sows the seed in various kinds of soil (a common occurrence given the poor and diverse soils); the fates of the seeds are determined by the type of soil they happen to strike; only the good soil produces a crop (and a bumper one at that). The historical Jesus might well have meant for the parable to convey some aspect (e.g. surprise, reversal) of the kingdom; whatever his intentions, however, they are now completely conditioned by the allegorical interpretation (and other observations) that Luke's Jesus adds to the parable.

Jesus' reflections and commentary (vv. 9-21) *focalize* reader attention on the issue of spiritual perception—how one hears the word and sees the light—and map a relevant hierarchy of values: attention–retention–production. First Jesus enjoins the crowds to pay strict attention. The fundamental importance of this step is underscored both by its placement in the text (right after the parable) and by the tense of the verb used to describe when Jesus expressed it. The narrator tells the reader that 'while [Jesus] said these things [i.e. told the parable], he would (repeatedly) call out, "He who has ears to hear, let him hear!"' (v. 8b). The imperfect (*ephōnei*) indicates continual or repeated action. Neither Jesus' story audience nor the authorial audience can afford to ignore this persistent call to attention, for *attentiveness* is the first step toward authentic apprehension of the sacred.[15]

But attentiveness, in and of itself, does not insure correct hearing. The mood of the passage changes as Jesus turns from the crowds and begins to address his disciples' questions about the parable. There are some

---

15. Jesus uses the call to attention, 'He who has ears to hear, let him hear', also at 14.35b, right after the metaphor about salt losing its saltiness and being thrown out.

who see but do not see, and hear but do not really hear, he tells them (vv. 9-10). The insider/outsider rhetoric is at work here even as it was in the prologue (see above). 'You (insiders) will see and hear', Jesus informs his followers, 'but to the rest (outsiders) it remains a puzzle (in parables)'. Why is it that some (like the Pharisees), despite paying rapt attention to Jesus, fail to apprehend him and his message, while others truly 'see and hear' immediately? That is the question raised for the disciples and the reader. Jesus answers with an allegorical exposition of the Sower parable.

> Now the parable is this: the seed is the word of God. And those along the road are those who have heard; then the devil comes and takes away the word from their heart, so that they may not believe and be saved. And those on the rocky [soil] are those who, when they hear, receive the word with joy; but these have no root; they believe for a while, and in time of temptation fall away. And [the seed] that fell among thorns are those who have heard, but, as they go on their way, they are choked with worries [*merimnōn*] and riches [*ploutou*] and pleasures [*hēdonōn*] of life, and so fail to bring fruit to maturity. But [the seed] in the good soil, these are those who, having heard the word in a good and noble heart, hold it fast and bear fruit with perseverance (8.11-15).

The interpretation moves in ascending order, from those who retain the word for the least amount of time (those who are along the road) to those who retain it permanently (those in good soil). But this does not mean that Jesus envisages a perceptional *scale*, an order of seeing and hearing that one may ascend as one learns better how to see and hear. Quite to the contrary, *only* the ones who retain the word in a good heart and bear fruit truly hear and see! Even those who internalize Jesus' word long enough to begin growing fruit (those among thorns) ultimately fail, for— so Jesus claims—genuine hearing always results in fruit. It is a 'closed system' in which the one with the good heart perceives the sacred and produces (an unbelievable amount of) fruit, while all others, despite any indications to the contrary, remain completely barren. This categorical, almost Calvinistic, scenario is made even more vivid by Jesus a few sentences later: 'Therefore watch how you listen, for whoever has, to him will [more] be given, and from him who has not, even what he seems to have will be taken away' (v. 18). The fruit (wheat) one produces is actually *more seed*, which, in turn, produces more seed in the agricultural cycle. The seed is thus both received and delivered by the good soil, much as the witness is to perceive correctly and then pass along the word she or he has heard. The word is thus both seed and fruit, and its dissemination is the highest value. All of this impresses upon the audience that the stakes are high, that hearing and seeing (reading) are not to be taken for granted, that how one perceives is of ultimate import, that a genuine hearer is, necessarily, *both spiritually receptive and productive.*

The latter lesson—that perception and action are linked—is clarified and reinforced by the addition of the short pericope of Jesus' mother and brothers trying to see him, but being unable to do so because of the crowd (8.19-21). This provides the platform for Jesus to claim, 'My mother and my brothers are *those who hear the word of God and do it*'. Hearing and doing the word is one of the narrative's most prominent themes. Authentic perception will always result in active obedience to the word (see Lk. 6.46-49; 11.27-28). One cannot be a true hearer without being a doer of the sacred revelation, for the word is at one and the same time a proclamation of freedom and a summons to decision, responsibility and action. Through such rhetoric, the authorial audience learns that there is an ethical dimension to reading this narrative, for it requires introspection, investment and personal response, not passive (or resistant) auditing.

Luke's drumbeat of hearing/doing is, however, qualified in a passage closely related to ours, the story of Jesus' visit to the house of Martha and Mary (Lk. 10.38-42). Like the story about the rich ruler (Lk. 18.18-26), the Martha and Mary episode dramatizes perceptional alternatives adumbrated by Jesus in his commentary on the Sower parable.[16] Mary, who sits at Jesus' feet in receptive posture, listens to his word (*ēkouen ton logon autou*, 10.39), and then is commended by the Lord for so doing (10.42), serves as a foil for the characterization of Martha, the central concern of the tale. Although Mary's portrait is sketchy, enough evidence is provided for the reader to identify her as 'good soil' (8.15). We never learn whether she finally bears fruit, but she is described as a

16. The Sower parable and its interpretation are programmatic in the sense that they establish for the reader standard patterns of response to Jesus by other characters. In encountering Jesus, who represents the rocky soil? Who the thorny ground? And who typifies the good earth? These are the questions readers now ask after reading the parable and its authoritative interpretation by Jesus. In other words, Lk. 8.4-21 sets up categories and reader expectations that are then dramatized in the story. Luke has, of course, borrowed (and modified) this narrative technique from Mark. For a full exposition of the Sower parable and its function in Mark's Gospel (with many insights for Luke–Acts as well), see Tolbert 1989: 127-230.

receptive listener, Jesus refers to her as having chosen the good (*agathēn*) portion, and he declares that it will not be taken away from her.[17] She is attentive, receptive and retentive—a veritable paradigm of Lukan perceptional values.

Martha, on the other hand, typifies the thorny ground (8.14), which, after receiving and beginning to nurture the word, chokes it off through the anxieties (*merimnōn*), riches or pleasures of life. Martha first receives (*hupedexato*) Jesus into her home (v. 38), but then is distracted with much service (*pollēn diakonian*). Her reception of Jesus signals an initial desire to hear his word (see Wall 1989: 24-25 for Lukan parallels). When she complains about Mary's failure to assist, however, and asks Jesus to tell her to help, he responds with a play on words:

> Martha, Martha, you are anxious (*merimnas*) and troubled by *many things*; but only *one thing* is necessary: for Mary has chosen the good portion (*merida*), which shall not be taken away from her (10.41b-42).

Jesus thus draws a contrast between many things and the one thing, between Martha's anxiety (*merimnas*—one of the 'thorns' mentioned by Jesus in his Sower allegory) and Mary's portion (*merida*). The similarity of the two Greek words (*merimnas//merida*) should not be missed, for by playing off that similarity Luke's Jesus helps cue the reader to process the story in terms of his earlier allegory, that is, as a contrast between good and thorny soils, between proper and improper modes of perception. Focusing reader attention on Martha's many duties and anxieties (rather than on riches and pleasures—the other 'thorns'), the Martha and Mary episode also helps to counterbalance Jesus' heavy emphasis on *doing the word*, an emphasis that could easily be misinterpreted to mean that doing the word is more important than listening to the word. Here Jesus sets the record straight. The proper sequence must be observed: in the overall process of engaging the word, listening (attention, reception, and retention) necessarily precedes doing. Anxiety-driven busy-ness will not do, for effective action arises from correct apprehension and appropriation of the revelation.

17. Note Luke's repeated emphasis on the word being *taken away* from individuals who are not prepared to retain it. The birds (the devil and his cronies) come and take away the seed from the first kind of soil in Jesus' parable, for example, and then Jesus warns that 'from him who has not, even what he seems to have will be taken away' (8.18). Here Jesus declares that Mary will not fall into that category.

*Monitoring the Sensors: Eyes, Ears and Heart*

The central lesson of Lk. 8.4-21 is that fecund reception of the sacred depends on the condition of one's eyes and ears, which, in turn, depends on one's heart. Readers are thus encouraged toward introspection, to identify their own values, to compare them with those being promoted in the narrative, and, ultimately, to align themselves with the norms of the story.[18] As we have observed, the values foregrounded in Jesus' interpretation of the Sower parable are attention to, retention of and (re)production of the divine revelation. Emphasis falls on perseverance (v. 15) in the face of life's contrary pressures. The audience realizes, of course, that a good heart exhibits many other qualities, some of which may be inferred by contrast with the anti-values raised by Jesus in his commentary: resistance to temptation (vv. 12-13); serenity or singleness of mind; willingness to live simply; and an orientation toward the spiritual aspects of human life instead of toward physical pleasures or fiscal concern (v. 14). The process of establishing the fundamental values (the good heart), however, continues throughout the entire narrative by means of a myriad of rhetorical strategies. Moving forward through Luke and Acts, the reader builds an image of the ideal heart—one that characterizes the ideal reader. This reader loves God and neighbor; has faith; is humble, repentant and loyal; shows compassion and mercy; and practices economic justice (among other virtues).[19]

The Lukan system of values and how it is communicated to the reader are large and complex topics with obvious implications for the present study. The scope of this project, however, requires that we restrict our inquiry to what the Lukan Jesus himself says about monitoring one's inner 'lenses' so that genuine perception can take place. Two passages are particularly pertinent in this regard. First, in his lengthy Sermon on the Plain, Jesus sternly warns the audience that the inspection or correction of character is, first and foremost, a personal matter, not an opportunity to criticize others.

---

18. As Johnson (1991: 134) aptly comments, 'this part of Luke's composition becomes a statement on the *internal* meaning of Jesus' prophetic ministry' (emphasis mine).

19. On the way Lukan values are communicated through characterization, see Darr 1992: 91-92.

> Why do you see the speck that is in your brother's eye, but do not notice
> the log that is in your own eye?... You hypocrite, first take the log out of
> your own eye, and then you will see clearly to take out the speck that is in
> your brother's eye (6.41, 42b).

Introspection is a delicate and often painful process. Given the human
tendency to self-deception, it is wise to concentrate first and foremost on
one's own inner state before attempting to assess that of another.
Everyone who wishes to see or hear is primarily responsible for
monitoring his or her own sensory apparatus.

Secondly, just before denouncing the Pharisees and lawyers who
consistently fail to 'see' him, Jesus exclaims,

> Your eye is the lamp of your body; when your eye is firmly focused
> (*haplous*), your whole body is full of light; but when it is evil (*ponēros*),
> your body is full of darkness. Therefore, be careful lest the light in you be
> darkness (11.34-35).

Susan Garrett has wisely directed scholarly attention away from a
fruitless quest for consistent anthropological categories in this saying
(1991: 95); it is fundamentally ethical in nature and uses an evocative
concatenation of light and eye imagery—rather than referential or
denotative language—to convey its meaning. Jesus here teaches once
again that spiritual perception is dependent on the condition of one's
inner self. In this instance, however, he promotes the value of singleness
of mind (*haplotēs*), of focusing on the good. 'The expression [*ho
ophthalmos haplous*] would have conveyed the notion that a given
individual *focuses his or her eye on God alone*. No worldly pleasures, no
competing masters, no evil spirits can cause the person of "the single
eye" to compromise his or her integrity toward the Lord' (Garrett
1991: 99). Readers are thus encouraged *to avoid distraction* and focus
sharply on values promoted by the narrative. Anything less leads to evil
(*ponēron*) and spiritual blindness, to seeing but not seeing and hearing
but not hearing.

### Conclusions

At the level of discourse, Jesus' words about perception serve to
*program* the authorial audience's hearing/reading of Luke's story. The
Nazareth episode and the parable of the Sower exhibit some of the
primary ways in which this authoritative voice guides readers as they

process the text: (1) Jesus' sayings about the immediacy of the revelation ('in your ears') draw the reader into the story world and break down resistance and disbelief; (2) his references to Scripture help control intertextual reading; and (3) various other sayings help link perception and the complex web of ethical values Luke weaves. Jesus' injunction to 'watch how you listen', therefore, is not only a warning to monitor how we read the text, but also a challenge to examine how we live before God.

## BIBLIOGRAPHY

Booth, Wayne C.
1983        *The Rhetoric of Fiction* (Chicago: University of Chicago Press, 2nd edn).

Buber, Martin
1946        *Moses* (London: Phaidon).

Chidester, David
1992        *Word and Light: Seeing, Hearing, and Religious Discourse* (Urbana: University of Illinois Press).

Darr, John A.
1992        *On Character Building: The Reader and the Rhetoric of Characterization in Luke–Acts* (Louisville: Westminister/John Knox Press).
1993        'Narrator as Character: Mapping a Reader-Oriented Approach to Narration in Luke–Acts', *Semeia* 63: 43-60.

Dillon, Richard J.
1978        *From Eye-Witnesses to Ministers of the Word: Tradition and Composition in Luke 24* (AnBib, 82; Rome: Pontifical Biblical Institute).

Fitzmyer, Joseph A.
1981        *The Gospel according to Luke, I–IX: Introduction, Translation, and Notes* (AB, 28; Garden City, NY: Doubleday).

Funk, Robert W.
1966        *Language, Hermeneutic, and the Word of God: The Problem of Language in the New Testament and Contemporary Theology* (New York: Harper & Row).

Garrett, Susan R.
1991        '"Lest the Light in You be Darkness": Luke 11.33-36 and the Question of Commitment', *JBL* 110: 93-105.

Hamm, Dennis
1986        'Sight to the Blind: Vision as Metaphor in Luke', *Bib* 67: 457-77.
1990        'Paul's Blindness and its Healing: Clues to Symbolic Intent (Acts 9; 22 and 26)', *Bib* 72: 63-72.

Harris, William V.
1989        *Ancient Literacy* (Cambridge, MA: Harvard University Press).
Johnson, Luke T.
1991        *The Gospel of Luke* (Sacra Pagina, 3; Collegeville, MN: The Liturgical
            Press).
Kelber, Werner H.
1983        *The Oral and the Written Gospel: The Hermeneutics of Speaking and
            Writing in the Synoptic Tradition, Mark, Paul, and Q* (Philadelphia:
            Fortress Press).
Kelley, Shawn
1991        ' "And Your Young Will See Visions": A Functionalist Literary
            Reading of the Visions to Saul and Peter in Acts', unpublished
            dissertation, Vanderbilt University.
Koet, B.J.
1986        'Today This Scripture Has Been Fulfilled in Your Ears', *Bijdragen* 47:
            368-94.
Landry, David T.
1992        ' "Promises, Promises": The Literary Function of the Birth Stories in
            Luke–Acts', unpublished dissertation, Vanderbilt University.
Lanser, Susan
1981        *The Narrative Act: Point of View in Prose Fiction* (Princeton, NJ:
            Princeton University Press).
Mailloux, Steven
1989        *Rhetorical Power* (Ithaca, NY: Cornell University Press).
Rabinowitz, Peter J.
1987        *Before Reading: Narrative Conventions and the Politics of
            Interpretation* (Ithaca, NY: Cornell University Press).
Sanders, Jack T.
1987        'The Prophetic Use of the Scriptures in Luke–Acts', in C.A. Evans
            and W.F. Stinespring (eds.), *Early Jewish and Christian Exegesis:
            Studies in Memory of William Hugh Brownlee* (Atlanta: Scholars
            Press): 191-98.
Siker, Jeffrey S.
1992        ' "First to the Gentiles": A Literary Analysis of Luke 4.16-30', *JBL*
            111: 73-90.
Tannehill, Robert C.
1972        'The Mission of Jesus according to Luke IV 16-30', in W. Eltester
            (ed.), *Jesus in Nazareth* (BZNW, 40; Berlin: Walter de Gruyter): 51-75.
1986        *The Narrative Unity of Luke–Acts: A Literary Interpretation.* I. *The
            Gospel according to Luke* (Philadelphia: Fortress Press).
Tolbert, Mary Ann
1989        *Sowing the Gospel: Mark's World in Literary-Historical Perspective*
            (Minneapolis: Fortress Press).
Tyson, Joseph B.
1987        'The Gentile Mission and the Authority of Scripture in  Acts', *NTS* 33:
            619-31.

1992       'Torah and Prophet in Luke–Acts: Temporary or Permanent?' *SBLSP* 31: 539-48.

Wall, Robert W.
1989       'Martha and Mary (Luke 10.38-42) in the Context of a Christian Deuteronomy', *JSNT* 35: 19-35.

# READING TABITHA: A FEMINIST RECEPTION HISTORY

## Janice Capel Anderson

### Introduction

In this essay I explore how a number of readers have read Acts 9.36-42. In doing so, I consciously write in the tradition of feminist reader-response criticism. I will begin with a brief review of feminist reader-response criticism. This will be followed by an interpretative reception history. Finally, I will consider a number of insights this reception history offers from the perspective of a feminist critic. All that I write is itself a reading of an Anglo-American, middle-aged, middleclass, heterosexual, Protestant feminist biblical scholar. I ally myself with other feminists who define feminism with bell hooks as 'a common resistance to all the different forms of male domination' (in Harding 1987: 188) and with Linda Alcoff as 'the affirmation...of our right and our ability to construct, and take responsibility for, our gendered identity, our politics and our choices' (1988: 432). Chandra Talpade Mohanty's description of Third World Feminism as 'imagined communities of women with divergent histories and social locations, woven together by the *political* threads of opposition to forms of domination that are not only pervasive but also systemic' (1991: 4) is a definition that, provided various social locations are remembered, could well serve as a definition embracing all feminisms.

### Feminist Reader-Response Criticism

Reader-response criticism has been one of the most important approaches to the Gospels and Acts in the eighties and nineties. Today most New Testament scholars have some notion of the 'reader' as developed in literary studies—whether they are most interested in actual or hypothetical, internal or external, first time or ideal readers (see Fowler 1991; Malbon and Anderson 1993 for references). Less attention has been paid to the social locations, to the gender, race, class and other particularities of actual readers and reader constructs. Feminist literary critics in English and biblical studies have raised these issues in very fruitful ways (see Fetterly 1978; Fulkerson 1991; Fuss 1989; Malbon and Anderson 1993; Martin 1989; Martin 1991; Ostriker 1993; Schweikart 1986; Showalter 1983; Tolbert 1990; Weems 1991). These critics have raised these issues because they have seen very clearly how social location affects interpretation—what, how and why one reads. Some of them emphasize the power of the text over the reader, others the power of the reader over the text. All of them explore what it means to read as a woman or a feminist, constructing what it means to be a woman or a feminist as they proceed. The difficulties in such a task can be glimpsed if one asks how a Guatemalan female peasant leader belonging to a base community, a white female middleclass urban German Lutheran biblical scholar, and a black female Holiness preacher in the rural southern United States might read the Lukan birth story— even if they all embraced a general understanding of feminism. There are differences between them, and even a single one of them belongs to multiple interpretative communities operating with different reading conventions and goals.

As females reading an androcentric and patriarchal text they may also be engaged in a process Judith Fetterley calls *immasculation.* Immasculation is the process of a woman reading and identifying as a male when reading an androcentric and patriarchal text such as 'Rip Van Winkle'. Fetterley writes,

> While the desire to avoid work, escape authority and sleep through the major decisions of one's life is obviously applicable to both men and women, in Irving's story this 'universal' desire is made specifically male. Work, authority, and decision-making are symbolized by Dame van Winkle, and the longing for flight is defined against her. She is what one must escape from, and the 'one' is necessarily male... In such fictions the female reader is co-opted into participation in an experience from which she is explicitly excluded; she is asked to identify with a selfhood that defines itself in opposition to her; she is required to identify against herself (1978: xii ).

In many cases, as Renita Weems points out, a text or a dominant reading practice may call for females to read not only as males but also 'like a certain kind of man' (1991: 67), an upperclass white Anglo male, for example. Once a reader recognizes this process, however, she can read self-consciously as a member of one or more resistant interpretative communities. As she reads she can recognize the process of immasculation and particular male reading strategies she uses. She can also recognize what the text excludes or tensions within it. She recognizes that she can affirm or resist, read with or against the text. She can read it with the interpretative conventions operative in liberative reading communities. She can ask what interests the text serves or may serve in particular social and historical circumstances. For biblical texts, many women readers have found that the texts can be both oppressive and liberative, depending upon the context in which they are read. Feminist reader-response critics struggle with how to read androcentric and patriarchal texts that nonetheless have evoked positive as well as negative responses. Schweikert writes,

> My point is that *certain* (not all) male texts merit a dual hermeneutic: a
> negative hermeneutic that discloses their complicity with patriarchal
> ideology, and a positive hermeneutic that recuperates the utopian
> moment—the authentic kernel—from which they draw a significant
> portion of their emotional power (1986: 43-44).

Within feminist biblical scholarship Schüssler Fiorenza, Tolbert and Weems have all—each from her own particular perspective—stressed the importance of this dual hermeneutic when dealing with the Scriptures. Schüssler Fiorenza has written of a hermeneutics of suspicion and a hermeneutics of re-vision (1993: 11).[1] A literary critic, the poet Alicia Suskin Ostriker, has written of a tri-partite hermeneutic for biblical texts. Taking a clue from feminist biblical critics and theologians, she speaks of a hermeneutics of suspicion, but she adds to this a hermeneutics of desire in which 'the reader finds in the text what she wants it to say' and a hermeneutics of indeterminacy that emphasizes the 'necessity for plural readings which won't cancel each other out' (1993: 57, 121-122). Ostriker approvingly cites Mieke Bal, who says in *Lethal Love*, 'Texts trigger readings; that is what they are; the occasion of a reaction...Every reading is different from, and in contact with, the text' (Ostriker 1993: 122).

## Reception History

As a practical matter the situated reading strategies and interests of readers can be seen in the reception history of particular texts. Below I

---

1.    Schüssler Fiorenza has also multiplied these categories, writing of a hermeneutics of suspicion, imagination, remembrance, proclamation and a hermeneutics of liberative vision and imagination (1992: 52-55).

will show how various readers have read Tabitha. First I will indicate the points of departure for differing interpretations in Acts 9.36-42. Then I will look at how modern male biblical scholars, key male interpreters of the past, several nineteenth-century women, and contemporary feminist scholars have read the text. I begin with modern biblical scholarship because most of the readers of this essay are members of that interpretative community, although they belong to others as well. I want to emphasize those reading conventions and then to show others by contrast. Those in the biblical guild may say that they have always known that the questions one poses determine the kinds of answers one receives. I want to go beyond this to indicate that one's social and historical location determine the questions one asks and the kind of answers one constructs. Feminist reception history shows that the context of discovery as well as the context of justification reflects individual and communal perspectives. [2]

*Jumping Off Points*

As we read, certain features of a text stand out and others recede in importance. Our own experiences, questions and interests as well as shared reading conventions shape which aspects of a text are central and which peripheral, which are puzzling and which are obvious, which are noticed and which ignored. They also influence connections we draw between the text we are reading and other texts we have heard or read. The case is no different with the story of Tabitha. The setting in Joppa is read as significant by some interpreters and ignored by others. Some interpreters focus on the meaning of the name Tabitha and its translation into Greek as Dorcas. Interpreters of the past often use it to characterize Tabitha; modern interpreters do not. Some interpreters place a great deal of significance on the use of the term *mathētria* (female disciple) to describe Tabitha; others downplay or ignore it. Many interpreters focus on the meaning of the description of Tabitha as someone who does 'good works and almsdeeds'. The giving of alms is an indication of Tabitha's social status as a wealthy independent woman for some. Various readers have puzzled over questions that the text raises for them: Why is Tabitha's corpse washed and placed in an upper room? Why do the disciples at Joppa wait until Tabitha is dead to send for Peter? Why does Peter heal Tabitha in private? Readers have made intertextual connections to various other texts and used them to

2. My point here rests on one made about science by Harding (1987: 183-84).

interpret this one. Some readers pair Tabitha's story with the preceding healing of Aeneas. Some readers connect the story to the healing of Jairus' daughter found in Mk 5.21-43 = Mt. 9.18-26 = Lk. 8.40-56. 'Tabitha, rise' reminds some of 'Talitha cum' ('Little girl, rise', Aramaic) in the Markan version, Talitha and Tabitha differing by only one letter. Some connect the Tabitha story to miracles Elijah and Elisha perform in 1 and 2 Kings. Those who look within Acts for parallels see a parallel between Peter's raising of Tabitha and Paul's healing/raising of Eutychus in Acts 20.7-12. The references to widows in vv. 39 and 41 set off other bells. Some readers think of Acts 6, some of 1 Timothy, where widows are mentioned. The mention of the widows also causes some interpreters to read Tabitha as a widow, although the text never directly refers to her as such. One of the biggest differences between various readings is whether the interpreter focuses primarily on Peter or Tabitha as the main character or divides his or her attention roughly equally. Finally, one major difference between readers of Acts is the degree to which they attend to the story of Tabitha, if they attend to the story at all. For many modern biblical scholars the story has little or no significance for the overall interpretation of Acts or for the reconstruction of early church history.

### Modern Male Biblical Scholarship

The reading conventions of modern biblical scholarship primarily arise out of historical-critical scholarship. In recent years Acts has been read predominantly in terms of the redactor's shaping and interpretation of previous traditions. Questions about the author's theology and the community he addresses are central. Usually, Luke and Acts are studied in the light of one another as parts of a two-volume work (although questions about this practice have been raised recently; see Parsons and Pervo 1993). Discussion of Tabitha's story rarely occurs in scholarly monographs on Luke–Acts.[3] The story fares better in scholarly commentaries, which must find something to say about each pericope. For the most part when traditional biblical scholarship reads Tabitha's story it reads it as the story of Peter. A brief review of titles for the section in which it is included is telling: '9.32-43 Peter's Journey to Lydda and

---

3. Exceptions are Dibelius (1956) and Pervo (1987), although their discussions are not lengthy. Jervell (1984) barely mentions Tabitha in his collection of essays entitled *The Unknown Paul*, but he does devote a whole chapter to a discussion of women in Acts.

Joppa' (Johnson 1977: 1332); 'Peter's Pastoral Visit to Lydda and Joppa' (Munck 1967: 87); 'Peter Continues the Prophetic Ministry of Healing (Acts 9.32-43)' (Tannehill 1986: 125); 'Acts 9.32-43 Peter Heals Aeneas and Raises Tabitha' (Haenchen 1971: 337 and Conzelmann 1987: 76); 'Petrus als Wundertater in Lod [Lydda] und Jafo [Joppa]: 9.32-43' (Schneider 1982: 46); and 'Peter's General Tour through Lydda to Joppa' (Packer 1966: 76). The focus on Peter may in part stem from the fact that most biblical scholars are male, but it also comes from looking for ways to connect various pericopes in Acts to one another or to other biblical texts.

Redaction critics look for connections between pericopes in which a single character appears or connections between characters who appear frequently. They also look for geographical, theological or thematic threads to tie Acts together and to link it to other texts. Most scholars tie the healing of Aeneas in 9.32-35 to that of Tabitha. Both stories demonstrate Peter's miraculous actions as preparation for the healing of Cornelius in Acts 10. These acts continue the spread of the gospel. The references to Lydda and Joppa in the two stories also enable a geographical and theological movement from Judaea, Samaria and Galilee to Caesarea where Peter will baptize Cornelius, often viewed as the first Gentile convert in Acts (e.g. Haenchen 1971: 341-42). The connection to the Holy Spirit, which is important in Acts, is preserved by Peter's prayer for Tabitha, which parallels his statement to Aeneas, 'Jesus Christ, he heals you' (Tannehill 1986: 126). Scholars find parallels between the story and the healing of Jairus's daughter (Lk. 8.40-46 = Mk 5.21-43 = Mt. 9.18-26), Elijah's healing of the widow's son (1 Kgs 18.17-24) and Elisha's healing of the Shunammite's son (2 Kgs 4.32-37). Peter's command, 'Tabitha rise' in v. 40 sounds like, and has an effect similar to, Jesus' command, 'Talitha cum', in Mk 5.41 (although the Aramaic is not used in Luke). Thus scholars read the story as authorizing Peter as a type of the ancient prophets and of Jesus. Haenchen, citing Loisy, notes, however, that 'it is out of the question for Peter to proceed with a woman as Elijah and Elisha with a dead boy' (1971: 339). Haenchen expresses some delicacy about physical connections between male and female. Comparisons sometimes are also drawn between Peter's raising of Tabitha and Paul's raising of Eutychus in 20.9-12 (Gasque 1989: 34). These readers read the story in the context of Acts as the parallel story of the missions of Peter and Paul. It is quite natural for scholarly readers who spend their time teaching and writing about *biblical* studies to make (or find) biblical parallels.

Apart from noting parallels to other similar biblical healings, modern scholars are not particularly concerned with details of the story, such as the washing of the corpse, which Conzelmann informs us was a common ancient custom (1987: 77), or the removal of the body to the upper room. Nor do they focus particular attention on the garments that the widows show to Peter.

Incidental curiosity does arise from the references to the widows who weep over Tabitha and to whom she is restored as a benefactor. Again, intertextual biblical bells go off. Since widows are mentioned in Acts 6.1-6 and in 1 Tim. 5.3-16, commentators sometimes feel compelled to discuss whether Tabitha's story should be read in the light of these passages. There is a dispute among interpreters over whether the widows in Acts 6 represent an official group with an official role. Most modern scholars read 1 Timothy as at least indicating an incipient church order of widows. In terms of Tabitha's story some simply announce that the widows are not members of an official group with a specific office (e.g. Conzelmann 1987: 77 and Bruce 1992: 199 nn. 83 and 85). Haenchen, citing Wellhausen, writes that 'in v. 39 the *chērai* [widows] appear only as a knot of women mourners, but in v. 41 they represent a social class in their own right' (1971: 341). He gives no reason for this distinction. Perhaps the grounds for it are the same as those that lead Stählin to suggest that the widows may represent a special class for whom Tabitha is raised. He takes the presence of the phrase 'saints and widows' in v. 41 to refer to two distinct groups (*TDNT*, IX, 452). Stählin also conjectures that Tabitha is a widow, since no husband is mentioned, and that she may have been commissioned by the church at Joppa to care for the other widows (*TDNT*, IX, 452).

Form-critical and narrative-critical approaches have somewhat different reading conventions. Form criticism's focus on the individual units of the tradition and the focus of both form criticism and narrative criticism on style produces slightly different readings of Tabitha's story. Dibelius classifies the Tabitha pericope as a legend coming from an independent tradition that the author had available. He argues that the story is told in an edifying style, like a gospel paradigm, but it is a legend because it has a personal interest in Peter and Tabitha (Dibelius 1956: 12-13). He notes an 'abundance of personal details: Tabitha's name is given, her character is described, the garments she made for widows are mentioned as evidence of her beneficence, and perhaps some reference to her appearance is implied by the particular mention of the care of the corpse' (Dibelius 1956: 13). Pervo, noting Dibelius's comments, highlights the details as producing pathos, something the sentimental readers of ancient romance novels would appreciate (Pervo 1987: 66-67). Tannehill, responsive to verbal and thematic connections, finds ties between Tabitha's concern for the poor and similar concerns in the rest of Acts. He also notes that Tabitha's practice of charity provides a 'bridge' to the charity of Cornelius in the next pericope (1986: 127), a point also noted by Schneider (1982: 49). Tannehill writes with more sensitivity to passages that concern wealth and ethnicity or feature female characters or males such as the Ethiopian eunuch and Cornelius. His use of narrative criticism and his theological/ideological concerns are all marks of more recent exegetical practice in the biblical guild. Reading Tabitha's story with a focus on the entire book of Acts or of Luke–Acts as a two-volume work, as redaction critics do, or in the context of the entire sweep of early Christian history, as many historical critics do, tends to eclipse Tabitha. One can easily see this in the comment of Johannes Munck: 'While the preceding and the following passages deal with decisive events, Paul's call and Peter's baptism of the first Gentile, this short passage [Acts 9.31-43] forms a pause in the account of the great climaxes' (1967: 89). Form criticism's focus on individual pericopes tends to bring Tabitha more into focus. Narrative criticism, like redaction criticism, reading either the narrative of Acts or Luke–Acts as a whole, tends to downplay Tabitha. However, narrative criticism's focus on characters may foreground 'minor' characters as well as major ones. In this respect form-critical and narrative-critical readings may have more in common with readings from the past, which focused on individual pericopes and on moral character for the purposes of preaching and edification.

## Male Readings from Church History
*Chrysostom: Tabitha 'as active and wakeful as an antelope'.* Chrysostom (c. 347–407), given the appellation 'golden-mouthed' in recognition of his preaching prowess, became Bishop of Constantinople in 398. He was soon embroiled in controversy, however, and ended his life in exile (Cross and Livingstone 1983: 285). Chrysostom was known for his homilies and his literalist method of interpretation (Grant 1984: 68-69). He reads Tabitha's story for what it might teach his listeners about how to behave rather than for any esoteric spiritual meaning. He reads the characters as models or types, which was a common practice

in the ancient world. While his reading might be considered too fanciful or personal by the modern biblical guild, he notes the similarity between this story and that of Jairus' daughter (as modern biblical scholars are wont to do.)

Chrysostom's reading begins with the sensible question: Why do the disciples wait until Tabitha is dead to send for Peter? His answer is that the disciples at Joppa did not want to trouble the disciples (Peter)

> about such matters, and to take them away from their preaching: as indeed this is why it mentions that the place was near, seeing they asked this as a thing beside his mark, and not now in the regular course (1956: 137).

Apparently, they did not want to interrupt Peter's preaching with concern about a sick person (woman?) unless she was dead and he happened to be nearby? Chrysostom's original question seems like a good one to me, but I am not so sure about his answer. The mid-nineteenth-century translators and editors of the homily think his answer makes perfect sense from Chrysostom's perspective. In a note they write, 'This is a hint to the hearers that they should show like forbearance and discretion, in not giving their Bishop unnecessary trouble' (1956: 137 n. 1). Chrysostom indicates that the disciples ask Peter not to delay because Tabitha is a disciple (*mathētria*). The weeping of the widows and the showing of garments, Chrysostom interprets as a 'cheering inducement to alms' (1956: 137). In contrast to the widows' weeping, Peter, he notes, took the circumstances calmly. Chrysostom then engages in an excursus on why the author 'informs us of the woman's name' (1956: 137). Her name matches her character, 'as active and wakeful was she as an antelope' (1956: 137). He notes she was full of good works as well as giving alms, making clothes with great humility along with the others. Returning to his recounting of the miracle, Chrysostom asks why Peter puts the widows out of the room. His answer is so that Peter is neither 'confused nor disturbed by their weeping' (1956: 137). Chrysostom notes that Peter reaches out his hand to Tabitha as Christ did to Jairus' daughter. Peter presents Tabitha alive to the saints and widows, 'to some for comfort, because they received back their sister, and because they saw the miracle, and for kindly support to others' (1956: 137). Chrysostom praises Peter's humility in that he stays in the home of a tanner, rather than with 'this lady', that is, Tabitha, 'or some other person of distinction...by all his acts leading men to humility, neither suffering the mean to be ashamed, nor the great to be elated!' (1956: 137).

Thus Chrysostom regards Peter as an important figure engaged in important work. Peter is a model. He is calm and collected, as well as attractively unassuming. Tabitha, who receives as much space in Chrysostom's reading as Peter, is also held up as a model. A disciple, she is active and wakeful as an antelope, full of good works as well as alms, and even though a person of distinction, suitably humble, working in company with the widows and saints. The widows come off as somewhat overly emotional, but as those to whom Peter shows compassion. In Chrysostom's homiletic reading, both Peter and Tabitha serve as edifying models for listeners. Peter, of course, is the one who is engaged in the important work of preaching and who shows compassion on the widows, healing Tabitha.

*Saint Basil the Great: 'The example of Dorcas'.* Basil the Great was one of the Cappadocian fathers of the church. He was the brother of St Gregory of Nyssa and St Macrina (Cross and Livingstone 1983: 857). Early in his career he was a hermit. Later he became Bishop of Caesarea and vigorously opposed Arianism (Cross and Livingstone 1983: 139-40). Eastern Orthodoxy groups Basil with Gregory of Nazianzus and Chrysostom as one of the three hierarchs (Norris 1990: 141). Like Chrysostom, Basil is concerned with community behavior. He reads Scripture to find examples.

In *The Morals* Basil sets forth a series of rules, each followed by scriptural supports. Rule 74 states, 'A widow who enjoys sufficiently robust health should spend her life in works of zeal and solicitude, keeping in mind the words of the Apostle and the example of Dorcas' (1950: 191). Basil supports this rule by references to Acts 9.36, recounting that Tabitha/Dorcas was 'full of good works and alms deeds', and to Acts 9.39, which refers to the coats and garments she made for the widows. He follows this with a reference to 1 Tim. 5.9-10 that lists the requirements for a true widow: chosen by the church for service and good works. Thus Basil reads Tabitha as a widow who serves widows and as a good example for widows to follow. A true widow perseveres 'day and night in prayer and supplication, with fasting' (1950: 192). The rules that precede and follow rule 74 concern the prohibition of divorce unless one of the partners commits adultery or is a hindrance to the other in the service of God (rule 73) and the requirements that bondservants obey their masters (rule 75). In elaborating the prohibition of divorce Basil cites biblical passages enjoining that women be subject to their husbands, refrain from adornment for the sake of beauty, and keep silent in church. Thus Basil is concerned, much in the mold of 1 Timothy and the New Testament household codes, with the 'proper' roles for Christian women. Tabitha/Dorcas is read as an example of the proper widow.

*Calvin: The author 'applies the same word to a woman'*. Calvin (1509–1564) was a prolific exegete, writing commentaries on most of the canonical books of the Bible. He sought to make clear the literal sense of the text in its original historical and literary context. He used the editions of the Bible and scholarly techniques available at the time. Theologically, the three reformation principles of *sola scriptura* (Scripture alone), *sola fide* (faith alone, rather than works) and *solo Christo* (Christ alone as the source of salvation) guided his interpretation (Schwöbel 1990: 98-99). The words of the Bible only become the Word of God for readers or hearers by the power of the Holy Spirit.

Calvin comments extensively on the story of Tabitha. While he notes such things as a possible parallel between Peter and Elisha (also seen by many modern biblical scholars), he sees the story as a powerful example of Christ's power. Calvin focuses on God's actions and purposes rather than upon Peter. He commends both Tabitha and Peter for their faithfulness to God, describing both as instruments of God. Calvin highlights the description of Tabitha as a disciple:

> Several times already he [the author of Acts] has used the word *disciple* for a Christian man, and in case we might think that it is suitable for men only, he applies the same word to a woman. But this title warns us that Christianity does not exist without teaching, and that the learning prescribed is of such a kind that the same Christ may be the only Teacher for all. This is the highest commendation, this is the basis of a holy life, this is the root of all virtues, to have learned from the Son of God what is the way to live, and what true life is (1965: 278).

He then argues that Tabitha's good works and almsgiving spring from her faith as a disciple, taking the opportunity in good Reformation fashion to stress faith before works and the equality before God of all believers. As with the term 'disciple', Calvin notes the translation of Tabitha's name into Greek as Dorcas, a point often made by interpreters of all periods and schools. He, however, offers a unique interpretation. He translates Dorcas as a wild she-goat, a name he views as 'far from complimentary' (1965: 278). But, he says, 'the sanctity of her life easily wiped out the stigma of a rather unbecoming name' (1965: 278). Calvin explains that the washing of Tabitha's body and the placing of the body in the upper room are proof that Tabitha was dead, although the placing of it in the upper room rather than in a tomb shows that the faithful had 'some hope of restoring her to life' (1965: 278). The washing of the body produces a long excursus on washing and burial practices on Calvin's part. It culminates in a condemnation of the washing and anointing practices of 'monks', that is, Roman Catholics. Calvin reads with an eye on how other readers may read the passage. As for the weeping widows and the poor distressed at Tabitha's death, Calvin argues that God had pity on their needs and also uses the miracle to strengthen their faith. The Spirit of God directs Peter's role in the whole affair. When Peter puts others out of the upper room in which Tabitha's body lies, he does so 'so that no one may ascribe to his power a work of God, of which he is only the agent' (1965: 281), not, as Chrysostom argues, in order to avoid distraction.

Calvin also responds to a charge, apparently made by some other readers, that the story of Tabitha proves that after death the soul is but a breath until the Resurrection Day. Otherwise, they ask, what good does it do Tabitha to be restored to bodily life, a prison house of suffering? Calvin again stresses God, arguing that God was 'more concerned about his own glory than about Tabitha herself', although since 'the advantage of the faithful is always connected to the glory of God, it was a greater blessing to her to be restored to life, in order to be a more illustrious instrument of the divine goodness and power' (1965: 282).

Thus, because Calvin's reading lens is theocentric and christocentric, Tabitha and her role as an agent receive more attention than in many modern scholarly readings. Both Peter and Tabitha are subordinated to God and God's purposes. Although one certainly could not call Calvin a feminist, Calvin is more open to accepting God's use of women than many of his male contemporaries.[4]

*Matthew Henry's Commentary: 'Tabitha was a great doer, no great talker'*. Matthew Henry (1662–1714) was a non-conformist, or dissenting, English minister. For several centuries English-speaking Protestant

---

4. For a discussion of Calvin's views on women, see Jane Dempsey Douglass (1985). Douglass argues that Calvin in his biblical interpretation evidences 'little explicit positive support for the traditional general subordination of women' (1985: 62). Calvin, for example, understands the command for women to keep silence in the church as human governance that can change, not eternal law (1985: 62).

ministers used his *Commentary on the Bible*. The *Commentary* is still popular among conservative Protestants today, often in its abridged version. Like Chrysostom, also a homilist, Henry focuses on Peter and Tabitha as models for believers to emulate. Tabitha is 'a disciple, eminent above many for works of charity' (Henry 1961: 1673). Like Calvin, Henry notes that her faith is shown by her works. Like a tree full of fruit, she is full of good works: 'Many are full of good words, who are empty and barren in good work; but Tabitha was a great doer, no great talker' (1961: 1673). Henry commends Tabitha at some length for her clothing of the needy. The widows are also praised for their gratitude to Tabitha for her charity and industry. They also do a good work in commending the dead, 'modestly, soberly, and without flattery' (1961: 1673). They repeat Tabitha's virtues 'not in word, but in deed' by showing the clothes she had made (1961: 1673). They weep to induce Peter to have compassion upon them, to restore Tabitha, who had likewise had compassion upon them. Although Henry devotes less space to Peter, Peter is praised because of his compassion and humility. Peter comes when called for help, even though he is a great apostle, and he raises Tabitha privately to avoid 'vainglory' (1961: 1673). Thus Henry solves one of the puzzles Chrysostom and Calvin also see in the passage: Why does Peter heal Tabitha in private? Henry's interpretation is similar to Calvin's, emphasizing Peter's humility.

Although Henry disagrees with Chrysostom on this point, Chrysostom and Henry, two preachers seeking to edify their hearers, have much in common. The praise of Tabitha is very welcome to my feminist ears, but there is a disturbing undertone. Tabitha is a great doer, but no great talker. From the perspective of putting her faith into practice rather than just being full of empty talk, this sounds good. From the perspective that a lot of men in Acts do a lot of talking and preaching, and women seem limited to good works and bankrolling the male talking, Henry's interpretation has a dark side.

### *Three Late Nineteenth-Century/Early Twentieth-Century Women's Readings: Stanton, Sangster and Foote*

Speaking very generally, two currents played important roles in the nineteenth- and early twentieth-century 'woman suffrage movement' in the United States. Liberal feminism emphasized the rationality and equal natural rights of women as individuals. Liberal feminists argued that women should have public-sphere legal rights to property, custody of children, control of inheritance, and the right to sue as well as the vote. Examples of nineteenth-century thinkers often classified as liberal feminists include Elizabeth Cady Stanton, Sarah Grimke, Sojourner Truth and Frances Wright. At the same time there was a great surge of what Josephine Donovan labels cultural feminism. A central thesis of cultural feminism was that women were different from men, and were in many ways, especially morally, superior. Motherhood and 'female' values were celebrated. This position was largely, but not entirely, a white middle and upperclass phenomenon. It was associated in some ways with the cult of True Womanhood. Donovan's examples of cultural feminists include thinkers such as Margaret Fuller, Charlotte Perkins Gilman, Jane Addams and, in some respects, Anna Julia Cooper and Elizabeth Cady Stanton, one of the most powerful figures in the 'woman suffrage movement'.[5] Although a gross oversimplification, in some ways one could say that cultural feminists took the binary oppositions that devalued women, such as reason–passion, aggression–peacefulness, public–domestic, and reversed the value polarity. In their particular historical circumstances, emphasizing female moral superiority was an effective tool to argue for women's suffrage and education. A negative and destructive use of this view occurred when it was tied to attempts to argue for women's suffrage as a way of countering the black male vote. Liberal feminists opposed this view because they had striven long and hard to establish that the rationality and agency of women were equal to those of men. This was the basis for their argument that women possessed the same natural rights as men. Many thinkers, such as Anna Julia Cooper and Elizabeth Cady Stanton, combined various elements of liberal and cultural feminism.

*Elizabeth Cady Stanton: 'What men teach in their high places, such women as Dorcas illustrate in their lives'.* Toward the end of her life Stanton (1815–1902) edited and wrote most of a commentary on the

5. How to view Cooper and Stanton in terms of liberal and cultural feminism is a matter of some controversy. For discussions of the ambiguities in Cooper's position see hooks 1981: 166-68 and Washington 1988: xlii-li. For Stanton see the debate between Offen (1988) and DuBois (1989). My own view is that there are elements of individualist/equality feminism as well as elements of relational/cultural feminism in both Stanton and Cooper, probably with equality feminism dominating. Both were products of the nineteenth century with its emphasis on the positive moral contribution of women. Stanton's *The Women's Bible* project, with its focus on passages concerning women, tends in many places toward a cultural feminism.

Bible designed to counter what she saw as reactionary elements in organized religion. In *The Woman's Bible* (1898) Stanton comments briefly on the Tabitha story:

> Tabitha was called by this name among the Jews; but she was known to the Greeks as Dorcas. She was considered an ornament to her Christian profession; for she so abounded in good works and alms-deeds that her whole life was devoted to the wants and the needs of the poor. She not only gave away her substance, but she employed her time and her skill in laboring constantly for the poor and the unfortunate. Her death was looked upon as a public calamity. This is the first instance of any Apostle performing a miracle of this kind. There was not witness to this miracle. What men teach in their high places, such women as Dorcas illustrate in their lives (1988 [1898]: 146).

Stanton pictures Tabitha as a woman devoted to the cause of the poor, a living example. Echoing in some respects Henry's comment about those who 'talk the talk but do not walk the walk', she sees Tabitha as the type of woman who practices what men merely teach. Her praise also raises the question of why there are no women teaching in high places.

*Margaret E. Sangster: 'Their names are inscribed in no Hall of Fame, but they are written in the Book of Life'.* Like Stanton, Margaret E. Sangster (1838–1912) produced a book on biblical texts concerned with women, including Tabitha. Sangster, a prolific popular author and editor, was much less radical than Stanton. Nevertheless, she wrote in favor of equal educational opportunity for women as well as advancing many tenets of cultural feminism.[6] The tenor of her writing can be seen in the conclusion to her book *The Women of the Bible* (1911):

> The portrait gallery of women, beginning with Eve in the Garden of Eden, shows us woman in every age essentially the same. The woman soul leads on. For good or for ill, for weal or for woe, woman influences man and, to a great extent, controls his destiny...
>
> Woman holds in her hand at this hour a great moral responsibility. If she choose to throw her influence in the scale in favor of peace, the knell of war will be sounded. If she awaken to the shame and infamy of child labor that the greed of Mammon may be satisfied, the children will cease to be enslaved before they have had time to play. Woman owes so much to Christ that it behooves her in a Christian land to remember the women in

---

6.    For more information on Sangster see Sangster (1980 [1909]) and Willard (1967 [1893]: 632).

lands that are still in the shadow of death. The work of woman for woman
and the work of woman for Christ should go hand in hand in this wonderful century in which we live (1911: 361-62).

Sangster's discussion of Tabitha is entitled 'The Raising of Dorcas'. The
discussion is much in the spirit of a cultural feminism that saw Woman
as a moral model who from the domestic sphere fights for justice and
cares for the poor. She also makes a point similar to that of Stanton that
women doers are often unsung heroines. She begins the chapter with a
comparison between Tabitha's work in the days of the early church and
the work of providing clothes for needy women and support for the
mission field in her own day. This is work women did 'conspicuously' in
Tabitha's day and 'have been doing all along the line ever since' (1911:
326). The needle is their weapon of choice. Sangster sees Dorcas as a
model that women can and have followed: 'In the course of my life I
have known not a few women who wrought for Jesus Christ after her
pattern. Their names are inscribed in no Hall of Fame, but they are
written in the Book of Life' (1911: 327). To Sangster's mind Dorcas fits
the picture of gentle and caring womanhood. She imagines Dorcas as
'gentle, tender, comforting and, I think, beautiful' (1911: 327). As for
Peter, Sangster humanizes him. She begins by recalling examples of
Peter's lack of faith from the Gospels. The Peter that prays for and
offers his hand to Dorcas, she writes, is not the Peter who walked on the
water and sank or who denied the Lord three times. It is the Peter
whom the Lord asks, 'Lovest thou Me?' and the Peter who heals the
cripple at the Beautiful Gate (1911: 328). Jesus, says Sangster, calls all
disciples to humble care for his lambs, men and women alike. She
concludes with the remark that the church in Joppa had a 'revival of
dead souls that day, when the living soul came back to Dorcas by the
grace of Jesus Christ at the summons of his servant' (1911: 329). As
with Calvin, the emphasis is on Christ's action rather than Peter's
power.

Sangster, however, operates with little hermeneutics of suspicion—or
at least not openly. She does not ask why women are wielding the
needle rather than ascending the pulpit stairs. Or why their names are
not inscribed in a Hall of Fame. On the other hand, she celebrates the
work of the little people who do the nitty-gritty work of caring for those
in need in a way that makes it clear that that work is indispensable and
might not get done otherwise. Her picture of Tabitha as a model woman
is essentialist, describing woman as a gentle caregiver and moral beacon.

It never poses a direct threat to a patriarchal social order. It certainly would permit men to continue to view women as those whose job it is to care for others and to protect moral values while the men handle the public sphere. The subject position that Sangster holds up as a model—'Woman works in fairs and bazaars, she sends boxes and barrels to missionary stations near and far, she clothes the orphans and cheers the destitute' (1911: 326)—is one that would most easily be filled by middleclass American Protestant women in her day. She does not write from the position of the destitute or of those to whom the missionaries go. At the same time, her description of unsung women church workers might be recognized with modifications for their own situations by many differently-situated women. Her women may wield the needle rather than the sword or pen, but they are agents nonetheless.

*Julia A.J. Foote: 'God is no respecter of persons'*. If we do look to nineteenth- and early twentieth-century American women differently situated from the white middleclass Stanton and Sangster, it is difficult to find records of their interpretation of Tabitha. One middleclass, educated, African American evangelist, Virginia W. Broughton, provides very brief topical outlines of several of her sermons. In one on the biblical authority for women's work she cites Acts 9.39 and Rom. 16.1 as examples of women as missionaries (1988 [1907]: 130). In a sermon on Christian work she offers Peter, Paul, Mary, Dorcas [Tabitha] and Lydia as illustrations that one's work is 'indicated by one's natural gifts and adaptability' (p. 132). Unfortunately, how Broughton developed these examples is not preserved. It seems safe to say that she was justifying women's work in fields traditionally understood as male.

If it is difficult to find examples of interpretations of Tabitha, it is not difficult to find examples of African American women's use of Acts.[7] A

---

7.    African American women interpreters of Acts include Jarena Lee, Anna Julia Cooper and Zilpha Elaw. The epigraph of Jarena Lee's autobiography, *The Life and Religious Experience of Jarena Lee*, is Joel 2.28, which is quoted in Acts 2: 'And it shall come to pass...that I will pour out my Spirit upon all flesh; and your sons, and your *daughters* shall prophecy [prophesy]'(Andrews 1986: 27, italics in original). Anna Julia Cooper makes use of the Cornelius episode. She considers Acts 10.34 (God is no respecter of persons) to be one of the Scripture passages that is key to the Christian message (Baker-Fletcher 1993: 45). Zilpha Elaw, after recounting a vision of Jesus guaranteeing the forgiveness of her sins, compares herself to the Ethiopian eunuch of Acts 8 (Andrews 1986: 57). Nineteenth-century English Methodist women preachers also found Joel 2.28 = Acts 2.17-21 especially empowering (Krueger

particularly striking example is found in the autobiography of Julia A.J. Foote (1823–1900), an African Methodist Episcopal female evangelist. Foote focuses not on female characters, but on males such as the Ethiopian eunuch of Acts 8 and the Roman centurion Cornelius in Acts 10. She also finds great inspiration as many feminists have done in Acts 2.16-21, which announces that the spirit of prophecy is poured out on daughters as well as sons. Foote's reading strategies illumine and enrich our understanding of possible approaches to texts like Acts. Foote reads from a very particular social and historical location but finds in that particularity universal implications. She intertwines her autobiography with, and sees parallels between her life and, these texts in Acts. She reads one in the light of the other. This practice, according to Renita Weems, is characteristic of the African American female interpretative community's hermeneutics. These readers, according to Weems, 'measure what they have been told about God, reality, and themselves against what they have experienced of God and reality and what they think of themselves as it has been mediated to them by the primary community with which they identify' (1991: 66).[8]

As Julia Foote describes her spiritual journey, a sense of sin and something missing troubled her as a young girl. She believed that if she was educated God would help her understand what she needed. Troubled by a lack of education and hampered by lack of educational opportunity for 'colored' children, the young Foote was forced to become self-taught after but a few weeks of school. She carefully studied the Bible. After a time she met an older man and woman who testified about their previous troubles overcoming sin and their experience of joy after sanctification. She interpreted herself as the Ethiopian eunuch and the older couple as Philip: 'I at once understood what I needed. Though I had read in my Bible many things they told me, I had never understood what I read. I needed a Philip to teach me' (1986 [1879]: 185). The female saint of the couple read and explained many passages of

1992: 7, 63-64), as did Katherine Zell during the Reformation in Strasbourg (Douglass 1985: 92-93).

8.    Weems is careful to note that her strategic use of the term African American women can obscure differences between African American women (1991: 59 n. 4). My placing Foote within the African American women's reading community can also elide differences. It would be more accurate to classify Foote as a member of a nineteenth-century African American A.M.E. female evangelistic/sanctification reading community.

Scripture to Foote, and shortly after Foote felt herself sanctified
(pp. 186-87). Neither Foote's parents nor her minister were much taken
with her keeping company with the elderly saints, her adoption of the
doctrine of sanctification, or her belief that she had been sanctified. Her
minister was particularly unhappy when she joyfully shared her beliefs
with others. He argued that she was too young 'to read and dictate to
persons older than yourself' (p. 188). But Julia Foote was not deterred
'by what man might think or say' (p. 189). Neither age nor sex were
barriers to the one who was no respecter of persons (Acts 10.34):

> Bless the Lord, O my soul, for this wonderful salvation, that snatched me
> as a brand from the burning, even me, a poor, ignorant girl! And will he not
> do for all what he did for me? Yes, yes; God is no respecter of persons
> (p. 189).

Acts 2.16-21, where Peter quotes Joel 2.28-29, is also significant for
Foote. She strongly felt her commission to preach came from the Holy
Spirit. The minister of the A.M.E. Zion church in Boston opposed her
efforts to preach sanctification and had her excommunicated. She made
an appeal to a higher level in the A.M.E. Zion church. Her appeal was
ignored, she argued, on the basis of her sex. In writing of this experience
she said that 'there was no justice meted out to women in those days.
Even ministers of Christ did not feel that women had any rights which
they were bound to respect' (p. 207). As William Andrews points out,
these words were a clear echo of the Supreme Court's words in the
Dred Scott decision, which held that black Americans 'had no rights
which the white man was bound to respect' (Dred Scott v. Sanford, 19
Howard 393, quoted in Andrews 1986: 20). Thus Foote tied together
unjust racism and sexism (Andrews 1986: 20). Immediately following
her discussion of her rejection she offers an entire chapter entitled
'Women in the Gospel'. There she writes of the authorization of Acts 2
for her preaching:

> I could not believe that it was a short-lived impulse or spasmodic influence
> that impelled me to preach. I read that on the day of Pentecost was the
> Scripture fulfilled as found in Joel ii. 28, 29; and it certainly will not be
> denied that women as well as men were at that time filled with the Holy
> Ghost, because it is expressly stated that women were among those who
> continued in prayer and supplication, waiting for the fulfillment of the
> promise. Women and men are classed together, and if the power to preach
> the Gospel is short-lived and spasmodic in the case of women, it must be
> equally so in that of men; and if women have lost the gift of prophecy, so
> have men (1986 [1879]: 208).

Many black Americans have been drawn to the Ethiopian eunuch as a 'culturally affirming and empowering tradition' (Martin 1989: 125). It may very well be that Foote found the story of an African Christian illuminating for that reason as well. At the same time Foote did not feel that she could not identify with the eunuch because he was male, or because he was a high official. She explicitly states that she identified with his need for inspired interpretative guidance. This reading did not mean that she assumed a position of racial or sexual subordination, however. The persons she saw in the role of Philip were an elderly African American couple, especially the female saint. At the same time as Foote looked to the Ethiopian eunuch, she turned to other passages in Acts where she read the Holy Spirit's authorization of women's preaching and teaching activities. While the story of Cornelius in Acts 10 (as well as the story of the Ethiopian eunuch in Acts 8.26-40; see Martin 1989 and Tannehill 1990: 107-112) marks the inclusion of Gentiles as previously excluded from Christianity, Foote reads the passage in the light of the exclusion of young girls who advocate sanctification. Her minister cannot exclude what God includes, whether pious Roman centurions or Julia Foote herself. According to Vincent Wimbush, Acts 2 and Acts 10, especially 10.34-35, were passages frequently used in African American biblical interpretation to argue for universal salvation, especially in relation to the racial situation in the United States (Wimbush 1993: 132). Foote's use of the passages marks her as a member of an African American reading community in the African American churches, particularly the A.M.E. churches. However, Foote extends the use of the passages to the impartiality of God in areas of gender as well as race. Her double perspective as an African American female enriches her reading. As Foote read the biblical text, she read it with a dual hermeneutic of suspicion and re-vision. She recognized and experienced biblical passages being used against her. She also found within Scripture what Schweikart (1986) calls utopian moments, for her the truer meanings vouchsafed by the Holy Spirit. Like the Ethiopian eunuch she had read many passages but only understood them after her eyes were opened by the elderly couple who served as her Philip. For Foote the gospel message of Acts spoke to her particular situation as an African American woman evangelist, but it did so because its message properly understood was universal. Universality did not mask a hidden male face, black or white, nor did it deny her particularity.

*Modern Feminist Scholars' Readings*

The most recent resurgence of readings of the New Testament by those who identified themselves as part of the women's movement or feminists began in the late sixties and early seventies. Many of these interpreters argued for an equal role in the churches for women. Often ordination and more power for women as well as combat against misogynism were goals. One of the most widely read works that contained interpretations of Luke–Acts, and Tabitha in particular, was Constance Parvey's essay, 'The Theology and Leadership of Women in the New Testament' (1974). In the eighties, feminist interpretation of the New Testament blossomed. Historical-critical, literary and social context methods were all employed. Bonnie Bowman Thurston's work, *The Widows: A Women's Ministry in the Early Church* (1989), arose out of the contrast she saw between the triple marginality of elderly poor women and the important role these women play in the service and support of churches today. She found that 'If women were marginal in church history, widows were invisible!' (1989: 7). Thus Thurston (citing Parvey) sought to recover the history of widows from the time of Jesus to 325 CE. The early nineties saw the publication of Mary Rose D'Angelo's 'Women in Luke–Acts: A Redactional View' in the flagship journal of the American biblical guild, the *Journal of Biblical Literature*, and Gail R. O'Day's commentary on Acts in *The Women's Bible Commentary*; both discuss Tabitha. D'Angelo, using redaction criticism, a well-accepted method in the guild, refers to Parvey's earlier work. She notes that Parvey and others have celebrated the significance of the role given to women in Luke–Acts. She also calls attention to subsequent feminist work that argues Luke–Acts 'appears to take a more conventional view of the role of women than do the other gospels' (1990: 442) and downplays women's leadership in the early church. D'Angelo wants to 'give a rationale for different feminist perceptions' (1990: 442) of Luke–Acts. O'Day, writing the commentary on Acts in *The Women's Bible Commentary*, continues a chain of feminist interpretation begun by Parvey, listing D'Angelo in her bibliography and depending on her for some of her arguments. In line with the pattern of the volume, she comments directly on women who appear in the narrative, including Tabitha. She notes the overall '*de facto* silencing' of women in Luke–Acts but also the subversive glimpses of women's experience and universal theology of Acts (1990: 312).

*Constance Parvey: Women in the New Testament.* Parvey notes the number of stories about women in Luke–Acts, highlighting the pairing of male and female illustrations. She argues that this served a pedagogical purpose, making 'the message clearly understandable to different groups—the female and the male listeners' (1974: 139). Here we have a hallmark of feminist readings, a concern for the effects upon hearers/readers, especially women. She interprets the story of Mary and Martha as a 'keystone': 'While previously the learning of scriptures was limited to men, now it is opened to women. The story of Mary and Martha allowed women to choose' (1974: 141). Parvey argues that the traditional role of a woman as a domestic servant is challenged when Mary is allowed to sit at the feet of a rabbi. Parvey notes what she sees as the more liberal educational policies of Christianity in contrast to those of rabbinic Judaism, a scapegoating and ill-informed move typical of many Christian feminists in the seventies and one that Plaskow (1978 and 1993) and Brooten (1985) have soundly criticized. Still, Parvey does note that 'cultural, religious, and legal impediments' are part of Christianity as well as part of Judaism (1974: 142). Parvey sees Acts as evidence for the prominent and active role of women in the early church. Parvey identifies Tabitha as a woman with a special status as a 'disciple'. She notes that, like Paul and Barnabas, Tabitha is never named as one of the Twelve, but 'unlike them, her designation as "disciple" has been minimized by the Church' (1974: 145). Whether Tabitha is 'merely a follower' or one of a 'small elite group' of Jesus' adherents, Parvey argues, she is clearly important. Parvey reads Tabitha as 'a Jewish woman of independent means', well-known for her charity, craftsmanship (Parvey, like Sangster, has an appreciation for Tabitha's needle) and 'graceful manner', since 'Tabitha' means 'gazelle'. Parvey reads the widows' weeping and Peter's swift arrival as evidence of Tabitha's importance:

> To be recorded as raised from the dead, and to be the focus of the first such miracle by a fellow disciple, she must have been considered indispensable to the congregation. Her exact status remains unknown, but that she was much more than merely one of the many followers is clear from the story about her (1974: 145).

This is quite a different reading of the story than that of modern scholars who see Tabitha as the incidental, if somewhat colorfully described, object of a miracle that demonstrates Peter's status as a prophet like Jesus, Elijah and Elisha. Parvey concludes her discussion of women in

Acts by noting that women of all social levels participated: 'In worship, teaching, institutional and missionary life, the Spirit, indeed, was poured out on both "sons and daughters"' (1974: 146).

Parvey's summary, concluding her entire article on women in the New Testament, restates the view seen in the section on Acts. Women, she argues, had prominent leadership roles in the early church, although not without the subordination coming from the Jewish cast of its cultural milieu. She also reiterates her interpretation of Paul as one who had preached a theology of equivalence in Christ. She sees the later church as struggling with a dualism of other-worldly spiritual equality and practical this-worldly subordination. The result has been that

> One might on rare occasion become a saint, but certainly not a priest; one might become a teacher, but certainly not a theologian or bishop. The consequence of this distorted spirituality and skewed social reality has been that women have been precluded from receiving or ever developing fully responsible and equal roles in the Church's spiritual, theological and institutional life (1974: 147).

*Bonnie Bowman Thurston: The Widows in the New Testament.* Thurston begins her discussion of Acts with a statement typical of much feminist New Testament scholarship. She reiterates the 'interestedness' of the New Testament: 'the writings of the early church were shaped in part by a struggle among opposing groups over the equality of women and therefore cannot be taken as an objective record of the actual condition of women in the early church' (1989: 28). With many other interpreters Thurston notes that the Tabitha story carries forward a favorite Lukan theme—paralleling apostles with Jesus—although with Parvey and Stanton she remarks that this is the first time an apostle raises someone from the dead. Her reading of Tabitha's story, however, centers, as does Parvey's, on the foci of the *hapax legomenon* of Tabitha as *mathētria* and on the status of the term 'widow'. She notes the ambiguity of the term 'disciple' in the early church but points out that it may indicate a special status as one of Jesus' early key followers, reading Peter's swift arrival and later use of the term *mathētria* in gnostic works as possible evidence of this. Thurston notes that the references to widows in Acts 9 as well as in Acts 4 and 6 may be read as referring simply to women whose husbands have died *or* as referring to a special group among these set aside for a special role in the church. Thurston takes issue with the interpretation of Jackson-Foakes and Lake that it is unlikely that the widows in Acts 9 represent an order that dispenses as well as one that receives charity. Thurston, along with Stählin (*TDNT*, IX, 452) and Swidler (1979: 305), reads the reference to 'saints and widows' in v. 41 as evidence for a distinction between the widows and the rest of the members of the early church. For Thurston, this suggests the possibility that a society of widows existed outside of Jerusalem as early as 43 CE. Thurston reads Tabitha herself as a woman of independent means, a caretaker of the group of widows. Since no husband is mentioned, Tabitha may herself be a widow, with the responsibility to care for the widows as a 'recognizable group' (1989: 34) as enjoined in 1 Tim. 5.16 and mentioned in later Christian writings. Thus Thurston is recovering the important role in New Testament history of older women, a role she sees modern women playing as well. She makes one of the classic moves of feminist historians, rendering visible women's agency in history. But this move is not simply compensatory, it is a rewriting of the history of the early church. Because Acts is a source for reconstructing women's agency, it can serve a liberatory function.

*Mary Rose D'Angelo: Women in Luke–Acts.* D'Angelo's study of the 'Women in Luke–Acts' is primarily redactional, focusing on the ideology, theology and community concerns of the editor—unlike Parvey's and Thurston's readings, which are primarily, although not exclusively, oriented to the reconstruction of early Christian history. As I noted above, D'Angelo announces that the goal of the essay is to give account of differences in feminist perceptions of Luke–Acts as liberatory or restrictive. Her thesis is captured in the following statement:

> On the one hand, the author of Luke does increase the number of stories about women in the Gospel, and the increase is a deliberate choice on the part of the author. On the other, the roles in which women appear are more restricted by what is acceptable to the convention of the imperial world than are the roles of women in Mark or John. It [the essay] will argue that the ambiguity results from the tension between the necessity of catechizing women converts who are still of real political importance to the church of Luke's day and the anxiety that an expanded role for women may cause Christians to be seen as practitioners of 'un-Roman activities'. Thus the Gospel offers to its women readers a wide variety of female role models who are the means at once of edification and of control (1990: 442-43).

Again we see the concern for effects on women readers, as well as an interest in the Lukan redactional purpose. D'Angelo agrees with Parvey that Luke–Acts shows a special concern for female illustrations and that these serve an educational purpose for women converts. However, these roles are rather conventional. Taking her cue from Schüssler Fiorenza's interpretation of the Mary and Martha episode (1986; see also now 1992: 51-76) as a story that criticizes Martha's active ministry as *diakonos* in favor of Mary's passive listening role, D'Angelo reads Tabitha's story as another example where 'women's ministry is not denied or forbidden, but rather avoided' (1990: 455). Although Tabitha is depicted as administering charity, it is from her own funds rather than the church's. 'Despite the manifest importance of Tabitha[,] the *mathetria* to her community, her work is described as making garments for widows (the ultimate in economic and matronal virtue, 9.36)' (1990: 455). D'Angelo sees the playing down of heroic roles for women in Acts as part of Luke's concern to show the safety of Christianity in a world where the prominent roles of women in oriental religions were viewed as a threat. But Luke's goal is not only to represent the role of women in Christianity as safe, it is to educate women to restricted roles. Luke's portrayals of women, however, have 'subversive potential', at times having 'given a message against his intention' (1990: 461).[9]

*Gail R. O'Day: Women in Acts.* O'Day begins her reading of the story of Tabitha by noting its pairing with the shorter story of the healing of a man in 9.32-33. She identifies the function of both stories in Acts as the same: 'to portray Peter as a miracle worker in the line of Elijah and Elisha and Jesus and to win converts to Christianity (9.35, 42)' (O'Day 1992: 309). Thus O'Day situates the stories in Acts much as any contemporary scholarly reader would. She goes on to highlight Tabitha's importance, reading the sending of two disciples to fetch Peter and the identification of Tabitha by the *hapax legomenon mathetria* as evidence. She also emphasizes Tabitha's good works and her acts of charity, the latter being the giving of alms. She emphasizes the importance of this female character. From this, however, she turns to the androcentrism of the text, exercising what Schüssler Fiorenza calls a hermeneutics of suspicion. She notes that the author does not use the term *diakonia* (ministry) to describe Tabitha's care for the widows, whereas he does so for men's care of widows in Acts 6.1, 4. This point echoes Schüssler Fiorenza's interpretation of the Mary and Martha story in Luke noted above. O'Day suggests that 'when Luke's description of Tabitha is read

9.   Schaberg (1992), focusing on the Gospel of Luke, advocates a similar interpretation of Luke–Acts. If anything, she stresses the negative aspects of Luke more than D'Angelo.

carefully, it becomes clear that Tabitha is valued as a philanthropist'
(1992: 309). Tabitha, who may be a widow herself, takes care of the
widows out of her own pocket. While these actions are praiseworthy and
make Tabitha a valuable model of discipleship, Luke's description of
Tabitha, O'Day implies, is not exactly revolutionary. Echoing D'Angelo,
O'Day describes Tabitha as 'the proper society matron, doing works of
charity and sewing clothes for the less fortunate' (1992: 309-10). Thus,
O'Day agrees with D'Angelo's assessment that Acts portrays women in
roles—including that of wealthy patronesses—that would be acceptable
to a patriarchal Greco-Roman world view. Luke conducts a 'silencing'
of the actual roles of women in the early church. 'One has to wonder,
however,' O'Day writes, 'why when men take care of widows, Luke
calls it "ministry" (6.4) but when Tabitha performs the same services
Luke calls it "good works"' (1992: 310). But, for O'Day, the limitation
of women's roles, including that of Tabitha in Acts, is not the whole
story. The 'heart of Acts' theology, the universal appeal of the gospel
and its spread to the Gentiles', subverts Luke's attempt to control
women (1992: 312). She writes of the Cornelius episode:

> The dissolution of cultic distinctions between clean and unclean refers to
> [Christian] Jews and Gentiles, but the implications are farther reaching.
> When Luke's theology is played out in a different context, this dissolution
> of cultic distinctions provides the theological grounds for removing cultic
> classifications of women as unclean or impure. Women and men can stand
> as equals before the impartial God of Acts (1992: 312).

O'Day's reading of the Cornelius episode is very similar to Foote's. For
both women Cornelius represents the excluded female. Provided that we
do not read the opening of Christianity to all nations and to all genders
in an anti-Jewish fashion, both readings make a powerful feminist point.
The danger in reading the Roman centurion as an unclean female Other
is that Judaism may be cast as exclusive–misogynist, Christianity as
inclusive–feminist. If we remember that Peter is a Jewish Christian, that
it was Jewish conversion of Gentiles that created proselytes and God-
fearers, and that Jonah and Ruth as well as Ezra–Nehemiah are part of
Hebrew Scripture, this pitfall may be avoided.

### Learning from Reception History

As one reviews the history of the reception of Tabitha's story it is clear
that readers' interpretative conventions, ideological commitments and

historical contexts shape their responses. Text and readers are partners in the dance of interpretation. One distinction between modern male-stream scholarship on the one hand and pastoral males, Stanton and Sangster, and recent feminists on the other is concern for pragmatic effects on hearers or readers. Reading the passage as exemplary literature shifts the emphasis from Peter to Tabitha. So does reading it to reconstruct the roles of women in early church history. Reading the story as exemplary literature is a practice scholars usually reject as leading to an ahistorical dogmatic interpretation. Oddly enough, however, this may actually provide a reading closer to the reading conventions of many first-century readers, who were taught to read characters as types.

Another shift in interpretation occurs depending on whether the reader reads the story in the context of Acts or Luke–Acts as a whole or independently. Reading the story independently, at least for a moment, before reinserting it, brings out a focus on Tabitha. Within the story itself Tabitha and Peter are dual centers of attention. Within the context of Acts, and even more so of Luke–Acts read as a two-volume work, Tabitha recedes in importance. Because the Gospels and Acts are andro-centric and patriarchal and women appear only here and there, it is not surprising that feminists have concentrated on the passages in which women appear. For historical critics these passages then become the basis for constructing a more accurate picture of Jesus' ministry, early Christian history in general, or even an evangelist's community. For literary critics the passages become occasions to reflect on women characters or ideological representation. For social context critics the passages become sociohistorical data or elements that contribute to the development of social models. For devotional readers these passages speak to experiences of oppression and liberation.

Reception history also reveals a contrast between reading Tabitha as a general model of discipleship and reading her as similar to or in contrast to Peter. The latter tends to keep her within the bounds of patriarchal subordination. Her service is not quite the same as Peter's preaching and healing power—after all, she, initially her inert body, is the object of Peter's healing action. The former highlights Tabitha's own actions, the power of her almsdeeds, oversight of others, and her needle. Reading and identifying with Peter involves immasculation.

Another point that reception history brings out is that discipleship and widowhood are contested categories. Tabitha as *mathētria* means different things to different readers. To Calvin it can be used against Rome to establish Christ as the only Teacher and the equal discipleship of all believers. Despite the fact that *mathētria* is a *hapax legomenon*, a phenomenon on which biblical scholars love to dwell, most malestream biblical scholars tend to pass over it, assuming women did not play prominent roles in the early church. Like the designation of Junia as a female apostle in Rom. 16.7 (see Brooten 1977), the designation of Tabitha as a *mathētria* and its dismissal as a title of significance without much consideration is an important example of androcentrism. The case of the widows who appear in Tabitha's story is similar. Whether the widows are read as a distinct order and whether Tabitha herself is read as a widow serve as signposts pointing to readers' interests and assumptions.

## The Feminist Readings

An examination of the feminist readings of Tabitha is enlightening because it reveals a tradition of our own, oscillation between equality and difference, and an emphasis on the multiplicity of texts and readers. Although more apparent in work on Pauline epistles and the Gospels, an examination of the reception history of Tabitha's story shows that we now have a tradition of our own, a tradition of feminist New Testament scholarly interpretation. In our writing we can cite and respond to the work of other feminists. The chains of citations no longer carry only male names. In addition we are beginning to recover women's readings of the New Testament from various historical settings (see e.g. Baker-Fletcher 1993; Gifford 1985; and Lerner 1993). Although these readings are not necessarily feminist, predating the modern use of the term, women's interpretation history is becoming visible. On the one hand, feminists can celebrate this discovery because we no longer have to reinvent the wheel, unaware of what our predecessors have done (Lerner 1993; Schüssler Fiorenza 1993). We can build upon what our predecessors have done as earlier women could not because the work of previous women interpreters was hidden in history (Lerner 1993). We can fruitfully enter dialogue with differing perspectives. On the other hand, it is a source of difficulty, especially for new graduate students and young scholars. It is no longer possible to write the first contemporary feminist scholarly interpretation of most pericopes, let alone of a whole Gospel or letter of Paul. Within the scholarly community, jobs, tenure and prestige are often based on innovation and sometimes on successfully savaging one's predecessors. As feminists become more prominent in the guild, we must now increasingly ensure that our criticism of other scholars, male and female, remains bold and also constructive.

Another enlightening aspect of the reception history of women's readings of Tabitha is how it highlights the alternation between the celebration and downplaying of female difference. One of the ongoing oscillations in feminist discourse in the United States has been between an emphasis on women's equality (in what respects and for what purposes) and the celebration of female difference (defined by whom, for what ends). It is an oscillation also related to oscillations between essentialism and anti-essentialism, 'American' and 'French' feminism, pro-sex and anti-pornography, and so on (see Alcoff 1988; Snitow 1990; de Lauretis 1990). With Sangster we see a celebration of Tabitha's female virtue, often unsung, but especially worthy and powerful. Although this move was essentialist, in her cultural context this provided a way to claim moral authority and a degree of influence for women. With figures like Foote and Parvey, who justify the service of women in roles usually reserved for men, we see the press for equality. We see the celebration of leadership roles of women in the early church, including Tabitha's importance as a disciple. She is an eminent figure, the first to be raised from the dead by an apostle. As women pressed for more power, especially in the role of ordained ministers in the 1960s and 1970s, the argument that women in the earliest church were not excluded from important spiritual or institutional roles supported the argument that they should not be excluded today. Women were and are not limited to the role of domestic servant. Thurston also highlights Tabitha as disciple and Tabitha as leader of an order of widows. Tabitha is one of the examples showing that women and, especially important for Thurston, older women, likely had official status positions in the early church. The position of women like Tabitha provides a strong argument for an equal role for women in modern churches. Parvey and perhaps Thurston represent what D'Angelo perceives to be a positive feminist scholarly reading of Luke–Acts.

Beginning with D'Angelo and O'Day writing in the early 1990s we see a backing away from celebration of early egalitarianism to highlighting the text's (or redactor's) androcentrism and domestication of women under a patriarchal umbrella, the re-patriarchalizing of what may have been more initial equality for women in the early church. There is a sarcasm about, rather than a celebration of, Tabitha's matronly (upperclass female) virtue. The emphasis is more on Luke's restriction of women.

So far in my reading I have emphasized the equality–difference oscillation, which interpreters often harden into a rigid dichotomy. Now I want to argue that my initial reading is complicated by multiple emphases occurring within feminist readings. Stanton, who emphasizes Tabitha's female virtue, also implicitly asks why there are no women teaching in high places. Even Sangster, who is most thoroughly a cultural feminist, emphasizes that males and females alike must feed Christ's lambs. Both see agency in 'female' tasks. The egalitarian Parvey, who approved of Mary as student over Martha as domestic servant, celebrates Tabitha's needlework and her gentle manner. D'Angelo and O'Day, who emphasize restriction rather than liberation in Luke–Acts, also recognize the text's subversive potential. They obviously are not keen on celebrating female virtues if this means a disallowing of women's non-traditional roles. At the same time they praise the importance of Tabitha's work on behalf of her community. This more complicated reading coheres with feminist reader-response criticism's hermeneutics of suspicion (its recognition of immasculation) and its hermeneutics of re-vision (its reading against the grain and/or reading for utopian moments).

The feminist readings are complex and multiplicative in other dimensions as well. Sangster and Stanton emphasize Tabitha's concern for the poor. Parvey notes that women of all social levels are empowered by the spirit in Acts. D'Angelo and O'Day also highlight class as an analytic category, noting Tabitha's position as a wealthy matron. They also read Acts recognizing the impact of the colonial context on the author and his desire to make Christianity acceptable to Roman imperial power. Thurston brings marital status and age to the fore. She emphasizes the position of widows, especially elderly widows, in the first-century Greco-Roman context as well as in contemporary society. Foote brings into clear focus the intersection of race and gender.

Reading the feminist reception history suggests that there is no first moment of naive celebration of female characters to be superseded by the wise eye that sees through the patriarchal devices immasculating us. Nor need we read Tabitha as only heroine or victim. Nor is there an easy way to separate egalitarian readings from those that represent and celebrate difference. An emphasis on either or both may be important in specific situations. Recent feminist theorists such as Patricia Hill Collins (1990) and in New Testament studies Elizabeth Schüssler Fiorenza

(1992) have emphasized that patriarchy involved and involves a pyramid of interlocking or multiplicative oppressions that takes different forms in different historical circumstances. With an awareness of this, feminists may choose to stress one or more of the following categories as they read Tabitha as female, a Jewish Christian, a person of wealth, and perhaps a widow. They also stress the importance of learning from a variety of readings from different particular social and historical locations. This is necessary for a hermeneutics of suspicion to locate exclusions and oppressive uses of biblical texts as well as to open possibilities for a hermeneutics of re-vision. Feminist readings, like that of Foote, for example, urge us not to restrict ourselves to passages with female characters or passages that discuss the roles of women. We can exercise a hermeneutics of re-vision as well as suspicion on all texts. At the same time we must exercise a hermeneutics of suspicion with regard to our own readings. As we have seen, even the celebration of universality in Foote and O'Day's readings could be misused. If we are concerned about the pragmatic effects of interpretation on women, we must be concerned about the pragmatic effects of all sorts of interpretations on all sorts of women and men.

## Conclusion

Biblical scholarship teaches scholarly readers to see how texts are multi-layered, often reflecting multiple historical situations. A text from a Gospel, for example, may reflect a setting in life in the ministry of Jesus, in the oral tradition of the early church, and in the evangelist's community. Reception history shows us the multiplicity of readers. Textual multiplicity and the multiplicity of readers also help us see the importance of multiple feminist readings in the service of critique and re-vision. In the reception history we have examined, an emphasis on the power of God or the Holy Spirit rather than on human authority strengthens the utopian moment for women. This is what we see in Calvin and Foote, for example. It is compatible with a theological understanding that rests authority in the *ekklēsia* of women, as with Schüssler Fiorenza, or in a Protestant understanding of the text as the Word of God, provided we understand with Calvin that the words written on the page only become the Word of God when the Holy Spirit illuminates the reader. If we follow Foote, the Bible can become the Word of God anew in each new historical and social context of reading, as the Holy Spirit—

rather than any oppressive human interpreter—leads. A single verse can be both oppressive and liberative. I may read Tabitha to commend the older women in my community who run the rummage sales, make baby clothes for those who need them, and are there with food when someone is too ill to cook. At the same time my celebration of caregiving may entail accepting the separation of public and private spheres, acquiescing in a limitation of women to the domestic sphere, to their 'proper' place. With Foote I may be bold to see myself as Cornelius, celebrating God as no respecter of persons, but when I do I read from a different position from Foote. I may also ignore the immasculation or apology for colonialism that Cornelius, the Roman centurion, might represent in certain circumstances. This is why it is important to examine readings from many different subject positions. For Christian feminist reader-response critics it is also why verse five of the hymn 'Holy is the Lamb' written by Julia Foote (Gates 1988 [1886]: 123) rings so true:

> Sometimes I read my Bible,
> It almost seems a task;
> Sometimes I find a blessing
> Wherever I do look.

## BIBLIOGRAPHY

Alcoff, Linda
  1988        'Cultural Feminism versus Post-Structuralism: The Identity Crisis in Feminist Theory', *Signs* 13: 405-36.
Andrews, William L. (ed.)
  1986        *Sisters of the Spirit: Three Black Women's Autobiographies of the Nineteenth Century* (Bloomington: Indiana University Press).
Baker-Fletcher, Karen
  1993        'Anna Julia Cooper and Sojourner Truth: Two Nineteenth-Century Black Feminist Interpreters of Scripture', in Schüssler Fiorenza (ed.) 1993: 41-51.
Basil, St
  1950        *Saint Basil: Ascetical Works* (Fathers of the Church: A New Translation, 9; trans. M. Monica Wagner; New York: Fathers of the Church, Inc.).
Brooten, Bernadette
  1977        'Junia...Outstanding among the Apostles', in L. Swidler and A. Swidler (eds.), *Women Priests: A Catholic Commentary on the Vatican Declaration* (New York: Paulist Press).
  1985        'Early Christian Women and their Cultural Context: Issues of Method in Historical Reconstruction', in Collins 1985: 65-92.

Broughton, Virginia W.
1988       *Twenty Year's Experience of A Missionary*, in Gates 1988: 1-140, orig.
           pagination (Chicago: The Pony Press, 1907, orig. edn).
Bruce, Frederick F.
1992       *The Book of the Acts* (New ICC; Grand Rapids: Eerdmans, rev. edn).
Calvin, John
1965       *The Acts of the Apostles*, I (Calvin's New Testament Commentaries;
           trans. John W. Fraser and W.J.G. McDonald; Grand Rapids: Eerdmans).
Chrysostom, St
1956       *Homilies on the Acts of the Apostles and the Epistle to the Romans*
           (Nicene and Post-Nicene Fathers, 11; ed. Philip Schaff; trans. with
           notes and indices by J. Walker, J. Sheppard and H. Browne; rev. with
           notes by George B. Stevens; Grand Rapids: Eerdmans).
Collins, Patricia Hill
1990       *Black Feminist Thought* (New York: Routledge & Kegan Paul).
Collins, Adela Yarbro (ed.)
1985       *Feminist Perspectives on Biblical Scholarship* (SBL Biblical
           Scholarship in North America, 10; Chico, CA: Scholars Press).
Conzelmann, Hans
1987       *Acts of the Apostles: A Commentary on the Acts of the Apostles*
           (Hermeneia; trans. J. Limburg, A.T. Kraabel and P. Juel; Philadelphia:
           Fortress Press).
Cross, F.L. and E.A. Livingstone (eds.)
1983       *Oxford Dictionary of the Christian Church* (Oxford: Oxford University
           Press, 2nd edn).
Culler, Jonathan
1982       *On Deconstruction* (Ithaca, NY: Cornell University Press).
D'Angelo, Mary Rose
1990       'Women in Luke–Acts: A Redactional View', *JBL* 109: 441-61.
de Lauretis, Teresa
1990       'Upping the Anti (sic) in Feminist Theory', in Hirsch and Fox Keller
           1990: 255-70.
Dibelius, Martin
1956       'Style Criticism of the Book of Acts', in H. Greeven (ed.), *Studies in
           the Acts of the Apostles* (trans. M. Ling; London: William Cloves &
           Sons; distributed in the United States by Charles Scribner's Sons).
Donovan, Josephine
1985       *Feminist Theory: The Intellectual Traditions of American Feminism*
           (New York: F. Ungar; paperback, New York: Continuum, 1990).
Douglass, Jane Dempsey
1985       *Women, Freedom, and Calvin* (Philadelphia: Westminster Press).
DuBois, Ellen Carol
1989       'Comment on Karen Offen's "Defining Feminism: A Comparative
           Historical Approach"', *Signs* 15: 195-97.
Felder, Cain Hope (ed.)
1991       *Stony the Road we Trod: African American Biblical Interpretation*
           (Minneapolis: Fortress Press).

Fetterly, Judith
  1978        *The Resisting Reader: A Feminist Approach to American Fiction*
              (Bloomington: Indiana University Press).
Foote, Julie A.J.
  1986        'A Brand Plucked from the Fire: An Autobiographical Sketch by
              Mrs Julia A.J. Foote', in Andrews 1986: 161-234 (originally
              published privately in 1879).
  1988        'A Brand Plucked from the Fire: An Autobiographical Sketch by Mrs
              Julia A.J. Foote', in Gates 1988: 1-124 (a facsimile of the 1886 edn).
Fowler, Robert M.
  1991        *Let the Reader Understand: Reader-Response Criticism and the
              Gospel of Mark* (Minneapolis: Fortress Press).
Fulkerson, Mary McClintock
  1991        'Contesting Feminist Canons: Discourse and the Problem of Sexist
              Texts', *Journal of Feminist Studies in Religion* 7: 53-74.
Fuss, Diana
  1989        'Reading Like a Feminist', *Differences* 1: 77-92.
Gasque, W. Ward
  1989        *A History of the Interpretation of the Acts of the Apostles* (Peabody,
              MA: Hendrickson Publishers).
Gates, Henry Louis Jr. (ed.)
  1988        *Spiritual Narratives: M.W. Stewart; J. Lee; J.A.J. Foote;
              V.W. Broughton* (introduction by Sue E. Houchins; The Schomburg
              Library of Nineteenth-Century Black Women Writers; New York:
              Oxford University Press).
Gifford, Carolyn De Swarte
  1985        'American Women and the Bible: The Nature of Woman as a
              Hermeneutical Issue', in Collins 1985: 11-34.
Grant, Robert M.
  1984        *A Short History of the Interpretation of the Bible* (Philadelphia:
              Fortress Press, 2nd edn).
Haenchen, Ernst
  1971        *The Acts of the Apostles* (trans. B. Noble and G. Shinn; rev. R.M. Wilson;
              Philadelphia: Westminster Press).
Harding, Sandra (ed.)
  1987        'Conclusion: Epistemological Questions', in S. Harding (ed.), *Feminism
              and Methodology* (Bloomington: Indiana University Press): 181-90.
Henry, Matthew
  1961        *Matthew Henry's Commentary in One Volume* (ed. L.F. Church; Grand
              Rapids: Zondervan).
Hirsch, Marianne and Evelyn Fox Keller (eds.)
  1990        *Conflicts in Feminism* (New York: Routledge & Kegan Paul).
hooks, bell
  1981        *Ain't I a Woman: Black Women and Feminism* (Boston: South End
              Press).
Jackson-Foakes, F. and Kirsopp Lake
  1933        *The Acts of the Apostles* (Vol. 4 of Part I, *The Beginnings of Christianity*;
              ed. Henry J. Cadbury and Kirsopp Lake; London: Macmillan).

Jervell, Jacob
1984          'The Daughters of Abraham: Women in Acts', in Jacob Jervell, *The Unknown Paul* (Minneapolis: Augsburg): 146-57, 186-90.

Johnson, Sherman E. (annotator)
1977          'Acts', in Herbert G. May and Bruce M. Metzger (eds.), *The New Oxford Annotated Bible, Revised Standard Version* (New York: Oxford University Press): 1319-60.

Krueger, Christine
1992          *The Reader's Repentance: Women Preachers, Women Writers, and Nineteenth-Century Social Discourse* (Chicago: University of Chicago Press).

Lerner, Gerda
1993          *The Creation of Feminist Consciousness: From the Middle Ages to Eighteen-Seventy* (Women and History, 2; New York: Oxford University Press).

Malbon, Elizabeth Struthers and Janice Capel Anderson
1993          'Literary-Critical Methods', in Schüssler Fiorenza (ed.) 1993: 241-54.

Martin, Clarice J.
1989          'A Chamberlain's Journey and the Challenge of Interpretation for Liberation', *Semeia* 47: 105-36.
1991          'The *Haustafeln* (Household Codes) in African American Biblical Interpretation: "Free Slaves" and "Subordinate Women"', in Felder 1993: 206-31.

Modeleski, Tania
1986          'Feminism and the Power of Interpretation: Some Critical Readings', in Teresa de Lauretis (ed.), *Feminist Studies/Critical Studies* (Bloomington: Indiana University Press).

Mohanty, Chandra Talpade
1991          'Cartographies of Struggle: Third World Women and the Politics of Feminism', in C. Talpade Mohanty, A. Russo and L. Torres (eds.), *Third World Women and the Politics of Feminism* (Bloomington: Indiana University Press): 1-47.

Munck, Johannes
1967          *The Acts of the Apostles* (AB, 31; Garden City: Doubleday).

Norris, Frederick W.
1990          'Basil of Caearea', in Everett Ferguson (ed.), *Encyclopedia of Early Christianity* (New York: Garland).

Newsome, Carol A. and Sharon H. Ringe (eds.)
1992          *The Women's Bible Commentary* (Louisville: Westminster/John Knox).

O'Day, Gail R.
1992          'Acts', in Newsome and Ringe 1992: 305-12.

Offen, Karen
1988          'Defining Feminism: A Comparative Historical Approach', *Signs* 14: 119-57.

Ostricker, Alicia Suskin
1993          *Feminist Revision and the Bible* (Bucknell Lectures in Literary History; Oxford: Basil Blackwell).

Packer, J.W.
1966        *The Acts of the Apostles* (The Cambridge Bible Commentary on the
            New English Bible; Cambridge: Cambridge University Press).
Parsons, Mikeal C. and Richard I. Pervo
1993        *Rethinking the Unity of Luke and Acts* (Minneapolis: Fortress Press).
Parvey, Constance F.
1974        'The Theology and Leadership of Women in the New Testament', in
            Rosemary Radford Ruether (ed.), *Religion and Sexism: Images of
            Woman in the Jewish and Christian Traditions* (New York: Simon &
            Schuster): 117-49.
Pervo, Richard I.
1987        *Profit with Delight: The Literary Genre of the Acts of the Apostles*
            (Philadelphia: Fortress Press).
Plaskow, Judith
1978        'Christian Feminism and Anti-Judaism', *Crosscurrents* 28: 306-309.
1993        'Anti-Judaism in Feminist Christian Interpretation', in Schüssler
            Fiorenza (ed.) 1993: 117-29.
Sangster, Margaret E.
1911        *The Women of the Bible: A Portrait Gallery* (New York: The Christian
            Herald).
1980        *From My Youth Up* (Signal Lives: Autobiographies of American
            Women; New York: Arno Press; repr. of the 1909 edn pub. New York:
            Revell Company under the title *An Autobiography: From My Youth
            Up: Personal Reminiscences*).
Schaberg, June
1992        'Luke', in Newsome and Ringe 1992: 275-304.
Schneider, Gerhard
1982        *Die Apostelgeschichte. II. Kommentar zu Kap. 9,1–28,31* (HTKNT, 5;
            Freiburg: Herder).
Scholes, Robert
1987        'Reading Like a Man', in A. Jardine and P. Smith (eds.), *Men in
            Feminism* (New York: Methuen).
Schüssler Fiorenza, Elisabeth
1986        'A Feminist Critical Interpretation for Liberation: Martha and Mary
            (Luke 10.38-42)', *Religion and Intellectual Life* 3: 16-36.
1992        *But She Said: Feminist Practices of Biblical Interpretation* (Boston:
            Beacon Press).
1993        'Introduction: Transforming the Legacy of the Women's Bible', in
            Schüssler Fiorenza (ed.) 1993: 1-28.
Schüssler Fiorenza, Elisabeth (ed.)
1993        *Searching the Scriptures. I. A Feminist Introduction* (New York:
            Crossroad).
Schweickart, Patrocino P.
1986        'Reading Ourselves: Toward a Feminist Theory of Reading', in
            Elizabeth A. Flynn and Patrocino P. Scheickart (eds.), *Gender and
            Reading: Essays on Readers, Texts, and Contexts* (Baltimore:
            Johns Hopkins University Press): 31-62.

Schwöbel, C.
1990 'Calvin', in R.J. Coggins and J.L. Houlden (eds.), *A Dictionary of Biblical Interpretation* (Philadelphia: Trinity Press International; London: SCM Press): 98-101.

Showalter, Elaine
1983 'Critical Cross-Dressing: Male Feminists and The Woman of the Year', *Raritan* 2: 130-49.

Snitow, Ann
1990 'A Gender Diary', in Keller and Keller 1990: 9-43.

Stählin, Gustav
1974 'χήρα', in *TDNT*, IX, 440-65.

Stanton, Elizabeth Cady
1988 *The Woman's Bible* (Salem, NH: The Ayer Company; repr. edn from Part II, New York: European Publishing Company, 1898).

Swidler, Leonard
1979 *Biblical Affirmations of Woman* (Philadelphia: Westminster Press).

Tannehill, Robert C.
1990 *The Narrative Unity of Luke–Acts*, II (Minneapolis: Fortress Press).

Thurston, Bonnie Bowman
1989 *The Widows: A Women's Ministry in the Early Church* (Minneapolis: Fortress Press).

Tolbert, Mary Ann
1990 'Protestant Feminists and the Bible: On the Horns of a Dilemma', in A. Bach (ed.), *The Pleasure of Her Text: Feminist Readings of Biblical and Historical Texts* (Philadelphia: Trinity Press International): 5-23.

Washington, Mary Helen
1988 'Introduction' to *A Voice From the South*, by Anna Julia Cooper, in Gates 1988: xxvii-liv.

Weems, Renita J.
1991 'Reading *Her Way* through the Struggle: African American Women and the Bible', in Felder 1991: 57-80.

Willard, Frances E. and Mary Livermore
1967 'Mrs Margaret Elizabeth Sangster', in *A Woman of the Century* (Detroit: Gale Research; repr. of the orig. edn, Buffalo: C.W. Moulton, 1893): 632.

Wimbush, Vincent L.
1993 'Reading Texts through Worlds, Worlds through Texts', *Semeia* 62: 129-39.

# THE GOSPEL OF MARK AS AN ORAL–AURAL EVENT: IMPLICATIONS FOR INTERPRETATION

## Joanna Dewey

Today many Christians experience the Gospel of Mark as a communal and aural event: they hear short portions of the Gospel read aloud at Sunday morning worship. What they know of Mark comes from hearing it in a communal context, but they hear only isolated snippets, not the whole story. In the last two decades, on the other hand, scholars have rediscovered the literary unity of Mark and now locate its meaning not in individual passages but in its narrative whole (e.g. Rhoads and Michie 1982; Tolbert 1989; Fowler 1991; Anderson and Moore 1992). However, scholars tend to read and analyze the text on the basis of individual silent readings of printed texts.

Ancient Christians neither heard isolated snippets, nor read the entire Gospel silently in isolation. In antiquity, people in groups would have heard the Gospel performed in its entirety. This was true for ancient literature in general. 'There is virtually no evidence to contradict the assertion that private, silent reading and writing simply did not exist in the period. Texts were produced to be read aloud in a communal setting' (Cartlidge 1990: 406 n. 37). But a written text was not even necessary. Brian Stock writes: 'What was essential for a textual community, whether large or small, was simply a text, an interpreter and a public. The text *did not have to be written*; aural record, memory, and reperformance sufficed' (1990: 37; italics mine). In many recitations or performances of a non-elite narrative such as the Gospel of Mark, there was probably simply an oral performer who had heard the story read aloud or heard the story performed, who in turn retold the story in interaction with a group of listeners. In this article I wish to address some implications of understanding Mark as an oral performance for a live audience rather than as a written text.[1] First, however, our assumptions,

---

1. In this article I use 'oral' to emphasize the aspect of composition or performance, 'aural' that of reception. At times I use both in order to stress both aspects.

based on our Western experience of widespread literacy and print media, require some preliminary remarks about literacy in antiquity.

## Orality and Literacy in Antiquity

Only a small minority of persons in the ancient world would have been literate. Using cross-cultural data on agrarian and advanced agrarian societies, scholars estimate that between two and four per cent of ancient Mediterranean people were literate (Malina and Rohrbaugh 1992: 3; Rohrbaugh 1993: 115; Bar-Ilan 1992: 56). Literacy would be higher in cities and among males, perhaps as high as fifteen per cent for urban males (Harris 1989: 267). But except for men among the ruling elite,[2] literacy in antiquity was unlikely to mean the ability to read and write fluently. Even among literates not many would be literate enough to read easily a relatively long narrative text such as Mark. Sometimes literacy meant simply the ability to sign one's name. Few if any early Christians belonged to the elite group for whom full literacy was normal. Furthermore, papyrus was very expensive (Harris 1989: 194-95), and a scroll the length of Mark would have been well beyond the resources of most early Christian groups.

Thus, if more than a very few people had any acquaintance with the Gospel, their acquaintance would have to have been from oral performance.[3] Oral performance was a very common phenomenon in the ancient world, as it is in other cultures today where widespread literacy is not the norm (Scobie 1979; Sjoberg 1960: 286-89). A composition the length of our text of Mark would take an hour and a half to two hours to tell, a quite customary duration for oral performances. Furthermore, good storytellers could easily learn the story of Mark from hearing it read or hearing it told (Ong 1967; Ong 1977; Ong 1982; Howe 1993). Oral performance and reception for the transmission of the Gospel of

2.    Percentages as always are elusive. The governing classes rarely exceed two per cent of the population in an agrarian society (Lenski 1974: 219; Duling and Perrin 1994: 56; Rohrbaugh 1993: 117). Since some of the higher status merchants and retainers may have participated in elite culture, a somewhat higher percentage may have been fully literate.

3.    The fact that Mark survived to be included in the canon suggests that it had wide popularity. Otherwise, after it was absorbed into Matthew and Luke, it would have been lost, as Q was lost.

Mark is not at all improbable; it would in fact have been the typical means.[4]

The Gospel of Mark shows evidence of its close connection to the world of oral performance and reception. I have argued elsewhere that Mark was composed for a listening audience using techniques of oral composition (Dewey 1989; Dewey 1991; see also Botha 1991). Recently, Richard Rohrbaugh has argued that Mark's intended audience consisted primarily of nonliterate peasants. Indeed the connection of Mark to the oral world is so great that we need to ask the question: Was it initially composed in writing (either by the author himself or herself or by the author dictating to a scribe), or was it initially composed and transmitted orally and only eventually put into writing?[5] That question, however, is a historical one, going beyond the scope of this article. Here my focus is on implications that oral performance and reception of Mark in a largely oral culture have for our understanding of the Gospel.

Literary analyses of Mark over the last two decades have greatly increased our understanding of the Gospel. Some have studied the narrative of Mark in light of first-century literary conventions of biographies (Robbins 1984) or romances (Tolbert 1989). Others have applied modern literary-critical methods directly to the Markan text: general literary criticism of plot, character and surface structure (Rhoads and Michie 1982; Malbon 1992; Malbon 1993; Dewey 1980), reader response criticism (Fowler 1991, 1992), structuralist criticism (Malbon 1986) and poststructuralist criticism (Moore 1992a; Moore 1992b).[6]

All of us have employed close reading of the printed text in our analyses. We have had access to the Markan text in ways that were impossible for ancient audiences. Modern readers can stop and reflect on the text at any point; ancient hearers could not. We can reread and

4.  On the first-century media world and its significance for understanding early Christian texts, see Kelber 1983; Kelber 1995a; Boomershine 1995; Dewey 1995.

5.  Most scholars assume the Gospel was initially composed in writing. Kelber (1983) saw its composition as a radical disruption of early Christian orality. Since Johann Gottfried Herder in the eighteenth century, Thorleif Boman, Albert B. Lord, Thomas E. Boomershine and P.J.J. Botha have argued for Mark as an oral composition (for references see Kelber 1983: 77-78; Botha 1991). I suspect there is a more complex interaction of oral and written composition involved in the creation of Mark. For a good discussion on issues the oral–aural culture poses for our understandings of synoptic development, see Kelber 1983: 1-43; Kelber 1995b; for the formation of Mark, see Keck 1978.

6.  The references cited are examples. Many additional works could be cited.

check back; they could not. We read the text silently and alone; they heard it spoken in community. Even ancient performers, if they had had contact with a written text at all, were more likely to have learned it from hearing it read aloud than from reading it themselves. We need now to ask: What difference or differences do our different modes of reception make? How would ancient composers have gone about composing differently from modern writers? How would ancient audiences have heard differently? What conventions of composition and of reception would such a highly oral–aural culture as that of first-century Christians have had? Of course not all cultures with the same communications media are going to have the same conventions;[7] nonetheless, oral performance and reception is likely to require some understandings substantially different from our modern reading assumptions, differences that affect interpretation and perceived meaning.

New Testament scholars are just beginning to explore the issues of how the oral/aural/textual media of antiquity influenced composition and reception of particular ancient texts.[8] Even anthropology and folklore studies, the loci for studies of oral literature, have not yet done much research on oral reception.[9] Thus, the following discussion is of necessity exploratory, in some instances suggesting areas for further research. Furthermore, in order to clarify some of the implications of orality, the following may overstate the disjunction between aural reception and silent print reading reception. But this discussion is a first step, and one that needs to be taken.

## *Characteristics of Oral Narratives*

Oral narratives, including written narratives performed orally for nonliterate audiences, tend to differ in characteristic ways from print narratives written for silent individual reading. Walter Ong summarizes these characteristics as follows: content is combined in additive rather

7.   Boomershine (1995) argues that post-70 CE Christianity and Judaism developed very different communications systems within the broader mix of ancient orality and textuality.

8.   Kelber's *The Oral and the Written Gospel* (1983) remains the basic work for New Testament scholarship. However, although he correctly grasped the differences in the two media, he at that time greatly overestimated their separation—and the written textuality of Mark—in the ancient media world.

9.   A collection of articles published in 1993 on the ethnography of *reading* provides a good beginning (Boyarin 1993).

than subordinating relationships; the structure is aggregative rather than analytic or linear; the content is also repetitious or 'copious', close to the human world, agonistically toned, and empathetic and participatory rather than objectively distanced (Ong 1982: 37-49). Recognition of some of these characteristics, particularly the additive and aggregative structures and the participatory character, helps us to interpret various aspects of Mark that have puzzled and divided scholars and literary critics of the Gospel.

*Additive and Aggregative Composition*
First, additive and aggregative composition results in non-linear plotting or, from our print perspective, lack of a climactic linear plot (Ong 1982: 141-44). Havelock describes the oral method of composition as the echo principle:

> What is to be said and remembered later is cast in the form of an echo of something said already; the future is encoded in the present. All oral narrative is in structure continually both prophetic and retrospective... Though the narrative syntax is paratactic—the basic conjunction being 'and then', 'and next'—the narrative is not linear but turns back on itself in order to assist the memory to reach the end by having it anticipated somehow in the beginning (1984: 183).[10]

Awareness of these structural characteristics helps us to make sense of Mark, which, on the one hand, consists of independent, often repetitive, episodes loosely connected without the linear climactic plot development we are accustomed to from modern novels and short stories, and, on the other, exhibits elaborate interweaving and development of themes (see Dewey 1989; Dewey 1991; Malbon 1993). Judged for effectiveness in oral communication, Mark may be seen as a sophisticated and adept composer, not as a somewhat inept compiler who, in the words of Bultmann, was 'not sufficiently master of his material' (1963: 350).

Understanding the additive and aggregative manner of composition also helps to make sense of the apparent tension between miracles and persecution in Mark. Today most scholars seem to read Mark with eyes trained on the internal consistency and linear plot development characteristic of print narrative. Since healings are numerous in the first half of the narrative, become rare after 8.26 and end entirely at 10.52, while suffering is increasingly foregrounded in the narrative after 8.27, they

10. Scholars using electronic media also create echoes. Some sentences of this article strongly echo Dewey 1989: 42-43 and 1992: 54-56.

read Mark as rejecting healing, miracle-based power, in favor of suffering (e.g. Kelber 1983; Tolbert 1989; Fowler 1991).[11] But in additive and aggregative narratives new information does not negate earlier information; it is added to it. Persecution at the hands of the powers of the world is added to the miracles of healing, sea crossings and feedings of thousands. The oral–aural logic is *both–and*, both miracles (which are to be prayed for in confidence, 11.22-25) and persecution (which is to be expected, 13.9-11). According to the narrative, *both* miracles *and* persecution are the lot of both Jesus and the disciples.

*Agonistic Tone*
A second characteristic of oral–aural narrative that helps us to interpret Mark is its agonistic tone. Ong writes:

> Many, if not all, oral or residually oral cultures strike literates as extra-ordinarily agonistic in their verbal performance... Bragging about one's own prowess and/or verbal tongue-lashings of an opponent figure regularly in encounters between characters in narrative (1982: 43-44).

What we perceive as negative treatment of the disciples in Mark may be considered agonistic. The disciples have trouble understanding Jesus and his teaching; they finally fail, deserting, denying and betraying him. The women disciples, introduced into the narrative once the male disciples have fled, remain faithful through the crucifixion and burial, but in their turn they fail at the empty tomb. Furthermore, the Markan Jesus at times treats the disciples rather agonistically, for example: 'Then are you also without understanding?' (7.18); 'Why do you discuss the fact that you have no bread? Do you not yet perceive or understand? Are your hearts hardened? Having eyes do you not see, and having ears do you not hear? And do you not remember?... Do you not yet understand?' (8.17-18, 21); 'Get behind me, Satan!' (8.33). Bragging is also found: Peter literally brags, 'Even though they all fall away, I will not...If I must die with you, I will not deny you' (14.29, 31)—which, of course, he fails to fulfil.

Modern scholars in general tend to take the negative portrait and the agonistic dialogue very seriously. Often they interpret the Markan disciples referentially: Mark aims to discredit the original disciples, their successors or some group in his own community (e.g. Weeden 1971; Kelber 1983). Even if they do not make historical inferences, literary

---

11. This is, of course, an oversimplification of their arguments. A few do not see suffering superseding miracles (Kolenkow 1973; Donahue 1982; Dowd 1988).

critics often see the conflict as fundamental enough to exclude the possibility of restoration of the disciples after they have deserted Jesus in Mark's narrative world (Tolbert 1989; Fowler 1991). Yet it is doubtful that ancient listening audiences would have interpreted the Markan disciples so negatively. Finding an adversarial atmosphere normal, they would not take the conflict as seriously, and they probably would not give the disciples' portrait much referential weight.[12] Furthermore, ancient hearers were accustomed to instruction by means of bad examples, 'warning examples of how not to behave' (Havelock 1963: 48).

> It should be noted that the examples which tend to predominate are in fact those in which the instruction fails to be carried out: the action that super-venes becomes 'heroic' or 'tragic' (or in the Hebrew case 'sinful') but no less effective as a warning as it preserves and conserves the underlying 'lesson' (Havelock 1986: 77).

The negative portrayal of the disciples may well have seemed to audiences merely part of a normal story.[13]

*Participatory Character*
Thirdly, the implications of the participatory character of oral–aural performance and reception are particularly important for our under-standing of Mark. Participation is at the heart of oral performance. Participation is not just on the part of an audience who responds to a fixed text but also on the part of the performer who constantly adapts his or her performance/text to the audience (Ong 1977: 69). Walter Ong writes that 'public verbal performance in an oral culture is participatory and essentially integrative. Speaker and audience and subject matter are raveled together in a kind of whole' (1977: 282). Thus, for the performer and the audience alike, the emphasis is on the *experience* of the performance event, not on new information learned from the performance. Oral culture 'tend[s] to be performance-oriented rather than information-oriented' (Ong 1982: 171).[14] Communication is often

12. Of course, how they would in fact interpret the Markan disciples would also depend on what traditions they knew about the actual disciples, information to which we have no access.
13. Given the agonistic character of ancient rhetoric as well, we probably also take too seriously the evidences of conflict in Paul's letters.
14. Ong finds this true even within more oral subgroups in highly literate cultures (1982: 171).

'an invitation to participation, not simply a transfer of knowledge from a place where it was to a place where it was not' (Ong 1977: 118). Thus, biblical scholars' reading of the Gospel for the information it gives us about the historical Jesus or the Markan community reads against the Gospel's genre of inviting participation in its story.

Here modern literary critics, analyzing Mark as a silent printed text, are closer to the genre function of the Gospel than historical critics are, for they analyze the Gospel as they would narrative fiction. John Barth writes, 'you hear it said that the novelist offers you an attitude toward life and the world. Not so, except incidentally or by inference. What he offers you is not a *Weltanschauung* but a *Welt*; not a view of the cosmos, but a cosmos itself' (1984: 17). Modern fiction, like oral narrative, creates a world that invites the reader in. What is true of print narrative today was even more true of oral narrative performance where the audience participated in the creation of the cosmos. David Barr writes about those who heard the book of Revelation in worship:

> [They] live in a new reality in which lambs conquer and suffering rules. The victims have become the victors. They no longer suffer helplessly at the hands of Rome; they are now in charge of their own destiny and by their voluntary suffering they participate in the overthrow of evil and the establishment of God's kingdom (1984: 50).

Similarly, hearing the Gospel of Mark performed is the experience of becoming part of a world in which both miracles and persecution are real. The hearers enter a world in which the courage to move forward in following the Markan Jesus—in spite of and through human failure as experienced through the disciples—becomes a possibility, even a reality. The oral–aural story does not primarily convey historical information; it gives meaning and power to a way of life, to a cosmos become real in performance.[15]

In the oral performance event, participation becomes 'empathetic identification' (Ong 1977: 18). According to Havelock, identification is necessary among nonliterates to enable both the performer and the audience to remember: 'You threw yourself into the situation of Achilles, you identified with his grief or his anger. You yourself became Achilles and so did the reciter to whom you listened' (1963: 45).

15. Of course, we may wish to read Mark for what we can learn about history. That is a legitimate enterprise, but not one that is likely to lead us to a better understanding of the Gospel itself.

> [The minstrel] recited effectively only as he re-enacted the doings and sayings of heroes and made them his own, a process...[of] making himself 'resemble' them in endless succession... His audience in turn would remember only as...they became his servants and submitted to his spell... Psychologically it is an act of personal commitment, of total engagement and of emotional identification (Havelock 1963: 160).

> [T]he whole experience becomes a kind of dream in which image succeeds image automatically without conscious control on our part, without a pause to reflect, to rearrange or generalize, and without a chance to ask a question or raise a doubt (Havelock 1963: 190).[16]

Similarly, the audience at a performance of Mark's Gospel, insofar as the narrative came alive for them, would identify sequentially with the various characters and events of the narrative. In the process of successively identifying with the different characters as they are portrayed in performance, the audience would identify alternately with the reality of miracle-based power and with the reality of suffering/persecution. And they would identify alternately with Jesus and with the disciples. The audience's processes of identification, then, would reinforce the effect of the *both–and* of healing and persecution, and the acceptance of both Jesus and the disciples, which the additive and aggregative nature of oral–aural narrative has engendered.

The process of identification in oral performance among nonliterates or highly aural cultures is central for the interpretation of oral–aural texts. Consideration of some theories of identification may help us to clarify the aural processes of participation. My aim here is not to provide a theoretical framework adequate to the complexity of types and levels of identification. Rather, it is to see if a theory, used heuristically, can help illuminate the differences between identification for oral and written media.[17] The observations of Ong and Havelock are basically descriptions

16. Havelock is speaking of the *Iliad*, which is in meter, while Mark is not. Nonetheless the process of *mimesis*, which is the term Plato uses for the act of composition, the performing, and the audience response, seems to refer to the quality of continual emotional identification and not to the style of the narrative (Havelock 1963: 22-25, 44-45, 145-64).

17. We can, of course, still experience an oral performance of Mark today. But our experience will be, at least in part, conditioned by our assumptions and perceptions formed by our highly literate training. We remain, if you will, literate hearers. Nonetheless, we can in such a way more closely proximate the ancient experience. The modern experience of performing Mark can also help us to understand oral processes (see Rhoads 1992).

based on ancient and modern *oral* literatures. Susan Sniader Lanser has developed a theory of narrative identification that at first seems promising in dealing with such literatures. In her study of narrative levels in *print* narratives, she argues that the reader identifies with the narrator in regard to values but with the narratee or character addressed in regard to situation. In reading the Gospel, then, the reader would identify with both Jesus and the disciples: with Jesus' values, on the one hand, and with the disciples' behavior, on the other. The theory explains how the reader can identify with both Jesus and the disciples: the reader *as reader* identifies with each in a different way (Dewey 1982). If Havelock is correct, however, about successive identification with each character in turn for oral narrative, Lanser's model does not apply to *hearing* the Gospel of Mark. Her model would require the hearer to distinguish between values and behavior, rather than to identify fully with each character.

More helpful is the work of Hans Robert Jauss on associative identification. In theorizing on the aesthetics of reception, Jauss posits five levels of identification of the audience with the hero. His first level, associative identification, fits the oral performance situation very well:

> By 'associative identification' we mean a type of aesthetic conduct which is realized at its purest by the assumption of a role in the closed imaginary world of a play-action. Play-action, however, does not here refer to a presentation for spectators. What the associative identification of the players does, rather, is suspend the opposition between presentation and contemplation, between actors and spectators (1974: 299).

Jauss locates associative identification in situations of 'Game/Competition (Ceremony)' (p. 298), that is, situations of ritual, celebration and what he calls 'play-action'. He cites in particular medieval religious drama. These are generally occasions of oral performance, which Ong also connects to celebration and play (1967: 30). For Jauss, associative identification is characterized by the suspension of the opposition 'between work and audience, between actors and spectators' (p. 296), and by 'placing oneself in the roles of all other participants' (p. 298).

For Jauss, associative identification can help create or reinforce shared group values:

> And since the player...can be a judge as well as an interested party, participation in the play-action leads beyond the acknowledgement of others' roles, and of the other party, to an acknowledgement and comprehension of the justice that prevails in the game... The constructive role that

the associative identification games play in the formation of social groups thus resides in the fact that the player can develop his own identity to the same extent that he, in the game, adopts the attitudes of others and exercises himself in modes of communication which, as expectations of behavior, can preorient social life (pp. 299-300).

Associative identification functions to preserve memory and 'can be employed by a class or institution of society in order to represent its ideal image of order' (p. 302). Associative identification enables the hearer to experience a new and better cosmos.

Jauss' understanding of 'associative identification' is very similar to Ong's and Havelock's descriptions of what happens when a performer (literate or nonliterate) interacts with a nonliterate audience. The hearer of Mark would identify fully, in terms of values *and* behavior, with both Jesus and the disciples. The process of sequential or associative identification explains the both–and of miracles and persecution; it enables us to understand how the audience could identify with both Jesus and the disciples rather than choose between them. With our ways of identifying formed in print culture and directly or indirectly influenced by Aristotle's thought, today we may read Mark according to Jauss' fourth level of identification, Aristotle's cathartic identification with the suffering hero: 'the spectator is...placed in the position of the suffering or hard-pressed hero in order to undergo, by way of tragic emotional upheaval or comic release, an inner liberation' (p. 310). Indeed, cathartic identification with the sufferings of Jesus may be a natural way to *read* Mark as a modern print narrative, and such a way of reading may undergird interpretations of Mark as exalting suffering over healing. But *hearing* the Gospel fosters associative identification, which helps to integrate both healing and suffering.

But hearing or experiencing Mark in associative identification presents the biblical scholar with new questions. If the audience truly identifies with all characters in turn, what is the effect of their identification with the Jewish leaders who recur throughout the narrative? How is the process of associative identification affected by the performer's evaluation of characters as sympathetic or hostile—or is it affected by it at all? Furthermore, how is the process of identification affected by the audiences' preconceptions and prior knowledge about characters in the story? How do differences of class, gender, psychology, and so on among individual members of an audience hearing Mark affect each person's reception of the Gospel? How does the shared context of the performance event affect the reception of the audience as a whole?[18] To what extent do the views of the audience in fact control the performer's presentation of characters as sympathetic or negative? Kelber writes,

> If a message is alien to an audience, or a matter of indifference, or socially unacceptable, it will not be continued in the form in which it was spoken. It will either have to be altered, that is, adjusted to prevailing social expectations, or eliminated altogether (1983: 28-29).

That is, how does the audience's influence over the performer affect the narrative standards and evaluations presented by the performer?

Answers to these and similar questions are beyond the scope of this article. The questions indicate areas that will benefit from new, cross-disciplinary research. The need to ask these questions suggests that a greater understanding of reception of oral performance, of the processes of participation and identification, may lead scholars to quite different 'readings' of the Gospel of Mark. Our full recognition of the orality-aurality of Mark may transform our interpretations of it.

The participatory character of oral performance also helps us to understand the apparently unfinished ending of Mark. The Gospel ends abruptly at Mk 16.8, with the women fleeing the tomb, saying nothing to anyone. From what we can infer from the scanty manuscript evidence, the written Gospel soon acquired longer endings that bring closure to the story. I suggest that in the situation of oral performance, with its sequential or associative identification of the audience with the events of the story, the unresolved ending at 16.8 functioned as a summons to the audience to follow Jesus in the way of discipleship, enjoying healings and risking persecution, failing and succeeding 'on the way'.[19] The ending would call the audience to *continue* the story, expecting both successes and failures.[20] The lack of closure helps to involve the hearer in the continuation of the story. As the process of associative identification blurs the boundaries of identification, so it also blurs the boundaries of actor–spectator, and, with an open ending such as Mk 16.8, it blurs the boundaries between story and everyday reality.

18.  Oral performance in highly oral–aural cultures tends to take place in a high context society, in which much is shared and assumed by the audience and the performer—in contrast to our low context literate culture, where much more information needs to be embedded in the written text (Malina and Rohrbaugh 1992: 9-13).

19.  For the Gospel ending 'on the way' see Malbon 1986.

20.  The ending functions orally much as a parable functions: see Dewey 1989: 43 and the literature cited there.

As the women disciples replace the male disciples when they are portrayed fleeing at Jesus' arrest, so the audience replaces the women disciples, and the story goes on.

Literary critics have suggested that this open ending is a challenge to readers to do better than the characters in the narrative (e.g. Petersen 1980; Tolbert 1989). I suggest that, as the narrative functioned orally, the audience would *not* compare themselves to the internal characters. A comparison requires distance between the characters and the audience, a clear distinction between actor and spectator; without distance, analysis or comparative evaluation is not possible. Associative identification stresses participation, indeed merging with the internal characters, thus leading to a continuation of the story into everyday life.

## *Instability of the Text: A Final Implication*

In the foregoing, I have tried to suggest ways that investigating Mark as oral performance–aural reception in a highly oral and aural culture may affect our interpretation of the Gospel. Recognition of the Gospel's oral and aural context alters our understanding of the relationship of miracles and persecution, our interpretation of the negative portrayal of the disciples, of the identification of the audience with the story, and, finally, of the ending of the narrative.

Lastly, I would like to suggest one more important implication of the oral setting of the Gospel, the one perhaps most disconcerting to biblical scholars. When we recognize how oral and aural the media world of early Christianity was, we also have to recognize the destabilization of the text itself. In oral–aural cultures, before there is any written text, or when a written text is recycled back into oral circulation, *there is no fixed text* that is used in oral performance. According to Ong, oral memory 'is never verbatim...the general story varies little from one telling to another. But the words always do' (1967: 24). Furthermore, performances vary radically in length, in what is included and what is excluded. Ong writes:

> A real audience controls the narrator's behavior immediately. Students of mine from Ghana and from western Ireland have reported to me what I have read and heard from many other sources: a given story may take a skilled or 'professional' storyteller anywhere from ten minutes to an hour and a half, depending on how he finds the audience relates to him on a given occasion... The teller reacts directly to audience response. Oral storytelling is a two-way street (1977: 69).

A recognition of the oral–aural milieu of early Christianity informs us that actual performances of the Gospel of Mark almost certainly differed significantly, one from another. The Gospels of Mark that first- and second-century Christians heard probably varied a good deal from each other *and* from the text we use today.

The question of the relationship of our written Markan text to oral performances of its story is a complicated and debated historical issue that cannot be argued in full here.[21] In brief, given the nature of oral memory and tradition (Keck 1978; Vansina 1985), it is likely that the original written text of Mark was dependent on a pre-existing connected oral narrative, a narrative that already was being performed in various versions by various people. If this is true, then we have in writing just one textual rendition of a living tradition,[22] one that at the time may have had little if any impact on the ongoing oral narrative tradition. In such oral contexts, the very concept of an original or authentic version makes little sense. Kelber writes of the Jesus tradition,

> The concepts of *original form* and variants have no validity in oral life, nor does the one of *ipsissima vox*, if by that one means the authentic version over against secondary ones. 'In a sense each performance is "an" original, if not "the" original' [quoting Lord 1960: 101]. Moreover, if each utterance constitutes an authentic speech act, then the question of transmission can never be kept wholly separate from composition (1983: 30; see also Kelber 1995b).

This observation would be equally true of the tradition of the Gospel of Mark. Each performance of Mark would be an original performance, and there would be no meaning in saying that one performance is truly Mark while another is not.

If, on the contrary, Mark was first composed in writing out of disparate pieces of tradition (Kelber 1983: 90-139), then one can argue that there was an 'original Mark', an original *written* creation. We would not know, however, how closely our text, be it UBS$^3$ or UBS$^4$,

---

21.  See n. 5 for references. I agree with Kelber (1983) that there is no natural evolution from orality to textuality; I would argue, however, that there was a complex and varied interaction between orality and textuality in the first centuries of the common era. Thus, *pace* Kelber, I do not view Mark as a disruption of an oral synthesis, creating a new textuality 'out of the debris of deconstructed orality' (1983: 95).

22.  If one takes account of Secret Mark, we have perhaps evidence for two textual versions; and if there were two texts, then perhaps there were more before the canon became fixed.

resembles 'original Mark', since our manuscript evidence is much later than 70 CE. Does our text actually represent Mark's 'original version', or does it reflect later oral tellings? Eusebius wrote, 'They say that this Mark was the first to be sent to preach in Egypt the Gospel which he had also put into writing' (*EH* 2.16, LCL edn vol. 1, p. 145). Regardless of his accuracy about how Christianity got to Egypt and Mark's role in bringing it there, Eusebius does attest to the continued importance of the storyteller even when a written text is available. And the storyteller who performs orally will alter his or her story from performance to performance; different storytellers will present different performances.[23] Furthermore, textual transmission is likely to have been heavily influenced both by oral performance traditions and by the preferences of the literate people who were using manuscripts.

All we can say with certainty is that our text likely represents only one version among many, one version that may or may not be characteristic of the Markan performance tradition. We do not know if, in our modern sense, there was an 'original Mark', and, if there was, precisely what 'original Mark' looked like. Nonetheless, our written text is the only text we have. Whether we are doing literary analyses of the text as an object to be read, or trying to reconstruct its meanings in the context of oral performance–reception, it is the text that of necessity we must use. Let us use it; but let us remember how differences between literate and oral–aural worlds affect how we understand Mark. Let us remember that it represents one version among many. Let us remember we do not know how typical it is, and that we do not know which audience it reflects at what time. With all its uncertainties—especially with all its uncertainties—the Gospel of Mark remains a fascinating narrative.

## BIBLIOGRAPHY

Anderson, Janice Capel and Stephen D. Moore (eds.)
1992    *Mark and Method: New Approaches in Biblical Studies* (Minneapolis: Fortress Press).
Bar-Ilan, Meir
1992    'Illiteracy in the Land of Israel in the First Centuries CE', in S. Fishbane and S. Schoenfeld, with A. Goldshläger (eds.), *Essays in the Social Scientific Study of Judaism and Jewish Society* (vol. 2; Hoboken, NJ: KTAV): 46-61.

23. As scholars using computers, we may be regaining some appreciation of the fluidity of texts.

Barr, David
  1984        'The Apocalypse as a Symbolic Transformation of the World: A
              Literary Analysis', *Int* 38: 39-50.
Barth, John
  1984        'How to Make a Universe', in *The Friday Book: Essays and Other
              Nonfiction* (New York: Putnam's Sons): 13-25.
Boomershine, Thomas E.
  1995        'Jesus of Nazareth and the Watershed of Ancient Orality and
              Literacy', in Dewey (ed.) 1995, forthcoming.
Botha, P.J.J.
  1991        'Mark's Story as Oral Traditional Literature: Rethinking the
              Transmission of Some Traditions about Jesus', *Hervormde Teologiese
              Studies* 47: 304-31.
Boyarin, Jonathan (ed.)
  1993        *The Ethnography of Reading* (Berkeley: University of California
              Press).
Bultmann, Rudolf
  1963        *The History of the Synoptic Tradition* (trans. John Marsh; New York:
              Harper & Row).
Cartlidge, David R.
  1990        'Combien d'unités avez-vous de trois à quatre?: What Do We Mean by
              Intertextuality in Early Church Studies?', in David J. Lull (ed.), *SBLSP*
              (Atlanta: Scholars Press).
Dewey, Joanna
  1980        *Markan Public Debate: Literary Technique, Concentric Structure, and
              Theology in Mark 2.1–3.6* (SBLDS, 48; Chico, CA: Scholars Press).
  1982        'Point of View and the Disciples in Mark', in K.H. Richards (ed.),
              *SBLSP* (Chico, CA: Scholars Press): 87-106.
  1989        'Oral Methods of Structuring Narrative in Mark', *Int* 53: 32-44.
  1991        'Mark as Interwoven Tapestry: Forecasts and Echoes for a Listening
              Audience', *CBQ* 53: 221-36.
  1992        'Mark as Aural Narrative: Structures as Clues to Understanding',
              *Sewanee Theological Review* 36: 45-56.
Dewey, Joanna (ed.)
  1995        *Orality and Textuality in Early Christianity* (*Semeia*; Atlanta: Scholars
              Press), forthcoming.
Donahue, John R.
  1982        'A Neglected Factor in the Theology of Mark', *JBL* 101: 563-94.
Dowd, Sharyn Echols
  1988        *Prayer, Power, and the Problem of Suffering: Mark 11.22-25 in the
              Context of Markan Theology* (SBLDS, 105; Atlanta: Scholars Press).
Duling, Dennis C. and Norman Perrin
  1994        *The New Testament: Proclamation and Parenesis, Myth and History*
              (Fort Worth: Harcourt Brace).
Eusebius
  1965        *The Ecclesiastical History* (LCL; 2 vols.; trans. Kirsopp Lake;
              Cambridge: Harvard University Press).

Fowler, Robert M.
    1991      *Let the Reader Understand: Reader Response Criticism and the Gospel of Mark* (Minneapolis: Fortress Press).
    1992      'Reader-Response Criticism: Figuring Mark's Reader', in Anderson and Moore 1992: 50-83.

Harris, William V.
    1989      *Ancient Literacy* (Cambridge, MA: Harvard University Press).

Havelock, Eric A.
    1963      *Preface to Plato* (Cambridge, MA: Belknap Press of Harvard University Press).
    1984      'Oral Composition in the *Oedipus Tyrannus* of Sophocles', *New Literary History* 16: 175-97.
    1986      *The Muse Learns to Write: Reflections on Orality and Literacy from Antiquity to the Present* (New Haven: Yale University Press).

Howe, Nicholas
    1993      'The Cultural Construction of Reading in Anglo-Saxon England', in Boyarin 1992: 58-79.

Jauss, Hans Robert
    1974      'Levels of Identification of Hero and Audience', *New Literary History* 5: 283-317.

Keck, Leander E.
    1978      'Oral Traditional Literature and the Gospels: The Seminar', in William O. Walker, Jr (ed.), *The Relationships among the Gospels: An Interdisciplinary Dialogue* (San Antonio: Trinity University Press): 103-22.

Kelber, Werner H.
    1983      *The Oral and the Written Gospel: The Hermeneutics of Speaking and Writing in the Synoptic Tradition, Mark, Paul, and Q* (Philadelphia: Fortress Press).
    1995a     'Modalities of Communication, Cognition, and Physiology of Perception: Orality, Rhetoric, Scribality', in Dewey 1995, forthcoming.
    1995b     'Jesus and Tradition: Words in Time, Words in Space', in Dewey 1995, forthcoming.

Kolenkow, Anitra Bingham
    1973      'Beyond Miracles, Suffering and Eschatology', in George MacRae (ed.), *SBLSP* (Cambridge, MA: Society of Biblical Literature): II, 155-202.

Lanser, Susan Sniader
    1981      *The Narrative Act: Point of View in Prose Fiction* (Princeton: Princeton University Press).

Lenski, Gerhard and Jean Lenski
    1974      *Human Societies: An Introduction to Macrosociology* (New York: McGraw–Hill Press).

Lord, Albert B.
    1960      *The Singer of Tales* (Cambridge, MA: Harvard University Press).

Malbon, Elizabeth Struthers
    1986      *Narrative Space and Mythic Meaning in Mark* (New Voices in Biblical Studies; San Francisco: Harper & Row; repr. The Biblical Seminar, 13; Sheffield: JSOT Press, 1991).

1992    'Narrative Criticism: How Does the Story Mean?', in Anderson and Moore 1992: 23-49.

1993    'Echoes and Foreshadowing in Mark 4–8: Reading and Rereading', *JBL* 112: 211-30.

Malina, Bruce J. and Richard L. Rohrbaugh

1992    *Social-Science Commentary on the Synoptic Gospels* (Minneapolis: Fortress Press).

Moore, Stephen D.

1992a    'Deconstructive Criticism: The Gospel of the Mark', in Anderson and Moore 1992: 84-102.

1992b    *Mark and Luke in Poststructuralist Perspective: Jesus Begins to Write* (New Haven: Yale University Press).

Ong, Walter J.

1967    *The Presence of the Word: Some Prolegomena for Cultural and Religious History* (Minneapolis: University of Minnesota Press).

1977    *Interfaces of the Word: Studies in the Evolution of Consciousness and Culture* (Ithaca, NY: Cornell University Press).

1982    *Orality and Literacy: The Technologizing of the Word* (London: Methuen).

Petersen, Norman

1980    ' "When Is the End Not the End?": Literary Reflections on the Ending of Mark's Narrative', *Int* 34: 151-66.

Rhoads, David

1992    'Performing the Gospel of Mark', in Björn Krondorfer (ed.), *Body and Bible: Interpreting and Experiencing Biblical Narratives* (Philadelphia: Trinity Press International): 102-19.

Rhoads, David and Donald Michie

1982    *Mark as Story: An Introduction to the Narrative of a Gospel* (Philadelphia: Fortress Press).

Robbins, Vernon K.

1984    *Jesus the Teacher: A Socio-Rhetorical Interpretation of Mark* (Philadelphia: Fortress Press).

Rohrbaugh, Richard L.

1993    'The Social Location of the Marcan Audience', *BTB* 23: 114-27.

Scobie, Alex

1979    'Storytellers, Storytelling, and the Novel in Graeco-Roman Antiquity', *Rheinishces Museum für Philologie* 122: 229-59.

Sjoberg, Gideon

1960    *The Preindustrial City: Past and Present* (New York: The Free Press, Macmillan).

Stock, Brian

1990    *Listening for the Text: On the Uses of the Past* (Baltimore: Johns Hopkins University Press).

Tolbert, Mary Ann

1989    *Sowing the Gospel: Mark's World in Literary-Historical Perspective* (Minneapolis: Fortress Press).

Vansina, Jan
    1985          *Oral Tradition as History* (Madison: University of Wisconsin Press).
Weeden, Theodore J.
    1971          *Mark—Traditions in Conflict* (Philadelphia: Fortress Press).

SOCIO-RHETORICAL CRITICISM:
MARY, ELIZABETH AND THE MAGNIFICAT AS A TEST CASE

Vernon K. Robbins

*The Emergence of Socio-Rhetorical Criticism*

Socio-rhetorical criticism is a textually-based method that uses programmatic strategies to invite social, cultural, historical, psychological, aesthetic, ideological and theological information into a context of minute exegetical activity. In a context where historical criticism has been opening its boundaries to social and cultural data, and literary criticism has been opening its boundaries to ideology, socio-rhetorical criticism practices interdisciplinary exegesis that reinvents the traditional steps of analysis and redraws the traditional boundaries of interpretation. Socio-rhetorical criticism, then, is an exegetically-oriented approach that gathers current practices of interpretation together in an interdisciplinary paradigm.

Both the textual base for the strategies and the interdisciplinary mode of analysis distinguish socio-rhetorical criticism from historical criticism, social-scientific criticism, sociological exegesis, social-historical criticism and the study of social realia and social organization—all of which are historical methods based on data external to texts. Historians and sociologists regularly focus on signs in texts that ostensibly refer to data outside of texts, and they criticize interpreters who appear to have an 'obsession' with the nature of texts themselves rather than the 'data' within texts. Socio-rhetorical critics are interested in the nature of texts as social, cultural, historical, theological and ideological discourse. They approach a text much like an anthropologist 'reads' a village and its culture (Peacock 1986). The interpreter perceives the dwellings and their arrangement; the interaction of the people and their rituals; and the sounds of the speech, the songs, the drums and the barking as signs that invite research, analysis and interpretation (Geertz 1973, 1983). Within this approach, historical, social and cultural data stand in an intertextual relation to the signs in texts. Socio-rhetorical interpretation, then, invites the data of the historical and social-scientific critic into exegesis at the stage where it explores the intertexture of a text.

Socio-rhetorical criticism differs from most types of literary criticism by a practice of 'revaluing' and 'reinventing' rhetoric rather than practicing one or more forms of 'restrained rhetoric' (Vickers 1982). Socio-rhetorical critics, perceiving texts to be 'thickly textured' with simultaneously interacting networks of signification, reinvent rhetoric by reading and rereading, interpreting and reinterpreting texts 'as forms of *activity* inseparable from the wider social relations between writers and readers, orators and audiences' (Eagleton 1983: 206; cf. Wuellner 1987: 453; Robbins 1993b: 443-44). Socio-rhetorical criticism reinvents the stages of interpretation by replacing George A. Kennedy's five stages of analysis—unit, situation, disposition of arrangement, techniques or style and rhetorical criticism as a synchronic whole (Kennedy 1984: 33-38; Wuellner 1987: 455-60)—with programmatic analysis of inner texture, intertexture, social and cultural texture and ideological texture (Robbins 1992a, 1992b, 1992c, 1992d, 1993b). Through this process, socio-rhetorical critics explore the full range of rhetorical figures and tropes in texts. Most modern literary critics, in contrast, reduce rhetoric to four master tropes—metaphor, metonymy, synecdoche and irony—and explore texts in the context of this 'restrained' rhetoric.[1] Socio-rhetorical critics differ from formalist and structuralist literary critics by exploring the rhetorical nature of the discourse both in the text and in traditional and nontraditional interpretations of the text. They differ from literary critics who invest primarily in anti-scientific and deconstructionist efforts by programmatically analyzing and interpreting texts within changing sets of boundaries. Socio-rhetorical criticism, then, is a form of literary analysis that invites programmatic, self-critical analysis and interpretation of the full range of rhetorical figures and tropes in texts. The goal is to nurture disciplined exploration, analysis and interpretation characteristic of *wissenschaftlich* research, but to do so in a manner that maintains a self-critical perspective on the data and strategies the interpreter uses to bring referents, meanings, beliefs, values, emotions and intentions to the signs in the text.

The beginnings of socio-rhetorical criticism lie in the goals for biblical

---

1. For a comprehensive discussion of the reduction of rhetoric in various centuries, see Vickers 1988: 435-79, and for the reduction to four tropes, pp. 439-42. For his definition of rhetorical figures and tropes, see pp. 491-98.

interpretation Amos N. Wilder set forth in his presidential address to the Society of Biblical Literature in 1955, entitled 'Scholars, Theologians, and Ancient Rhetoric' (Wilder 1956). Wilder began by raising 'the basic question of the nature of religious symbol and of symbolic discourse' (p. 1). Referring to New Testament eschatology as 'a tremendous expression of the religious imagination, an extraordinary rhetoric of faith' (p. 2), he quoted Theodor Gaster's statement that 'our task must be to get behind the words to what semanticists call their "referents"; and this is the domain of Cultural Anthropology and Folklore rather than of Philology' (p. 3, quoting Gaster 1950: 112). Asserting that we have much to learn 'from what is now known of the "mythic mentality" or "mythic ideation" as explored by the anthropologists and by students of the origins of language and myth' (p. 5), Wilder turned to an analysis of the strengths and weaknesses of Bultmann's demythologization of myth, Dodd's 'Platonizing tendency', and Cullmann's conforming of disparate expressions in biblical texts to a pattern in a selected body of material (pp. 6-8). In the end, Wilder's focus on biblical texts as literature causes him to limit the source for new insights into myth and symbol to aesthetic criticism, because 'workers in aesthetics... have learned much from anthropology and psychology' (pp. 8-9). As a result, it has taken New Testament interpreters a quarter of a century to begin to integrate analysis of the inner imaginative and argumentative aspects of early Christian texts with analysis of the social aspects of their discourse. Most New Testament interpreters who responded to Wilder's call to use new forms of literary criticism have resisted the insights of social scientists into myth, the social construction of reality and the ideological nature of culture.

In 1972, Wayne A. Meeks moved Wilder's vision of interpretation decisively forward in an article entitled 'The Man from Heaven in Johannine Sectarianism' (Meeks 1972). Meeks analyzed both 'the special patterns of language' in the Gospel of John and the special logic of the myth of the descending and ascending redeemer (p. 44), integrating a close, rhetorical reading of the text with anthropological and sociological insights into the formation and maintenance of sectarian communities. His interpretation demonstrates the profound relationship in Johannine discourse between the redeemer who belongs to the 'world of the Father' yet comes into the 'world which does not know or comprehend' him, and those who are 'in the world' yet are drawn to the redeemer by 'believing' in him. In the end, the reader sees that the redeemer's foreignness to the world is directly related to the sect's perception of itself as foreign to the world—'in it but not of it'. In Meeks's words,

> The Fourth Gospel not only describes, in etiological fashion, the birth of that community; it also provides reinforcement of the community's isolation. The language patterns we have been describing have the effect, for the insider who accepts them, of demolishing the logic of the world, particularly the world of Judaism, and progressively emphasizing the sectarian consciousness. If one 'believes' what is said in this book, he is quite literally taken out of the ordinary world of social reality (Meeks 1972: 71).

This article, in my view, is a superb initial step toward socio-rhetorical criticism, since it attends equally to exegesis and to social and cultural dimensions of early Christian discourse. In the intervening years Meeks has written a number of important articles that advanced this kind of analysis yet further (see bibliography in Meeks 1993: 254-55). His books, however, have featured rather conventional exegetical practices to exhibit social and moral aspects of early Christianity rather than developed new practices to exhibit the social, cultural and ideological dimensions of Christian discourse in its Mediterranean context (Meeks 1983, 1986a, 1993).[2]

The year after the appearance of Meeks's article, Jonathan Z. Smith presented a paper on 'The Social Description of Early Christianity' that called for the incorporation of highly developed anthropological theory in analysis and interpretation of early Christian data (Smith 1975).[3] In his

2. Three explanations for this, I suggest, are ready to hand. First, Meeks began his work when the traditional exegetical tools of historical criticism completely dominated New Testament interpretation. Secondly, the overwhelming majority of Meeks's colleagues were, and still are, historians who emphasize data they perceive to be referred to by texts rather than methods that explore the nature of texts themselves. Thirdly, it has taken much diligent work to develop rhetorical and social analysis to a level advanced enough to guide analysis of texts that do not evoke the same kind of countercultural, sectarian ideology as the discourse in the Fourth Gospel.

3. Despite Smith's four books since that time (1978, 1982, 1987, 1990), New Testament interpreters have been slow to adopt the critical insights of cultural anthropology. There are numerous reasons. First, a full picture of Smith's agenda emerges only through a careful reading of the complete corpus of his work, much of which first appeared in articles that were later gathered into book form. Secondly, Smith has published books with an obviously unified agenda only since 1987. Prior to this, his books contained articles that revealed only part of his agenda at a time. Thirdly, Smith

article, Smith referred to an 'almost total lack of persuasive models' (p. 19), a seduction 'into a description of a *Sitz im Leben* that lacks a concrete (i.e. non-theological) seat and offers only the most abstract understanding of "life"' (p. 19), the writing of social histories of early Christianity 'in a theoretical vacuum in which outdated "laws" are appealed to and applied...which no longer represent a consensus outside the New Testament or church history fields' (p. 19), and 'unquestioned apologetic presuppositions and naive theories' (p. 20). He suggested, however, that there were many resources available to move ahead, including a few 'major syntheses, lacking only the infusion of new theoretical perspectives' (p. 20). Calling for 'careful attention to the inner history of the various religious traditions and cults' (p. 20) and analysis and interpretation that are 'both richly comparative and quite consciously situated within contemporary anthropological and sociological theory' (p. 21), he pointed to Meeks' article on the Johannine Man from heaven as a 'happy combination of exegetical and sociological sophistication' (p. 21). Smith's critical agenda introduces theoretical practices that move socio-rhetorical interpretation beyond aesthetic criticism toward a comprehensive, critical method for constructing a new picture of the social and religious nature of early Christianity.

In the midst of these beginnings, Helmut Koester and James M. Robinson proposed a dynamic, pluralistic model for investigating early Christian groups, communities and cultures that interacted with one another in a context that, after two to three centuries, produced a Christianity with its own sacred scriptures, theological systems, ecclesiastical offices and institutional structures (Robinson and Koester 1971). Hans Dieter Betz contributed to this endeavor by bringing widespread

---

works at the 'critical' end of interpretative discourse, the high end that calls for a deeply informed self-consciousness about one's own work. Most New Testament interpreters who devote time to theory have preferred to generate formal theories about deep linguistic structures and self-referential features of narrative than to generate self-critical theories about interpretative practices. Fourthly, Smith's work challenges the innermost nature of the discipline itself, including the 'myth of origins' in which biblical interpreters embed their interpretative practices. Since one of the characteristics of scientific (*wissenschaftlich*) analysis is to hide its ideological foundations, it is natural that New Testament interpreters have been reluctant to evaluate their deepest commitments programmatically and submit them to public scrutiny. Socio-rhetorical criticism calls for interpretative practices that include minute attention to the ideologies that guide interpreters' selection, analysis and interpretation of data.

rhetorical practices of Mediterranean speakers and writers into interpretation of New Testament texts (1972, 1975, 1979, 1985a, 1985b,
1986), and Wilhelm H. Wuellner began to apply insights from 'the new
rhetoric' to argumentation in New Testament literature (1976a, 1976b,
1978, 1979, 1986). Meanwhile, Robert C. Tannehill produced an
aesthetic, rhetorical analysis and interpretation of sayings of Jesus with
unusual sensitivity to the forcefulness of their vivid images and tensive
patterns (1975).

The same year as the appearance of Smith's initial paper (1975),
Betz's first rhetorical analysis of Paul's letter to the Galatians (1975) and
Tannehill's aesthetic, rhetorical analysis of sayings of Jesus (1975),
John G. Gager's *Kingdom and Community: The Social World of Early
Christianity* introduced models from twentieth-century sociology and
anthropology for the study of early Christianity (1975). Gager's analysis
was part of the same intellectual world as Smith's; but this was a world
distant from the work of Betz, Wuellner and Tannehill. Many interpreters knew that these intellectual worlds should come together, but
they also knew that the road would be steep and rocky. Gager broached
the issue with a well-placed quotation from Peter Brown: 'The need to
link disciplines is frequently expressed among us. Discussion of this need
takes place in an atmosphere, however, that suggests the observation of
an African chieftain on a neighboring tribe: "They are our enemies. We
marry them"' (P. Brown 1970: 17; quoted in Gager 1975: xii; cf. Gager
1982).

Gager himself used social anthropological studies of millennialist cargo
cults in Melanesia, social psychological studies of cognitive dissonance
and a merger of cultural anthropological and 'history of religion' interpretations of myth to approach 'the end of time and the rise of community' in first-century Christianity (Gager 1975: 19-65). Then he
discussed the transition from charismatic authority to canon and orthodoxy (pp. 66-92), the social class or status of early Christians (pp. 93-
113), and the challenge of the success of Christianity for interpreters of
early Christianity (pp. 114-58). Rich with sociological and anthropological insight as well as information about the first four centuries of early
Christianity, this book established a new paradigm of investigation and
interpretation. While a number of its agendas have been pursued in one
way or another, the task of incorporating the insights of this paradigm
programmatically into exegesis of New Testament texts still lies in the
future. Socio-rhetorical criticism sets forth a programmatic set of

strategies to pursue, test, enrich and revise the provisional conclusions Gager advances in his book.

At the beginning of the 1980s, then, various approaches and analyses had advanced a program of investigation and interpretation of the social, cultural, religious and theological dimensions of early Christian discourse. It would take another decade, however, for these activities to come together in a programmatic, critical method. As the 1980s began, John H. Elliott developed 'sociological exegesis' (1981), and Bruce J. Malina introduced widespread topics of Mediterranean social and cultural life into New Testament studies under the name of cultural anthropology (1981). A few years later, a *Semeia* volume appeared on *Social Scientific Criticism* (Elliott 1986), and soon after, Philip Esler's study of the social and political motivations of Lukan theology became available (1987). Recently, an edited volume on *The Social World of Luke–Acts* (Neyrey 1991a) and a volume on *Social Scientific Criticism and the New Testament* (Elliott 1993) have displayed the results of more than a decade of work by Malina, Neyrey, Elliott, Rohrbaugh and others on honor–shame, dyadic personality, limited good, kinship, purity and other widespread features of Mediterranean society and culture. Meanwhile, Norman R. Petersen has produced studies of Paul and the Gospel of John that merge formalist literary criticism and sociology (1985, 1993). Both the formalist approach to the text and the use of sociology without the rich resources of social and cultural anthropology limit the studies to a conventional view of the historical and social nature of early Christianity.

In 1984 and 1987, I used the term 'socio-rhetorical' in the title of a book and in an article that merged rhetorical analysis with insights from anthropologists, sociologists and social psychologists to interpret early Christian texts. Works by Kenneth Burke provided an initial rhetorical framework (Robbins 1984: 5-14, 20-48; Robbins 1987: 502, 505, 508-509) and first-century BCE and CE rhetorical treatises provided insights from the Mediterranean social environment of early Christianity (Robbins 1984: 29, 64; Robbins 1987: 503, 506-509, 512). Writings by Clifford Geertz, in turn, provided an initial anthropological framework for comparative analysis and interpretation (Robbins 1984: 5-6), and folklore studies and social psychological role theory guided the interpretation of the relation of the teacher to his disciples (Robbins 1984: 7-8, 39, 83, 110, 112-14, 158, 162, 165). Then, in 1987, Wilhelm H. Wuellner introduced the terms 'reinvented' or 'revalued' rhetoric for rhetorical analysis that interprets biblical texts as 'social discourse' and biblical hermeneutics as 'political discourse' (Wuellner 1987: 453, 456, 462-63). Elisabeth Schüssler Fiorenza's presidential address to the Society of Biblical Literature at the end of that same year (1988) and her article on 'The Rhetorical Situation in I Corinthians' (1987) placed the issue of ideology in the text and in the interpreter's strategies directly before biblical scholars. Burton L. Mack's *Myth of Innocence* (1988), *Rhetoric and the New Testament* (1990) and *The Lost Gospel* (1993) have advanced rhetorical, textual practices informed by insights about myth and ritual from cultural anthropology and about social discourse and ideology from modern and postmodern criticism.

I presented the framework for developing socio-rhetorical criticism as a programmatic, comprehensive method within biblical studies in the introduction to the 1992 paperback edition of *Jesus the Teacher* (Robbins 1992a) and in an article for the Society of Biblical Literature later that year (1992b). These essays introduced a 'four-texture' approach to socio-rhetorical criticism: (a) inner texture, (b) intertexture, (c) social and cultural texture and (d) ideological texture. A four-texture approach was also utilized in Clarice J. Martin's interpretation of the Ethiopian eunuch in Acts 8 (1989) and in Bernard Brandon Scott's comprehensive interpretation of the parables of Jesus (1989). Other socio-rhetorical studies have appeared during the last few years, usually with some reference to the socio-rhetorical nature of their investigation and interpretation.[4] The remaining part of this essay exhibits practices associated with socio-rhetorical criticism utilizing the four-texture approach. The goal is both to explain strategies and to illustrate them in actual exegesis. The text under consideration is the account of Mary's encounter with the angel Gabriel and Elizabeth in the Gospel of Luke.

### *Inner Texture: Every Reading has a Subtext*

The overall goal of 'inner' textual analysis and interpretation in a socio-rhetorical mode is to attain initial insight into the argumentation in the text (Perelman and Olbrechts-Tyteca 1969; Perelman 1982). Any strategies of analysis and interpretation, from the most simple repetition of signs to the most subtle argumentative strategies, may contribute to

4. See the works of Altenbaumer (1992), Braun (1993), Huie-Jolly (1994), Kloppenborg (1989, 1990, 1991, 1993), Robbins (1991a, 1992b, 1992c, 1992d, 1992e, 1993b), Sisson (1994), Wachob (1993), Webber (1992), York (1991).

readings of the inner texture of a text. Every reading of the 'inner' text, even a reading that an interpreter calls 'intrinsic' to the text itself, is guided by 'extrinsic' interests, perspectives and meanings. These extrinsic dimensions may derive from disciplinary codes or 'subtexts' for the reading. A disciplinary code is a master discourse like history, anthropology or theology, which is guided, sanctioned and nurtured by authorized institutional structures, groups and organizations (Bal 1988a: 2-13). A subtext, in contrast, is a theory, approach or other text that somehow helps to illumine an aspect of the text a person is interpreting (Bal 1988b: 42, 51-65). Socio-rhetorical criticism calls for critical consciousness about the codes and subtexts an interpreter brings to 'intrinsic' readings. It also investigates the boundaries interpreters set that limit subtexts to 'Jewish' modes of thinking rather than opening them to 'Hellenistic-Roman' modes of thinking; theological modes rather than social, cultural, psychological and religious modes; formal literary modes rather than argumentative, interactive, rhetorical modes; and modes of the mind alone rather than modes that include both body and mind.

One important subtext is the basic rhetorical nature of language as explained by Kenneth Burke: language has repetitive, progressive, conventional and minor rhetorical form (Burke 1931: 123-83). The basic question related to this subtext is: On the basis of sign repetition and patterns of progression, where are the beginning, middle and end of a significant span of text? A strategy in answering this question is the giving of 'basic lexical sense' to signs signifying 'narrative agents' in Lk. 1.26-56.

In terms of sign repetition and progression, the priest Zechariah and his wife Elizabeth, who live in the region of Judea, are the first characters to appear in the Gospel of Luke (1.5), and they are the center of attention through Lk. 1.25. In a sentence that constitutes Lk. 1.26-27, the name Mary occurs for the first time in the text, and twice in this verse the text refers to this woman as a *parthenos*, which is regularly translated 'virgin' in English. The occurrence of these signs signals the potential beginning of a span of text with special focus on 'a *parthenos* named Mary'.

It is noticeable that the name Zechariah, which appears six times (1.5, 12, 13, 18, 21) prior to the occurrence of the name Mary (1.27), reappears only once in the phrase 'house of Zechariah' (1.40) until it recurs twice in Lk. 1.59, 67. This means that a significant span of text occurs in which two women interact with one another in the absence of the husband Zechariah or any other man. A programmatic display of the names of narrative agents reveals repetition of four words or phrases that refer to deity and two that refer to two women named Mary and Elizabeth.

*Narrative Agents in Luke 1.26-56*

| | | | | | |
|---|---|---|---|---|---|
| 26 | God | angel | | | |
| 27 | | | | Mary | |
| 28 | | the Lord | | | |
| 30 | God | angel | | Mary | |
| 32 | God | the Lord | | | |
| 34 | | angel | | Mary | |
| 35 | God | angel | Holy Spirit | | |
| 36 | | | | | Elizabeth |
| 37 | God | | | | |
| 38 | | angel | the Lord | Mary | |
| 39 | | | | Mary | |
| 40 | | | | | Elizabeth |
| 41 | | | Holy Spirit | Mary | Elizabeth |
| | | | | | Elizabeth |
| 43 | | my Lord | | | |
| 45 | | the Lord | | | |
| 47 | God | the Lord | | | |
| 56 | | | | Mary | |

As this display shows, there is reference to God and the angel Gabriel in Lk. 1.26 before there is reference to Mary in Lk. 1.27. This signifies that something with reference to God and the angel Gabriel establishes the context of utterance (Fowler 1986: 86-88, 93-96) for the circumstances in which Mary functions. In addition to God and an angel, the discourse refers to 'the Lord' and 'the Holy Spirit'. While references to God, the Lord and Mary span the entire unit (1.26-56), a basic 'beginning' pairs Mary with the angel Gabriel through 1.38. A basic 'middle' for this span of text appears in the double occurrence of the phrase 'the Holy Spirit' (1.35, 41) and four occurrences of the name Elizabeth (1.36-41); and a basic 'end' appears with references to Mary, my/the Lord, and God in the absence of reference to the angel, Elizabeth and the Holy Spirit (1.42-56). Basic repetition of names of narrative agents, therefore, exhibits a span of text with a basic beginning, middle and end.

In the first step of analysis 'voice' has not been given to the sign patterns in the text. In order to locate the narratorial boundaries of the beginning, middle and end of this unit, it is necessary for the interpreter to give 'voice' to the signs in the text.[5] Narratorial voice in Lk. 1.26-56 differentiates narration from attributed speech. There are two and one half verses of narration (1.26-28a) that open the beginning of the unit. In the context where the language refers to Elizabeth, there is a span of three and one half verses of narration (1.39-42a) that open the middle of the unit. A short 'And Mary said' in 1.46a opens the final unit, which contains nine and one half verses of attributed speech before a final verse of narration (1.56). This reveals the narratorial boundaries of the beginning (1.26-38), middle (1.39-45) and end (1.46-56); and the voicing leads the interpreter to strategies of argumentation that occur throughout the unit.

The voice of the narrator, the first level of narration (Tolbert 1989: 90-106), introduces Mary to the reader/hearer within a narrative pattern that features an angel sent from God. This pattern begins when the narrator asserts that an angel of the Lord appeared to Zechariah while he was praying inside the Temple at the hour of incense (Lk. 1.10-12), and it recycles with the assertion that the angel Gabriel appeared to Mary at Nazareth in the sixth month of Elizabeth's pregnancy. At the second level of narration, the level of the voices of characters that are embedded in the voice of the narrator (first level), the angel Gabriel tells Mary that she is God's 'favored one' and that the Lord is with her (1.26-28). The narrator tells the reader/hearer that Mary was troubled at the statement and debated in her mind concerning what it might mean (1.29), much as the narrator's voice says that Zechariah was troubled and afraid when he first saw the angel of the Lord (1.12). The implied reader begins to detect, then, a dialogue between the voice of the narrator and the voices of characters in the story. In the context where the narrator focuses on Mary's puzzlement, the angel tells her she has found favor with God, she will conceive and bear a son, and the son

---

5.    'Narrative critics' give 'voice' to signs in the text by generating a subtext of an 'implied' author and reader whom they perceive to be 'presupposed by the narrative' itself (Powell 1990: 19-21). It is important to be attentive to the 'meanings' narrative critics embed in the voices they give to the signs. It is customary for narrative critics to embed twentieth-century, post-industrial values, meanings, convictions and perspectives in the voices while insisting that these meanings are 'in the text'. Socio-rhetorical criticism attends programmatically to this issue in the intertextual, social and cultural, and ideological arenas of analysis.

(a) will be called Jesus;
(b) will be great;
(c) will be called Son of the Most High;
(d) will be given the throne of his father David by God;
(e) will reign over the house of Jacob forever; and
(f) will have a kingdom that has no end (Lk. 1.30-33).

The narrator tells the reader that Mary is 'a virgin betrothed' to 'Joseph, of the house of David' (1.27). The angel tells Mary the Holy Spirit will come upon her, the Most High will overshadow her, and therefore the child will be called holy, the Son of God. In addition, the angel tells Mary that her kinswoman Elizabeth is six months pregnant after being barren, because with God no word will be impossible.[6]

When Mary speaks, she presents a different perspective from the narrator and the angel. The first time she speaks, she tells the angel she has no man (1.34). The second time, she refers to herself as a maid-servant of the Lord and says, 'Let it be according to your word' (1.38). Mary has believed and consented, then, in a context of concern that she has no man. From the point of view of the angel, Mary is a fortunate young woman with everything she could hope for on her side. She has been specially favored by God, and the child within her is specially blessed. The narrator, however, says Mary is troubled, and when Mary tells her story in song, the reader gets a somewhat new insight into things.

Mary's voice in the Magnificat uses and reconfigures other characters' voices in the text. First, Mary repeats language the angel speaks to Zechariah about joy and gladness (1.14, 47). Secondly, Mary reconfigures language Elizabeth uses when Elizabeth says that the Lord has shown regard for her and taken away her own reproach among men (1.25, 48a). Thirdly, Mary reconfigures language Elizabeth uses when she tells Mary that she, Mary, is blessed because she has believed in the fulfilment of the things spoken to her (1.45, 48b). Fourthly, Mary uses, reconfigures and embellishes language the angel Gabriel spoke to her about the power of the Most High (1.35, 49). Fifthly, Mary reconfigures the angel's statements about her son's 'father David' and about his reigning 'over the house of Jacob forever' (1.32-33, 54). Mary asserts that God 'puts down the mighty from their thrones', and 'exalts those who live in humiliation' (1.52). Thus, Mary's voice not only introduces a

6. See Troost 1992 for the importance of 'word' throughout Lk. 1-2.

dialogue with the narrator's voice but with the voices of the angel that appeared to Zechariah, of the angel Gabriel who appeared to her, and of her kinswoman Elizabeth. Is Mary simply perpetuating the views of these other narrative agents, or does she have a somewhat different perspective? This will be a point at issue as we proceed to other arenas of interpretation. From a narratorial perspective, Mary's Magnificat engages in dialogue with other voices in the discourse.

Robert Tannehill has produced a compelling reading of the inner texture of the Magnificat by using Hebrew poetry as a subtext to give meaning to Mary's voice (Tannehill 1974; Tannehill 1986: 26-32). Tannehill emphasizes parallelism, repetition and the natural rhythm of reading, and his analysis yields two stanzas or strophes: (a) 1.46-50 and (b) 1.51-55. The division is marked, he says, by two concluding lines for each strophe (1.49b-50; 1.54b-55), which resemble each other in thought and form. For Tannehill, then, the inner texture of the poem yields a traditional hymn, which opens with a statement of praise and follows with a series of reasons for this praise. To reiterate, the subtext for this compelling reading of the inner texture of the hymn comes from presuppositions about Hebrew poetry. Tannehill observed that the opening statement of the hymn is a statement of praise and the following statements provide reasons for the praise, but he did not analyze the nature of the reasons. Lucy Rose, in an unpublished paper written at Emory University, approached the Magnificat with a very different subtext, namely argumentation in Hellenistic-Roman rhetoric (Rose 1989). The argumentative texture of the Magnificat comes into view if one follows guidelines from the *Rhetorica ad Herennium*, which was written in the 80s BCE.

*Theme* or *Topic*:
My soul magnifies the Lord,
And my spirit has gladness in God my Savior (Lk. 1.46b-47).

*Rationale*:
because he has shown regard for the humiliation of his maidservant (Lk. 1.48a).

*Confirmation of the Rationale*:
For behold, henceforth all generations will call me blessed (Lk. 1.48b).

*Embellishment*:
(1) For he who is mighty has done great things for me,
and holy is his name,
and his mercy is on those who fear him from generation to generation.

(2) He has done a strong thing with his arm,
he has scattered the proud in the imagination of their hearts,
he has put down the mighty from their thrones,
and exalted those of low degree;
he has filled the hungry with good things,
and the rich he has sent empty away (Lk. 1.49-53).

*Conclusion*:
He has helped his servant Israel,
in remembrance of his mercy,
as he spoke to our fathers,
to Abraham and to his posterity for ever (Lk. 1.54-55).

After Mary's announcement of her topic of magnifying the Lord (1.46b-47), she provides an initial rationale for her speech-action: (because) 'God has shown regard for the humiliation of his maidservant' (1.48a). These two steps set the stage for 'the most complete and perfect argument', to use the words of *Rhetorica ad Herennium* 2.18.28–19.30 (Robbins 1993a: 123-25). With this announcement, Mary has started her hymn with an enthymeme—a rhetorical syllogism that provides a minor premise for her topic and leaves the major premise unstated. The unstated major premise appears to be embedded in ritual logic that suggests that when the Lord God focuses special attention on the humiliation of a woman, such a woman responds naturally with hymnic speech from her glad heart. This produces the following underlying syllogism:

*Implied Major Premise*:
When the Lord God shows regard for the humiliation of the soul and spirit of one of his maidservants, the favored woman praises the Lord God as her savior.

*Minor Premise*:
God has shown regard for the humiliation of the soul and spirit of his maidservant Mary.

*Conclusion*:
Mary's soul magnifies the Lord and her spirit rejoices in God her savior.

From a rhetorical perspective, the hymn begins syllogistically rather than paradigmatically. In other words, the beginning of the speech introduces the deductive logic of a rhetorical syllogism rather than the inductive logic of a rhetorical example. This raises the fascinating issue of whether there was a specific instance of 'humiliation' that Mary could narrate if asked, or whether Mary's 'humiliation' was some general state common to most, if not all, women.

After the opening enthymematic argument in 1.46-48a, v. 48b voices a confirmation of the rationale. This is a natural next step for a 'most complete and perfect argument'. The confirmation that 'God has given regard to my humiliation' lies in the future: 'From now on, all generations will bless me' (or, 'will call me blessed'). In 1.48b, then, Mary buttresses her initial rationale with a *rationis confirmatio*, a confirmation of the initial rationale.

After stating the theme, rationale and confirmation to open her argument (1.46-48), Mary embellishes the opening statements (1.49-53). This move fulfils the next step in a most complete and perfect argument. The embellishment contains two stanzas (1.49-50, 51-53), each beginning with what the mighty one 'has done' (*epoiēsen*). The first stanza links what God has done for Mary with what God does for 'those who fear him'; the second stanza presents a series of basic actions by God:

(a) God has scattered the proud in the imagination of their hearts;

(b) God has put down the mighty from their thrones and exalted the humiliated;

(c) God has filled the hungry with good things and sent the rich away empty (Lk. 1.51-53).

These statements assert that God watches over all generations (1.48b, 50) and that God has been especially attentive to those who live in humiliation (1.48a, 52); and they imply that God welcomes those with a rejoicing, praising spirit, since he 'scatters' those who are 'proud in the imaginations of their hearts' (1.46b-47, 51). These statements amplify and more deeply ground the opening assertions of the speech. Mary concludes with a recapitulation that refers to the help God gave to Israel in the past, to Abraham and his seed forever (1.54-55). Thus Mary, standing in the line of 'Abraham's posterity forever', praises God with reasoning that fulfils Hellenistic-Roman guidelines for 'the most complete and perfect argument'.

The final part of the inner-textual reading has proposed the presence of argumentative features that did not appear when Hebrew poetry provided the only subtext for the reading. This suggests a bi-cultural nature for the discourse that will be important to pursue in additional interpretative steps. The unit ends with an argument by Mary that God's benevolence to her has a relation to God's benevolence in the past and God's plans for the future. Yet Mary has come to this point only through a troubling encounter with the angel Gabriel and a supportive encounter with Elizabeth. It will be necessary to investigate additional dimensions of meaning in the context of other textures of the language in this unit.

The present discussion of the inner texture of Lk. 1.26-56 has introduced a limited number of subtexts for its reading. Socio-rhetorical criticism invites any number of subtexts to approach the unit, with the goal of enriching the understanding of the topics, voices and arguments in it. Readings from yet other angles can explore the interchange between male and female voices and the reverberation of topics about different classes and statuses of people. Analysis of inner texture has introduced an initial set of strategies to identify topics and get a glimpse of the argumentative interaction in the unit.

### Intertexture: Every Comparison has Boundaries

A second arena of rhetorical criticism is intertextual comparison, analysis and interpretation. Here the strategies emerge from the following questions: From where has this passage adopted its language? With what texts does this text stand in dialogue? Comparison takes us into canonical issues, understood in the broad terms introduced by postmodern criticism (Eagleton 1983: 1-53). All interpretations can be characterized in terms of the data with which they allow a particular text to be compared. These issues appear in an interpreter's observation, analysis and interpretation of reference, recitation, recontextualization, reconfiguration and echo in a text.

An initial dimension of intertexture is reference. Reference to proper names in Lk. 1.26-56 indicates explicit dialogue with people and places in Israelite tradition. There is reference to the angel Gabriel, God, a city of Galilee, the house of David, the Most High, the Lord God, the throne of David, the house of Jacob, the Holy Spirit, the Son of God, a city of Judah, his servant Israel, and our fathers, Abraham and his posterity. There also is reference to a virgin betrothed to a man (1.27), a woman called barren (1.36) and a maidservant of the Lord (1.37, 48). With what texts and textual traditions are these phrases in dialogue? We will see that this is a highly-contested issue in interpretation.

A second dimension of intertexture is recitation, which includes rehearsal of attributed speech in exact, modified or different words from other accounts of the attributed speech, and rehearsal of an episode or series of episodes, with or without using some words from another account of the story. Recitation appears in the form of generalized summary in 1.51-55: in the past God has shown strength with his arm, scattered the proud, put down the mighty from their thrones, exalted those in humiliation, filled the hungry with good things, sent the rich empty away, helped his servant Israel, and spoken to our fathers, to Abraham and his posterity. It is not clear exactly what events are being rehearsed; this is recitation of past events in a generalized, summary form. Such recitation allows an interpreter freedom to draw boundaries in various ways around episodes recounting God's interaction with Israel; an interpreter may include or exclude stories according to the interpreter's inclination.

A third dimension of intertexture is recontextualization, which is the placing of attributed narration or speech in a new context without announcing its previous attribution. There is a long list of recontextualized speech from the Septuagint in this unit (R.E. Brown 1977: 357-62; Fitzmyer 1981: 356-57), which we will discuss below.

A fourth dimension of intertexture is reconfiguration. Certainly the Lukan unit is reconfiguring the long tradition of barren Israelite women who have conceived in their old age and borne a son. Exactly which stories are the strongest intertexts is an important issue. But what of accounts of virgins? Does this account of the virgin Mary reconfigure any accounts of virgins in the Septuagint? Are there any Mediterranean accounts of virgins that this account of Mary may be reconfiguring? We will see below that the established boundaries for discussion of reconfiguration in traditional New Testament interpretation not only suppress discussion of the stories of virgins in the Septuagint but completely exclude well-known stories about virgins impregnated by gods in Mediterranean society. Here a purity system has been functioning with the intensity of all purity systems, keeping stories about the immoral Hellenistic gods raping virgins on earth out of 'scientific' exegesis. The result is an absence of biblical monographs that programmatically compare the Lukan account of the conception of the virgin Mary, when the Holy Spirit comes upon her and the power of the Most High overshadows her (Lk. 1.34), and accounts of the conception of virgins in Mediterranean literature, when gods come upon them in different forms and circumstances. It is highly likely that the account of Mary is multicultural, reconfiguring Mediterranean stories about virgins as well as Israelite stories about virgins and barren women. We will return to this below in the discussion of the social and cultural texture of the account.

A fifth dimension is intertextual echo. Beyond specific configuration of traditions and episodes lie echoes (Hollander 1981; Hays 1989). When the Lukan account of Mary and Elizabeth is recounted in Greek toward the end of the first century CE, the echoes in its intertexture are manifold. Again, the traditional boundaries in New Testament exegesis have been drawn in such a way that interpreters saturate the discussion with echoes from Israelite and Jewish tradition but suppress echoes from broader Mediterranean tradition, society and culture.

The spectrum of intertexture, from reference to echo, intensely raises the issue of canon in interpretation (Eagleton 1983: 1-53). For most interpreters, canonical boundaries for interpretation of the Lukan account of Mary and Elizabeth have been drawn in a manner that intentionally excludes comparison of the Magnificat with hymns of praise in Hellenistic-Roman culture and the conception of Mary with accounts of the conception of other virgins in Mediterranean literature. The strategy that keeps such data out is a 'canonical strategy', and the elements of this strategy are basic canon, canon within the canon (or 'inner canon') and near canon (Myers 1991: 53-54). The basic canon for New Testament interpretation of this unit is comprised by the Old and New Testaments. Central to any canonical strategy, however, is the establishment of a canon within the canon, an 'inner' canon. The canon within the canon for interpretation of this unit comprises the Israelite tradition of barren women and the account of Hannah and her hymn of praise in 1 Sam. 1.1–2.10. This strategy produces an interpretative near canon comprised of material from Psalms (35.9; 111.9; 103.17; 89.11; 107.9; 98.3) and other passages in the Old Testament, Apocrypha and Pseudepigrapha (R.E. Brown 1977: 358-60; Fitzmyer 1981: 356-69). It is noticeable that this inner canon and near canon exclude any stories about virgins in Israelite tradition. Beginning with the tradition of barren Israelite women, it opens its boundaries to hymns of praise within the book of Psalms and within prophetic, apocalyptic, pseudepigraphic and Qumran literature. If interpreters open the boundaries of near canon further they may bring in information from rabbinic literature and from the church fathers, monastics and mystics in Christian tradition. But all of this opening of the boundaries carefully avoids stories about virgins who are forced to conceive, either by gods or by men fulfilling the will of a god. The absence of significant comparative work on Hellenistic-Roman hymns to gods and goddesses and on accounts of virgins who are overpowered and made pregnant by gods makes it impossible to redraw those boundaries here. Instead, the discussion will focus on the one major, recent attempt to open these boundaries in New Testament interpretation.

The Lukan account is susceptible to non-conventional boundaries. In Luke, the angel appears to the husband Zechariah concerning the conception and birth of the son John the Baptist to the barren wife Elizabeth (Lk. 1.11-20); but the angel appears to the betrothed virgin Mary, and to her alone, concerning the conception and birth of Jesus (Lk. 1.26-38). In the Matthean account, in contrast, the angel appears to the man Joseph rather than to the virgin Mary (Mt. 1.20; 2.13, 19). In Luke, no male is part of Mary's scene unless the reader genders Gabriel as male (Brenner and van Dijk-Hemmes 1993; Troost 1993). The Lukan account is closer to the account of the birth and conception of Samson in Judg. 13.2-25 than to any other account of conception by a barren woman, since the messenger of God appears to the future mother in the account and tells her that she will conceive and bear a son. In Luke, a kinswoman Elizabeth, whose barrenness has been removed by God, in effect replaces the role that the husband Manoah plays in the story of the conception and birth of Samson. The function of Elizabeth raises another issue, namely the relation of one blessed woman to another blessed woman in Israelite tradition. This essay will turn to that issue in the section on ideology; for now the discussion turns to the Lukan reconfiguration of a 'dishonorable' Israelite tradition about the over-powering of virgins by embedding it in the 'honorable' tradition of the perpetuation of Israel's patriarchal line through barren women.

The special dynamics of a 'canon within the canon' are at work in Mary's reference to her 'humiliation' in the rationale she provides for her joyful soul and spirit (Lk. 1.48b). Her humiliation is different from the humiliation of a barren woman: Mary is pregnant before marriage, and conventional social logic presupposes that a male causes a female to become pregnant. When a male causes a female to become pregnant outside of marriage, he is said to have 'humiliated (*tapeinoō*) her'. Interpreters suppress the difference between the humiliation of a married, barren woman and an unmarried, pregnant woman in the Lukan account by establishing boundaries of intertexture that keep the accounts of Israel's dishonored virgin women outside the interpretative 'canon within the canon' and, indeed, outside the interpretative near canon. In essence, the interpretative strategy erases the accounts of dishonored virgins from Israelite, Jewish and Mediterranean literature. It erases the accounts by displacing them with accounts of honorable barren women. This may, indeed, be a natural effect of Lukan narration on readers. But interpreters should exhibit the nature of Lukan discourse in exegetical practice rather than simply replicating its discursive strategies.

Jane Schaberg has challenged the traditional inner canon of inter-texture for the Lukan account of Mary by calling attention to legislation about and accounts of sexually dishonored women in Israelite tradition. Deut. 22.23-24 (cf. 22.29) presents specific legislation about betrothed virgins who are dishonored:

> And if there be a young virgin betrothed (*pais parthenos memnēsteumenē*) to a man (*andri*), and a man (*anthropos*) has found her in the city and lain (*koimethē*) with her, you shall take them both out to the gate of their city and they shall be stoned with stones, and they shall die; the young woman because she did not cry out in the city, and the man because he humiliated (*etapeinōsen*) his neighbor's woman (*gunaika*) (Deut. 22.23-24 LXX).

The language of virgin, betrothal and humiliation in this legislation is precisely the same as in the Lukan account. Mary is a virgin betrothed to a man (Lk. 1.27: *parthenon emnesteumenēn andri*), and when she becomes pregnant she refers to that pregnancy as humiliation (Lk. 1.48: *tēn tapeinōsin*). From her perspective, her pregnancy has humiliated her.

As stated above, this humiliation of Mary perpetuates a 'dishonorable' tradition of important women in Israel's history. In Gen. 34.2, Dinah, the daughter of Leah and Jacob, was 'humiliated' (*etapeinōsen*) by 'Shechem the son of Hamor the Hivite, the prince of the land', when he seized her and lay with her. In Judg. 19.24 and 20.5 the father of the Levite's concubine offers both 'my virgin daughter' (*hē thugatēr mou hē parthenos*) and the Levite's concubine to the men of the city that 'you might humiliate' (*tapeinōsate*) them. In 2 Sam. 13.12, 14, 22, 32 David's daughter Tamar pleads with Amnon not to humiliate her, but he overpowers her and lies with her, and his death was considered to be a punishment for this act. Deut. 21.14 is an additional, instructive form of legislation. When Israel goes forth to war, and an Israelite captures a beautiful woman and desires her and takes her for a wife,

> Then, if you have no delight in her, you shall send her out free, and you shall not sell her for money; you shall not treat her with contempt, since you have humiliated (*etapeinōsas*) her.

An Israelite is given the right to humiliate a foreign woman whom he has taken captive, but certain regulations govern his activity, including the recognition that he has humiliated her. Lam. 5.11 offers a cry of anguish over the 'dishonorable' tradition of humiliated women:

> They humiliated (*etapeinōsan*) women in Zion,
> Virgins (*parthenous*) in the cities of Judah.

In Ezek. 22.10-11 the prophet indicts the princes of Israel themselves:

> In you men uncover their fathers' nakedness; in you they humiliate (*etapeinoun*) women who are unclean in their menstruation. One deals unlawfully with his neighbor's wife; another has defiled his daughter-in-law in ungodliness; and another in you has humiliated (*etapeinoun*) his sister, the daughter of his father.

The humiliation to which Mary refers in Lk. 1.48a refers to this 'dishonorable' tradition. In Jane Schaberg's words: 'The virgin betrothed to a man (Lk. 1.27) was sexually humiliated. But her humiliation was "looked upon" and reversed by God' (Schaberg 1987: 100; Schaberg 1992: 284-85). This information suggests the importance of including Deut. 22.24; Gen. 34.2; Judg. 19.24, 20.5; 2 Kgs 13.12-32 and Lam. 5.11 as inner canonical intertexts for interpretation of Lk. 1.26-56. Yet these texts are never mentioned by Raymond Brown and Joseph Fitzmyer, to mention two interpreters who have worked in detail with the intertexture of the Lukan account.

If the inner canon included all the information in the Bible about virgins who were overpowered by males, then new data would emerge from the near canon of the apocrypha, pseudepigrapha and other Mediterranean literature. The beginning point for the strategy that keeps this information out is the suppression of a dimension of the 'inner texture' of the Lukan account itself. Namely, the virgin Mary refers to 'her' humiliation in Lk. 1.48a, not Elizabeth's. Mary's 'low estate', as it is often translated, results from conception outside of marriage, not absence of conception within marriage. Mary's rationale for praising God is that God has shown special regard for the pregnancy that was forced upon her. Unfortunately, there is no space to develop this further here; it is necessary to summarize and move on to social and cultural texture.

Socio-rhetorical criticism calls for a detailed assessment of the manner in which inner canonical boundaries have been established for interpretation in relation to the inner texture of a unit itself. In the instance of the Magnificat, New Testament interpreters have suppressed the intertexture of Mary's speech with virgins overpowered by men or male gods by changing the reference of her speech to barrenness instead of pregnancy outside of marriage. Once an 'inner canon' for interpretation has excluded all discussion of overpowered virgins in the Bible, it can easily push back any comparison with accounts of virgins in extracanonical Jewish texts and other Mediterranean literature.

## *Social and Cultural Texture: Every Meaning Has a Context*

The social and cultural texture of a text raises questions about the response to the world, the social and cultural systems and institutions, and the cultural alliances and conflicts evoked by the text (Fowler 1986: 85-101). These social and cultural phenomena are primary topics in rhetorical theory (Aristotle, *Ars Rhetorica* 1.2.21-22; 2.22.1–23.30; 3.15.1-4; Kennedy 1991: 46-47, 186-204, 265-68). Particular social data regularly are 'material' topics in discourse, specific 'subject matter'. Social and cultural systems and institutions are common topics, those that span all subject matter in society and culture. Cultural alliances and conflicts are 'final' topics, those that function specially to make one's own case to other people. These topics functioning together evoke the social and cultural nature of a particular discourse (Robbins 1993b; Wuellner 1991; Elliott 1993: 36-51).

Bryan Wilson's analysis of types of religious sects can assist an interpreter initially in ascertaining the social response to the world in the discourse of a particular New Testament text. James A. Wilde introduced Wilson's sociological typology of sects into New Testament study in his dissertation and an article (Wilde 1974, 1978), and in 1981 John H. Elliott incorporated Wilson's insights into the method he called sociological exegesis (Elliott 1981: 75-77, 96, 102-106, 122; cf. Elliott forthcoming). Later, Philip Esler used them for an initial test of Lukan discourse, and his lead can be helpful in our analysis. Since this essay is designed to introduce the reader to socio-rhetorical criticism, it seems good to describe all seven of Wilson's types briefly, each of which, from our perspective, is evoked by specific topics that occupy the discourse.

1. The *conversionist* response views the world as corrupt because all people are corrupt: if people can be changed then the world will be changed.
2. The *revolutionist* response assumes that only the destruction of the world, of the natural but more specifically of the social order, will suffice to save people.

3.      The *introversionist* response sees the world as irredeemably evil and presupposes that salvation can be attained only by the fullest possible withdrawal from it.

4.      The *gnostic* (*manipulationist*) response seeks only a transformed set of relationships—a transformed method of coping with evil—since salvation is possible in the world if people learn the right means, improved techniques, to deal with their problems.

5.      The *thaumaturgical* response focuses on the concern of individual people for relief from present and specific ills by special dispensations.

6.      The *reformist* response assumes that people may create an environment of salvation in the world by using supernaturally-given insights to change the present social organization into a system that functions toward good ends.

7.      The *utopian* response presupposes that people must take an active and constructive role in replacing the entire present social system with a new social organization in which evil is absent (Wilson 1969; Wilson 1973: 22-26).

Most historical manifestations of religious communities exhibit a tensive relation among two, three or four of these responses to the world. A strong focus on only one regularly signals the manifestation of a cult—a group organized around a new idea or an imported alien religion—rather than a sect (Stark 1986). Esler concludes that the thaumaturgical, conversionist and revolutionist types of response are relevant for Luke–Acts (Esler 1987: 59). Let us test his conclusion in the context of analysis of Lk. 1.26-56.

First, the miraculous intervention of God upon both Elizabeth and Mary signals thaumaturgic rhetoric. This essay will explore a few of the details below, but perhaps it is sufficient at this point to cite the statement of the angel: 'For with God no word will be impossible' (1.37). Secondly, the change of Mary from being 'greatly troubled' (1.29) to her agreement to 'let it be to me according to your word' (1.38) exhibits conversionist rhetoric. Mary changes from a young woman who does not believe she can conceive a son apart from a man to a young woman who accepts the promise of the angel, and this seems to introduce a model for people's response to God's miraculous intervention in the affairs of the world. Other stories, like Zaccheus' change of heart, distribution of half of his wealth to the poor and fourfold restoration of all he has defrauded (Lk. 19.1-10), exhibit fully this kind of rhetoric in Luke and Acts. The view is that changes of heart produce salvation. Thirdly, 'reversal rhetoric' is prominent in Mary's speech (York 1991). In the past, God 'has put down the mighty from their thrones, and exalted those who have been humiliated; he has filled the hungry with good things, and the rich he has sent empty away' (Lk. 1.52-53). God is overturning, and promises further to overturn, the world, and specifically the social order. Esler considers this to be revolutionist rhetoric, but we will need to return to this below. The 'reversal' rhetoric may be utopian or reformist rather than revolutionist in the context of Lukan thaumaturgical and conversionist rhetoric that brings salvation to people in the world (1.69, 71, 77).

Let us deepen this initial perception of the social response to the work in the text with analysis of common social and cultural topics in the text—kinship, honor and shame, limited good, purity codes, patron–client relations and hospitality codes—what David B. Gowler calls 'cultural scripts'. These common topics have been the special domain of New Testament social scientific critics for more than a decade (Malina 1981; Elliott 1986; Elliott 1993; Neyrey 1991) and they can help us to make the analysis more precise.

The concern about 'humiliation' (*tapeinōsis*) in Lk. 1.26-56 especially concerns kinship, honor and shame. The narrative leaves the ascribed family status of Mary unstated, in contrast to that of Elizabeth, who was 'of the daughters of Aaron' (Lk. 1.5). Mary's honor is embedded in her betrothal to a man 'of the house of David' (Lk. 1.27). Her humiliation derives from pregnancy before marriage has occurred (Lk. 1.34, 48a). But God has removed this humiliation by communicating honor through the angel Gabriel beforehand and through the responses of the honored Elizabeth to her pregnancy. When the angel Gabriel comes to Mary in her private chambers, however, the speech on the lips of the angel attributes fear to Mary. Malina and Rohrbaugh, gendering both God and Gabriel as male in their reading of this text, evoke a social situation in which a man encounters a young woman and threatens her virginity. In their view, the male angel has persuaded her to consent to be overpowered by the Holy Spirit, the Most High. They comment as follows (1992: 289):

> Notice how readily Mary gives in when 'cornered' by the angel. While
> obviously no lust is involved in this case, the scenario still points to tradi-
> tional Mediterranean urgency to keep women duly encompassed. And
> Mary's answer in this difficult situation is: 'Let it be with me according to
> your word' (v. 38). What this means in typical Mediterranean fashion is:
> 'As you like!'

Serious questions are being raised in current interpretation about this
kind of male gendering of biblical texts (Brenner and van Dijk-Hemmes
1993). Both traditional and nontraditional readers have implicitly, if not
explicitly, gendered God as male in relation to Mary. Malina and
Rohrbaugh's reading is highly similar to Schaberg's reading in
gendering Gabriel as well as God as male. This is, without a doubt, one
of the most explosive issues of our time. The gendering of both God and
Gabriel as male takes us to the heart of ideology. Would it be possible
for us to read this text in such a manner that neither God nor Gabriel
are gendered as male in relation to Mary? The work of Brenner, van
Dijk-Hemmes and Troost promises to give us such a reading in the near
future. Let us look more closely at the text itself to see the nature of the
social and cultural topics in it.

When the angel Gabriel first told Mary this visit meant that she was
being favored by God with conception and birth of a special son, she
protested that she had no man (1.34). Here, then, the text explicitly
evokes the traditional perception that a woman becomes pregnant only
as the result of the presence of a man. When the angel draws an analogy
between the honorable conception of her barren kinswoman Elizabeth
and her own impending conception, Mary believes the angel's word of
promise to her (1.36-38). We lack comparison of the argumentation the
angel uses to persuade Mary with argumentation by gods who visit
virgins in Mediterranean antiquity. But we should not be surprised to
find similar strategies of persuasion. The angel has confronted Mary with
powerful words and she has been persuaded by them. The 'central'
concern for a woman in this situation in Mediterranean antiquity is
honor, and the powers have provided for her honor. This appears to be
the primary reason for her praise of God: God has shown regard for the
humiliation of this maidservant; from now on, all generations will call her
blessed—instead of a dishonorable woman (1.48).

The result of this analysis suggests an inner relation between thaumaturgy and conversion: Mary will encounter a miracle just like Elizabeth
has experienced a miracle; acceptance of this miracle requires a deep
change of heart on behalf of Mary. Mary's first response to Gabriel was

that she had no man, therefore she could not imagine how she could have a son (1.34). The answer of the angel persuades her to change her mind and accept the possibility (1.35-37), and Elizabeth's statements affirm her new point of view (1.42-45). Thus, argumentation that features honor and kinship confirms and deepens our understanding of the centrality of thaumaturgy and conversion in the discourse. But what about the reversal of the powerful and the lowly in Mary's Magnificat? Let us turn to cultural alliances and conflicts to deepen our understanding of this discourse.

A beginning framework for investigating cultural interaction in a text emerges in the distinction sociologists of culture make between dominant culture, subculture, contraculture, counterculture and liminal culture. On the one hand, a cultural system has its own set of premises and rationales (Peacock 1986: 35). On the other hand, every cultural system is comprised of multiple 'local cultures' (Geertz 1983). Local cultures interact with other local cultures, either by dominating or embedding themselves in another culture. Each culture develops its own premises and rationales within this context of domination and/or embedding.

The rhetorics of dominant culture, subculture, counterculture, contraculture and liminal culture are a factor in producing these cultures, and in turn these cultures generate these kinds of rhetoric. The relation of rhetoric to culture and culture to rhetoric, then, is reciprocal. What kind of culture rhetoric is at work in Lk. 1.26-56? To pursue this issue it is necessary to have definitions of these types of culture rhetoric (Robbins 1993b).

(a) *Dominant culture rhetoric* adopts a point of view according to which its own system of attitudes, values, dispositions and norms are supported by social structures vested with power to impose its goals on people in a significantly broad territorial region.

(b) *Subculture rhetoric* imitates the attitudes, values, dispositions and norms of dominant culture rhetoric, and it claims to enact them better than members of dominant status.

Ethnic subculture rhetoric is a particular kind of subculture rhetoric. It has origins in a language different from the languages in the dominant culture, and it attempts to preserve and perpetuate an 'old system' in a dominant cultural system in which it now exists, either because a significant number of people from this ethnic culture have moved into a new cultural environment or because a new cultural system is now imposing itself on it (Roberts 1978; Gordon 1970).

(c) *Counterculture rhetoric* is a 'heretical' intra-cultural phenomenon that articulates a *constructive* image of a better way of life in a context of 'rejection of *explicit* and *mutable* characteristics' of the dominant or subculture rhetoric to which it is responding (Roberts 1978: 114). It is not simply a reaction formation to another form of culture, but it builds on a supporting ideology that provides a relatively self-sufficient system of action (Roberts 1978: 121; Roberts 1976; Yinger 1982).

(d) *Contraculture rhetoric* is 'groupculture' rhetoric that is deeply embedded in another form of culture to which it is a reaction formation. It asserts 'more negative than positive ideas' (Roberts 1978: 124, citing Bouvard 1975: 119) in a context where its positive ideas are simply pre-supposed and come from the culture to which it is reacting. It often is possible to predict the behavior and values evoked by contraculture rhetoric if one knows the values evoked by the culture to which it is reacting, since the values are simply inverted (Roberts 1978: 123-24; Yinger 1960: 629; Stark 1967: 141, 153; Ellens 1971).

(e) *Liminal culture rhetoric* is 'disjunctive and multiaccentual' speech that evokes a cultural space 'outside the sentence'. It uses cacophonic, syncopated sounds and articulations in 'heterogeneous and messy array' to evoke a possibility of 'enunciation' and 'identity'. It is a liberating strategy 'articulated at the liminal edge of identity' to create the possibility for an emergent cultural identity (Bhaba 1992: 443-45).

If we analyze the text that features Mary and Elizabeth from the per-spective of culture rhetoric, we begin to test the dynamics of revolution-ist rhetoric in relation to reformist and utopian rhetoric. The angel Gabriel represents the power of God, and the speech of the angel represents a form of dominant culture rhetoric. After Mary accepts Gabriel's promise to her she speaks about the nature of God's power in terms of making the mighty low and the low mighty. Is Mary simply amplifying the dominant culture rhetoric Gabriel has introduced to her, or is this a different kind of culture rhetoric? Let us remain in touch with the topics that concern the social response to the world in the discourse as we pursue this issue. Does Mary's discourse introduce a revolutionist vision in which God's power 'destroys' the present evil world, a utopian vision in which God's power 'replaces' the present social structures and powerful people with a new kind of structure and role for leaders, or a reformist vision in which God's power 'changes' something within the present system to make it function benevolently?

The answer to this question must come from the overall rhetoric of

Luke and Acts. For this reason, it is important to embed Lk. 1:26-56 in the discourse of both volumes. In a recent study of the social location of the implied author of this two volume work, I drew the conclusion that

> the thought of the implied author is located in the midst of the activities of adult Jews and Romans who have certain kinds of power in cities and villages throughout the Mediterranean world from Rome to Jerusalem... The arena of socialization reveals an upwardlooking use of technology toward Roman officials with political power. Jewish officials, however, are considered equal in social status and rank... Thus, the thought of the implied author is located socially in a place where it seems advantageous, and perhaps necessary, to tell 'these foreign affairs' to people slightly higher in social rank who read Greek and appreciate a people who strive to be devout, righteous, and lettered... Accepting a position of subordination, Christians speak with politeness and care upwards to those who dominate the system. Yet, bolstered by God's sanctioning of their diversity and by their ideology of 'at homeness' in the Roman empire, they not only tell their story to those above but engage in vigorous and continued confrontation with those from whom they claim their Jewish heritage and those with whom they enjoy the benefits of Greco-Roman culture (Robbins 1991a: 331-32).

The exchanges among the angel Gabriel, Mary and Elizabeth exhibit a subset of these dynamics. The angel Gabriel represents the power and will of God in much the same way that King Agrippa represents the power and will of the emperor (Acts 25.13–26.32), thus they both use dominant culture rhetoric. When the angel Gabriel speaks to Mary, he uses command and 'name dropping' characteristic of representatives of hierarchical structures. He is fully authorized by dominant power and he fills his discourse with the authorities that stand behind him as he works.

Since both Gabriel who represents God and King Agrippa who represents the emperor use dominant culture rhetoric, there is an inner tension in the discourse of Luke–Acts. Do two dominant cultures stand in unmitigated opposition in Luke–Acts, or does the dominant rhetoric of one of the cultures accept a subordinate position in relation to the other? It seems clear from the relation of the discourse in the prefaces to the discourse in the speeches of Paul in Acts that representatives of Christianity accept a subordinate role to the emperor and his representatives (Robbins 1979). The discourse in Luke–Acts adopts a position according to which people like Theophilus and King Agrippa are likely to view the story of Christianity as a matter of 'foreign affairs', but it challenges such a view by embedding the affairs of Christianity within the affairs of the emperor and his representatives. When a decree of the emperor creates a movement of people whereby Jesus of Nazareth is born in the city of David (Lk. 2.1-5), the stage is set for a cooperative relation between the power of the emperor and the power of God throughout the story. As the story progresses, events among early followers of Jesus work symbiotically with power structures within the Roman empire to create a story in which power that travels from Rome to Jerusalem creates the environment for Christianity to travel from Jerusalem to Rome (Robbins 1991b: 218-21). In this context, representatives of Christianity adopt subcultural rhetoric as they converse with representatives of the emperor.

The dominant culture rhetoric Gabriel uses with Mary, then, stands in an ethnic subcultural relation to the dominant culture rhetoric King Agrippa uses with Paul. After Mary's encounter, she takes the initiative to go alone to the honored, no longer barren, woman Elizabeth, much like Paul goes to synagogues in cities in Asia Minor, Macedonia and Greece. When Mary speaks in the presence of Elizabeth, she speaks a high form of Jewish rhetoric, a form containing the poetic qualities of royal Davidic and classical prophetic speech. At the highpoint of Mary's speech, however, she speaks a rhetoric of reversal: those who are powerful will be made low, and those who live in humiliation will be exalted (Lk. 1.52). In other words, while speaking the highest level of this ethnic subculture rhetoric, Mary introduces a contracultural phenomenon in her rhetoric—a phenomenon that 'inverts' some aspect of another cultural system. Whose culture is Mary's speech inverting, and what is she inverting in that culture? Is Mary's rhetoric counter-cultural rather than contracultural? In other words, are the inversions part of an overall positive vision, or does her speech emphasize more negative than positive things?

The strategy of the narrative is to present a form of dominant Jewish culture rhetoric primarily on the lips of Pharisees (Moxnes 1988; Gowler 1989; Gowler 1991; Gowler 1993). In these contexts, Lukan discourse regularly presents itself as Jewish contraculture rhetoric. This rhetoric claims to represent Jewish tradition authentically by inverting certain behaviors in dominant Jewish culture. From the perspective of dominant Jewish culture rhetoric as Lukan discourse presents it, Christian discourse is a 'dishonorable' tradition. But Lukan discourse also presents sources of power within Jewish tradition investing this 'dishonorable' tradition with honor. In other words, Lukan discourse claims that

Christianity does not reject the central values of Jewish tradition; it simply inverts objectional dominant Jewish culture thought and behavior. The Gospel of Luke, then, embeds Mary's rhetoric in a narrative context that inverts hierarchies within its own presentation of dominant Jewish culture rhetoric, and Mary herself embodies an inversion of 'dishonored' and 'honored' traditions in dominant Jewish tradition. She asserts that God authorizes the honoring of her dishonor, and in other parts of the narrative God authorizes the honor of Jesus, Stephen and Paul, who also represent 'dishonorable' traditions within dominant Jewish culture rhetoric as Lukan discourse presents it.

But now let us pursue the relation of Mary's rhetoric to Roman culture. When the angel speaks to Mary, the language is Greek and Mary responds in Greek. Even the greeting of the angel is Greek, *chaire* (1.28), rather than Hebrew, *shalôm*. Mary's rhetoric, then, uses the *lingua franca* of the dominant culture and is emboldened by it. Moreover, when Mary praises God, she uses high level Jewish hymnic verse that incorporates a form of reasoning and confirmation of its reasoning that reaches upward toward a subcultural form of Hellenistic-Roman argumentation. Mary's rhetoric reaches up in social status, like the narratorial voice reaches up toward Theophilus in the preface (Lk. 1.1-4; Robbins 1979; 1991a: 321-23). The hierarchical structure of the social order seems not to be in contention, but only the benevolence of those who hold positions of power in that structure. This rhetoric, then, seems not to reject 'explicit and mutable characteristics' of Roman culture, which claims peace, salvation and benevolence as central values. Rather, Mary's rhetoric has a subcultural relation to Roman culture— her discourse claims that God fulfils central values of Roman culture better than the kingdom of the emperor does. In the end, the discourse of Luke and Acts perpetuates a contracultural Jewish rhetoric as an ethnic subcultural form of Roman culture. How close is Mary's speech to dishonored virgins who bore the heroes, gods and goddesses of Mediterranean culture? Only future investigation, analysis and interpretation can tell us. New Testament interpreters have not yet confronted the issue and explored it.

Returning to the social response in the discourse, then, the issue is whether the discourse perceives evil to be present in the people or in the structures that run society. Mary's rhetoric evokes an image of changing the people in power: God will remove those who now have power and put the lowly in those positions. Mary does not assert that the structures of power themselves should be changed but only the people who have the power. Nor does Mary claim that God will destroy the people who have the power—God will depose and scatter them. This means that her discourse probably is not appropriately described as revolutionist, which would imply destruction of both the structures of the social order and the powerful people who run it. Nor does the discourse appear to be utopian, where an entirely new social system will replace the present one. Rather, Mary's discourse is reformist, with an emphasis on changing the people in power. When Lukan discourse embeds this reformist vision in thaumaturgical, conversionist discourse, the vision is significant reform indeed. As God's thaumaturgic powers raise the lowly to positions of power, the vision is that God's conversionist powers change the hearts of the honored ones to goals of benevolence and mercy. The changes in the social order, then, will occur as leaders use power structures to 'show mercy' and to 'fill the hungry with good things'. Mary's discourse, then, shows no desire that hierarchical power structures be taken away. She simply has her own view of how those who hold the positions of power should embody the thaumaturgical and conversionist powers of God.

### Ideological Texture: Every Theology Has a Politics

Exploration of the ideological texture of a text focuses on self-interests. What and whose self-interests are being negotiated in this text? If the dominant voices in the text persuade people to act according to their premises, who will gain and who will lose? What will be gained and what will be lost (Elliott 1993: 119-21; Eagleton 1991; McGowan 1991)?

These questions move into the realm of ideology, point of view and theology. And here the motto is that every theology has a politics. Ideology is 'an integrated system of beliefs, assumptions and values, not necessarily true or false, which reflects the needs and interests of a group or class at a particular time in history' (Davis 1975: 14). This integrated system proceeds from the need to understand, to interpret to self and others, to justify, and to control one's place in the world. Ideologies are shaped by specific views of reality shared by groups—specific perspectives on the world, society and people, and on the limitations and potentialities of human existence. Inasmuch as all religious groupings and movements have specific collective needs, interests and objectives that they seek to relate to ultimate sacred norms and principles—in Christianity, to the will and action of God as revealed in Jesus Christ—all religious movements, including early Christianity, develop ideological positions and perspectives (Elliott 1981: 268; Elliott 1993: 51-53; Schüssler Fiorenza 1983; Schüssler Fiorenza 1985; Schüssler Fiorenza 1992).

Who, we must ask, is benefitting by having Mary speak as she does in the Magnificat? Who is benefitting by having Mary speak out about raising the lowly up to power and driving the powerful away empty-handed? Whose ideology is being advanced, for whose benefit, by Mary's dialogue with the angel and Elizabeth and by the argumentation in the Magnificat? Let us approach the issue from three angles: (a) the voices of the narrator and the angel, (b) the dialogue between Mary and Elizabeth and (c) the monologue by Mary to God.

The narratorial voice throughout Luke and Acts presents a case for Christianity as a healing, peace-loving group of people who encounter conflict when Jewish leaders attempt to run them out, imprison or kill them. This narratorial voice presents a case for certain Christian leaders throughout the Mediterranean world from Ethiopia throughout Syria-Palestine, Asia Minor, Macedonia, Greece and Rome. The rhetoric of Luke and Acts offers a certain group of Christian leaders the benefit of a bi-cultural founder and leader. Simultaneously, Jesus functions both as a messiah, who launches high level contraculture rhetoric against established Jewish leaders, and as a Hellenistic-Roman benefactor-savior who engages in high artisan, low elite subculture rhetoric that challenges all leaders. Social identity is at stake for Christians. From a social perspective, Christians look to an outsider like subversive troublemakers. The narratorial voice, with the voices of characters embedded in it, argues the case that all the troubles Christians have arise with Jewish leaders who are proud, greedy and lovers of money. Jesus and his followers, in contrast, enact humility and benevolence.

Social and political benefits are at stake in Luke and Acts, and wherever its narratorial rhetoric is successful Christians will attain positive social identity and will receive accompanying political benefits. Material benefits also are at stake. Of key importance are the resources in cities throughout the Mediterranean world, the location of storing and distributing of grain supplies and the like (Robbins 1991a). If Christians can be Roman citizens, as the converted Pharisee Paul is, then Christians have the right to receive a portion of the grain dole and other services of the cities. Individual benefits also are at stake. Christian leaders, both individually and in pairs, receive the right to travel freely throughout the empire, entering regions, villages and cities at will.

This is the overall context in which the voice of the narrator and the voice of the angel function in Luke 1. According to the narratorial voice, the God of the Jews, whom the angel calls 'Most High' and 'Lord God', initiates Mary's pregnancy through the agency of the power of God and the 'Holy Spirit' (1.32, 35). When it is made clear to Mary that this pregnancy outside of marriage will bring her honor through her prestigious son, she accepts the action in the obedient mode of a client responding to a powerful patron. Mary cannot refuse God's offer; she accepts the role of an obedient servant/client and expresses gratitude that she will be held in honor by all people. The rhetorical effect is to claim that Christians are specially favored with the benefits of the patron God of the Jews. This God works contraculturally within Jewish tradition, at times creating human situations that are traditionally dishonorable in order to bring honor to certain dishonored people. God's activity presupposes and advances hierarchical structures within a patriarchical ideology, yet it inverts certain dishonored conditions within the context of those structures. In Luke 1, God advances the ideology of patrilineal honor in the form of prestigious sons who have political power (1.32-33) and holy status (1.35). But God also offers an inversion of weak and powerful, hungry and well-fed (1.51-53). Patrilineal hierarchy remains in place, but there is reform within it.

This ideology among first-century Christians proved to be highly successful. On the one hand, this kind of rhetoric presents a willingness to accept the patronage system within Hellenistic-Roman culture and work within it. Luke and Acts, therefore, share much of the ideology of a document like Plutarch's *Alexander*, which challenges patrons to be generous. Yet, Luke and Acts are reformist within that system. They activate reformist practices by means of contraculture rhetoric against Jewish leaders. In other words, through aggressive criticism of Jewish leaders, Lukan discourse calls for reform within the established political system of patronage and the centralized economic system of distribution (Rohrbaugh 1984; Rohrbaugh 1987; Rohrbaugh 1991; Moxnes 1988; Esler 1987; Braun 1993). This Christian discourse, then, calls for selected reform at the expense of established Jewish leaders. The people who will benefit present themselves as leaders of an ethnic subculture that fulfils the highest claims of dominant Roman government, namely salvation (*sōtēria*) and peace.

The dialogue between Mary and Elizabeth features the mothers of the founders of the Christian movement supporting one another in a manner that overturns the usual competition that accompanies the births of specially endowed sons who are potential rivals over power and leadership. The 'honorable' tradition of barren women characteristically contains rivalry between kinswomen. The dialogue between Mary and Elizabeth engages this rivalry and reconfigures it. When Elizabeth became pregnant, she said the Lord had looked upon her to take away her reproach 'among men' (Lk. 1.25). She tells Mary, in contrast, that she, Mary, is blessed 'among women' (Lk. 1.42). Mary rephrases Elizabeth's statement to claim: 'all generations will call me blessed' (Lk. 1.48b).

The exchange between Mary and Elizabeth reverberates with Israelite traditions of rivalry among women in a context where they are trying to win the special place of favor from their husbands. Leah speaks of 'being called blessed' in a context of desperation after she has been unsuccessful in getting her husband Jacob to love her. Leah had hoped that her bearing of Reuben for Jacob would cause him to love her (Gen. 29.32). But this did not happen. Leah's rivalry with Rachel over Jacob's love continued as Rachel gave her maidservant Bilhah to Jacob and she had two sons, Dan and Naphtali (Gen. 20.3-8). Leah in turn gave her maidservant Zilpah to Jacob, and she bore Jacob two sons, Gad and Asher (Gen. 30.9-13). The name Asher means 'happy, blessed'. Leah called him Asher, because, as she said, 'the women will call me *asher*' (in Greek, *makaria*, Gen. 30.13). With this statement Leah gave up on removing the reproach from 'her man'. Instead, she looked to women, who would look at her and 'call her *makaria* happy, blessed'. Mary's rationale for her joy in the Magnificat captures the dynamics of this tradition and reconfigures them. When she asserts that 'all generations will call me blessed' (Lk. 1.48b), she is embodying the rivalries of the past and the hopes for the future. If men and women can honor each other as God takes away their reproach and manifests powers of mercy and benevolence, then both the people and the social order may receive God's promises from the past.

What does this mean for interpretation in this paper? It means, on the one hand, that Mary's assertion holds the potential for evoking a sense of rivalry between herself and Elizabeth. Rivalry between 'knowing only the baptism of John' and 'knowing the way of God' as taught by Jesus is well-known in the Lukan narrative (Acts 18.24-26), and readers could expect rivalry between the mothers of John and Jesus. The narrator implies, on the other hand, that there is no rivalry; in the context of the narration, Mary appears to be trying to overcome a division between receiving honor among men and among women. The narrator may also be trying to overcome this division by featuring Simeon's blessing of both Mary and Joseph (Lk. 2.34) followed by Anna's thanks to God and interpretation of the redemption Jesus brings to Jerusalem (Lk. 2.38).

The overall rhetoric of the interchange between Mary and Elizabeth, then, suggests an attempt to remove rivalry between the mothers of the specially honored sons who stand at the beginning of the story of Christianity. In contrast to the rivalry between Sarah and Hagar, Rachel and Leah, Hannah and Penninah, Mary takes her body to Elizabeth, and together they celebrate and honor their pregnant bodies. The rhetoric of Lukan discourse is to claim that Christians perpetuate a culture of the body, impregnated by the Holy Spirit, that overcomes rivalry, division and hatred. Christians confront other people with their bodies for the purpose of overcoming hatred, healing illness, enacting forgiveness and calling for generosity without expectation of return.

Mary's monologue to God in the presence of Elizabeth offers additional social and individual benefits to Christian women. When Elizabeth says that 'all women' will call Mary blessed and Mary asserts that she herself will be called blessed by 'all generations', there is a special claim of honor for women both among Christian men and among Christian women. This is ambiguous honor, to be sure, since the primary base of it is honor from men. Mary's hymnlike speech emulates the tongue of David, which, of course, befits a woman betrothed to a man 'of the House of David'. Her body is forced to perpetuate dominant Jewish tradition in a dishonorable manner that is declared honorable by a God who maintains patrilineal tradition. Mary upholds the male line of tradition, and through her appropriate consent and expression of gratitude she receives honor. In other words, Mary receives honor in the great tradition in which men protect the reputation of 'their women'.

But does Mary's voice say something more? Does anyone hear, or notice, her initial cry that she will become pregnant without a man? She has no real choice in the matter. From the perspective of patriarchal tradition, this is God's doing and Mary is fortunate, blessed, the mother of the messiah. What about Mary's perspective? She says she has been afflicted, dishonored. Why? Not because she is barren and wants a child, but because she is with child outside a marriage contract. If someone, benevolent or otherwise, decides she is to have a son, is that to be her station in life?

We need an ethnography of virgins in Mediterranean culture in order to explore the further nuances of Mary's speech to God. So far we do not have a comprehensive study of virgins in Mediterranean society and their speech to gods. What would the implications be for a virgin to speak like Mary speaks? Through the help of Mieke Bal, we are coming closer to an understanding of virgins in Israelite tradition (1988b: 41-93). In her study, Bal distinguishes between *na'arah* (young girl), *'almah* (mostly already married woman before her first pregnancy), and *bethulah* (a woman confronted with the passage from young girl to almost married woman). What does it mean for a woman who is going through this transitional phase of insecurity and danger in a patriarchal society to speak of being humiliated, of having God show regard for her humiliation, and of having a conviction that from now on all generations will call her blessed? New Testament interpreters have yet to gather the data and programmatically address this issue.

Male interpreters regularly celebrate Mary's speech as liberating for her and for all who are poor in social, political or economic status. Victor Turner, however, shows that rituals of announcement and enactment of reversal by those of lower status support and reaffirm the hierarchical system that is in place. People of higher status, if they are wise, permit, indeed encourage, those of lower status to speak out and enact their frustrations in a context of reversal. The key is to establish boundaries, either spatially or temporally, for these announcements and enactments. In other words, those in power establish a clear definition of these people as a subculture or counterculture with an important but limited function in society *or* they designate a period of time during the year when the lower classes celebrate a reversal whereby they experience power and humiliate those of higher status.

The enactment of reversal, either within a subculture or within a designated time period, strengthens the ideology of hierarchy, the necessity of having powerful people over weak people. The weak have their momentary experience of being powerful or they have their limited social domain in which to perform their powerful acts. Either strategy allows and encourages the weak to turn their energy toward the work of service, and perhaps reconciliation, which is welcomed by the established hierarchy.

## Conclusion

Socio-rhetorical criticism suggests that we need to look carefully outside many of the boundaries within which we customarily interpret the Magnificat. I am aware that I, like others, speak from within a bounded context. My approach to this text is socially located, as is anyone else's approach. I consider it important, however, to establish clear boundaries for the purpose of programmatic analysis. But then I consider it essential to subject those boundaries to analysis and criticism and to look through and beyond those boundaries for additional insight, even if those insights explode and reconfigure insights I had within that other context of analysis and interpretation. This, for me, is the nature of language, whether it is oral or written. Since different sets of boundaries establish different contexts for meanings, language signifies complexly interwoven textures of signification that appear only when analysis explores language from the perspective of multiple contexts. Socio-rhetorical criticism invites the interpreter to establish more than one set of boundaries for interpretation because multiple interpretations will bring into sight, sound and feeling aspects of oral and written discourse that otherwise will remain hidden.

Mikhail Bakhtin observed that speech is a social possession, and for this reason much, in fact most, of our speech comes from other people. He speaks, then, of many voices in our speech, *heteroglossia*. Exploration of Lk. 1.26-56 from the perspective of multiple contexts reveals that 'each word (text) is an intersection of words (texts) where at least one other word (text) can be read' (Kristeva 1986: 37). 'Intertextuality' is the current term for this observation that 'any text is constructed as a mosaic of quotations; any text is the absorption and transformation of another' (Kristeva 1986: 37; Kristeva 1974; Bakhtin 1981; Draisma 1989; Robbins 1992c). Intertextuality is not, therefore, limited to explicit presentation of other texts as second or third level narration (as Acts 2.26). Speaking, writing and reading are social acts. This means that social meanings surround the words at all times. A speaker, writer and reader play with boundaries they themselves establish and transgress for their own purposes. The interplay between boundaries and transgressions of boundaries, then, is the very nature of communication. If one person tries to keep someone's voice out, another is likely to let it in.

When Mary refers to her 'humiliation', she uses a word that can connote a wide range of meanings, and the question is what range of meanings any reader entertains for the signs in the text. At this point, the text is extremely vulnerable; an interpreter must remember that every sign should be viewed 'as an active component of speech, or text, or sign, modified and transformed in meaning by variable social tones, valuations, and connotations it condenses within itself in specific social conditions' (Wuellner 1989: 43). Since the community that uses language is a heterogeneous society, Mary's 'humiliation' is 'a focus of struggle and contradiction. It is not simply a matter of asking "what [this] sign means"...but of investigating its varied history', since 'conflicting groups, classes, individuals, and discourses' contend with each other for its meaning (Wuellner 1989: 43).

John York (1991) has analyzed the manner in which Jesus picks up and embellishes the language of reversal Mary introduces in the Magnificat. This means that Mary does not have the last word in Luke. Her male son, Jesus, picks up and reconfigures Mary's language in the beatitudes, parables and sayings. When, in Lk. 11.27-28, a woman in the crowd tries to restore the importance of Mary by saying to Jesus, 'Blessed is the womb that bore you, and the breasts that you sucked!', Jesus replies, 'Blessed rather are those who hear the word of God and keep it!' Mary does not have the last word with the language she uses in the Magnificat. In Lukan discourse, her male son takes over her language and determines much of her future by his use of it. Who is the narrator who speaks in this way, and what is the narratorial voice trying to achieve by this refiguring of Mary's language in the narrative? The reader is asked to believe that Mary speaks in the Gospel of Luke, but does she? She tries to speak, and it may be possible to recover a voice that has been trying desperately to speak but cannot because it is continually drowned out by men's voices, my own included. In Lukan discourse, Mary seeks solace from another woman, going to Elizabeth who is an honored, no longer barren, woman. In this context, she finally directs her speech to God. As she argues her case, she expresses her gratitude to God for declaring her pregnancy outside of marriage to be honorable and continues with an embellishment that appeals to the God who reforms traditions of patronage so that particular forms of dishonor are removed within them. In this manner, Mary becomes the mother of a Christian discourse that envisions the possibility of winning its way in the Roman Empire through aggressive speech against established Jewish leaders that contains implications for reform within actual practices of patrons, patronesses, leaders and members of all ranks within Christianity—be they Jewish, Roman, Phrygian or Lycaonian.

## BIBLIOGRAPHY

Altenbaumer, James E.
1992        'The Salvation Myth in the Hymns in Revelation' (PhD dissertation, Emory University).

Bakhtin, M.M.
1981        *The Dialogic Imagination* (ed. M. Holquist; trans. C. Emerson and M. Holquist; Austin: University of Texas Press).

Bal, Mieke
1988a       *Murder and Difference: Gender, Genre, and Scholarship on Sisera's Death* (Bloomington & Indianapolis: Indiana University Press).
1988b       *Death and Dissymmetry: The Politics of Coherence in the Book of Judges* (Chicago: University of Chicago Press).

Betz, Hans Dieter
1972        *Der Apostel Paulus und die sokratische Tradition: Eine exegetische Untersuchung zu seiner 'Apologie' 2 Kor 10–13* (BHT, 45; Tübingen: Mohr–Siebeck).
1975        'The Literary Composition and Function of Paul's Letter to the Galatians', *NTS* 21: 353-79.
1979        *Galatians: A Commentary on Paul's Letter to the Churches in Galatia* (Hermeneia; Philadelphia: Fortress Press).
1985a       *2 Corinthians 8 and 9* (Hermeneia; Philadelphia: Fortress Press).
1985b       *Essays on the Sermon on the Mount* (trans. L.L. Welborn; Philadelphia: Fortress Press).
1986        'The Problem of Rhetoric and Theology according to the Apostle Paul', in A. Vanhoye (ed.), *L'Apôtre Paul* (BETL, 73; Leuven: Leuven University Press): 16-48.

Bhaba, Homi K.
1992        'Postcolonial Criticism', in S. Greenblatt and G. Gunn (eds.), *Redrawing the Boundaries: The Transformation of English and American Literary Studies* (New York: Modern Language Association of America).

Bouvard, Margarite
1975        *The Intentional Community Movement: Building a New Moral World* (Port Washington, NY: Kennikat Press).

Braun, Willi
1993        'The Use of Mediterranean Banquet Traditions in Luke 14.1-24' (PhD dissertation, University of Toronto).

Brenner, Athalya and Fokkelien Van Dijk-Hemmes
1993        *On Gendering Texts: Male and Female Voices in the Hebrew Bible* (Biblical Interpretation Series, 1; Leiden: Brill).

Brown, Peter
1970        'Sorcery, Demons and the Rise of Christianity from Late Antiquity

into the Middle Ages', in M. Douglas (ed.), *Witchcraft Accusations and Confessions* (London: Tavistock Publications): 17-45.

Brown, Raymond E.
1977        *The Birth of the Messiah: A Commentary on the Infancy Narratives in Matthew and Luke* (Garden City, NY: Doubleday).

Burke, Kenneth
1931        *Counter-Statement* (Berkeley: University of California Press).

Davis, David Brian
1975        *The Problem of Slavery in the Age of Revolution 1770–1823* (Ithaca, NY: Cornell University Press).

Draisma, S. (ed.)
1989        *Intertextuality in Biblical Writings Essays in Honour of Bas van Iersel* (Kampen: Kok Press).

Eagleton, T.
1983        *Literary Theory: An Introduction* (Minneapolis: University of Minnesota Press).
1991        *Ideology: An Introduction* (New York: Verso).

Ellens, G.F.S.
1971        'The Ranting Ranters: Reflections on a Ranting Counter-Culture', *CH* 40: 91-107.

Elliott, John H. (ed.)
1986        *Social-Scientific Criticism of the New Testament and its Social World* (*Semeia* 35).

Elliott, John H.
1981        *A Home for the Homeless: A Sociological Exegesis of 1 Peter, its Situation and Strategy* (Philadelphia: Fortress Press). Reprinted in a paperback edition with new introduction and subtitle changed to *A Social Scientific Criticism of 1 Peter, its Situation and Strategy* (Minneapolis: Fortress Press, 1990).
1993        *Social Scientific Criticism and the New Testament* (Minneapolis: Fortress Press).
Forthcoming  'Phases in the Social Formation of Early Christianity: From Faction to Sect. A Social-Scientific Perspective', in *Recruitment, Conquest, and Conflict in Judaism, Christianity, and the Greco-Roman World* (Emory Studies in Early Christianity, 6; Atlanta: Scholars Press).

Esler, Philip Francis
1987        *Community and Gospel in Luke–Acts: The Social and Political Motivations of Lucan Theology* (SNTSMS, 57; Cambridge: University of Cambridge Press).

Fitzmyer, Joseph A.
1981        *The Gospel according to Luke* (AB, 28; Garden City, NY: Doubleday).

Fowler, Roger
1986        *Linguistic Criticism* (Oxford: Oxford University Press).

Gager, John G.
1975        *Kingdom and Community: The Social World of Early Christianity* (Englewood Cliffs, NJ: Prentice–Hall).
1982        'Shall we Marry our Enemies? Sociology and the New Testament', *Int* 36: 256-65.

Gaster, Theodor H.
  1950        *Thespis: Ritual, Myth and Drama in the Ancient Near East* (New York:
              Schuman).
Geertz, Clifford
  1973        *The Interpretation of Cultures* (New York: Basic Books).
  1983        *Local Knowledge: Further Essays in Interpretive Anthropology* (New
              York: Basic Books).
Gordon, Milton M.
  1970        'The Subsociety and the Subculture', in D. Arnold (ed.), *Subcultures*
              (Berkeley: Glendessary Press): 150-63.
Gowler, David B.
  1989        'Characterization in Luke: A Socio-Narratological Approach', *BTB*
              19: 54-62.
  1991        *Host, Guest, Enemy, and Friend: Portraits of the Pharisees in Luke and
              Acts* (Emory Studies in Early Christianity, 1; New York: Peter Lang).
  1993        'Hospitality and Characterization in Luke 11.37-54: A Socio-
              Narratological Approach', *Semeia* 64: 213-51.
Hays, Richard B.
  1989        *Echoes of Scripture in the Letters of Paul* (New Haven: Yale University
              Press).
Hollander, John
  1981        *The Figure of Echo: A Mode of Allusion in Milton and After*
              (Berkeley: University of California Press).
Huie-Jolly, Mary R.
  1994        'The Son Enthroned in Conflict: A Socio-Rhetorical Analysis of John
              5.17-23' (PhD dissertation, University of Otago, New Zealand).
Kennedy, George A.
  1984        *New Testament Interpretation through Rhetorical Criticism* (Chapel
              Hill: University of North Carolina Press).
  1991        *Aristotle on Rhetoric: A Theory of Civic Discourse* (New York: Oxford
              University Press).
Kloppenborg, John S.
  1989        'The Dishonoured Master (Luke 16.1-8a)', *Bib* 70: 474-95.
  1990        'Alms, Debt and Divorce: Jesus' Ethics in their Mediterranean
              Context', *Toronto Journal of Theology* 6/2: 182-200.
  1991        'Literary Convention, Self-Evidence and the Social History of the Q
              People', *Semeia* 55: 77-102.
  1993        'The Sayings Gospel Q: Recent Opinion on the People behind the
              Document', *Currents in Research: Biblical Studies* 1: 9-34.
Kristeva, Julia
  1974        *La Révolution du langage poétique* (Paris: Seuil).
  1986        *The Kristeva Reader* (ed. T. Moi; New York: Columbia University
              Press).
Lentricchia, Frank and Thomas McLaughlin (eds.)
  1990        *Critical Terms for Literary Study* (Chicago: University of Chicago
              Press).

Mack, Burton L.
1988    *A Myth of Innocence: Mark and Christian Origins* (Philadelphia: Fortress Press).
1990    *Rhetoric and the New Testament* (Minneapolis: Fortress Press).
1993    *The Lost Gospel: The Book of Q and Christian Origins* (San Francisco: Harper).
Mack, Burton L. and Vernon K. Robbins
1989    *Patterns of Persuasion in the Gospels* (Sonoma, CA: Polebridge Press).
Malina, Bruce J.
1981    *The New Testament World: Insights from Cultural Anthropology* (Atlanta: John Knox Press, rev. edn, 1993).
Martin, Clarice J.
1989    'A Chamberlain's Journey and the Challenge of Interpretation for Liberation', *Semeia* 47: 105-35; repr. in N.K. Gottwald and R.A. Horsley (eds.), *The Bible and Liberation: Political and Social Hermeneutics* (rev. edn; Maryknoll, NY: Orbis Books, 1993).
McGowan, John
1991    *Postmodernism and its Critics* (Ithaca, NY: Cornell University Press).
Malina, Bruce J. and Richard L. Rohrbaugh
1992    *Social-Science Commentary on the Synoptic Gospels* (Minneapolis: Fortress Press).
Meeks, Wayne A.
1972    'The Man from Heaven in Johannine Sectarianism', *JBL* 91: 44-72.
1983    *The First Urban Christians: The Social World of the Apostle Paul* (New Haven: Yale University Press).
1986a   *The Moral World of the First Christians* (Philadelphia: Westminster Press).
1986b   'A Hermeneutic of Social Embodiment', *HTR* 79: 176-86.
1993    *The Origins of Christian Morality: The First Two Centuries* (New Haven: Yale University Press).
Moxnes, Halvor
1988    *The Economy of the Kingdom: Social Conflict and Economic Relations in Luke's Gospel* (Philadelphia: Fortress Press).
Myers, William H.
1991    'The Hermeneutical Dilemma of the African American Biblical Student', in Cain Hope Felder (ed.), *Stony the Road we Trod: African American Biblical Interpretation* (Minneapolis: Fortress Press): 40-56.
Neyrey, Jerome H. (ed.)
1991    *The Social World of Luke–Acts: Models for Interpretation* (Peabody, MA: Hendrickson Publishers).
Peacock, James L.
1986    *The Anthropological Lens: Harsh Light, Soft Focus* (Cambridge: Cambridge University Press).
Perelman, Chaim
1982    *The Realm of Rhetoric* (Notre Dame: University of Notre Dame Press).
Perelman, Chaim and L. Olbrechts-Tyteca
1969    *The New Rhetoric: A Treatise on Argumentation* (Notre Dame: University of Notre Dame Press).

Petersen, Norman R.

1985    *Rediscovering Paul: Philemon and the Sociology of Paul's Narrative World* (Philadelphia: Fortress Press).

1993    *The Gospel of John and the Sociology of Light: Language and Characterization in the Fourth Gospel* (Valley Forge, PA: Trinity Press International).

Powell, Mark Allen

1990    *What is Narrative Criticism?* (Minneapolis: Fortress Press).

Robbins, Vernon K.

1979    'Prefaces in Greco-Roman Biography and Luke–Acts', *Perspectives in Religious Studies* 6: 94-108.

1984    *Jesus the Teacher: A Socio-Rhetorical Interpretation of Mark* (Philadelphia: Fortress Press). Reprint with new introduction and additional indexes (Minneapolis: Fortress Press, 1992).

1987    'The Woman who Touched Jesus' Garment: Socio-Rhetorical Analysis of the Synoptic Accounts', *NTS* 33: 502-15.

1991a    'The Social Location of the Implied Author of Luke–Acts', in Neyrey 1991: 305-32.

1991b    'Luke–Acts: A Mixed Population Seeks a Home in the Roman Empire', in L. Alexander (ed.), *Images of Empire* (JSOTSup, 122; Sheffield: JSOT Press): 202-21.

1992a    'Introduction to the Paperback Edition', in reprint of Robbins 1984: xix-xliv.

1992b    'Using a Socio-Rhetorical Poetics to Develop a Unified Method: The Woman who Anointed Jesus as a Test Case', in Eugene H. Lovering, Jr (ed.), *SBLSP* (Atlanta: Scholars Press): 302-19.

1992c    'The Reversed Contextualization of Psalm 22 in the Markan Crucifixion: A Socio-Rhetorical Analysis', in F. Van Segbroeck *et al.* (eds.), *The Four Gospels* (BETL, 100/2; Leuven: Leuven University Press): 1161-83.

1992d    'A Male Reads a Feminist Reading: The Dialogical Nature of Pippin's Power—A Response to Tina Pippin, "Eros and the End"', *Semeia* 59: 211-17.

1992e    'A Socio-Rhetorical Look at the Work of John Knox on Luke–Acts', in M.C. Parsons and J.B. Tyson (eds.), *Cadbury, Knox, and Talbert: American Contributions to the Study of Acts* (Atlanta: Scholars Press): 91-105.

1993a    'Progymnastic Rhetorical Composition and Pre-Gospel Traditions: A New Approach', in Camille Focant (ed.), *The Synoptic Gospels: Source Criticism and the New Literary Criticism* (BETL, 110; Leuven: Leuven University Press): 111-49.

1993b    'Rhetoric and Culture: Exploring Types of Cultural Rhetoric in a Text', in Stanley E. Porter and Thomas H. Olbricht (eds.), *Rhetoric and the New Testament: Essays from the 1992 Heidelberg Conference* (Sheffield: JSOT Press): 443-63.

Roberts, Keith A.

1976    *Religion and the Counter-Culture Phenomenon: Sociological and*

*Religious Elements in the Formation of an Intentional Counter-Culture Community* (Ann Arbor: University Microfilms).

1978 'Toward a Generic Concept of Counter-Culture', *Sociological Focus* 11: 111-26.

Robinson, James M. and Helmut Koester

1971 *Trajectories through Early Christianity* (Philadelphia: Fortress Press).

Rohrbaugh, Richard

1984 'Methodological Considerations in the Debate over the Social Class Status of Early Christians', *JAAR* 52: 519-46.

1987 ' "Social Location of Thought" as a Heuristic Construct in New Testament Study', *JSNT* 30: 103-19.

1991 'The Pre-Industrial City in Luke–Acts: Urban Social Relations', in Neyrey 1991: 125-49.

Rose, Lucy A.

1989 'A Rhetorical Analysis of the Magnificat' (PhD Seminar Paper, Emory University).

Schaberg, Jane

1987 *The Illegitimacy of Jesus: A Feminist Theological Interpretation of the Infancy Narratives* (New York: Crossroad).

1992 'Luke', in Carol A. Newsom and Sharon H. Ringe (eds.), *The Women's Bible Commentary* (Louisville, KY: Westminster/John Knox Press).

Schüssler Fiorenza, Elisabeth

1983 *In Memory of Her: A Feminist Theological Reconstruction of Christian Origins* (New York: Crossroad Press).

1985 *Bread Not Stone: The Challenge of Feminist Biblical Interpretation* (Boston: Beacon Press).

1987 'Rhetorical Situation and Historical Reconstruction in I Corinthians', *NTS* 33: 386-403.

1988 'The Ethics of Interpretation: De-Centering Biblical Scholarship', *JBL* 107: 3-17.

1992 *But She Said: Feminist Practices of Biblical Interpretation* (Boston: Beacon Press).

Scott, Bernard Brandon

1989 *Hear Then the Parable: A Commentary on the Parables of Jesus* (Minneapolis: Fortress Press).

Sisson, Russell B.

1994 'The Apostle as Athlete: A Socio-Rhetorical Interpretation of 1 Corinthians 9' (PhD dissertation, Emory University).

Smith, Jonathan Z.

1975 'The Social Description of Early Christianity', *RSR* 1: 19-25.

1978 *Map is not Territory: Studies in the History of Religions* (Leiden: Brill).

1982 *Imagining Religion: From Babylon to Jonestown* (Chicago: University of Chicago Press).

1987 *To Take Place: Toward Theory in Ritual* (Chicago: University of Chicago Press).

1990 *Drudgery Divine: On the Comparison of Early Christianities and the Religions of Late Antiquity* (Chicago: University of Chicago Press).

Stark, Werner
    1967        *Sectarian Religion* (New York: Fordham University Press).
    1986        'The Class Basis of Early Christianity: Inferences from a Sociological
                Model', *Sociological Analysis* 47: 216-25.
Tannehill, Robert C.
    1974        'The Magnificat as Poem', *JBL* 93: 263-75.
    1975        *The Sword of His Mouth* (Philadelphia: Fortress Press and Missoula,
                MT: Scholars Press).
    1986–89     *The Narrative Unity of Luke-Acts: A Literary Interpretation* (2 vols.;
                Philadelphia: Fortress Press).
Tolbert, Mary Ann
    1989        *Sowing the Gospel: Mark's World in Literary-Historical Perspective*
                (Minneapolis: Fortress Press).
Troost, Arie
    1992        'Using the Word in Luke 1–2' (Short Paper, Colloquium Biblicum
                Lovaniense).
    1993        'Reading for the Author's Signature: Genesis 21.1-21 and Luke
                15.11-32 as Intertexts', in Athalya Brenner (ed.), *A Feminist
                Companion to Genesis* (The Feminist Companion to the Bible, 2;
                Sheffield: Sheffield Academic Press): 251-72.
Vickers, Brian
    1982        'Introduction', in B. Vickers (ed.), *Rhetoric Revalued* (Medieval &
                Renaissance Texts and Studies, 19; Binghamton, NY: Center for
                Medieval & Renaissance Studies): 13-39.
    1988        *In Defence of Rhetoric* (Oxford: Clarendon Press).
Wachob, Wesley
    1993        'The Rich in Faith and the Poor in Spirit: The Socio-Rhetorical
                Function of a Saying of Jesus in the Epistle of James' (PhD
                dissertation, Emory University).
Webber, Randall C.
    1992        '"Why were the Heathen so Arrogant?" The Socio-Rhetorical
                Strategy of Acts 3–4', *BTB* 22: 19-25.
Wilde, James A.
    1974        *A Social Description of the Community Reflected in the Gospel of
                Mark* (Ann Arbor: University Microfilms).
    1978        'The Social World of Mark's Gospel: A Word about Method', *SBLSP*
                2: 47-67.
Wilder, Amos N.
    1956        'Scholars, Theologians, and Ancient Rhetoric', *JBL* 75: 1-11.
Wilson, Brian
    1969        'A Typology of Sects', in R. Robertson (ed.), *Sociology of Religion*
                (Baltimore: Penguin Books): 361-83.
    1973        *Magic and the Millenium: A Sociological Study of Religious
                Movements of Protest among Tribal and Third-World Peoples* (New
                York: Harper & Row).
Wuellner, Wilhelm H.
    1976a       'Paul's Rhetoric of Argumentation in Romans: An Alternative to the
                Donfried–Karris Debate over Romans', *CBQ* 38: 330-51; repr. in

K.P. Donfried (ed.), *The Romans Debate* (Minneapolis: Augsburg, 1977): 152-74.

1976b     'Methodological Considerations concerning the Rhetorical Genre of First Corinthians' (Seminar Paper, SBL Pacific Coast Regional, Paul).

1978     'Der Jakobusbrief im Licht der Rhetorik und Textpragmatik', *LB* 43: 5-66.

1979     'Greek Rhetoric and Pauline Argumentation', in W.R. Schoedel and R.L. Wilken (eds.), *Early Christian Literature and the Classical Intellectual Tradition* (FS R.M. Grant; Paris: Beauchesne): 177-88.

1986     'Paul as Pastor: The Function of Rhetorical Questions in First Corinthians', in A. Vanhoye (ed.), *L'Apôtre Paul: Personalité, Style et Conception du Ministère* (BETL, 73; Leuven: Leuven University Press): 49-77.

1987     'Where is Rhetorical Criticism Taking Us?' *CBQ* 49: 448-63.

1988     'The Rhetorical Structure of Luke 12 in its Wider Context', *Neot* 22: 283-310.

1989     'Is There an Encoded Reader Fallacy?', *Semeia* 48: 43-54.

1991     'Rhetorical Criticism and its Theory in Culture-Critical Perspective: The Narrative Rhetoric of John 11', in P.J. Martin and J.H. Petzer (eds.), *Text and Interpretation: New Approaches in the Criticism of the New Testament* (New Testament Tools and Studies, 15; Leiden: Brill): 171-85.

Yinger, J. Milton

1960     'Contraculture and Subculture', *American Sociological Review* 25: 625-35.

1982     *Countercultures: The Promise and the Peril of a World Turned Upside Down* (New York: Free Press).

York, John O.

1991     *The Last Shall be First: The Rhetoric of Reversal in Luke* (JSNTSup, 46; Sheffield: Sheffield Academic Press).

# 'SINCE GOD IS ONE': RHETORIC AS THEOLOGY AND HISTORY IN PAUL'S ROMANS

## Antoinette Clark Wire

Literature has for years held itself aloof from other studies in the humanities, seeking truth from the inexhaustible interplay of whole and parts within the text. History and theology have been noticeably ignored. Now literature emerges at the door, eager to play but fearful of losing its purity in the world's power struggles. Literary analysts make forays into cultural criticism, historians use popular literature to do microhistory, and theologians reach for novels as their sources. Yet the traditional boundaries between disciplines remain formidable and literature is still hesitant to see itself as shaper of a culture's past and contender in debates about ultimate reality. Perhaps rhetoric can hold out a hand to show the persuading text how it can be theology and history without losing its integrity as literature.

In a 1980 essay the literary critic Jane Tompkins observes that in classical times language was understood as a form of power to affect behavior, whereas today we have come to see language as signification. We interest ourselves in interpreting its meaning without relation to its social impact. In Tompkins's view even Renaissance poetry saw itself as a means toward social ends, and literature became a separate realm of aesthetic experience with its own standards of truth only when widespread printing severed the social relation of writer and audience. She argues that although reader-oriented approaches have recently undercut the claims to objectivity of both scientific and aesthetic truth statements, this has not challenged the assumption that the task of criticism is to determine meaning, and we still take the text as an object of study rather than a force exerted upon the world. Tompkins proposes that post-structuralists practice the study of language in its political character, taking as seriously their own talk of language being constitutive of reality as did the Greek rhetoricians who saw mastery of language as mastery of the state.

Some response to this kind of challenge has appeared in recent studies of the rhetoric of Paul's letters, especially 1 Corinthians (Betz 1986; Schüssler Fiorenza 1987; Wuellner 1989; Wire 1990; Castelli 1991). But Romans presents such difficulties in determining Paul's intended audience that little progress has been made in understanding its function as social power, in spite of many recent studies of its rhetoric (Wuellner 1974; Moxnes 1980; Siegert 1985; Elliott 1990). In this essay I frame the question somewhat differently, asking how the persuasive literary text of Paul's letter to Rome is also theology and history, at once message and event. Paul's Romans is a good test case for this question because its modern literary quarantine has not been tight, allowing some advances in its theological and historical research without reverting to naive assumptions that it is a history book or a book of doctrine. A text that argues from the nature of ultimate reality to persuade certain readers is bound to be an important theological and historical document. The question is what kind of theology and history such persuasion can be, and what its reading with these purposes in mind means for the text as literature. My thesis is that a reading of Romans that takes it as persuasion from start to finish allows it to be a very useful kind of theology and history in ways that do not compromise its literary character.

Theology will be taken here as human understanding of God, ideology in its ultimate sense. There are multiple ways one can pursue the theology of Romans as persuasion. Paul's theological appeals indicate the nature of the theological storehouse he is drawing upon (Dahl 1977; Moxnes 1980: 117-206; Bassler 1982: 7-119; Johnson 1989). His arguments about Christ or the church allow inferences concerning his understanding of God (Wire 1974). His approaches to the people he wants to persuade betray his audience's theological stance (Wire 1990). Here I will be asking strictly how theology functions in Paul's own attempt to persuade in this letter (as also Dahl 1977; Moxnes 1980; Bassler 1982; Dunn 1988; Johnson 1989; Elliott 1990), focusing on two central types of argument: argument by explanation and argument by repelling of blasphemy. This limited review of Paul's rhetoric as theology should give a sufficient basis for asking in turn whether theology developed as rhetoric can be taken seriously and what its uses are.

History will be interpreted as human study of the human past, which by its nature is self-study and self-formation, even when it appears to be focused on an alien world. Historians can take very different approaches to an argumentative text, all of which are legitimate as long as they take into account its effort to persuade. Such study may search for historical data in all the author's appeals; it may ask the historical implications of certain arguments; it may ask what can be known about the author and audience. My study here of two major arguments in Romans will consider what they reveal about Paul's relation to his audience and the persuasion he hopes to effect. Recognizing Paul's rhetoric as history will pose the question of the status and uses of history as rhetoric. The final question will be how theological and historical study of Paul's argument strengthens or weakens the integrity of Romans as literature.

### Rhetoric as Theology and History in Paul's Argument by Explanation

Most descriptions of Paul's argument in Romans identify his announcement that the gospel is God's righteousness revealed from faith to faith as the programmatic theme of the letter (1.16-17), a theme that is then developed in terms of God's wrath and God's righteousness (Wuellner 1974; Käsemann 1980). This view of the letter's structure ignores the fact that the supposed thematic statement about God's righteousness appears in the text as an explanation of an explanation of an explanation of Paul's eagerness to tell his gospel to the Romans. This is represented in the triple *gar* ('for') in 1.16a, 16b, 17a:

> I owe it to Greeks and barbarians, wise as well as dull, so I am eager to proclaim the good news also to you in Rome. For I am not ashamed of the good news, for it is God's power to save everyone who trusts, the Jew first and also the Greek. For God's justice is revealed in it from trust to trust, as it is written, 'The just will live by trust' (1.14-17).

Is the particle *gar* ('for') an insignificant connecting-word between these sentences, or does its repeated use show that the structure of Paul's argument has been improperly identified? In questions, answers and wishes *gar* may have the adverbial sense of 'in fact', 'indeed', but when appearing as the second word in declarative sentences it is a causal coordinating conjunction that offers a reason for or an explanation of a preceding statement.[1] Yet *gar* appears 143 times in Romans, more often

1.  See Smyth 1920: §§2803-11 and BDF, §452. For our purposes it is not crucial to distinguish the explanatory use that normally follows verbs of speaking and may account for 1.16a, 'for I am not ashamed of the gospel', from the causal uses that appear in 1.16b and 17, 'for it is God's power...for God's righteousness is revealed...' Causation is a more precise kind of explanation.

than in any other New Testament book (Morgenthaler 1958), and one might therefore surmise that its meaning is weak. But study of the syntax and usage proves otherwise. The 16 uses of the particle in ch. 8 appear in groups of sentences heavy with theological explanation following immediately after each of four affirmations about the believers' present experience: the experience of freedom from condemnation (v. 1), of life in the Spirit (v. 12), of suffering (v. 18) and of triumph (vv. 28, 37). Although Paul's subject is quite different in ch. 15, here similarly each of four instructions or claims about present conduct (15.1-2, 7, 17, 25) are followed by explanations that immediately—or in one case finally—explain what has already been said in terms of Christ. There is reason, therefore, to ask about the explanatory function of Paul's theology and to reconsider the structure of Paul's argument in the first chapter and in the letter as a whole.

When Paul initially presents his theological claim of God's justice revealed to trust as an explanation of his previous statement that he wants to tell them good news (1.16-17), he shows at the very least that he is writing a letter. Because a letter is personal persuasion, it subordinates all information provided—including theology—to the relation of speaker with hearers that the letter is cultivating. (I assume the ancient context in which letter writing and reading are specialists' tasks that carry a speaker's word to hearers.) So Paul begins Romans with the standard three-point salutation—A to B, greeting—and yet manages under the first cypher to explain himself as carrier of good news, which God first promised through prophets, then realized by appointing one of the Davidic line to be God's son by resurrection, and now spreads by making Paul Christ's slave and an apostle of this news to all Gentiles including those in Rome. This authorizes Paul to address them in the next part of his salutation: 'to all God's loved ones in Rome, called to be saints'—though the 'all' suggests a wider audience than the Gentiles just referred to. He concludes with a blessing from the Father God and Master Jesus.

In this way the single-sentence salutation (1.1-7) manages without any *gar* to become an argument by explanation, tracing this speaker back to a sequence of three divine acts of speaking through the prophets, instating Christ and sending Paul to the Gentiles, the last act now about to reach Rome through God's blessing in this letter. When Paul has assured them by divine oath of his prayers and his longing to come there to fulfill his Gentile mission, modestly praising their faith and speaking of mutual encouragement (1.8-14), he again asks for fruit among them because he owes this to every Gentile. His eagerness is explained by his not being ashamed, which is in turn explained by this news being God's power to save all who trust—Jew first and also Greek, which is itself finally explained by God's justice being revealed from the trust of some people to the trust of others (cf. 3.30)—and everything is confirmed from prophetic Scripture, 'The just will live from trust' (1.15-17). So Paul has traced his impetus for coming to Rome back to God's justice, which he then explicates at length.

From a rhetorical perspective one must say that the entire extended explanation of his gospel on the basis of God's justice (1.18–11.36) is a digression in the letter, from which he returns to instruct them at some length (12.1–15.13) before repeating his plans to come and adding greetings and blessings (15.14–16.23). A digression in argument always has its purpose, and the speaker expects to return to the main argument stronger for having taken the detour. The purpose of this digression has been shown to be explanation. Here Paul will provide the background that demonstrates the nature and validity of his confidence in this gospel to the Gentiles. This view that Paul's argument in Rom. 1.16–11.36 is explanatory digression can be confirmed by several kinds of supporting evidence: Paul's return after the explanation and the instruction to the same statement of his Gentile mission in Rome, and now beyond (15.14–29); the intermittent incursions of Paul's claim on the Romans during his explanation, especially in the first-person plural forms in chs. 5 and 8 and in his address to Gentiles in 11.13-32; and Paul's use of analogous explanatory disgressions in other letters such as the explanation of wisdom in 1 Cor. 1.18–2.16 (Wire 1990: 47-62).

To understand Paul's argument for God's justice as an explanation of his Gentile gospel is at once a historical and a theological task. The key theological question is what understanding of God Paul presents in this argument. The related historical question is whom Paul is seeking to persuade, which should be clear in the way he presents this theology. The challenge is to pursue these questions by taking into account all relevant historical and theological data without losing from sight that the issue here is the right reading of Paul's persuasion in this argument.

As in the salutation, in which Paul explains his calling in terms of God's acts, the major explanation of his Gentile gospel in Rom. 1.16–11.36 is theological. But here God's acts are presented as a revelation of God's nature, so that 'the power of God for salvation to all who trust, to

Jew first and also to Greek' is explained finally as 'the justice of God revealed from trust for trust' (1.16-17). This is in turn explained in terms of a revelation of God's wrath or judgment against all injustice (1.18–3.20), which seems to be preparatory in nature to assure that 'every mouth is stopped' that might claim another justice and that 'the whole world be made accountable to God' (3.19). This makes way for God's justice to be revealed gratis to whomever is willing to trust (3.21–4.25). It is this initial explanation of his gospel that I will consider for its theological and historical ramifications.

Paul's rhetorical development of the theology of God's wrath or judgment is very specific in its unraveling the varieties and disguises of injustice, and especially in its descriptions of two different ways in which accountability occurs. Injustice is first described as suppression of the truth of God's invisible power and divinity, known so plainly in what God has made that every human creature is accountable for recognizing God. Here Paul reverses the order of explanation from effect to cause to provide a narrative sequence from cause to effect, as he does periodically for dramatic impact (4.11-12, 18-25; 6.3-4, *passim*). He argues that the different ways people do not recognize their Creator are the cause of corresponding acts of human injustice—such as adultery, pederasty and deceit—owing to a divinely-conceded retribution in kind ('God delivered them up...').[2]

But immediately Paul reverts with a double *gar* to his argument by explanation (2.1), 'Therefore you (singular) are inexcusable, whoever you are who judge, for by judging another you condemn yourself, for you who judge do the very same things' (2.1). The one who judges while doing the same is shown to be self-indicting, because doing these things has been identified as the effect of not honoring the God one knows. What makes a person just is not privileged knowing the right but doing the right. Those who deny the Creator with the consequence of sin and those who sin and expose their denial of the Creator are equivalent, and at this point Paul identifies them as Gentile and Jew respectively (2.9-29). The Jew who rejoices in the Law but breaks it stands condemned with the Gentile, whereas the circumcised in heart—Jew or Gentile—receives God's praise (2.17, 28-29). Paul brings his assertion of God's judgment of Gentile and Jew to a climax with a chain of quotations from Ecclesiastes, the Psalms and Isaiah to the effect that 'No

2. See Klostermann 1933 on the triple *ius talionis* in this passage and also the recent review of this thesis in Bassler 1982: 201-202.

one is just, not one'. This is taken as sufficient demonstration that knowledge of God has not led to doing God's will and the conclusion is drawn that the Law's holy task is to make those who read it accountable to God who alone is just (3.9-20).[3]

At this point God's justice, witnessed to by the Law and Prophets, is announced to be revealed through the trust of Jesus Christ (in God) for all willing to trust (3.21-28). This is explained in terms of Gentile and Jew: 'for there is no distinction', which is itself explained: 'for all have sinned and lack God's glory and are made just gratis through emancipation in Christ'. The purpose of this is that 'God might be just and justify whoever lives out the trust of Jesus'. Paul does not immediately explain what it means for a Jew—or a Gentile—to be justified from the trust of Jesus in God because his immediate interest is in the parity this establishes between the two groups. He returns to this issue, 'Then where is the boast?' and answers that it is excluded not by the law of working but by the law of trusting. Such reinterpreting of Law, like the earlier reinterpreting of circumcision, appeals to those who respect the Law. Paul is seeking to draw in the Jew to see how a boast in special access is now impossible because people are made just strictly by trust and apart from the Law's works.

The next question brings all this explanation of God's justice back to the nature of God: 'Is God the Jews' God only and not the Gentiles' God? Surely also the Gentiles' God, since God is one, justifying circumcision from trust and uncircumcision through trust' (3.21-30). Although many Gentiles were monotheists in this period, as Dahl has demonstrated, Paul's questions here are addressed to the Jew. This is clear in the order in which the two groups are mentioned and in the way Gentile inclusion is legitimated on the basis of God's unity. The distinction between Jew and Gentile based on the Jews' privilege is shown to be impossible because of who God is—'since God is one'.

Having revealed the parity of Jew and Greek based on the single point of access—trust in the one God—Paul returns to the question that he did not take up earlier concerning what such trust means. He takes Abraham, 'our ancestor according to the flesh', as the model of this trust (4.1-25). The physical identity of the Jew descended from Abraham is thus explained in terms of trust in the God who justifies the ungodly

---

3.    The intermediate argument from blasphemy repelled, in which Paul makes the transition from all being judged impartially by their works to no one being righteous, will be considered in the next section.

and gives life to the dead. Because this identity is established before Abraham's circumcision, it can be shared by the uncircumcised who live out Abraham's trust in God and count on God's promise. In contrast to the very narrow explanation of Abraham's seed as Christ, which Paul developed in Galatians, the Romans are given a broad explanation of inheritance by trusting the one God who makes life from the dead at Isaac's birth and Jesus' resurrection. The trust in God that justifies human beings is thus the foundation of both Jewish and Christian identity. Paul's explanation of his gospel goes on from here in subsequent chapters to incorporate language from Christian confessions, but not before it has conceded the primary model of this trust to be Abraham, the Jewish 'ancestor according to the flesh'.

Paul's apparent address to Jews here, whether or not they are Christian Jews, raises all the more accutely the historical question of whom Paul is trying to persuade throughout this extended argument from explanation. The fact that this letter speaks four times in the second-person plural to address Gentiles (1.1-6, 13-14; 11.13-33; 15.15-29), in three cases locating them in Rome, seems to prove that Paul is explaining his gospel to Roman Gentiles. This is plausible because the letter shows he has not yet been in Rome (1.10; 15.22-24), so that Christ may have been preached there in some different way. But can we account for the many appeals Paul makes to the Law, Prophets, Scripture and Jewish tradition if he is persuading Gentile Christians in Rome? Were the Gentiles Jewish proselytes or had they been converted to a Jewish Christianity?

Because Roman Jews in this period gathered in multiple synagogues, largely Greek-speaking but some apparently Aramaic-speaking and with no known central organization (Philo, *Leg. ad Gai.* 152-61; Lietzmann 1961: II, 132-33; Barrett 1957: 6; Santucci 1980: 26-56; Wiefel 1991), it is conceivable that some of these people or groups were also believers in Christ, as is suggested by Suetonius's note on the exile from Rome in 49 CE, 'since the Jews constantly made disturbances at the instigation of Chrestus' (*Claud.* 25). By the fourth century, Ambrosiaster writes, 'It is established that in the apostles' time there were Jews residing in Rome since they lived under Roman rule, and that those Jews who believed transmitted to the Romans that they ought to profess Christ while keeping the law' (Ambrosiaster, *Ad Romanos*, introduction). The lack in Romans of any polemic against keeping specific laws such as we find in Paul's Galatians might seem to counter the thesis of a Jewish Christianity in Rome, but it may be that Paul chose to deal with the Roman situation differently, namely, by proclaiming the good news in Christ as a true law and circumcision now available to all by trust.

One major problem in explaining Paul's address to Jews in terms of a single Judaism-practicing Gentile audience is the repeated indication of some kind of a rift between Jewish and Gentile Christians in Rome. This is suggested in Paul's instruction to 'welcome one another, and not for arguments over opinions', where the arguments he mentions concern meat and special days (14.1-6; 15.7). A rift may be hinted in Paul's broader irenic counsels of mutual love and subjection to the state, since conflicts brought government suppression down on all Jews (12.1–13.10). Tension is also implied in Paul's explaining his gospel in terms of one God whose justice excludes distinctions and boasting, so that Jews are not to consider themselves more righteous, and Gentiles are not to despise the root into which they are grafted (3.21-30; 10.1-4; 11.17-24).

Yet at the same time as Paul reflects tension by arguing for the salvation of all—'circumcision from faith and uncircumcision through faith' (3.30)—he never collapses the two groups as if they could both be addressed in the same way. And in spite of Paul's repeated claim that his Gentile gospel will bring him to Rome, the explanation of this gospel that follows cannot be said to be directed to Gentiles, not even equally to Jews and Gentiles until perhaps his closing image of the olive tree (11.13-24)—though of course he insists that both Jew and Gentile are made just by trust. A primary address to Jews for almost ten chapters cannot be demonstrated without a comprehensive review of all the arguments in those chapters, which is not possible here, but it is indicative that the entire argument from explanation reviewed above (1.18–4.25) is directed to Jewish hearers. This is certainly true for the attack on Gentile sin that highlights Gentile culpability and degeneracy in order to attract and convict a judge who does the same things (1.18-32). The judge caught in self-condemnation in soon identified as a Jew who lives as if knowing the Law is sufficient without doing it (2.1-29). This conviction of the judge demonstrates to the Jew that Gentiles with 'circumcision in heart' and 'the Law of trust' are not less just, since no human is just before God except by trust in God's justifying. The very fact that Paul carries the explanation of his gospel back to God's nature as the one just judge and giver of life (3.26, 29-30; 4.16-23) is the ultimate appeal to the Jew.

But how can such a Jewish address be brought in line with Paul's multiple claims to Gentiles in Rome that they are part of his Gentile mission at large? It is possible that Paul's very description of his right as apostle to the Gentiles to come to Rome is intended for Jewish ears. It would assure that he has no agenda but to preach Christ to Gentiles and therefore would not stir up conflict in the synagogues that could incur political repression. He may hope that with such assurance they will come to terms with his Gentile gospel, especially if it is explained in a way that they can respect: Jewish priority, doing rather than merely knowing the right, justice of God alone, Abraham's trust in God, citations from Scripture as numerous as in any Pauline letter, and the God of Israel as the God of all.

Finally, Paul's account of his prayers for the Romans at the letter's start and his request for their prayers at the close as he faces probable Jewish and Jewish-Christian opposition in Jerusalem would have a special persuasive power for Jewish Christians as part of a diaspora people linked by prayer, whose fate is never independent of what happens in Jerusalem (1.8-10; 15.30-32). If they accept his extended explanations and instructions between the two prayers, it could lead to greater toleration of his Gentile gospel among Roman Jews and Jewish Christians, and even, possibly, to support for Paul in Jerusalem. The background of Paul's concern may be a growing alienation of Jews from his gospel as attested particularly in Romans 9–11. Is it too much to say that Paul's failure soon after this letter to receive support for his work from Jerusalem, followed in 64 CE by Nero's scapegoating of Christians as distinct from Jews, together suggest that Roman Jews probably rejected this explanation of his Gentile gospel and continued in increasing numbers to dissociate themselves from Gentiles in Christ? Romans indicates that Paul would have taken this as a mortal blow to his gospel grounded in the one God of Jews and Gentiles who makes each group just by trust and thus overcomes the alienation between them.

## *Rhetoric as Theology and History in Paul's Argument by Blasphemy Repelled*

Ten times in Rom. 1.16–11.36 Paul's explanation of his Gentile gospel provokes him to ask a blasphemous question that he immediately rejects with the phrase *mē genoito*, 'let it not be!' or as the KJV translates with the proper sacral tone, 'God forbid!' (Wire 1974: 148-222; Boers 1981;

Johnson 1989: 139-75). To turn back possible scandalous consequences of a position with this phrase as a kind of aversion charm was not an uncommon practice in Greek diatribe, witness Epictetus's 'Does a man then not differ at all from a stork? *mē genoito*' (*Diss.* 1.29, 19; cf. 2.5, 6). But the fact that Paul's questions all threaten sacred traditions suggests they are probably adaptions of a type of argument used by the rabbis to protect the inviolable. The rabbis voiced blasphemies of the most sacred things, 'Was our mother Sarah a whore?', 'Could there be two authorities (at the final judgment)?', 'Shall the Torah of Israel be forgotten?' (*Ruth R.* 1, 2; *b. Ḥag.* 15a; *b. Šab.* 138b) and rebuked the blasphemies with the silencing *ḥās wᵉšalōm*, 'hush and keep peace!', in order to lead into the necessary and opposite truth.

Two kinds of blasphemous questions are provoked by Paul's explanation of his gospel. His proclamation of God's wrath against all injustice puts in question God's faithfulness to Israel and God's right to judge (3.3, 5-6; 9.14; 11.1, 11), whereas his proclamation of God's justice for all who trust puts in question human responsibility to keep the Law (3.31; 6.1-2, 15; 7.7, 13). I will focus on the former charge, showing how Paul states, averts and counters the attacks against God's faithfulness and judgment and pointing out how this rhetoric is both theology and history. I will then consider the character of this theology and history as rhetoric and its implications for literature.

The five short questions that propose scandalous conclusions about God because of the strict impartiality of God's judgment all include the negative particle *mē*, signifying already in the asking that the answer must be 'no'. In one case the scandal is further warded off by an intermediate 'I speak in a human way', before the *mē genoito*.

The first two questions appear in ch. 3 in Paul's explanation of his gospel as God's wrath against all injustice, both the injustice done by those who know God through creation and yet have no respect, and the injustice done by those who receive God's Law but do not keep it. It is this parity of the two groups, Gentiles and Jews, that provokes the question of what advantage the Jew then has. Paul insists they are privileged and explains that they were entrusted with the oracles of God. The theological question is then forced, 'If some did not trust, could their lack of trust cancel out God's trustworthiness? Let it not be! Let God be true though every person lie!' (3.3-4). God's being true here means that God's oracles and acts are fully integrated, that God does not give up before actualizing the divine word, with the result that no lack of human trust can cancel what God entrusts. Yet this seems to make God just at the cost of condemning those without trust, so Paul continues, 'Could God be unjust in carrying out his wrath? (I speak in a human way). Let it not be! Or how could God judge the world?' (3.5-6). For Paul God's impartial judgment is axiomatic; it is the ground for the possibility of all trust. God can only be just, even at the expense of God's people who are not. When Paul then asks the second time if the Jews have an advantage, he responds in the opposite way, 'Not at all!' (3.9), apparently because the impossible blasphemy has proven the irrevocability of God's justice, which exposes all human lack of trust.

Historically this rhetoric is geared precisely to ask the questions a faithful Jew might bring to a gospel of God's impartial judgment of all: Then what priority has the Jew? Can anything cancel God's promises? If you say our injustice sets off God's justice, why blame us? Though of course the discourse is rhetorical and not an actual person's dialogue with Paul (Stowers 1981; Santucci 1980: 5-23, 85-86), he shapes it to persuade those he wants to persuade. He sets up and disarms the 'one who judges' by repelling the very blasphemies that the Jew knows can only be repelled, ending with every mouth's claim stopped. The Gentile mouth is no less stopped, but Paul's argument effects that only in passing, by statement not by persuasion, as if it were not contested.

After the chapters in which Paul announces God's justice, confirming (and reinterpreting) the Law through declaring Abraham's trust in God to be justice (3.21-4.25), followed by the celebration of life from death in Christ through the Spirit (5.1-8.39), Paul is overtaken by a lament for the Jews who are alienated from Christ (9.1-5). This lament takes up the unfinished business in Paul's previous arguments from blasphemy where God's impartial judgment fulfilled the curses but not the blessings of God's oracles entrusted to the Jews. At first Paul cannot state the blasphemy and simply rejects it—'It is not such that God's word has failed' (9.6)—giving Sarah's and Rebecca's sons as explanation that God's mercy has never been programmed. Yet this only provokes the blasphemy, 'Could there be injustice from God?' Its rejection—'Let it not be!' (9.14)—carries the hearer into Scripture, including the potter image that celebrates and brooks no contest to the freedom of God's mercy (9.15-29). Next Paul tries to face the worst, the idea that perhaps those most seeking God's justice have simply not received it with trust (9.30-10.21). But he interrupts himself, 'Has God repudiated God's people? Let it not be!' (11.1), and the revulsion from the blasphemy against God's trustworthiness again carries the hearer into assurance from Paul's own story and Elijah's that there are many chosen by grace. But not all, which provokes the final unthinkable thought: 'I ask, then, could they have tripped so as to fall?' (11.11). Here the end of God's people stands for God's desertion of them.

The retort, 'Let it not be!', culminates Paul's explanation of his gospel by attributing the Gentiles' salvation to this tripping by the Jews, in such a way that the Gentiles themselves turn out to be God's instrument of the Jews' inclusion. Having suggested such a high role for the Gentiles, Paul immediately addresses them, now for the first time since his opening chapter, and warns them not to become proud, because they are not the original branches and can only depend on the root. In fact, his instrumental view of them never hints that they will convert the Jews and make them into Christians like themselves. Rather Paul says that it was God who converted the Gentiles, or 'grafted them in', so as to somehow to provoke Israel and allow fulfilment of the divine oracles. It is the experience of exclusion that Paul sees as enabling God's mercy, first for the Gentile and then the Jew (11.30-32). But Christ is not mentioned in this chapter and Paul's gospel remains a Gentile gospel: 'In terms of the gospel they are enemies on your account, but in terms of election they are loved ones on the ancestors' account, for God's gifts and calling are irrevocable' (11.28).

The historical significance of this argument depends on the recognition that Paul wards off Gentile pride that is based on a potential—too soon actual—misunderstanding of their role vis-à-vis Israel, but he does this only after completing his ten-fold argument from blasphemy repelled. Every aspect of the argument from averting blasphemy is shaped to draw the Jewish objector to the double proclamation of salvation by trust—perhaps particularly the Jewish Christian who is becoming an isolated breed. Through each terror that Paul is forcing himself and his Jewish audience to face, he presses on to God's triumph on Israel's behalf that he is confident will emerge. Because all this occurs within the explanation of Paul's Gentile gospel as the revelation of God's impartial and faithful justice, which Paul insists that Jews understand in their own terms, the Gentile gospel paradoxically culminates in its own limitation to Gentiles, its own historical particularity.

The entire argument also points in an inchoate way to the historical particularity of God's mercy to Israel, which is in no sense strictly future but was present concretely prior to Paul's gospel in Abraham and Sarah

and Rebecca and Elijah—to mention only some of those Paul names—
and is now eschatologically taking place in new provocation and mercy
(11.31). One can almost say that Paul switches from addressing Jews to
addressing Gentiles in order to talk about a proclamation to Jews that is
not the focus of *his* apostolate but that he sees as the mission of other
Jewish Christians. It is not clear historically whether Paul is challenging
Jewish Christians in Rome alone or also in Jerusalem. To the Romans he
goes on to propose thinking in new ways of Christ:

> Therefore welcome each other just as Christ welcomes you to God's
> glory. For I tell you that Christ became a helper of the circumcised on
> behalf of God's truth to confirm the promises to the ancestors, and the
> Gentiles have given God glory for mercy (15.7-8; see Boers 1981: 8-9).

Yet Paul simultaneously pleads for the Romans' prayers on his behalf,
that Jewish Christians in Jerusalem will receive the Gentile offering and
send him on through Rome to Spain (15.30-32). Whatever else, Paul has
tried to explain his Gentile gospel to Jews in a way that confirms God's
continual faithfulness to Israel. In that sense this argument represents
what is close to a first and last effort in Christian history.

Theologically, Paul's explanation of his gospel, including these arguments by stating and repelling blasphemy, ends in a doxology to the
unsearchable wisdom of God. The concerted effort to figure out what
God is doing, which gropes toward a mystery of a parallel but different
trust in God by Jews and Gentiles, does not claim any definitive success.
What survives is the confidence, expressed in these words of praise, that
God knows what God is doing. So the historical battle that Paul is
fighting to keep the Christian church integral to Judaism rests its case
finally on the confession, 'from God and through God and to God are
all things' (11.36). 'Since God is one', (3.31) God's people can only be
one.

## Theology and History as Rhetoric

It is clear that rhetoric can be pursued in the form of theology and of
history, but it still remains unclear whether theology and history will
recognize themselves in this rhetoric. If theology is human understanding of God, is that not more universal, or at least subject to more
rigorous standards of evaluation than the persuader will employ? And if
history is human understanding of the human past, is that not more
comprehensive and critically controlled than any one persuasive
discourse? Must true theology and history not distance themselves from

the power struggles that dominate persuasive discourse and seek in the academy or monastery for a broader perspective inaccessible to the speaker in council, court or cult?

The assumption behind these questions is that theology and history proper occur at the final stages of human reflection, when events are past and interests have cooled. Then the human mind is best able to take the thoughts of many opponents and weigh them without bias in order to discern the truth. The truth is therefore not itself embedded in any particular situation but hovers above, and the human task par excellence is not to make history—or live out theology—but to understand both once they are made by those of more limited vision.

Aside from the obvious bias of this position, which privileges the reflective professions and institutions (Tompkins 1980: 221-26), the fallacy here is that truth is general. On the contrary, the most creative work in theology or history is generated by specific situations that demand thought. Whether on the street or at the computer, the person who is intent on a situation of human need is forced to see new connections and contribute to the advance of knowledge. Yet more basic than this is the pressure on such persons to persuade others to meet this need, thereby shaping historical events and theological experience in ways that many will later ponder. Beyond specific creative contributions of persons and groups struggling to define their right to exist and make their way in history, there are also cultural periods that are especially creative. They often involve juxtapositions of different cultures. Such cultural periods may often have a more open market in understanding the human past and understanding God, something approaching a genuine dialogue in which persuasion is seriously attempted, multiple types of people are in argument, and the competition to appeal to tradition in different ways stimulates new social structures, religious experience and historical consciousness.

The study of literature today is increasingly open to the world outside the text, whether by recognizing the text as an artifact in its society and hence a witness to human theology and history, or by seeing the text as an aspect of the reader's experience and thus of the society impacted by the text. Perhaps particularly those texts that focus their persuasion on a specific audience—though the nature of most publishing today makes this difficult—might be taken as test cases of the implications for literature of theology and history as rhetoric. Editorials in a local paper, avant-garde drama and the essays in professional journals are all working to persuade relatively defined groups. I would suggest that, where the authors' depth and breadth of knowledge and their writing skills are at all equivalent, the interest of these writers in persuading their audiences will be the key factor that focuses the writing in content, style and tone, and at its best makes literature of prose.

In reading ancient texts we fumble about to compensate for the knowledge readers were then expected to have, and we never fully understand the rhetoric as history or theology. But the text sharply and finely focused on persuading a specific audience—could we say the literary text par excellence?—has the greatest possibility, because of its integration, to bring that world to life. Nor does the fact that the rhetoric is always a specific human persuasion diminish its potential as theology or history when these are recognized as a certain human understanding of God and of the human past. Words that seek to shape history and theology may be the best evidence of that history and theology.

Romans I take to be this kind of text. Paul worked in the text of Romans to use traditional theological commitments, which Jews could not deny and remain recognizable to themselves, in order to explain his Gentile gospel as integral to but distinct from Judaism. It may be true that he more nearly makes Judaism over into his experience of faith in Christ than vice versa, yet he pulls back from this repeatedly. His real achievement is that his explanation of the Gentile gospel ends in the mystery of its own historical particularity rather than universality, alongside and inextricably related to the historical particularity of Israel. What binds the two—Jew and Gentile—Paul calls the revelation of God's justice from trust to trust, from the trust of one group in God to the trust of the other in God (1.17). There is an analogy between the two, even an essential commonality, in so far as it is one God in whom both trust. So what is on the one hand God's unfathomable mystery can on the other hand be explained in human argument: 'since God is one, who makes the circumcised just by trust and the uncircumcised just through that trust' (3.30).

It must be conceded that Paul's argument was not effective to persuade in his own time, at least not effective in a way that survived the tragedy of the next decades. And in the years since, his letter has been made a tool of very different purposes. But we still read it, and it could yet become a creative stimulus for Christians and Jews willing to take stock and pursue historical and theological change.

## BIBLIOGRAPHY

Bassler, Jouette M.
1982    *Divine Impartiality: Paul and a Theological Axiom* (SBLDS, 59; Chico, CA: Scholars Press).
Barrett, Charles Kingsley
1957    *A Commentary on the Epistle to the Romans* (New York: Harper & Row).
Betz, Hans-Dieter
1986    'The Problem of Rhetoric and Theology according to the Apostle Paul', in A. Vanhoye (ed.), *L'apôtre Paul: personalité, style et ministère* (Leuven: Leuven University Press): 16-48.
Boers, H.
1981    'The Problem of Jews and Gentiles in the Macro-Structure of Romans', *Neot* 15: 1-11.
Castelli, Elizabeth A.
1991    *Imitating Paul: A Discourse of Power* (Louisville, KY: Westminster/ John Knox).
Dahl, Nils Alstrop
1977    'The One God of Jews and Gentiles', in *Studies in Paul* (Minneapolis: Augsburg): 178-91.
Donfried, Karl P. (ed.)
1991    *The Romans Debate* (rev. edn; Peabody, MA: Hendrickson).
Dunn, James D.G.
1988    *Romans 1–8* (WBC, 38A; Dallas: Word Books).
Elliott, Neil
1990    *The Rhetoric of Romans: Argumentative Constraint and Strategy and Paul's Dialogue with Judaism* (Sheffield: JSOT Press).
Johnson, E. Elizabeth
1989    *The Function of Apocalyptic and Wisdom Traditions in Romans 9–11* (SBLDS, 109, Atlanta: Scholars Press).
Käsemann, Ernst
1980    *Commentary on Romans* (Grand Rapids: Eerdmans).
Klostermann, E.
1933    'Die adäquate Vergeltung in Rm 1.22-31', *ZNW* 32: 1-6.
Lietzmann, Hans
1961    *History of the Christian Church* (4 vols.; trans. B. Woolf; London: Lutterworth).
Morganthaler, R.
1958    *Statistik des neutestamentlichen Wortschatzes* (Zürich: Gotthelf).
Moxnes, Halvor
1980    *Theology in Conflict: Studies in Paul's Understanding of God in Romans* (NovTSup, 53; Leiden: Brill).
Santucci, John
1980    'Romans 13.1-7 and the Situation of the Early Roman Church' (MA thesis, Graduate Theological Union).

Schüssler Fiorenza, Elisabeth
1987    'Rhetorical Situation and Historical Reconstruction in 1 Corinthians', *NTS* 33: 386-403.

Siegert, Folker
1985    *Argumentation bei Paulus, gezeigt an Römer 9–11* (Tübingen: Mohr [Paul Siebeck]).

Smyth, H.W.
1920    *Greek Grammar* (Cambridge, MA: Harvard University Press).

Stowers, Stanley Kent
1981    *The Diatribe and Paul's Letter to the Romans* (Chico, CA: Scholars Press).

Tompkins, Jane P.
1980    'The Reader in History: The Changing Shape of Literary Response', in *Reader-Response Criticism: From Formalism to Post-Structuralism* (Baltimore: The Johns Hopkins University Press): 201-32.

Wiefel, Wolfgang
1991    'The Jewish Community in Ancient Rome and the Origins of Roman Christianity', in Donfried 1991: 85-101.

Wire, Antoinette Clark
1974    'Pauline Theology as an Understanding of God: The Explicit and the Implicit' (PhD dissertation, Claremont Graduate School).
1990    *The Corinthian Women Prophets: A Reconstruction through Paul's Rhetoric* (Minneapolis: Fortress Press).

Wuellner, Wilhelm
1974    'Paul's Rhetoric of Argumentation in Romans: An Alternative to the Donfried–Karris Debate over Romans', *CBQ* 38: 330-51, reprinted in Donfried 1991: 128-46.
1989    'Hermeneutics and Rhetorics: From "Truth and Method" to "Truth and Power"', *Scriptura*, Special Issue: 1-54.

## ALLEGORIES OF HAGAR:
## READING GALATIANS 4.21-31 WITH POSTMODERN FEMINIST EYES*

### Elizabeth A. Castelli

> Allegory may dream of presenting the thing itself...but its deeper purpose and its actual effect is to acknowledge the darkness, the arbitrariness, and the void that underlie, and paradoxically make possible, all representation of realms of light, order, and presence... Allegory arises...from the painful absence of that which it claims to recover...
>
> Stephen Greenblatt

> Allegories are, in the realm of thoughts, what ruins are in the realm of things.
>
> Walter Benjamin

In postliterate, postmodern, postfeminist America, what possible reading of Hagar? Hagar, allegory of foreign territory, a space passed through on the way towards a mythical home; allegory of Sinai, the source of the first inscription; allegory of slavery, of flesh, of the past—loss, absence, ruin? In this critical space—America with its 'Post-' Age stamp (Moore)—what possible reading of a biblical allegory? *Allegory may dream of presenting the thing itself...*

This essay originates in my struggle with two puzzles: the nagging persistence in the collective imagination of the West of the figure of Hagar and the interpretative character of allegory. Working in the complex matrix formed by postmodernism, feminism and liberal biblical studies, I have sought to understand how these two puzzles work

\* A very different earlier version of this essay benefited greatly from readings by Professors Jenifer Ward (German and Women's Studies, The College of Wooster), Christina Crosby (English and Women's Studies, Wesleyan University) and David Dawson (Religion, Haverford College). That earlier version was presented in November 1991 at the Society of Biblical Literature annual meeting in a joint session sponsored by the Rhetoric and the New Testament Section and the Semiotics and Exegesis Section.

together in Paul's allegorical rendering of the Hagar–Sarah–Abraham narrative of Genesis. When I first started thinking about this problem, I understood the allegory as a figural intensification of the violence done Hagar in the original narrative. In this, my interpretation differed little from post-Romantic indictments of allegorical readings as doing violence to innocent original texts. In pursuing the matter further, I have shifted my focus to reading allegory as itself undermining the fixed character of meaning (even as it insists upon it) *and* therefore as a more ambivalent interpretative strategy whose effects are tentative, circumstantial, and tied to immediate contexts. This essay, then, is a kind of multiple reading—a simultaneous reading of allegory, Paul's uses of allegory, Hagar, and theoretical interventions into the practices and politics of interpretation. This reading cannot simply embrace allegory in its historical practice, as will become clear, nor can it simply resist allegory, lest the resistance become an enactment of the very procedures this essay attempts to call into question. This reading must occupy some third, strategic position, a position embedded in the paradox that is allegory—a rendering of truth that asserts that truth is always somewhere else, something other than where or what appears. In short, there are times when allegory is to be resisted, and times when allegory may fruitfully function as a form of resistance. Allegories of Hagar provide examples of both workings of allegory.[1]

1. A brief comment about the shape and order of the argument of this essay is in order. In its penultimate formulation, the essay was organized with the theoretical discussion of allegory preceding the reading of Paul's allegory of Sarah and Hagar. The editors of the volume, in the interests of offering a 'reader-friendly' book, suggested that I switch the order of these two sections, placing the more concrete (and perhaps, to the reader, more familiar) exegetical analysis before the more abstract (and perhaps more exotic) theoretical material Because of the intersecting discussion in the two sections, the essay poses a difficulty for the reader; as one of the editors put it, 'Parts one and two fit together in such a way that each one should be read before the other!' I was persuaded by the editors' arguments that switching the order of the first two sections of the essay would make the piece more accessible to readers unfamiliar with the theoretical debates afoot in literary and cultural studies around the problem of allegory. Moreover, I found myself actually delighted at the postmodern character of the problem, having apparently (if inadvertently) created a text in which two parts of the argument require that the other one be read first—a logical impossibility, of course. Still, it was not my desire to write an unapproachable text, and therefore I hope that the editors' practical resolution to the potential difficulty has contributed to the essay's clarity.

## Reading Paul's Allegory[2]

Paul's allegory of Sarah and Hagar concludes an extended proof from Scripture that begins in ch. 3 of Galatians.[3] Having already invoked traditions concerning Abraham, Paul here expands his focus to include the stories of the two women and concludes his argument with his allegory. The placement of the allegory within the larger argument is noteworthy for, as Betz points out, the persuasive force of allegorical interpretations was a subject of considerable controversy in ancient rhetorical theory. While some, such as Quintilian and the anonymous author of the *Rhetorica ad Herennium*, read the indirectness and potential ambiguity of allegory as weakening the argument, others, like pseudo-Demetrius, held that indirect arguments were sometimes more effective than straightforward ones.[4] Furthermore, an indirect argument (like allegory) might have the effect of flattery by allowing the hearer to make explicit the connections implied by the allegory.[5]

Allegory as a rhetorical trope possesses a capacity to persuade its reader or hearer to reimagine the meanings of a text or tradition. Allegory draws the reader into the argument and constructs a kind of complicity between the interpreter and the reader. Like other forms of rhetorical persuasion, allegorical interpretation depends upon what is familiar to the reader. In the course of the interpretation, the familiar is

2.    I am, of course, not the first to attempt a reading of this text. In addition to the commentary literature cited in the bibliography, see Barrett 1976; Callaway 1975; Hansen 1989: 141-57; Janzen 1991; Martyn 1990; Wagner 1991.

3.    This is the view, at least, of the great majority of commentators on the text (Betz 1979; Burton 1920; Fung 1988; Lagrange 1950; Neil 1967—who nevertheless describes the passage as 'what on the face of it seems to be a masterpiece of irrelevancy' [p. 71]; Oepke 1973; Ridderbos 1953; Rohde 1989), though recently Borse (1984) and Hansen (1989) have argued that the text actually belongs with that which follows, the discussion of freedom. Most recently, Matera (1992: 172-74) has summarized the problem's various solutions, appealing ultimately to Martyn's 1990 essay, which ties 4.21-31 thematically with what comes before. I have sided with the traditional, majority view on the question; yet, I believe my reading of the allegory is not tied to the ultimate solution of this question.

4.    One might turn fruitfully here to de Man's discussion of the relationship between allegory and mimesis, where the obliqueness of allegory calls into question the apparent directness of mimesis.

5.    Betz 1979: 239-40, citing Quintilian, *Inst.* 5.12; *Rhetorica ad Herennium* 4.34.46; Pseudo-Demetrius, *Eloc.* 2.99-101, 151, 222, 243.

refigured, and what is familiar is translated into something new, different, and often remarkable. It is crucial that the interpreter and the reader share some common understanding about the elements of the allegory. In other words, allegory presumes a kind of pre-existing, if not absolute, consensus between writer and reader. In the case of Paul's allegory of Sarah and Hagar, the interpreter begins with a familiar tradition, one whose conventional interpretation accords identification between the reader and the figure of Sarah, the mother of the free and legitimate heir, and her offspring. The interpreter and the reader share this conventional understanding of the tradition. By the end of the allegory, a second consensus or complicity between the interpreter and the reader is articulated, for Paul concludes with a statement using the first-person plural: *dio, adelphoi, ouk esmen paidiskēs tekna alla tēs eleutheras* (4.31)— 'Therefore, brothers, we are not the children of the slave woman but of the free woman'. The consensus Paul's allegorical interpretation of the story depends on is thematically tied to the embrace of the figure of Sarah and the rejection of the figure of Hagar. Framed by this consensus concerning the straightforward meaning of the tradition, the allegorical interpretation proceeds to produce the real, hidden meanings of 'Sarah' and 'Hagar'. Rhetorically, this consensus between Paul and his readers draws the readers into the persuasive sweep of the allegory; as Betz interprets it,

> The conclusion in 4:31, stated in the first person plural, includes the readers among those who render judgment. In formulating not merely the conclusion to the 'allegory' but to the entire *probatio* section (3:1–4:31) Paul anticipates that the whole argument has convinced his readers (Betz 1979: 240).

Allegory here serves as a consensus-building trope. Yet this is only part of the way that allegory transforms an earlier biblical tradition into a convincing argument on behalf of Paul's larger attempt to persuade his audience to abandon their attraction to the law. Allegory, as part of a broader rhetorical repertoire, contributes to Paul's continued attempts to translate from one interpretative language into another, and to promote a set of new interpretative conclusions as both inherent to the tradition itself and inevitable results of the interpretative process. The process of allegory as translation is distinguished by both violence and foreclosure, enacted here by means of three interpretative operations: the schematizing or reduction of the original text or tradition; the (often implicit) assertion of an essential connection between the two planes of meaning that constitute the allegory; and the elimination of alternative meanings. In the case of Paul's allegory of Sarah and Hagar, one can trace out the paths of each of these operations in the text.

Allegory often schematizes or reduces the original text or tradition it seeks to interpret. In this movement, one could claim that all interpretation is, in some measure, a form of allegory, since no interpretation can engage a text without focusing on some parts of the text and ignoring others. Yet, allegorical interpretation may tend toward a more exaggerated selection process than other forms of interpretation because of the requirements of the second interpretative operation—the establishment of an essential connection between the literal and the figurative planes of signification. Whatever elements may be found in the original text that do not lend themselves to the allegorical framework will be eliminated in the process of interpretation. In Paul's treatment of Sarah and Hagar, we see just this kind of reduction take place.

This process begins early in the allegory, when Paul introduces the scriptural source he will then interpret. As Betz points out, in 4.22 Paul makes use of the standard formula to signify quotation from Scripture (*gegraptai gar hoti*), but instead he summarizes selected parts of the Sarah and Hagar narrative from Genesis 16 and 21 (Betz 1979: 241). In doing so, he emphasizes the parts of the tradition that contribute to his allegory while eliding complicating dimensions of the two narratives. Furthermore, Betz rightly remarks that Paul's interest is not historical accuracy, but the construction of the stark contrast between the two women and their sons; therefore, the existence, for example, of other sons of Abraham neither figures in Paul's account nor presents any difficulty for him (pp. 241-42). This process of schematization or reduction is crucial to allegorical interpretation as well as to arguments dependent upon allegory. The elimination of complicating details sets the elements of the tradition in sharper relief while at the same time allowing the allegory to present itself as a complete interpretation, leaving no remainder.

The schematization or reduction of the tradition also results in the reduction of the two women characters into ciphers in the service of the argument. Of course, the Genesis narrative that is the source for Paul's allegory is not itself 'about' Sarah and Hagar but rather 'about' Abraham; nevertheless, the circumstances and details of the narrative open the story to some kind of resisting reading, as the work of

Renita Weems has ably demonstrated.[6] In a non-allegorical narrative, Sarah and Hagar may be read in multiple, even competing ways; in the context of the allegory, they have become essentialized embodiments of abstracted concepts set in irrevocable and absolute opposition. This process of reduction and abstraction is a foundational characteristic of the allegorical method, as Betz points out,[7] and it fixes the relationship between the two as utterly unchangeable.

This violence of reduction smooths out the complexities of the narrative tradition Paul is glossing, so that the next step in the allegorical process can take place: the lining up of the two planes of meaning and the assertion of the essential connection between the two. Allegory presupposes two overlapping planes of signification, the literal and the figurative, and the pattern of equivalences between these two planes claims to account fully for all elements, leaving no remainder. Furthermore, according to the logic of allegory, the correspondence between the literal and the figurative elements is essential rather than arbitrary. The allegorical method is the key that unlocks the deep meaning trapped below the surface of the text. For Paul's allegory of Sarah and Hagar, this function of allegory is particularly poignant because, once each has been fixed into her signifying role, the meanings that accrue to her are also fixed. The distance between 'seeming' and 'being', between representation and essence is collapsed, and accidents of history, situation and circumstance are rewritten onto the women as inevitabilities. Textually, this collapse of distinction between the representative and the ontological can be seen in v. 24: *hautai gar eisin duo diathēkai*, where *eisin* literally means 'are' but is translated frequently 'represent' or 'stand for'.[8] Furthermore, the theological resonances of the term *diathēkai* contribute to the sense of inevitability of the two sets of correspondences that are attributed to these two women/signifiers. As Betz puts it: '*diathēkē*...

---

6. Weems, for example, points out the resonance of the Genesis story (despite its focus on Abraham) for many African American women readers (1991: 75-76). She also engages the Genesis account of Sarah and Hagar more extensively in her earlier work on womanist interpretation of Scripture (1988: 1-19).

7. Betz 1979: 239: '...[A]llegory takes concrete matters mentioned in Scripture and tradition (mythology) to be the surface appearance or vestige of underlying deeper truths which the method claims to bring to light. Thereby concrete matters in the texts are transposed into general notions of philosophical or theological truth.'

8. Betz 1979: 238 n. 1: '*NEB*: "stand for"'. See also Burton 1920: 257: 'From this point of view *eisin* is to be interpreted as meaning in effect "represent", "stand for"'; and Lightfoot 1981: 180: '*Eisin* "are" not actually, but mystically or typically'.

amounts to a world order decreed by divine institution; it contains God's definition of the basis and purpose of human life' (Betz 1979: 244). Defining the women as 'covenants' fixes their status in the allegorical relationship, thus Paul's allegory forecloses questions of 'how', 'why' and 'toward what end' with respect to Sarah's status as a free woman and Hagar's status as a slave woman. These are questions that themselves might serve to undercut the surety of Paul's reading, but there is no room for them in an interpretation that collapses representation and essence. The circumstances of Sarah's 'freedom' and Hagar's 'slavery' are not relevant for the allegory; Sarah simply *is* free and Hagar simply *is* a slave, and these statements about social status take on ontological force, as well as theological significance. The fixed character of the meanings associated with each of the women in the story is rearticulated through the very structure of allegory, insofar as it makes claims about the intentional and essential qualities of the narrative it interprets.

The apparent arbitrariness, then, of the allegory is for the allegorist an illusion. The meanings produced by allegorical interpretation, which seem to the uninitiated to be contrived, become true and eliminate any other associative meanings. Meanwhile, the structuredness of allegorical meanings—the essential bond between the surface signifier and its deep referent—promotes a clearly dualistic interpretative stance. In the context of Paul's allegory of Hagar and Sarah, this theoretical or structural dualism underwrites a conceptual dualism in the content of Paul's argument. Throughout the letter, stark oppositions are being constructed, and they reach a particularly powerful intensity in the allegory where two sets of correspondences (*systoichia*) are spelled out:

| Hagar | Sarah |
| --- | --- |
| Mount Sinai | — |
| slavery | freedom |
| present Jerusalem | Jerusalem above |
| — | 'our mother' |
| 'according to the flesh' | 'according to the Spirit' |
| [Ishmael] | Isaac |
| [Judaism/the 'agitators'?][9] | 'we, brethren' |
| old covenant | new covenant |
| children of the slave | children of the free woman |

9.    There is a significant debate in the literature concerning the unexpressed opposite of Paul's 'we, brethren' in this passage. Is the opposition being drawn between 'Christians' and 'Jews', or between those on Paul's side and 'the troublemakers in Galatia' (Hansen 1989: 149) or the 'agitators' (Matera 1992: 174)? For

The dualism inherent in the structure of allegory fortifies the conceptual dualism that Paul constructs in the letter and that reaches its most acute articulation in these eleven verses. While one cannot know whether Paul himself was conscious of how the structure and content of his allegory reinforce each other, it is clear that masters of rhetoric and practitioners of allegory who were Paul's predecessors and contemporaries thought of allegory as grounded in structural dualism. As with other articulations of dualism from antiquity, these oppositions were not seen as arbitrary or capricious, but rather as inherent and essential. The intersection of dualism in the structure and content of Paul's argument, then, contributes to the growing sense that what is being attributed to Hagar and Sarah is integral to them.

## The Nature of Allegorical Interpretation[10]

Allegory, once a jewel in the crown of interpretation, is cast aside during the Romantic period as garish, contrived, unnatural. Ephemeral, apparitional, without substance, allegorical meanings come to be understood by the critic Coleridge (and then by everybody else) to be 'but empty echoes which the fancy associates with apparitions of matter' in contrast to symbol, which 'abides itself as a living part in that Unity of which it is the representative' (Coleridge 1936: 30, cited in Culler 1975–76: 262-63). Symbol is organic and intuitive, allegory mechanical and forced (Culler 1975–76: 263). While symbol fuses subject and object, allegory highlights their hopelessly irreconcilable difference (Culler 1975–76: 263).

Into the practice of modern biblical interpretation the resistance to allegory is itself translated. As a rhetorical trope, allegory is seen as polemical rather than descriptive, and its claims to a special route to the

the purposes of this reading, the solution to this problem is perhaps less pressing, for it is the dualistic structure of the argument that is crucial to this interpretation. Yet, the problem points to the ongoing presence of allegorical sensibilities in the interpretation of Scripture, for have not, traditionally, Jewish figures in New Testament texts been interpreted allegorically to stand for 'the Jews' and 'Judaism', most often for polemical ends?

10. This section has benefitted from a range of theoretical investigations into the problem of allegory. See especially Bloom 1951; Bloomfield 1972; Clifford 1974; Culler 1975–76; Dawson 1990; Dawson 1992; de Man 1979; de Man 1981; de Man 1983; Fineman 1981; Fletcher 1964; Greenblatt 1981a; Hanson 1959; Honig 1972; Miller 1981; Nuttall 1967; Pépin 1976; Quilligan 1979; Whitman 1987.

truth are seen to mask its behind-the-scenes maneuvering to produce that truth. Allegorical interpretation is most often characterized as naïve, disingenuous, contrived, ahistorical or interested. Consider the terms in which one early twentieth-century critic of allegorical interpretation writes of it:

> the rule comes to be that in allegorical interpretation *an entirely foreign subjective meaning is read into the passage* which has to be explained. In this way *allegory is almost always a relative, not an absolute, conception, which has nothing to do with the actual truth of the matter*...(Geffcken 1908: 327, emphasis mine).

Hans Dieter Betz, in his commentary on Galatians, portrays the method that produced the Sarah and Hagar allegory in this fashion:

> The method rests upon the assumption that the material to be interpreted contains a 'deeper meaning' not visible on the surface. The allegorical method was believed to be able to bring this deeper meaning to light. *The fact is, however, that for the most part the deeper meaning is secondary to the material which it claims to explain, and that the deeper meaning has its origin in the interpreter and his ideas and frame of reference* (Betz 1979: 243, emphasis mine).

Both writers claim a knowledge of the truth of texts, a truth sullied when 'foreign', 'subjective' and 'secondary' meanings supplant meanings that, one is led to infer, are indigenous, objective and primary. Moreover, both writers imagine texts and their meanings as entities under the threat of allegorical invasion or displacement. Such imperiousness on the part of allegory originates in a suspicious locale ('the interpreter and his ideas and frame of reference') and, worse yet, carries with it falsehood because it 'has nothing to do with the actual truth of the matter'. As Andrew Louth puts it, in a curious theological reclamation of allegory, 'There seems to be a fundamental distaste for, or even revulsion against this whole business of allegory...because we feel that there is something *dishonest* about [it]' (Louth 1983: 97).

Louth goes on to suggest that the abhorrence of allegory is grounded in two intellectual and theological presuppositions: first, the notion that the meaning of a text 'is a past historical event', accessible through objective scientific means such as the historical-critical method (1983: 97-98); and, secondly, the notion of *sola scriptura*, a mainstay for Protestantism as well as an implicit foundation of historical criticism. From this point of view, allegory seems to be a way of obscuring the clarity of revelation, 'a way of adulterating the purity of divine revelation with human opinions and conjecture' (1983: 98). Louth's recuperation of allegory has as one of its goals the rejuvenation of theology, and in this it shares Pascal's theological interest in the rescue of Scripture through a process of totalizing reading, using allegory to reconcile scriptural contradictions.[11] While this goal is quite apart from the interests of this discussion, it nevertheless points tantalizingly toward a postmodern engagement of interpretation and textuality. De Man has suggested that the very occurrence of allegory lays bare the straightforward referential claims of representation itself, asking,

> Why is it that the furthest reaching truths about ourselves and the world have to be stated in such a lopsided, referentially indirect mode? Or, to be more specific, why is it that texts that attempt the articulation of epistemology with persuasion turn out to be inconclusive about their own intelligibility in the same manner and for the same reasons that produce allegory? (1991: 2)

Indeed, postmodern readers will probably be drawn to pose the question of whether any reading is anything *but* an allegory—literally, a way of saying something else (*allo* + *agoreuō*).[12] And, indeed, could one not go further to point out that the critique of allegory launched by historical-critical scholarship—though resonant with earlier Protestant critiques (Luther 1953 [1535]: 414)—is itself allegorical, a way of saying something else about the status of interpretation itself? Like other forms of allegorical interpretation, historical-critical scholarship's critique of allegory also 'has its origin in the interpreter and his ideas and frame of

11. See the discussion of this allegorical maneuver in de Man 1981: 13, which treats Pascal's

> principle of totalizing reading, in which the most powerful antinomies must be brought together, in the *Pensée* headed 'Contradiction' (257-*684*, 533): 'One can put together a good physiognomy only by reconciling all our oppositions. It does not suffice to follow a sequence of matched properties without reconciling contraries: in order to understand an author's meaning, one must reconcile all the contradictory passages'... Applied to Scripture, which Pascal here has in mind, this reconciliation leads directly to the fundamental opposition that underlies all others: that between a figural and a true reading. 'If one takes the law, the sacrifices, and the kingdom as realities, it will be impossible to coordinate all passages (of the Bible); it is therefore necessary that they be mere figures'.

12. Such a view is expressed in a good deal of the literature emerging in literary studies on allegory. See Bloomfield 1972; Culler 1975–76; de Man 1979; de Man 1981; Fineman 1981; Greenblatt 1981a; Greenblatt 1981b; Miller 1981.

reference', as the historical-critical interpreter strives to separate 'him'self from 'his' predecessors.[13]

If allegory and interpretation are, broadly conceived, oscillating mirror images, what can be said of allegory as one specifiable form of interpretation? Allegory as a way of reading is a form of translation—a departure, a journey, a carrying across (Falk 1990: 91). Both procedures, allegory and translation, are characterized by violence, critique, creation and movement, and imbedded in painful practices—abandonment, refiguration, transformation. Both produce new texts whose relation to the texts in which they are rooted is often troubled, fraught with anguished struggle for authority, engaged in an irresolvable conflict over the truth of the matter. The truth that ultimately remains elusive, lost in translation, remaindered. Hagar.

If allegory is akin to translation, then perhaps it shares with translation the movements and tensions that are a part of meaning's migration from one language to another. Ultimately, neither of these operations— allegorical interpretation or translation—is truly absolute, complete, or final; yet, each strives for and values such closure. In the pursuit of closure, each participates in violence and *fore*closure, in the reduction of meaning for the purposes of producing new meaning. Violence and foreclosure occur, in allegory, through a range of operations.

Allegory constructs a relationship of equivalences between subjects that occupy different planes of meaning. In so doing, allegory posits a natural or truth-embued connection between each pair of equivalent elements. Between the surface signifier and its hidden referent exists a bond of meaning that is not capricious, but rather essential.[14] Although allegory may appear to the uninitiated to be contrived, fundamental to its success is its claim that the meaning exposed by the allegory is the foundationally true and complete meaning. This aspect of allegory is crucial to a consideration of its effects, for the explicit claim articulated by allegory is that meaning is not negotiable, situational, or mediated by

13. This struggle with precursors is, according to Dawson (1992: 1), a central characteristic of the allegorical tradition emergent in the work of the Alexandrians Philo, Valentinus and Clement. One hears echoes here of Harold Bloom's anxiety of influence. In relation to this expansion of the concept of allegory, one might even pose the further question, is not all history-writing, at varying levels of explicitness, allegorical?

14. See the discussion of the notion of innate correspondence in relation to allegory in Fletcher 1964: 70.

history or circumstance; it is static, and resident within a system whose full range of elements may be discerned and decoded with the proper tools for interpretation. Meaning resides hidden in the text, awaiting the allegorical key that will open it up to view. This 'rightness' of allegory is at the heart of its polemical power.

Ordinarily, allegorical interpretation does not, of course, simply solve the puzzle of meaning in quite so facile a fashion. Indeed, as theorists of allegory increasingly insist, a crucial dimension of the allegorical relation is the tension by which signifier and referent are bound. For J. Hillis Miller, this tension produces the paradox that what allegory reveals it simultaneously hides (1981: 358), while for Jon Whitman,

> the more allegory exploits the divergence between corresponding levels of meaning, the less tenable the correspondence becomes. Alternatively, the more it closes ranks and emphasizes the correspondence, the less oblique, and thus the less allegorical, the divergence becomes (1987: 2).

Still, if the relationship between the signifier and its allegorical referent is tensively wrought, allegory must work especially assiduously to eliminate other meanings that might be associated with the signifier, the first term in the comparative relation. Mundane, diffused, polysemic meanings must be deferred, repressed, set aside in allegory in favor of the singular, deeply embedded meaning.[15]

Furthermore, allegory inscribes dualism at a conceptual level, setting up a clear opposition between the commonplace meaning and the privileged allegorical meaning and undergirding a whole series of further oppositions: literal–analogical, surface–depth, letter–spirit. Ancient handbooks on rhetoric and ancient practitioners of allegory saw this dualism as residing at the heart of allegory. The first-century BCE *Rhetorica ad Herennium* defines allegory as 'a manner of speech denoting one thing by the letter of the words, but another by their meaning'.[16] Philo, the preeminent allegorist of the first century, frequently writes of this essential quality of allegory; in his laudatory account of the Therapeutae and Therapeutrides, he describes their allegorical interpretative method:

---

15. I disagree here with Betz who argues that allegory is characterized by ambiguity (1979: 240).

16. *Rhetorica ad Herennium* 4.34.46, cited by Betz (1979: 240 n. 14): 'Permutatio [*allēgoria*] est oratio aliud verbis aliud sententia demonstrans'.

> The exposition of the sacred scriptures treats the inner meaning conveyed in allegory. For to these people the whole law book seems to resemble a living creature with the literal ordinances for its body and for its soul the invisible mind laid up in its wording. It is in this mind especially that the rational soul begins to contemplate the things akin to itself and looking through the words as through a mirror beholds the marvellous beauties of the concepts, unfolds and removes the symbolic coverings and brings forth the thoughts and sets them bare to the light of day for those who need but a little reminding to enable them to discern the inward and hidden through the outward and visible (*De vita contemplativa*, 78).

Moreover, allegory is fundamentally linked to the production of new authority within the interpretation. Allegory accomplishes its task when the interpretation supersedes the text, when the allegorical rendering becomes the definitive location of the truth of the text. In his classic study of literary allegory, Edwin Honig puts it this way:

> An allegory succeeds when the writer's re-creation of the antecedent story, subject, or reference is masterful enough to provide his work with a wholly new authority; such an achievement draws deeply on his ability to project an ideal by manifold analogies in the larger design of the whole work. The subject matter already stands, in whatever form, as true or factual by common acceptance. When the subject is taken over by the writer...it bears a certain general but muted authority, mythical, religious, historical, or philosophical, depending on the range of its acceptance. To come alive, the subject must be recreated, completely remade by the writer. To remake the subject the author creates a new structure and, inevitably, a new meaning. To the extent that the subject is thus remade, it exists for the first time and has an authority independent of that of the antecedent subject (1972: 13).

David Dawson, more recently, has argued—though from a somewhat different orientation—that the allegorical interpretation and composition taking place in ancient Alexandria enacted just this kind of authoritative remaking. As he characterizes the work of Philo, Valentinus and Clement at the beginning of his masterful study of allegory and cultural revision in Alexandria, each participates in a process of critique and challenge of precursors:

> These three authors claimed authoritative originality for their allegorical readings and compositions, which they used as a means of enabling certain privileged perspectives...to challenge cultural and religious precursors and contemporaries and to promote alternative ways of being in the world (1992: 1).

As this statement suggests, Dawson's reading of allegory concerns itself less with the textual relations foregrounded by allegorical interpretation than with the cultural effects of allegory, which he argues are primarily cultural critique and cultural revision. Allegory is particularly useful in this regard because it opens up the possibility of other meanings. 'The allegorical potential ensures that meaning does not so exclusively become a function of one sort of reading (or one group of readers) that it seems to become an attribute—a "sense"—of the text itself' (1992: 237), he argues. Moreover, allegory, within the framework of cultural critique, can be shown to produce counterhegemonic interpretations of texts and traditions. Allegory can, in short, become a form of cultural resistance.

### Resisting Allegory/Allegory as Resistance

The passage of Sarah and Hagar from their traditional narrative into Paul's allegory is a process of smoothing over and eliding complexities, eliminating potential contradictions, and reducing them to fixed and absolute opposites. In the course of this transformation, the meanings that accrue to them are, in one sense, inverted. That is, while the traditional interpretation holds that the offspring of Sarah is the nation of Israel, Paul has argued that the rightful heirs to God's promise are himself and other believers in Christ. In so doing, Paul has deposed the reigning interpretation and has set his own up in its place. As suggested earlier, a successful allegory displaces its antecedent, remakes its subject, and constitutes its own independent authority. Claiming a new and independent meaning, the allegory supersedes the antecedent and replaces it. By analogy, Paul's allegory of Sarah and Hagar enacts this process not simply on the tradition of the two women but on the tradition as a whole. In superseding the claims of the traditional interpretation of their story, Paul also constructs his own new and authoritative version. Once again, the structure, form and content of his argument intersect and reinforce one another.

One of the effects of this quality of allegory and argument is to reinforce the marginalization of Hagar, a process already at work in the traditions Paul draws upon but heightened in this retelling. Just as Hagar was cast out and rejected in the traditional story, so too those whom Hagar represents in Paul's allegory are to be repudiated. Yet the stakes seem somewhat higher in Paul's version because of the dialectical character of the allegorical process: the intensification of Hagar's rejection through the rhetoric of persuasion and consensus fundamentally transforms the earlier narrative figure of Hagar. For the readers and hearers of this allegory, Hagar *becomes* her allegorical refiguration. Moreover, while her rejection and banishment are narrated in the first account, in the allegory they function as conceptual presuppositions, as foundational elements in the allegorical consensus. Whereas, narratively, there might have been some room for negotiation (that is, the story could conceivably have had a different ending), allegorically, the narrative elements become fixed and immutable.

The question arises whether this immutability of the new Hagar is itself a function of allegory or whether it is a function of Paul's particular use of allegory. David Dawson has formulated the intriguing thesis that allegorical interpretation served, in the Alexandrian context at least, to unseat reigning interpretations and to replace them with antihegemonic ones, with the result that the world and culture might be seen and made anew (1992). In short, allegorical interpretation can be a potent form of cultural critique. Is it possible to transpose this thesis into a different setting, the one in which Paul wrote and where allegorical interpretation had not quite the hegemonic role to which it could lay claim in Alexandria? If so, then one way of reading Paul's allegory of Sarah and Hagar is as an interpretation leading its readers to reorient their understanding of the world through the shift from the literal realm to the allegorical. Dawson describes how this process works:

> Cultural revision through an allegorical reading of scripture demands that one relate scripture and the world while refusing to identify them. If 'the given' and 'the obvious' function as the sole criteria for textual meaning and reference, scripture will depict and reinforce the everyday assumptions of the readers' world. On the other hand, if such a text were read in a way that bore no relation at all to the 'given' and 'obvious', it would have no relevance for the reader, at least insofar as he or she desired to retain and endorse some elements of the given world... If a text is to depict any recognizable world at all, it must be susceptible to a reading determined in part by the 'given' and 'obvious'—a 'literal' reading. But if that text is to enable readers to challenge or escape the given world, it must also be susceptible of another reading, which denies the hegemony of the first reading—and perhaps as a consequence the hegemony of the given order of things (Dawson 1992: 236-37).

The complicating factor for reading Paul's allegory in this fashion is that Paul's interpretation may initially have been an antihegemonic reading of Hagar and Sarah, but over time it has become itself a hegemonic reading. In this, it has perhaps lost the tensive relationship between the literal and the figural that both Dawson and Whitman understand to be crucial to the maintenance of allegory.

My reading of this allegory is predicated on the tendency of allegory toward foreclosure, reification and ossification of meaning. That is, I have argued that allegory as both a genre and a form of persuasion tends toward the creation of a closed system of signification and, that in the case of Sarah and Hagar, the two women are reduced to essences to which are attributed singular, authoritative meanings. In the process, Paul's allegorical interpretation becomes inevitable, normative, fixed.

The irony of this process, of course, is that allegory is itself a response to inevitable, normative, fixed meanings—an attempt to speak otherwise, to say something else publicly and openly (*allo* + *agoreuō*). As Stephen Greenblatt puts it, characterizing the analysis of Paul de Man (and, implicitly, other postmodernist theorists of allegory),

> Allegory in this view then is quite the opposite of what it often pretends to be: the recovery of the pure visibility of the truth, undisguised by the local and accidental. Allegory may dream of presenting the thing itself...but its deeper purpose and its actual effect is to acknowledge the darkness, the arbitrariness, and the void that underlie and paradoxically make possible, all representation of realms of light, order, and presence (Greenblatt 1981b: vii).

In other words, allegory calls into question the clarity and self-evident character of meaning's production and therefore ultimately undercuts its own project by positing that meaning always resides elsewhere, truth eludes its seeker. Given this function of allegory, its claims to articulate the truth of a text through its processes of displacement and substitution must ultimately call the very interpretation into question or, alternately, cease to be allegory and become, rather, hegemonic. It is this second move that, I would argue, indicts Paul's allegory in its new form as hegemonic, normative discourse.

Is this the inevitable outcome of allegorical interpretation, or are there occasions when allegory does not become ossified and hegemonic? There are compelling reasons to hope so: for one thing, if all interpretation is, in some measure, a form of allegory, as many critics and theorists believe, then it is crucial to the practice of engaged criticism that allegory not always tend toward hegemony. There are also compelling examples of how such nonhegemonic allegory might be practiced, and not surprisingly, these examples emerge from subaltern discourses and articulations of theory that view interpretation and the use of theory as strategic, partial, situational, and always open to rephrasing and rereading. Perhaps not surprisingly, there are numerous allegories of Hagar that challenge the hegemonic readings of both Genesis and Galatians, in the service of creating a new way of viewing the world, to put it in Dawson's terms.

For example, the story of Sarah and Hagar has been read in allegorical fashion as a dramatization of the limits and inadequacies of a feminist strategy that focuses only on the abstraction 'woman' or that posits a naïve category of 'sisterhood', as though women were not also always constituted by other, often competing, always complicating identities. Renita Weems's reading of the story is, in fact, an allegorical reading focused on African American women as readers of the Bible:

> While the details of Hagar's story offer for the African American female reader minimal positive strategies for survival, the story, by way of a negative example, reminds such a reader what her history has repeatedly taught her: *That women, although they share in the experience of gender oppression, are not* natural *allies in the struggles against patriarchy and exploitation* (Weems 1991: 76; emphasis in the original).

Hagar's story here becomes an allegory for two other narratives: that of African American women's experience and that of hegemonic strands of feminism; reading the two together produces a new interpretation of discourses of 'women', one that accounts for the African American woman reader's history.[17]

Hagar's story has also been retold allegorically within the frame of North American womanist and feminist fictional literature. Pauline Elizabeth Hopkins' nineteenth-century novel, *Hagar's Daughter*, allegorically appropriates the Hagar narrative to recount a tale of loss and redemption.[18] In the work of Canadian novelist Margaret Atwood, the story of Hagar becomes the springboard for an elaborated allegorical narrative about the appropriation of women's reproductive capacity by

17.    Delores S. Williams places the story of Hagar at the center of her new book on (African-American) womanist theology. Unfortunately this book appeared too late for me to incorporate a discussion of her 'allegory of Hagar', but readers should note this important work; see Williams 1993.

18.    Hopkins 1988: 1-284. I first learned of Pauline Hopkins' work, along with that of many other nineteenth-century African American women novelists, from Carby 1987; on Hopkins, see Carby 1987: 121-62.

the religiously-sanctioning state (1986). Each of these novels makes fruitful use of the Sarah and Hagar narrative by challenging the hegemonic view that Hagar's primary function is simply as a counterpoint to Sarah. Their allegories are nonhegemonic precisely because they shift the point of view to that of Hagar.

This change in perspective allows other allegories of Hagar to function as nonhegemonic interpretations of tradition. In a recent midrash, Margo Hittleman, a Jewish feminist poet, has imagined the reconciliation of Jewish and Arab women through an allegorical poem reinterpreting this tradition.[19]

1.
And still the battle rages,
replaying the ancient script of Sarah and Hagar
banishment and exile.

What if
the story had ended thus:

And Sarah seeing that she had erred, took her servant and her mule laden with food and drink and went out into the desert after Hagar to beg her forgiveness. Three days and three nights she traveled, stopping only to rest the mule. On the afternoon of the fourth day, Sarah came upon Hagar and Ishmael sleeping in the shade of a young tree. Sarah drew close, calling to the woman that she needn't be afraid. But Hagar, thinking Sarah had come only to taunt her further, rose up and cursed her, vowing that their sons and their sons' sons and their sons until the seventieth generation would bear arms against each other. Sarah listened and waited and when Hagar fell silent, she spoke from her heart, begging her sister's forgiveness. And when Hagar saw Sarah spoke in truth, her heart softened and she wept, for she knew the curse contained only bitterness and death. And she welcomed Sarah into her arms and the two women embraced and cried, each telling the other of her loneliness and grief. And at the spot where their tears fell, an iris bloomed. And they called that place 'where peace bloomed'. On the evening of the seventh day, Sarah and Hagar returned to Hebron and they dwelt there together. And their sons grew strong and bold, bound as brothers, learning the wisdom of the world, older from younger, younger from older. And peace filled the house.

Moreover, in an apparently broad-based movement among fundamentalist Muslim women in Egypt, gender activists have taken up the name Hagar[20] while Islamist theorists grappling with the conjunction of Islam and postmodernism have also begun to read Hagar allegorically:

19. Hittleman 1990/5751: 60. This first section of the poem 'Words' is reprinted with the permission of the author.

20. A recently formed fundamentalist Islamic women's organization in Egypt has

> We invoke the metaphor of Hagar...as the voice of counterdiscourses—
> discursive systems created by women, blacks, and Muslims from diverse
> backgrounds—and as the dialectic between assertiveness in defense of
> fulfilling important needs versus cooperative submission to collectively
> undertaken goals and projects. Hagar's voices, in this sense, are powerful
> and omnipresent (Fischer and Abedi 1990: 315).[21]

In all of these cases, the allegories of Hagar function strategically in
the fashion of Dawson's antihegemonic allegories of ancient Alexandria.
Here, allegory retains its edge and its crucial tension between literal and
figurative. Pointing outward, away from the traditional, literal, normative, these allegorical readings elaborate a new vision of a world remade
by the possibility of reading otherwise. This remains possible, of course,
because all of these allegorical readings are situated explicitly on the
margins of interpretative discourse. They are antihegemonic because
they remain contingent, situational, partial. They embody the possibility
of saying something else in public that is allegory's heart. If Fischer and
Abedi's understanding of Hagar as herself the figure for voices of
multiplicity (1990: 221) is accepted, then allegories of Hagar offer,
perhaps, a keenly critical example of the radical potential of political
interpretation as allegory.

taken the name Hagar; while the intent of such a self-naming is unclear, it is certainly
different from various other Muslim women's groups that have taken the names of
Mohammed's wives (Margot Badran, personal communication, Fall 1990). The term
'gender activism' is Badran's and seeks to name in a somewhat neutral and inclusive
fashion parallel strains of political activity among women in Egypt, some of whom
identify themselves explicitly as 'feminists' and some who draw their primary identities from fundamentalist forms of Islam; both groups of women work toward goals of
the empowerment of women, though in radically different settings.

21. In general, see Fischer and Abedi's reading of the centrality of Hagar in the
practice of *hajj* (1990: 150-221), especially the claim that Hagar herself stands for
sublimated discourses:

> Hagar, perhaps, is of particular import as a sign not only of the slow but
> insistent growth of a feminist consciousness in the Muslim world...but more
> generally of the form of alternative submission/self-assertion of alternative
> discourses from the street, from the lower classes, from oral life worlds, from
> the world of women heard and felt as vigorous in life albeit little represented
> in textual worlds (p. 220).

See also their reading of Hagar as the embodiment of multiplicitous voices engaging a
range of political and religious anxieties (p. 221).

# BIBLIOGRAPHY

Atwood, Margaret
1986        *The Handmaid's Tale* (Boston: Houghton Mifflin).
Barrett, Charles Kingsley
1976        'The Allegory of Abraham, Sarah, and Hagar in the Argument of
            Galatians', in J. Friedrich, W. Pöhlmann, and P. Stuhlmacher (eds.),
            *Rechtfertigung: Festschrift für Ernst Käsemann zum 70. Geburtstag*
            (Tübingen: Mohr [Siebeck]; Göttingen: Vandenhoeck & Ruprecht):
            1-16.
Benjamin, Walter
1977        *The Origin of German Tragic Drama* (trans. J. Osborne; London: New
            Left Books).
Betz, Hans Dieter
1979        *Galatians* (Hermeneia; Philadelphia: Fortress Press).
Bloom, Edward A.
1951        'The Allegorical Principle', *ELH: A Journal of English Literary
            History* 18: 163-90.
Bloomfield, Morton W.
1972        'Allegory as Interpretation', *New Literary History* 3: 301-17.
Borse, Udo
1984        *Der Brief an die Galater* (Regensburg: Verlag Friedrich Pustet).
Burton, Ernest De Witt
1920        *A Critical and Exegetical Commentary on the Epistle to the Galatians*
            (ICC; New York: Charles Scribner's Sons).
Callaway, Mary C.
1975        'The Mistress and the Maid: Midrashic Traditions behind Galatians
            4.21-31', *Radical Religion* 2(2-3): 94-101.
Carby, Hazel
1987        *Reconstructing Womanhood: The Emergence of the Afro-American
            Woman Novelist* (New York: Oxford University Press).
Clifford, Gay
1974        *The Transformations of Allegory* (London: Routledge & Kegan Paul).
Coleridge, Samuel Taylor
1936        *Miscellaneous Criticism* (ed. T. Raysor; London: Constable & Co.).
Culler, Jonathan
1975–76     'Literary History, Allegory, and Semiology', *New Literary History* 7:
            259-70.
Dawson, David
1990        'Against the Divine Ventriloquist: Coleridge and De Man on Symbol,
            Allegory, and Scripture', *Journal of Literature and Theology* 4: 293-
            310.
1992        *Allegorical Readers and Cultural Revision in Ancient Alexandria*
            (Berkeley: University of California Press).
De Man, Paul
1979        *Allegories of Reading: Figural Language in Rousseau, Nietzsche,
            Rilke, and Proust* (New Haven: Yale University Press).

| 1981 | 'Pascal's Allegory of Persuasion', in Greenblatt 1981a: 1-25. |
|------|------|
| 1983 | 'The Rhetoric of Temporality', in *Blindness and Insight: Essays in the Rhetoric of Contemporary Insight* (Minneapolis: University of Minnesota Press, 2nd rev. edn): 187-228. |

Falk, Marcia
    1990    *The Song of Songs: Love Lyrics from the Bible* (San Francisco: Harper Collins).

Fineman, Joel
    1981    'The Structure of Allegorical Desire', in Greenblatt 1981a: 26-60.

Fischer, Michael M.J. and Mehdi Abedi
    1990    *Debating Muslims: Cultural Dialogues in Postmodernity and Tradition* (Madison: University of Wisconsin Press).

Fletcher, Angus
    1964    *Allegory: The Theory of a Symbolic Mode* (Ithaca: Cornell University Press).

Fung, Ronald Y.K.
    1988    *The Epistle to the Galatians* (Grand Rapids: Eerdmans).

Geffcken, Johannes
    1908    'Allegory, Allegorical Interpretation', in J. Hastings *et al.* (eds.), *Encyclopaedia of Religion and Ethics*, I (New York: Charles Scribner's Sons): 327-31.

Greenblatt, Stephen J. (ed.)
    1981a    *Allegory and Representation* (Selected Papers from the English Institute, NS, 5; Baltimore: Johns Hopkins University Press).
    1981b    'Preface', in Greenblatt 1981a: vii-xiii.

Hansen, G. Walter
    1989    *Abraham in Galatians: Epistolary and Rhetorical Contexts* (JSNTSup, 29; Sheffield: JSOT Press).

Hanson, R.P C.
    1959    *Allegory and Event: A Study of the Sources and Significance of Origen's Interpretation of Scripture* (Richmond, VA: John Knox).

Hittleman, Margo
    1990 [5751]    'Words', *Bridges: A Journal for Jewish Feminists and our Friends* 1 (2): 60-62.

Honig, Edwin
    1972    *Dark Conceit: The Making of Allegory* (Providence, RI: Brown University Press).

Hopkins, Pauline Elizabeth
    1988    *The Magazine Novels of Pauline Hopkins* (The Schomburg Library of Nineteenth-Century Black Women Writers; New York: Oxford University Press).

Janzen, J. Gerald
    1991    'Hagar in Paul's Eyes and in the Eyes of Yahweh (Genesis 16): A Study in Horizons', *Horizons in Biblical Theology: An International Dialogue* 13.1-22.

Lagrange, M.-J.
    1950    *Saint Paul: Epitre aux Galates* (Paris: Gabalda).

Lightfoot, J.B.
1981      *St. Paul's Epistle to the Galatians* (repr.; Peabody, MA: Hendrickson).
Liptzin, Sol
1980      'Princess Hagar', *Dor le-Dor* 8 (3): 114-26.
Louth, Andrew
1983      *Discerning the Mystery: An Essay on the Nature of Theology* (Oxford: Clarendon Press).
Luther, Martin
1953 [1535] *A Commentary on St Paul's Epistle to the Galatians* (repr.; London: James Clarke).
Martyn, J.L.
1990      'The Covenants of Hagar and Sarah', in J.T. Carroll *et al.* (eds.), *Faith and History: Essays in Honor of Paul W. Meyer* (Atlanta: Scholars Press): 160-92.
Matera, Frank J.
1992      *Galatians* (Sacra Pagina, 9; Collegeville, MN: Liturgical Press).
Miller, J. Hillis
1981      'The Two Allegories', in M.W. Bloomfield (ed.), *Allegory, Myth and Symbol* (Cambridge, MA: Harvard University Press): 355-70.
Moore, Stephen D.
1989      'The "Post-" Age Stamp: Does it Stick? Biblical Studies and the Postmodernism Debate', *JAAR* 57: 543-59.
Neil, William
1967      *The Letter of Paul to the Galatians* (Cambridge: Cambridge University Press).
Nuttall, A.D.
1967      *Two Concepts of Allegory: A Study of Shakespeare's* The Tempest *and the Logic of Allegorical Expression* (London: Routledge & Kegan Paul).
Oepke, Albrecht
1973      *Der Brief des Paulus an die Galater* (THKNT, 9; Berlin: Evangelische Verlagsanstalt).
Pépin, Jean
1976      *Mythe et Allégorie: Les origines grecques et les contestations judéo-chrétiennes* (Paris: Etudes Augustiniennes, nouv. edn, rev. et aug).
Philo
1967      *Philo in Ten Volumes* (trans. F.H. Colson; LCL; Cambridge, MA: Harvard University Press).
Quilligan, Maureen
1979      *The Language of Allegory* (Ithaca: Cornell University Press).
Ridderbos, Herman N.
1953      *The Epistle of Paul to the Churches of Galatia* (Grand Rapids: Eerdmans).
Rohde, Joachim
1989      *Der Brief des Paulus an die Galater* (Berlin: Evangelische Verlagsanstalt).

Wagner, Guy
1991        'Les enfants d'Abraham ou les chemins de la promesse et de la liberté: exégèse de Galates 4.21 à 31', *RHPR* 71: 285-95.

Weems, Renita
1988        *Just a Sister Away: A Womanist Vision of Women's Relationships in the Bible* (San Diego: LuraMedia).
1991        'Reading *Her Way* through the Struggle: African American Women and the Bible', in C. Hope Felder (ed.), *Stony the Road we Trod: African American Biblical Interpretation* (Minneapolis: Fortress Press): 57-77.

Whitman, Jon
1987        *Allegory: Dynamics of Ancient and Medieval Technique* (Cambridge, MA: Harvard University Press).

Williams, Delores S.
1993        *Sisters in the Wilderness: The Challenge of Womanist God-Talk* (Maryknoll: Orbis Books, 1993).

PEERING INTO THE ABYSS:
A POSTMODERN READING OF THE BIBLICAL BOTTOMLESS PIT

Tina Pippin

## Introduction:
### Locating the Abyss in the Apocalyptic Landscape

Consider a map of the Apocalypse of John. The geography of the text is broadly divided into the two spheres of heaven and earth. In heaven is the dwelling place of God. On earth are the cities: the sites of the seven churches, Jerusalem (Mount Zion) and Babylon. There are deserts, waters and mountains. There are rural and urban areas and natural and supernatural realms.

Look around at the terrain of utopia: there is the New Jerusalem where God and the faithful dwell, but outside the city walls remains the active lake of fire and sulphur and the bottomless pit. There is a definite division of insider and outsider, and the focus of the textual map is split. After the great victory of God's army over evil, a 'holy city, the New Jerusalem' (Rev. 21.2) descends from heaven with new water and a tree of life (Rev. 22.1-5). The old earth with all its waters, dry land and mighty cities is destroyed. Even Death and Hades are no more after they are thrown into the lake of fire (Rev. 20.13).

Is creation really new if chaos still abides outside the garden gates? Why does this breach, this rupture, this gaping hole remain in the textual landscape? Is not God's future meant to be seamless and faultless, with all the evil powers and chaos destroyed for all time? Does the text throw the world back into an endless cycle of eternal return—out of chaos to creation and back again and again and again, never-ending? Is the textual map constantly deconstructing itself, falling into its own abyss?

Consider the following texts: 'Death will be no more; mourning and crying and pain will be no more, for the first things have passed away' (Rev. 21.4). 'Let the evildoer still do evil, and the filthy still be filthy, and the righteous still do right, and the holy still be holy' (Rev. 22.11).

In other words, watch your step. The text is not ending neatly; rather, it is opening itself to the chaotic all over again.

As a postmodern reader of the Apocalypse I want to locate myself at the point on the textual map labelled ABYSS and enter the text from this place. The dot on the map is itself part of the rupture and is the site of an impossible location. The abyss is a place of difference—different from any other place. The abyss is a place that is totally 'Other'. To locate oneself at/in the pit means to be at a place that is no place, no ground, no bottom, no context.

The subject and the method of this paper coincide. The abyss is a postmodern site because it is a site of conflict and struggle and chaos—the center that collapses. The abyss is an entry point into a strange and fragmented reading of the Apocalypse, a reading that is postmodern because it is not rooted in any historical-critical starting point. A reading from the abyss is not 'rooted' at all. In fact, to begin at the abyss is an 'unnatural' starting point. As Ihab Hassan defines postmodernism, 'Indeterminacy elicits participation; gaps must be filled. The postmodern text, verbal or nonverbal, invites performance: it wants to be written, revised, answered, acted out' (1987: 10). The abyss represents what in postmodernism is the unrepresentable, the indeterminate, the fragmented, the self-less and the depth-less.

The mythic place of the abyss on the textual map of the Apocalypse redefines space and location. The abyss is an imagined spot on the map—the impossible made possible in the fantasy of the end of time. The abyss is a dip in the landscape of the possible; it is the 'jumping-off-point' into nothingness. Its presence on the apocalyptic landscape is undeniable—and chilling. In the Apocalypse the abyss is a place of both warning and assurance for the believers. But even when assuring the believers of the safekeeping of the evil powers in the abyss, there is always the possibility that the angel with the key will open the entrance door.

The abyss makes the landscape unstable. In their study of postmodern landscape, Trevor Barnes and James Duncan call attention to the development of landscape as a 'social and cultural production':

> Thus a landscape possesses a similar objective fixity to that of a written text. It also becomes detached from the intentions of its original authors, and in terms of social and psychological impact and material consequences the various readings of landscapes matter more than any authorial intentions. In addition, the landscape has an importance beyond the initial situation for which it was constructed, addressing a potentially wide range of readers (1992: 6).

Locating the abyss on the map of the Apocalypse is a particular way of reading and a way of entering the textual landscape. This gaping hole/pit is a starting point, an ending point, a bottomless point and thereby no point at all on the map. Reading for/at the abyss is a postmodern reading because it is a different positioning at the place of absolute difference (or *différance*, in the Derridean sense of both differ and defer). The abyss defers the closure of the text. There is no authorial control over the depths of this abyssmal space. John measures the heavenly city, but the pit is measureless.

The map of the Apocalypse is a political map, for the destruction of the 'world' (the Mediterranean basin) and its reconstruction as the political center of God's power in the New Jerusalem are all central.[1] In the margins are danger, evil, pollution, dishonor, exploding and endless disorder. The abyss is in the margins of the text. But there are no set boundaries. There is a door to heaven (Rev. 4.1) as there is on the pit (Rev. 9.1-2), but there is movement in and out of each domain. The reader is shown the pit in all its horror; if persons were not marked on the forehead with the seal of God, the locusts that come out of the abysmal smoke would 'torture them for five months, but not to kill them, and their torture was like the torture of a scorpion when it stings someone. And in those days people will seek death but will not find it; they will long to die, but death will flee from them' (Rev. 9.5-6). This description of torture is good propaganda for becoming a servant of God!

Does the Apocalypse of John privilege order? Traditional readings of the text assert the final order of the end of time and God's victory over the forces of evil. I want to argue that this text is unbound in its own disorder—that the New Jerusalem as an ordered space is decentered by the well of chaos, which is seen as the abyss and the whole area outside the holy city where the evil powers dwell (in different states of punishment and tortured existence). The order is tenuous at best, with evil lurking outside the walls. The walls do not hold, they crumble, they 'cave' in, so to speak. The city itself is on the edge of the abyss, and its ordered economy and demographics are constantly threatened. There is a prison for the evil beings and a lake of torture and death. The vision of a protective state is interrupted by the presence of horror, and horror is interrupted by the presence of the ordered state, and on and on.

---

1. For a discussion of maps working in a society 'as a form of power-knowledge', see J.B. Harley's article (1992) on deconstructing geography.

### *The Abyss as Prison-House: Defining its Intertextual Dimensions*

In the Apocalypse of John the stories of destruction and creation swirl around the landscape. The supernatural and the natural collide and intersect. And this apocalyptic text collides with other biblical texts, other apocalyptic texts, readers and the cultural values and manifestations of imagining the end of the world. Text and texts—text(s) and worlds—interface. This basic definition of intertextuality as the relations of texts comes from Kristeva (1980; drawing from Bakhtin), Barthes (1977) and Derrida (1979). These textual relations and signification are often vague, problematic, warring or with permeable boundaries. With the signifier a–b–y–s–s, the boundaries are broken through; in fact, there are no boundaries, since the abyss has no boundaries. To write about the abyss is to write about nothingness, space turned upon space, the ground knocked out of meaning. As Kristeva states about the abject, the abyss is 'the place where meaning collapses' (1982: 2).

Nonetheless, the abyss has had its own history of interpretation. The abyss is part of all the apocalyptic action; it is a prison-house[2] for evil monsters:

> Then I saw an angel coming down from heaven, holding in his hand the key to the bottomless pit and a great chain. He seized the dragon, that ancient serpent, who is the Devil and Satan, and bound him for a thousand years, and threw him into the pit, and locked and sealed it over him, so that he would deceive the nations no more, until the thousand years were ended. After that he must be let out for a little while (Rev. 20.1-3).

Abyss, *abussos* in Greek, has many definitions. As seen from the passage above, the abyss is a spirit prison (from which the Antichrist and his evil cohorts ascend). Even more basic, the abyss is a bottomless pit, a well, the deep (Hebrew *tᵉhôm*), the interior of the earth, a place of exile, the original flood waters under the earth, chaos, the primordial Goddess, the source of the universe, the underworld (but not the place of eternal punishment).[3] In Gnosticism the abyss is 'the Supreme Being and the author of the Aeons' (Cooper 1978: 10). Christian mystics dwelt on the 'creation out of nothing' aspect of the abyss; one descends into the

---

2.    Northrop Frye defines 'prison-house' from Wordsworth as a descent theme from the innocent state of birth into a state 'of corruption or confusion' (1976: 100).

3.    Most of these basic definitions can be found in Bible dictionaries; see Jeremias for a brief discussion of the idea of the abyss as a spirit prison (1964: 10).

abyss to experience the pure essence of God (McRay 1986: 18-19).

Although the abyss is not Sheol, Gehenna or hell, the post-biblical tradition begins to merge these metaphors into an underworld place of eternal punishment. In some early Christian apocalypses, the abyss is more than a holding cell; it is also a torture chamber. The image of the mouth of hell develops during this period and is fully imagined in the medieval hell mouth iconography of a beast's or bird's (owl's) mouth (see Davidson and Seiler 1992; Wickham 1987). One of the most graphic images of the abyss as hell mouth appears in the *Apocalypse of Paul*:

> The abyss has no measure; moreover there also follows on it the (gulf, void?) which is below it. And it is as if perhaps someone takes a stone and throws it into a very deep well and after many hours it reaches the ground; so is the abyss. For when these souls are thrown in they have scarcely reached the bottom after five hundred years (ch. 32).

This well in the *Apocalypse of Paul* is 'sealed with seven seals'. When Paul desires to look in the well, his guide angel says,

> Open the mouth of the well that Paul, God's dearly beloved, may look in, because power has been given him to see all the punishments of the underworld. And the angel said to me: Stand at a distance, for you will not be able to bear the stench of this place. Then when the well was opened there came up immediately a disagreeable and very evil smell which surpassed all the punishments. And I looked into the well and saw fiery masses burning on all sides, and the narrowness of the well at its mouth was such that it was only able to take a single man (ch. 42).[4]

This hell mouth is a narrow passage that spews smoke and odors. Compare *1 En.* 88.1, 'that abyss was narrow, and deep, and horrible and dark'. But in Isa. 5.14 the mouth is opened wide: 'Therefore Sheol has enlarged its appetite and opened its mouth beyond measure'.[5]

The biblical deep is not just full of water; a large variety of sea monsters and serpents reside in the watery chaos. The basis for this view of the dangerous depths of the abyss is found in Ps. 42.7: 'Deep calls to deep at the thunder of your cataracts'. In the Apocalypse of John the

---

4. See also the discussion in Pippin 1993.

5. Michael Goldberg states that medieval representations of the hell mouth come from the Isa. 5.14 image of a large, wide open, mouth. He cites 'the Psalter of St Swithin's Priory, the famous York Minster Mouth of Hell' and Tennyson's *Charge of the Light Brigade* (25-26): 'Into the mouth of hell/Rode the six hundred' (1992: 342).

depths spit out smoke that contains locusts, who are monstrous winged figures on horses with human faces, women's hair, lion's teeth and scorpion tails that sting and torture their victims (Rev. 9.3-10).[6] The beast who kills the two witnesses comes out of the abyss (Rev. 11.7). The abyss is the place of monsters and all sorts of impurities. Evil angels are the inmates of the abyss in *1 En.* 21.10: 'This place (is) the prison of the angels, and there they will be held for ever'. This text echoes 2 Pet. 2.4, in which the sinful angels are cast into Tartaros (hell) until judgment day. In Jude 6 the angels are bound in chains for safekeeping until their trial.

From the orifice of the pit come horrible bodily discharges. The *Apocalypse of Peter* 8 gives a particularly graphic image of the

> very deep pit and into it there flow all kinds of things from everywhere: judgment (?) horrifying things and excretions. And the women (are) swallowed up (by this) up to their necks and are punished with great pain... And the milk of the mothers flows from their breasts and congeals and smells foul, and from it come forth beasts that devour flesh...

The excretions and foul smells are part of the torture. Most of all, 'there are wheels of fire, and men and women hung thereon by the power of their whirling. Those in the pit burn' (*Apoc. Pet.* 12; cf. *1 En.* 90.24-25).

The angel in charge of the abyss is identified in the Apocalypse of John 9.1, 'And the fifth angel blew his trumpet, and I saw a star that had fallen from heaven to earth, and he was given the key to the shaft of the bottomless pit', and more specifically in 9.11, 'His name in Hebrew is Abaddon, and in Greek he is called Apollyon'. Abaddon is the name of the destroyer angel and king of the underworld but is not Satan.[7] In Albrecht Dürer's 1498 woodcut Abaddon/Apollyon is throwing the Dragon down the narrow entrance of the abyss (Rev. 20.1). The stories of the fallen angels from Gen. 6.1-4 and *1 Enoch* 6–8 tell of more than two hundred angels falling to earth. Eventually these fallen angels fall even further into the interior of the earth. Leonard Thompson points out that the evil beasts in the Apocalypse (Apollyon, beast from the sea, scarlet beast) are 'variations on one another' (1990: 80). Evil monsters are difficult to tell apart, especially in the heat of the apocalyptic moment, with the beast in hot pursuit or disappearing into the bottomless pit into

6. In the *Shepherd of Hermas* Vision 4.1.6, fiery locusts come out of the mouth of the beast 'like some Leviathan'.

7. Leonard Thompson notes, 'Abaddon parallels death, the grave, and Sheol' (1990: 220 n. 11).

destruction—or rather, a limited prison sentence.

The abyss is imagined as a place of pain, or, to borrow Robert Detweiler's phrase, as a 'text of pain',[8] which describes texts that are written on the body (1989: 123). The abyss is both a part of the earth and a part of the body, the female sexual organs. As with Marduk's defeat of Tiamat in the *Enuma Elish*, the body of the Mother Goddess is divided into pieces, into a fragmented body; the male triumphs.[9] In the Apocalypse the female body is used to create the New City, and the triumphal males enter to live in this well-ordered place. All that remains outside the city are the 'remains', the sexual center of the female. So does the male triumph completely and absolutely? Or does the presence of the abyss create such desire and terror because the ultimate Fall from grace, Eve's 'sin', is (re)presented? As long as the abyss remains on the textual landscape, there is no certainty and no Truth. The text and the body are dismembered. The abyss is a body part laid bare and strewn throughout the text.

Is there a source to the abyss? Its concept of bottomlessness is an impossibility. In *1 En.* 21.7 the abyss is 'full of great pillars of fire which were made to fall; neither its extent nor its size could I see, nor could I see its source'. This concept of no origin relates to the Derridian idea that there is no source or origin to meaning, and that it is a false direction to search for an origin. The abyss appears and disappears on the map. The abyss is the black hole in space; what happens when an abyss is entered is still only speculation. Is the abyss where eroticism and death are linked? (Can this also be said of the New Jerusalem?) Could the bottomless pit be the ultimate joyride in the apocalyptic amusement park? Is its repeating presence for the reader's pleasure, always placing the reader on the brink of disaster? Or is the abyss the vanishing

8.    The idea of pain is expressed in Korean Minjung theology. A. Sung Park defines Han as the 'boiled-down feeling of pain caused by injustice and oppression. It is the deep-seated lamentation or bitterness of the suffering Minjung' (1989: 50). And 'Han is the abyss of grief which is deeply embedded in the collective unconscious history of the Korean Minjung' (p. 51). As the abyss of pain, Han is a text of pain in Korean liberation hermeneutics.

9.    Paul Ricoeur focuses on the creation of evil in the *Enuma Elish*: 'If the divine came into being, then chaos in anterior to order and the principle of evil is primordial, coextensive with the generation of the divine'. Of Tiamat and Apsu representing the waters of the earth, Ricoeur adds, 'But this liquid chaos has a surcharge of meaning, in which the myth of the origin of evil takes shape. For Tiamat is more than the visible immensity of the waters; she has the power to produce' (1967: 177).

(or infinity) point on the canvas, with everything disappearing into a postmodern nihilism?

Approaching the mouth of the abyss is dangerous. The abyss is a cave, an endless serpent. Does this mouth have lips? Could this be the poison kiss—the kiss of death? Or are these 'lips' the vulva? Does this mouth devour? Does this mouth have teeth—the *vagina dentata*, the agent of castration? Here is the prison-house of language, under lock and key. Usually words or sounds come out of a mouth; here there is only oral residue, the trace of the spoken, the trace of Wisdom, the hiss of signification.

### Representing Nothingness

The whole idea of chaos has been played out recently in the fields of science and literature. In science and mathematics chaos theory seeks to find the order out of disordered systems; the repeating systems are called 'strange attractors', or patterns of order found in the deep structure of chaos. The unpredictable aspects of our world have a certain order to them; hidden inside the 'random' changes in nature (e.g. natural disasters) is a pattern of order in the midst of chance. According to Antonio Benítez-Rojo in his study of Caribbean literature, 'Chaos looks toward everything that repeats, reproduces, grows, decays, unfolds, flows, spins, vibrates, seeths' (1992: 3). Instead of filling the chaos of a text with an ordered or structured reading, poststructuralist and postmodernist readings allow for chaos to have precedence, to create its own space and disorder. In other words, meaning is indeterminant, and signifier and signified are unbound in an endless spiral.

This connection between chaos theory and postmodernism has best been made by Katherine Hayles. She investigates chaos theory, fractal geometry, the deconstructive theory of Jacques Derrida, Roland Barthes' reading of Sarrazine and Michael Serres' philosophical interpretations. The main connection is that these 'discourses invert traditional priorities: chaos is deemed to be more fecund than order, uncertainty is privileged above predictability, and fragmentation is seen as the reality that arbitrary definitions of closure would deny' (1990: 176). The rifts, holes, fissures and ruptures of texts are the focal points of postmodernism. In discussing Derrida's *Of Grammatology*, Hayles notes that texts 'are reservoirs of chaos' that are 'always already' chaotic. These terms from Derrida refer to iteration, a word having different meanings in different contexts (p. 180). Iteration occurs in the 'folds' of a text—textual spaces of repetition. 'The fold can be thought of as a way to create the illusion of origin', Hayles adds, while iteration 'unfolds' the text so that there is no point of origin (p. 181). Hayles summarizes, 'For deconstructionists, chaos repudiates order; for scientists, chaos makes order possible' (p. 184).[10]

For Hayles, postmodernism constructs a 'denaturing process' in which language, context, time and the human are denatured (1990: 266). The new world created in the Apocalypse is a denatured world where nature and history collapse. The tree and waters of life in the New Jerusalem are repetitions of their Eden versions in Genesis. The origin of the world created out of the depths/chaos is repeated in the abyss, where there is no bottom, no origin. Perhaps there is a 'future shock' (Alvin Toffler) where the future is used up before it happens (1990: 280),[11] and any human concept of time expands. John is a sort of time traveller who is able to break loose of his prison on Patmos to explore future worlds, while the horror of his present world is forever seeping into the future visions of hope and vice versa. There is no escaping chaos in the Apocalyse. Chaos is everywhere, past, present and future.

Chaos represents Otherness (*différance*), and chaos, like the abyss in the Apocalypse, is a female concept. Hayles criticizes the chaos theoretician James Gleick for his reification of male-based scientific knowledge and the ignoring of women scientists in his discussion of chaos. Hayles accuses Gleick of maintaining science as exclusively male, while 'it is the particular project of this domain to have intercourse with a feminine principle' (1990: 174). Hayles further observes:

> But otherness is also always a threat, arousing the desire to control it, or even more extremely to subsume it within the known boundaries of the self, thus annihilating the very foreignness that makes it dangerously attractive... The desire to control chaos is evident in the search for ways to rationalize it. By finding within it structures of order, these scientists have in effect subsumed chaos in the familiar. But if this incorporation were entirely successful, chaos could no longer function in its liberating role as a representation of the other (p. 173).

---

10. Dudley Young examines the mythological roots of chaos as 'the yawning womb-tomb abyss from which Mother Earth arose to deliver the cosmos' and as 'a deathly hole just waiting to grab the inattentive or unlucky' (1991: 182).

11. Hayles lists some recent films to illustrate the point of a 'false future': '*Back to the Future, Brazil, Terminator [I, II]*, and *Peggy Sue Got Married*' (1990: 280).

The otherness of the abyss in the Apocalypse represents the ultimate threat, the ultimate dangerous female. The abyss is the ruptured female, the ruptured hymen, no longer virgin, nor virgin mother, but the place of the vaginal birth of the universe. The evil women in the Apocalypse, Jezebel and the Whore of Babylon, are clearly not virgins. The Woman Clothed with the Sun is a repeating of the Mary/Mother of God myth. The Bride of Christ is a virginal bride, but when she becomes the New Jerusalem she is entered by the believers and the company of God, including her husband, the Lamb. Still, the virginal women have maintained shame, which is represented by the hymen (see Malina 1981: 42-48). The abyss is yet another female character in the Apocalypse, representing the primordial female, chaos, the deep waters under the earth.

The presence of the abyss in the text seduces the reader. Like drivers who slow down to stare in fascination at an automobile accident, the gaze of the text on the monstrous and the horrible shows the pull of desire to look in that direction. There is a definite gaze on the female in the Apocalypse, and this gaze is controlling. The female is marked and sectioned off, and violence follows, either by death, exile, or the use of the body to create a new city. The abyss also receives this gaze. The abyss as female is Other, and the Other in the Apocalypse is feared and desired all at once. Demons enter the abyss, while only the purified people and spirits of God enter the Bride.

To return to the notion of the abyss as the female organ, as vagina and ruptured hymen—what is also present in this line of thinking is what the abyss is *not*, or what it lacks, which is the phallus. Following a Freudian line, the abyss represents castrated woman/mother. The female must hide her shame, her lack. According to Jacques Lacan, 'the phallus can play its role only when veiled' (1977: 288).[12] Elizabeth Grosz comments on this Lacanian concept of veiling:

> This gap or lack is also the founding trace of the unconscious, constituted as such by the repressed signifier: It is the ultimately significative object which appears when all the veils are lifted. Everything related to it is an object of amputations and interdictions… When the veils are lifted, there is only the Medusa—women's castrated genitals, lacking, incomplete,

12. Jane Gallop adds in her discussion of male castration desire: 'Desire shall henceforth be wed to castration because the phallic signifier is the mark of desire' (1985: 145).

horrifying (for men). Salomé's dance, like strip-tease, can only seduce when at least one veil remains, alluring yet hiding the *nothing* of woman's sex (1990: 121).[13]

Is the sealing door to the abyss a type of veil? For Kristeva that which horrifies, the abject, is veiled: 'The time of abjection is double: a time of oblivion and thunder, of veiled infinity and the moment when revelation bursts forth' (1982: 9). So, too, for Derrida: 'Truth, unveiling, illumination are no longer decided in the appropriation of the truth of being, but are cast into its bottomless abyss as non-truth, veiling and dissimulation...' (1979: 119). The door to the abyss is a locked and sometimes lifted veil.

The abyss represents both the Unconscious and unconscious desires. Only the angel has the key (on 'a great chain'!) with which he can unlock the covering over the mouth. This focus on lack and on castration is a phallocentric way of imagining the abyss. Grosz follows Irigaray's definition of phallocentrism as the centering of the male as normative for human behavior. She states:

> As the sexual other to the One sex, woman has only been able to speak or to be heard as an undertone, a murmur, a rupture within discourse; or else she finds her expression in a hysterical fury, where the body 'speaks' a discourse that cannot be verbalized by her (1990: 174).

As a 'rupture within discourse' the abyss is a hysterical place when the veil or lid is taken off. Or is it a place of *jouissance*? God places an angel guard in control of the entrance/mouth of the abyss. Only the mouth is bound and maintained. But the rupture is deep, so that there is no end to chaos (or revelation) in the 'end'.

The rupture is not the rupture caused by castration (or clitorectomy), but rather it is the rupture caused by (sexual experience and) the birthing process. Still, the abyss represents chaos and must be controlled under lock and key.[14] What remains is the murmur, the rupture that the presence of the abyss places in the text. The abyss remains a gendered space, a female space.

13. Hélène Cixous also criticizes Lacan's phallocentric focus or 'phallogocentric sublation'. The male myth is that women are between 'two horrifying myths: between the Medusa and the abyss' (1991: 341).

14. Thompson reveals the function of controlling the abyss: 'Through images of locks, keys, chains, seals, loosing, and binding John is able to describe controlled movement between earth and Hades (9.1; 20.1-3). Since the realm below represents not only the demonic but also death, movement to and from that realm may also occur in the form of transformation from death to life, or resurrection' (1990: 83).

## Conclusion: Transgressing Boundaries
### Who Will Descend into the Abyss? (Rom. 10.7)

The apocalyptic abyss is part of the western cultural landscape.[15] In literary, theological and philosophical traditions, the fascination with the abyss has taken the imagination into new realms of the supernatural underworld—in particular, into one realm that is a more ordered chaos, that of hell. Eventually, the concept of hell developed into a hierarchically structured place, in direct opposition to the hierarchy of heaven. But the abyss remained in the margins of the apocalyptic imagination as the true chaos, with no order, no form, no plot, no characters, no narrator—and so on. The abyss crosses all boundaries; it is boundless. How does something that ruptures all form fit into an apocalyptic vision of how God is going to re-form the world?

The visions of the Apocalypse of John are of a world with an imposed order. The mouth of the abyss is guarded and only opened under divine command. There is a pre-designed plan for the boundaries of the new world. This aspect of fixity in Christianity is criticised by philosopher Georges Bataille:

> The Christian God is a highly organised and individual entity springing from the most destructive of feelings, that of continuity. Continuity is reached when boundaries are crossed. But the most constant characteristic of the impulse I have called transgression is to make order out of what is essentially chaos. By introducing transcendence into an organised world, transgression becomes a principle of an organised disorder (1986: 119).

The presence of the abyss in the text makes all boundaries useless. Continuity disintegrates when the mouth of the abyss is transgressed. The original chaos survives with all its depths intact.

The philosophical roots of a postmodern reading of the abyss come from Friedrich Nietzsche's question, 'Is seeing itself—not seeing abysses?' (1961: 177; quoted in Watson 1985: 245), which reflects the nihilism resulting from any attempt to ground knowledge in God. Nietzsche is responding to the Kantian idea of 'der Wahre Abgrund', which translates as 'true abyss. The truth of grounding, to be *without* grounds' (Watson 1985: 229). This loss of ground is the loss of truth and knowledge. In other words, there are some things that cannot be known

---

15. In Eastern religions such as Buddhism and Hinduism, the concept of nothingness (or sunyata, emptiness) is positive and represents freedom.

completely, despite science and reason, and this groundlessness is the problem of abysses for philosophers such as Kant, Hegel, Heidegger, Nietzsche and Derrida. Stephen Watson traces the line of philosophical thinking about the abyss back to the essence of God (a focus of the mediaeval mystics); deconstructionists (following Nietsche) say that this essence or origin is the abyss; still the abyss is continually problematized. The abyss is a problem in philosophical thought because it represents infinity, the endless repetition of time, being and knowledge that is never fixed or rooted or rational.

The abyss is what one sees when one sees the Other. Watson understands the Nietzschean abyss as affirming difference:

> There is a refusal to reduce all attributes to an univocity. A refusal, there-fore, of ontology, of 'Being'; all is interpretation and exegesis. The world is, in short, an abyss, and *Ab-grund*... It is a chasm of infinite alterity, the infinite return of this Other with a Same. It is the return of the Other, of becoming, of difference (1985: 233).

When the abyss is faced, the Other is faced. Perhaps the abyss should be written abyss, crossed through to point to the non-origin, the absence the abyss represents.[16] This Other of the abyss in the Apocalypse is the abject (Kristeva 1982)—that which is horrible and profane. In the abyss are linked Female–Other–Death, the trinity of the sacrificial mode. The body of the female is sacrificed throughout the Apocalypse, but with the abyss is left a body part, a chasm that devours horrors and spews forth some of the most horrible evil beasts imaginable. The interior of the abyss is not described; it is too horrible to imagine. So the text stops at the mouth, and the opening is perhaps the scariest part of all.

The desire for primordial creation, the big birth, repeats itself in the apocalyptic narrative. The abyss is the creative power of the female. The boundaries of the dualism of male–female, culture–nature and mind–body are disrupted. The whole text is left in ruins. The boundaries of the New Jerusalem seem impenetrable, but they are not a stable entity in the text, for this future city is always not yet. The abyss is always already.

16. John Caputo asserts that Derrida's understanding of absence is an absence of signs. He states, 'Is not the *sur-prise* [of Rousseau] the way we are taken-in, or drawn-out, by the movement of with-drawal?... Is not this play the play of Being, of the abyss, the world-play which plays without why across the epochs?... Instead of the substitute, Derrida should speak of the aboriginal abyss; instead of the supplement, the hidden depths; instead of masturbation, the primal birth of things in *lethe*' (1985: 199).

The abyss is the excess of desire, surplus erotic power. The focus at the end of the twentieth century is on human power to destroy the world through nuclear holocaust and/or environmental poisoning. In the Apocalypse of John the focus is on God's power to destroy the world. Of course, Christian fundamentalists still hold diligently to this theology.[17] They have a fascination with the horror of the endtime; they stand close to the edge of the abyss, straining to peer in as Paul did in the *Apocalypse of Paul*. Current historical events in the Middle East are read with anticipation of the soon-to-come horrors. The evil beast is soon to be spit out of the hell mouth.

In the abyss 'all is interpretation and exegesis', and there is no end to this process. So, to say that in the Apocalypse of John the abyss means such-and-such is ultimately to say nothing. Historical-critical exegesis desires a grounding in meaning, which is no ground. The Apocalypse is not a history book of the late twentieth or the late first century. The exegete is left with no place to stand, for to stand in the abyss is to stand no place.

The end of the Bible returns to the beginning. There is an echo or trace of the nothingness, the formless void, from the beginning. There is the possibility of a new and different creation, another text. Leaving the void intact creates the possibility of change. Maybe this time the story will be different.

### BIBLIOGRAPHY

Altizer, Thomas J.J.
    1990    *Genesis and Apocalypse: A Theological Voyage toward Authentic Christianity* (Louisville: Westminster/John Knox Press).
Barnes, Trevor J. and James S. Duncan
    1992    'Introduction: Writing Worlds', in Barnes and Duncan 1992: 1-17.
Barnes, Trevor J. and James S. Duncan (eds.)
    1992    *Writing Worlds: Discourse, Text and Metaphor in the Representation of Landscape* (New York: Routledge).
Barthes, Roland
    1977    'The Death of the Author', in *Image, Music, Text* (trans. S. Heath; New York: Hill & Wang): 142-48.
Bataille, Georges
    1986    *Eroticism: Death and Sensuality* (trans. Mary Dalwood; San Francisco: City Lights Books).

17.   One common theme in contemporary millenarian thought is that of television as the hell mouth (Boyer 1993: 237).

1989        *The Tears of Eros* (trans. P. Connor; San Francisco: City Lights Books).

Blanchot, Maurice
1986        *The Writing of the Disaster* (trans. A. Smock; Lincoln: University of Nebraska Press).
1992        *The Step not Beyond* (trans. L. Nelson; Albany: State University of New York Press).

Benítez-Rojo, Antonio
1992        *The Repeating Island: The Caribbean and the Postmodern Perspective* (Durham: Duke University Press).

Boyer, Paul
1993        *When Time Shall Be No More: Prophecy Belief in Modern American Culture* (Cambridge, MA: Harvard University Press).

Caputo, John D.
1985        'From the Primordiality of Absence to the Absence of Primordiality: Heidegger's Critique of Derrida', in Silverman and Ihde 1985: 191-200.

Cixous, Hélène
1991        'The Laugh of the Medusa', in Robyn R. Warhol and Diane Price Herndl (eds.), *Feminisms: An Anthology of Literary Theory and Criticism* (New Brunswick: Rutgers University Press): 334-49.

Cooper, J.C.
1978        *An Illustrated Encyclopedia of Traditional Symbols* (London: Thames & Hudson).

Davidson, Clifford and Thomas H. Seiler (eds.)
1992        *The Iconography of Hell* (Kalamazoo, MI: Medieval Institute Publications).

Derrida, Jacques
1974        *Of Grammatology* (trans. Gayatri Chakravorty Spivak; Baltimore: Johns Hopkins University Press).
1979        *Spurs: Nietzsche's Styles* (trans. Barbara Harlow; Chicago: University of Chicago Press).
1981        *Dissemination* (trans. B. Johnson; Chicago: University of Chicago Press).

Detweiler, Robert
1989        *Breaking the Fall: Religious Readings of Contemporary Fiction* (San Francisco: Harper & Row).

Duensing, Hugo (trans.)
1966        *The Apocalypse of Paul*, in Schneemelcher and Hennecke 1966.
1966        *The Apocalypse of Peter*, in Schneemelcher and Hennecke 1966.

Frye, Northrop
1976        *The Secular Scripture: A Study of the Structure of Romance* (Cambridge, MA: Harvard University Press).

Gallop, Jane
1985        *Reading Lacan* (Ithaca, NY: Cornell University Press).

Game, Ann
1991        *Undoing the Social: Towards a Deconstructive Sociology* (Toronto: University of Toronto Press).

Gleick, James

1987          *Chaos: Making a New Science* (New York: Viking).
Goldberg, Michael
1992          'Hell', in David Lyle Jeffrey (ed.), *A Dictionary of Biblical Tradition in English Literature* (Grand Rapids: Eerdmans): 340-43.
Grosz, Elizabeth
1990          *Jacques Lacan: A Feminist Introduction* (London: Routledge).
Haraway, Donna J.
1991          *Simians, Cyborgs, and Women: The Reinvention of Nature* (London: Routledge).
Harley, J.B.
1992          'Deconstructing the Map', in Barnes and Duncan 1992: 231-47.
Hassan, Ihab
1987          *The Postmodern Turn: Essays in Postmodern Theory and Culture* (Columbus: Ohio State University Press).
Hayles, N. Katherine
1990          *Chaos Bound: Orderly Disorder in Contemporary Literature and Science* (Ithaca, NY: Cornell University Press).
Jameson, Frederic
1972          *The Prison-House of Language: A Critical Account of Structuralism and Russian Formalism* (Princeton: Princeton University Press).
1991          *Postmodernism, or, The Cultural Logic of Late Capitalism* (Durham: Duke University Press).
Jeffrey, David Lyle (ed.)
1992          *A Dictionary of Biblical Tradition in English Literature* (Grand Rapids: Eerdmans).
Jeremias, Joachim
1964          'ἄβυσσος', *TDNT*, I, 9-10.
Knibb, M.A. (trans.)
1984          *Animal Apocalypse [1 Enoch 85–90]*, in Sparks 1984.
1984          *Book of the Watchers [1 Enoch 1–36]*, in Sparks 1984.
Kristeva, Julia
1980          *Desire in Language: A Semiotic Approach to Literature and Art* (ed. L.S. Roudiez; trans. T. Gora, A. Jardine and L.S. Roudiez; New York: Columbia University Press).
1982          *Powers of Horror: An Essay on Abjection* (trans. L.S. Roudiez; New York: Columbia University Press).
Lacan, Jacques
1977          *Ecrits: A Selection* (trans. Alan Sheridan; New York: Norton).
Lake, Kirsopp (trans.)
1913          *The Shepherd of Hermas*, in *The Apostolic Fathers*, II (LCL; Cambridge, MA: Harvard University Press).
McCaffery, Larry (ed.)
1991          *Storming the Reality Studio: A Casebook of Cyberpunk and Postmodern Fiction* (Durham: Duke University Press).
McRay, John R.
1986          'Abyss', in William H. Grentz (ed.), *The Dictionary of Bible and Religion* (Nashville: Abingdon Press): 18-19.

Malina, Bruce
1981        *The New Testament World: Insights from Cultural Anthropology*
            (Atlanta: John Knox Press).
Nietzsche, Friedrich
1961        *Thus Spoke Zarathustra* (trans. R.J. Hollingdale; New York: Penguin
            Books).
Park, A. Sung
1989        'Theology of Han (the Abyss of Pain)', *Quarterly Review* (Spring):
            48-62.
Payne, Robert
1960        *Hubris: A Study of Pride* (New York: Harper & Brothers).
Pippin, Tina
1992        *Death and Desire: The Rhetoric of Gender in the Apocalypse of John*
            (Louisville: Westminster/John Knox Press).
1993        'Wisdom and Apocalyptic in the Apocalypse of John: Desiring
            Sophia', in Brandon Scott and Leo G. Perdue (eds.), *In Search of
            Wisdom* (Louisville: Westminster/John Knox Press): 293-303.
Ricoeur, Paul
1967        *The Symbolism of Evil* (trans. Emerson Buchanan; Boston: Beacon
            Press).
Ruf, Frederick J.
1991        *The Creation of Chaos: William James and the Stylistic Making of a
            Disorderly World* (Albany: State University of New York Press).
Schüssler Fiorenza, Elisabeth
1991        *Revelation: Vision of a Just World* (Minneapolis: Fortress Press).
Schneemelcher, Wilhelm and Edgar Hennecke (eds.)
1966        *The New Testament Apocrypha*, II (Philadelphia: Westminster Press).
Silverman, Hugh J. and Don Ihde (eds.)
1985        *Hermeneutics and Deconstruction* (Albany: State University of New
            York Press).
Sparks, H.F.D. (ed.)
1984        *The Apocryphal Old Testament* (Oxford: Clarendon Press).
Thompson, Leonard L.
1990        *The Book of Revelation: Apocalypse and Empire* (New York: Oxford
            University Press).
Watson, Stephen H.
1985        'Abysses', in Silverman and Ihde 1985: 228-46.
Wickham, Glynne
1987        *The Medieval Theatre* (Cambridge: Cambridge University Press).
Young, Dudley
1991        *Origins of the Sacred: The Ecstasies of Love and War* (New York: St
            Martin's Press).

Rembrandt, *The Anatomy Lesson of Dr Nicolas Tulp*

# How Jesus' Risen Body Became a Cadaver

Stephen D. Moore

## Prologue

In the beginning was the Word, and the Word was in a book, and the Word was the book.

There was a book sent from God, whose name was John. It came as a witness to testify to the light, so that all might believe through it. It was not the light, but it came to bear witness to the light.

And the Word became flesh—human flesh at first, then, eventually, animal flesh, parchment, processed sheepskin. Later still it became paper, processed wood pulp, the blood-drenched wood of a Roman cross.

Why did the Word become flesh, according to John? In order to reveal his glory (1.14), the glory bestowed on him by the Father (8.54; 13.31-32; 17.1, 5, 22, 24). How did the Word reveal his glory? By means of the 'signs' (*semeia*) that he performed (2.1-11; 4.46-53; 5.2-9; 6.1-13, 16-21; 9.1-12; 11.17-44; cf. 2.18-19; 20.30). He 'manifested his glory, and his disciples believed in him' (2.11; cf. 2.23; 4.48; 6.14, 30; 11.18; 12.37).

Why did the Word become writing, according to John? For precisely the same reason that the Word performed signs: so that his audience might come to believe, and believing 'have life in his name' (20.31; cf. 19.35; 21.24). Each time the book is read, Jesus re-enacts his signs. The book extends Jesus' mission beyond the tomb. In short, the book is Jesus' risen body. Here is how the book was found:

> Peter and the other disciple set out and went toward the tomb. The two were running together but the other disciple outran Peter and reached the tomb first. He bent down to look in and saw the linen wrappings lying there, covered with writing, but he did not go in. Then Simon Peter came, following him, and went into the tomb. He saw the linen wrappings lying there, and the cloth that had been on Jesus' head, not lying with the linen wrappings but rolled up in a place by itself, and likewise covered with

> writing. Then the other disciple, who reached the tomb first, also went in,
> and he saw and believed; for as yet they did not understand that, as
> scripture, he must rise from the dead (Jn 20.3-9, NRSV, modified).

'Read me', urges the book, 'that you may have life'. 'Eat me', urges
the Word, in the book; 'whoever eats me will live because of me' (6.57;
cf. 6.51-58). Eat me, ingest me, digest me—but don't excrete me!

As biblical scholars, we have learned not to devour the book, nor
even the Word. Instead we have learned to dissect the book and the
Word.

As biblical scholars, we have learned to be doubting Thomas's doubly
dubious twin. Invited to subject the Risen Body to a physical examination, Thomas declines, and for the same reason that so many believers
decline to subject the Word to a critical examination. Convinced that the
Word is of God, Thomas refuses to put his finger in the mark of the nib
in its hands, or place his hand in the paper-cut in its side (20.27-28).
Jesus commends Thomas for his rejection of the empirical method:
'Have you believed because you have seen me? Blessed are those who
have not seen and yet have come to believe' (20.29). Biblical scholarship, in contrast, is the science that subjects the written body of Jesus to
a rigorous examination. As such, biblical scholarship has medicine as its
sibling science.

## Ecclesia Abhorret a Sanguine

> ... [I]f the old beliefs had for so long such prohibitive power, it was
> because doctors had to feel, in the depths of their scientific appetite, the
> repressed need to open up corpses (Foucault 1973: 125-26).

Michel Foucault's *The Birth of the Clinic: An Archaeology of Medical
Perception* examines the process by which the human body was
reinvented as an object of scientific scrutiny in eighteenth- and
nineteenth-century Europe.[1] During the same period, as we know, the
Bible was being reinvented as an object of scientific scrutiny. What is the
relationship between these two gazes, these two glances, the medical and
the exegetical?

In order for modern medicine to emerge, the medical gaze, long
blunted by 'the black stone of the body' (Foucault 1973: 117), had to

---

1 .　In French the subtitle of Foucault's book reads *une archéologie du regard
médical*, 'an archaeology of the medical gaze'. It begins: 'This book is about space,
about language, and about death; it is about the act of seeing, the gaze' (p. ix).

hone itself, had to become scalpel-sharp. Throughout the eighteenth century, in particular, medicine beheld a new space opening up before it, 'the tangible space of the body', 'that opaque mass in which secrets, invisible lesions, and the very mystery of origins lie hidden' (p. 122). The age of pathological anatomy had arrived, but so had the age of biblical criticism. The pen took its place beside the scalpel.

Critical dissection of the biblical text has often been seen as an irreligious act. Examples from the history of biblical scholarship abound, such as the public outcry that greeted the publication of D.F. Strauss' *Life of Jesus* in 1835. The author was abruptly dismissed from his post at Tübingen, his conservative colleagues 'incensed that a theologian of this persuasion was aspiring to teach prospective ministers' (Baird 1992: 247; cf. Kümmel 1972: 120). Four years later, the attempts of liberal supporters to secure a chair for Strauss at Zürich were foiled by the good people of the town, who held noisy protest meetings and circulated outraged petitions (Baird 1992: 247-48). More than a hundred and fifty years later, as we all know, institutions of learning can still be found that harbor dark suspicions regarding biblical criticism, although the public no longer burns our books, or even reads them. And even when one's institution is not wary of biblical criticism, one's students often are. To give a simple example from my own recent experience, my first day at Wichita State University began with a student solemnly putting this question to me: 'Dr Moore, I'm tempted to take your New Testament course, but first I need to know if you're an atheist'. My reply, although heavily qualified, was enough to enable him to overcome the temptation.

If critical dissection of the Bible has sometimes been seen as a sacrilegious act, however, the dissection of cadavers has been only slightly less suspect throughout much of Christian history. Foucault puts it memorably:

> Medicine could gain access to that which founded it scientifically only by circumventing, slowly and prudently, one major obstacle, the opposition of religion, morality, and stubborn prejudice to the opening up of corpses. Pathological anatomy had no more than a shadowy existence, on the edge of prohibition, sustained only by that courage in the face of malediction peculiar to seekers after secret knowledge; dissection was carried out only under cover of the shadowy twilight, in great fear of the dead: 'at daybreak, or at the approach of night', Valsalva slipped furtively into graveyards...; later, Morgagni could be seen 'digging up the graves of the dead and plunging his scalpel into corpses taken from their coffins' (1973: 124-25, quoting an early nineteenth-century source).

Although Foucault himself is skeptical of these tales from the crypt, the religious dread that ultimately gave rise to them can hardly be denied.

Throughout the Middle Ages, in particular, the Church frowned upon anatomical dissection 'as showing a lack of respect for the human body, "the temple of the soul"...' (Castiglioni 1958: 409). At times this dogmatic scruple extended even to surgical practice. *Ecclesia abhorret a sanguine* was the dictum—'the Church abhors blood' (Starobinski 1964: 38). And as most physicians happened to be members of the clergy, the study of medicine in this period 'was largely confined to the library' (p. 33; cf. p. 64).

If the Church had its Bible, the medical profession too had its Scripture, the writings of Claudius Galen (138–201 CE), who was universally regarded as the greatest physician of late antiquity, on a level with Hippocrates himself.[2] Anatomy was taught in the schools exclusively from the text of Galen, 'which was regarded as a canon about which there could be no dispute' (Castiglioni 1958: 340). The phrase *sicut asserit Galenus* ('thus does Galen declare') carried a weight of authority that was second only to that of the Bible itself (cf. pp. 317, 344, 519).

Not surprisingly, therefore, the critique of Galenism had to await the Renaissance, and an intellectual climate when the interrogation even of biblical dogma was, to an extent, possible (cf. Castiglioni 1958: 502). 'The first branch of medicine to feel the impact of the Renaissance spirit was anatomy', a study that would henceforth be based on meticulous observation as opposed to reliance on tradition (Starobinski 1964: 41). 'Public dissections were practiced carefully and in greater numbers than heretofore. The ancient custom of reading from a text of anatomy, while often a clumsy assistant mishandled the organs, was going out of fashion....' (Castiglioni 1958: 490). More teachers of anatomy began to perform their dissections in person. Anatomy began to take its place in the medical curriculum. And '[s]oon dissection of the cadaver was prescribed as an essential and regular part of the instruction' (p. 491).

Increasingly, these sanctioned assaults on the dead were accompanied by a rhetoric of light and enlightenment: 'Open up a few corpses: you will dissipate at once the darkness', declared Xavier Bichat in his *Anatomie générale* of 1801 (quoted in Foucault 1973: 146). Compare a fairly standard description of the Enlightened mindset that gave rise to

2.    In *The Care of the Self*, Foucault comments at length on Galen's theories (1986: 105-23).

the critical study of the Bible: '...[A]lmost nothing was sacred—all was secular, everything was open to human scrutiny... Humanity had progressed out of darkness and into a new light...' (Baird 1992: 5).

Of course, there was more to reading than mere seeing. One also touched the Book, if only to turn the page. One listened, if only to one's inner voice murmuring the words on the page. The biblical scholar, like his medical counterpart, soon began to read with a *stethoscope*, an instrument that exercised the eyes, the fingers and the ears, while conferring an appearance of detachment on the examination.

How did the stethoscope originate? Johann Zimmermann, an eighteenth-century physician quoted by Foucault, expresses the view that 'doctors should be free to make their observations...by placing their hands directly on the heart', but adds that 'our delicate morals prevent us from doing so, especially in the case of women' (Foucault 1973: 163; cf. Starobinski 1964: 65). The stethoscope, which emerged in the early nineteenth century, enabled the male physician to maintain a decorous distance from his female patient, even while placing a cold prosthetic ear against her bare breast and listening intently to the secret sounds of her body. Thus, the decorous distance was something of a sham from the start. For the biblical scholar, too, the semblance of distance became all important as he probed the text, stripping back its many layers. But because the stethoscope was limited in its powers of penetration, the scholar came to rely even more on the scalpel.

## A 'Gray's Anatomy' of the Fourth Gospel

> ...we seem to see the scalpel uncovering the organs themselves (Starobinski 1964: 42).

Developments in the field of anatomy were crucial for the emergence of medical science, as we have seen. The question therefore arises: What is the relationship between Alan Culpepper's *Anatomy of the Fourth Gospel*, and its many precursors, and Henry Gray's *Anatomy of the Human Body*, and its many successors? Can we map the arterial network that connects these two volumes?

*Gray's Anatomy* begins,

> In ancient Greece, at the time of Hippocrates (460 BC), the word anatomy (*anatome*) meant a dissection, from *tome*, a cutting[,] and the prefix *ana*[,] meaning up. Today anatomy is still closely associated in our minds with the dissection of a human cadaver...(p. 1)

Is this what Dr Culpepper had in mind when he decided to entitle his examination of the Fourth Gospel an *Anatomy*? Apparently not, for Culpepper frowns on dissection. He quotes disapprovingly Klaus Koch's source-critical definition of the literary critic as one who 'approaches the text with, so to say, a dissecting knife in his hand...' (Koch 1969: 69, quoted in Culpepper 1983: 10). Indeed, as Culpepper rightly remarks, the dominant model of Johannine scholarship in general 'depends on dissection' (p. 3). Traditionally in our field, the art of dissection has been passed down from doctor-father to doctor-son. Robert T. Fortna, for example, preparing to cut into the Fourth Gospel in his important source-critical study, *The Gospel of Signs*, acknowledges his personal and professional debt to his 'critical and demanding "doctor-father"', J. Louis Martyn (p. ix). For Culpepper, however, 'dissection and stratification have no place in the study of the gospel and may distort and confuse one's view of the text' (p. 5). What view of the text does Culpepper himself have? Here Foucault, ever the optometrist, may be of help.

In *The Birth of the Clinic*, Foucault distinguishes sharply between the medical *glance* and the medical *gaze*. The glance follows the path of the knife; it cuts beneath the surface, opens up the corpse, 'that opaque mass in which secrets...and the very mystery of origins lie hidden' (1973: 122). The glance feeds on fresh cadavers; its instrument is the scalpel, and its domain is the anatomical theater or the mortuary. The gaze, in contrast, is content to graze (on) the surface of the body; its 'correlative...is never the invisible, but always the immediately visible...'. (p. 107). It consists 'of a general examination of all the visible modifications of the organism' (p. 111). Its domain is the doctor's examining room.

Literary criticism, for Culpepper, far from being something performed with a dissecting knife, 'is basically an inductive method in that one works from observations on the text being studied' (p. 9). On Culpepper's own account, therefore, *Anatomy of the Fourth Gospel* is not an *Anatomy* at all, not the result of an anatomical dissection; rather, it is a physical examination. 'Let's have a good look at you', is what Dr Culpepper intends to say to John—not 'Let's open you up and have a look'. Visibly relieved, John removes his outer clothing and stretches out on the examining table—which in this case is a rectangular slab of paper.

And yet I wonder if Culpepper's methods are really so bloodless. By the time he is through with his examination, does he too not hold a dripping scalpel in his hand? Culpepper suggests as much in his

Conclusion: 'we have explored the "anatomy" of the Fourth Gospel, tracing its rhetorical form and studying the function of each of its organs' (p. 231). Organs can be thoroughly studied only under the knife, however. Is John's chest an open cavity, then, overflowing with excised organs, which have been carefully removed, inspected, and then replaced? If so, *Anatomy of the Fourth Gospel* may indeed be an *Anatomy* after all.

But what kind of *Anatomy* is it? Here Gray provides the clue. Already in the 1850s Gray could write, 'The whole field of anatomy has become very large, and as a result a number of subdivisions of the subject have been recognized and named, usually to correspond with a specialized interest or avenue of approach' (p. 1). Following Gray, Culpepper's enterprise can be termed *Gross Anatomy*, 'the study of morphology by means of dissection with the unaided eye', a major branch of which is *organology*, the study of the structure of organs (*ibid.*). Gray also notes that 'a considerable amount of disagreement and confusion has arisen because of conflicting loyalties to teachers, schools, or national traditions' (p. 2). Evidence of such disagreement can be found in Culpepper's *Anatomy*, as we have seen; the subspecialization that Culpepper criticizes may be termed *Embryology* or *Developmental Anatomy*, the study of an organism's growth from inception to birth (Gray 1973: 1). For Culpepper, this would encompass 'the history of the material, the process by which the gospel was composed, and developments within the Johannine community' (p. 3). In effect, Gray enables us to see that historical criticism and narrative criticism, far from being radically different enterprises, are but two divergent branches of a general anatomy of the Bible.

(The biblical texts speak to us. Their voices raised in chorus, they chant: 'The aim of the anatomists is attained when the opaque envelopes that cover our parts are no more for their practised eyes than a transparent veil revealing the whole and the relation between the parts' [Foucault 1973: 166].)

### Culpepper's Eye-agram

...the triumph of the gaze that is represented by the autopsy... (Foucault 1973: 165).

*Anatomy of the Fourth Gospel* is an organology, then—but there is one organ that occupies it more than any other. That organ is the *eye*. In recent years, a certain diagram from Seymour Chatman's narratological study, *Story and Discourse*, has become a familiar sight in literary studies of the Bible (Chatman 1978: 151):

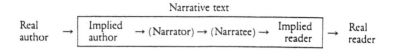

Remarkably, Chatman's rectangular diagram of narrative communication becomes, in Culpepper's free adaptation of it, an oval containing three concentric circles—an outsized eye, in other words (Culpepper 1983: 6):

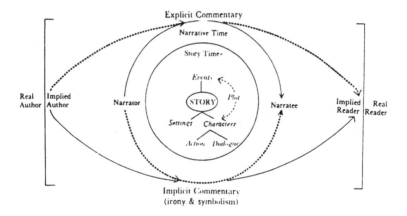

'Between author and reader is the text, enclosed above in brackets', explains C. (*ibid.*), or better, *See*. The text is an eye, then. More precisely, the text is an eyeball (*bulbus oculi*), snug in its bony cavity (*orbit*), represented here by the brackets (cf. Gray 1973: 1040). Absent from *See*'s eye-agram are the text's cover and dustjacket, its eyelids (*palpebrae*). Gray describes the eyelids as 'two thin movable covers' that protect the eye from injury 'by their closure' (p. 1064).

*See*'s eyeball neatly diagrams several of his enabling assumptions. It indicates, for example, that the real (historical) author and the real (original) readers are properly the objects of peripheral vision only for the narrative critic. '...[T]he interests and theology of the real author is not our primary concern', states *See* (p. 15). Later it emerges that the real reader is not *See*'s central focus either (p. 212). Of course, a skeptic might respond that the eye-agram could equally be interpreted to suggest that the real author and audience are the blind spot of *See*'s narrative theory. The blind spot is located on the periphery of the eyeball, in the optic disk (Gray 1973: 1050).

With uncanny precision, *See* has positioned 'story' in his eye-agram to correspond with the lens of the eye, while the narrator and narratee are positioned on the circumference of the retina. The lens serves to focus the external world, along with the retina, 'a delicate nervous membrane, upon which the images of external objects are received' (Gray 1973: 1049). Correspondingly in the eye-agram, the external world is focused, processed and relayed to the narratee through the agency of the narrator and the medium of the story.

Our word 'theory' comes from Greek *theoria*. Etymologically, therefore, a theory is a sight, a spectacle, a speculation. *See*'s narrative theory, however, is not a spectacle or sight so much as an *instrument* of sight: an unblinking eye that attempts to take in the Fourth Gospel at a glance. Trapped by the eye, the text is forced to assume its contours.

Arguably, however, the Fourth Gospel lends itself to this sort of reduction. The Gospel is also the risen body of Jesus, as we have seen. And as much as anything else, the Johannine Jesus is himself an instrument of vision. 'No one has ever seen [*horaō*] God', the narrator announces programatically; it is the Son alone who has made him known (1.18; cf. 6.46; 8.38a; 12.45; 14.8-9; 15.24b). The Son focuses the radiant glory of the Father and relays it to the believer (cf. 11.40; 17.22); in this respect, the Son is an eye. 'I am the light of the world', declares the eye; 'whoever follows me will never walk in darkness but will have the light of life' (8.12; cf. 9.5; 3.19-21; 9.39; 11.9-10; 12.35-36, 40, 46).

The theory that the Johannine Jesus is an eye also sheds fresh light on 19.34, the enigmatic flow of water from Jesus' side. All the features of the eye that we looked at earlier—lens, retina and the rest—are located on the exterior of the vitreous body (*corpus vitreum*), a transparent, semigelatinous fluid that accounts for most of the volume of the eyeball (Gray 1973: 1045):

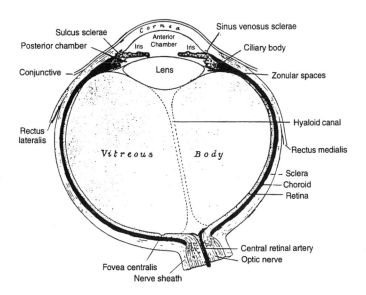

It is only to be expected, therefore, that when Jesus' dead body—a dull, lifeless eye—is pricked with the point of a lance a colorless, waterlike liquid should gush forth from it, in addition to blood: 'One of the soldiers pierced his side with a spear, and at once there flowed out blood and water' (Jn 19.34).

### Opening the Corpus

> Late at night, under the flickering light of a kerosene lamp, the Doctor
> labors at the writing table…(Schweitzer 1933: 212).

If biblical scholarship has often taken the form of a paramedical science, medicine, for its part, has sometimes taken the form of biblical scholarship. Over the years, in particular, a diverse body of medical specialists has converged on Jesus' still-warm corpse as it is removed from the cross—inspired, perhaps, by the anonymous soldier who has just initiated an autopsy with the point of his spear.[3] One thinks of such monographs as Pierre Barbet's *A Doctor at Calvary: The Passion of Our Lord Jesus Christ as Described by a Surgeon* (1953; see also

---

3.  Cf. Starobinski, 1964: 36: 'Surgical experience could…be gained at. gladitorial schools or with the armies'.

Stroud 1871), and numerous articles in a similar vein.[4] To my mind, these studies can be read as inadvertent but instructive caricatures of biblical scholarship, considered as a paramedical science.

Take 'The Wound in the Side of Christ', for example, whose author, A.F. Sava, appears to be up to his elbows in blood as he writes. This curious article is punctuated with gory statements such as the following:

> I have repeatedly pierced lungs of cadavers less than six hours after death....(p. 344). I have collected into glass cylinders blood from different cadavers from 2 to 4 hours after death...(p. 345). A stab wound through the chest directed to the heart, after [I] had previously filled the pericardial sac with 1000 cc. of water, failed to produce any of the water at the chest wound. Rather, inside the chest and especially around the right lung, the water literally flooded the area (p. 346).

These grisly confessions, which, to the nonmedical ear, are more evocative of Dr Frankenstein than of Dr Welby, perhaps, are all the more startling for the fact that they appear in the ordinarily anemic pages of *The Catholic Biblical Quarterly.*

When these articles appear in a medical journal, the effect is no less surreal. An excellent case in point is W.D. Edwards, W.J. Gabel and F.E. Hosmer's 'On the Physical Death of Jesus Christ', a blow-by-blow medical account of Jesus' scourging and crucifixion, which appeared in *The Journal of the American Medical Association* side by side with glossy advertisements for pain medication, on the one hand, and papers on such topics as 'Self-induced Vomiting and Laxative and Diuretic Use among Teenagers', on the other.

Dr Edwards and his associates begin by frankly admitting that the subject of their autopsy is not an actual corpse: 'The source material concerning Christ's death comprises a body of literature and not a physical body or its skeletal remains' (p. 1455). Laid out on the slab, in other words, is not a fresh cadaver but a moldering pile of paper. And this literary corpus is composed not only of ancient sources but also of modern scholarship on the historical Jesus, as the authors go on to explain.

As it happens, this is the same chaotic pile of paper that the Fourth Evangelist mentions at the end of his Gospel: 'There are also many

4. Edwards, Gabel and Hosmer list 14 English-language articles of this sort (p. 1463), although even this is only a partial list. In general, these articles tend to treat the passion narratives as historical reports, accurate down to even the smaller details. Edwards, Gabel and Hosmer's own treatment is no exception in this regard.

other things that Jesus did; if every one of them were written down, I suppose that the world itself could not contain the books that would be written' (21.25). In recent years, innumerable dissections of this corpus have been performed by biblical surgeons in search of the historical Jesus. The first great dissection of this sort, however, was performed by Albert Schweitzer in Strasbourg in 1905. Leaving no cavity of the colossal cadaver unexplored, Schweitzer carefully removed all the vital organs and placed them in neat piles around his study. Here is his own account of the autopsy:

> When I had worked through the numerous 'Lives' of Jesus, I found it very difficult to group them in chapters. After attempting in vain to do this on paper, I piled all the 'Lives' in one big heap in the middle of my room, picked out for each chapter I had planned a place of its own in a corner or between the pieces of furniture, and then, after thorough consideration, heaped up the volumes in the piles to which they belonged, pledging myself to find room for all the books belonging to each pile, and to leave each heap undisturbed in its own place, till the corresponding chapter in the Sketch should be finished. And I carried out my plan to the very end. For many a month all the people who visited me had to thread their way across the room along paths which ran between heaps of books (1933: 39).[5]

As the paper whale rose up to swallow Schweitzer, Schweitzer proceeded to dissect the whale with a paperknife, confident that the corpse of the historical Jesus was interred deep in its innards (cf. Mt. 12.40).

Just how close is the connection between the post mortem and the historical examination? The word 'autopsy' has its origins in *autopsia*, which Liddell and Scott render as 'a seeing with one's own eyes'. The cognate noun, *autoptēs* ('eyewitness'), was used by Herodotus (2.29; 3.115) as a term for the first-hand historical researcher (cf. Lk. 1.2). It would appear that autopsy and historiography are blood relations, then.[6] The opening of Jesus' corpse with a lance can be regarded as an autopsy, since the author of the incision knows that the subject is already dead (Jn 19.33a). Significantly, this autopsy is accompanied by an *autopsia*: 'He who saw it has borne witness...that you also may believe' (19.35). Autopsy, historiography, evangelical witness... Albert Schweitzer, who went on to become a medical practitioner—and a medical

5. The 'Sketch' in question was, of course, *The Quest of the Historical Jesus* (Schweitzer 1964).

6. My thanks to Stuart Lasine for alerting me to this fact.

missionary to boot—exemplifies the curious combination of these three elements that has so characterized modern biblical scholarship.

## *Epilogue*

As scholar-surgeons, we subject the Book and the Word to examination by dissecting them. Do we carve them up only in order to prepare them for the dinner table? Less and less, I suspect, although the Book has always begged us to devour it, and the Word has always urged us to ingest him. Why do we decline these urgent invitations to dine? Is it because we fear that the Book and the Word, if swallowed whole, will have mind-altering effects that we will be unable to control? Admittedly, such fears are not without foundation. In the end, perhaps, it all amounts to the covert execution of a tyrant by his physicians. He dies on the operating table, which has imperceptibly become a dissecting table. What began as an appendectomy ends as an autopsy.

## BIBLIOGRAPHY

Baird, William
1992    *History of New Testament Research.* I. *From Deism to Tübingen* (Minneapolis: Fortress Press).

Barbet, Pierre
1953    *A Doctor at Calvary: The Passion of our Lord Jesus Christ Described by a Surgeon* (Garden City, NY: Doubleday).

Castiglioni, Arturo
1958    *A History of Medicine* (trans. and ed. E.B. Krumbhaar; New York: Alfred A. Knopf).

Chatman, Seymour
1978    *Story and Discourse: Narrative Structure in Fiction and Film* (Ithaca, NY: Cornell University Press).

Culpepper, R. Alan
1983    *Anatomy of the Fourth Gospel: A Study in Literary Design* (Philadelphia: Fortress Press).

Edwards, William D., Wesley J. Gabel and Floyd E. Hosmer
1986    'On the Physical Death of Jesus Christ', *Journal of the American Medical Association* 255: 1455-63.

Fortna, Robert Tomson
1970    *The Gospel of Signs: A Reconstruction of the Narrative Source Underlying the Fourth Gospel* (Cambridge: Cambridge University Press).

Foucault, Michel
1973    *The Birth of the Clinic: An Archaeology of Medical Perception* (trans. A.M. Sheridan Smith; New York: Pantheon Books).

1986        *The History of Sexuality*. III. *The Care of the Self* (trans. Robert
            Hurley; New York: Pantheon Books).

Gray, Henry
1973        *Anatomy of the Human Body* (ed. Charles Mayo Goss; Philadelphia:
            Lea & Febiger, 29th American edn).

Koch, Klaus
1969        *The Growth of the Biblical Tradition: The Form-Critical Method*
            (trans. S.M. Cupitt; New York: Charles Scribner's Sons).

Kümmel, Werner Georg
1972        *The New Testament: The History of the Investigation of its Problems*
            (trans. S. McLean Gilmour and Howard C. Kee; Nashville: Abingdon
            Press).

Liddell, Henry George and Robert Scott (eds.)
1966        *A Greek–English Lexicon* (Oxford: Clarendon Press).

Sava, A.F.
1957        'The Wound in the Side of Christ', *CBQ* 19: 343-46.

Schweitzer, Albert
1933        *Out of My Life and Thought: An Autobiography* (trans. C.T. Campion;
            New York: Holt, Rinehart & Winston).

1964        *The Quest of the Historical Jesus: A Critical Study of its Progress from
            Reimarus to Wrede* (trans. W. Montgomery; New York: Macmillan).

Starobinski, Jean
1964        *A History of Medicine* (trans. Bernard C. Swift; New York: Hawthorn).

Strauss, David Friedrich
1835        *Das Leben Jesu, kritisch bearbeitet* (2 vols.; Tübingen: C.F. Osiander
            [ET: *The Life of Jesus, Critically Examined* (ed. Peter C. Hodgson;
            trans. George Eliot; Philadelphia: Fortress Press, 1973)]).

Stroud, William
1871        *Treatise on the Physical Cause of the Death of Christ and its Relations
            to the Principles and Practice of Christianity* (London: Hamilton &
            Adams).

# THE ETHICS OF READING DECONSTRUCTIVELY, OR SPEAKING FACE-TO-FACE: THE SAMARITAN WOMAN MEETS DERRIDA AT THE WELL

## Gary A. Phillips

> There can be no denying that the critical exegesis of the Holy Scriptures has had an unsettling effect upon religious minds—Emmanuel Levinas
>
> ...TAKE IT HERE I AM EAT...DRINK—Jacques Derrida

### Reading Responsibly for the Other

In the face-to-face encounter with the Bible deconstruction offers readers a way to be ethically responsible.[1] Deconstructive reading aspires to be responsible—to the specific text, to its historical contexts, to its readers—in ways that traditional critique and method are not. This claim must sound quite jarring indeed to readers who may agree with the formidable literary critic M.H. Abrams that deconstruction does not treat the text as 'a human document' (1991: 332), or respected biblical scholars like Robert Morgan and John Barton who caution that 'the radical indeterminacy of deconstructive criticism, which denies to any text a fixed and stable meaning, is scarcely compatible with the ways religious communities use their scriptures as a norm' (1988: 256-57). After all, these critics say, any method as self-absorbed, negative and ahistorical as deconstruction can only be destructive of established readings, interpretative practices and institutions.[2] This view, I want to argue, fails in important ways to grasp what is distinctive about the way deconstructive reading calls for a certain kind of critical accountability on the

---

1.  On the positive reception of Derrida's deconstructive project by biblical scholars see Beardslee 1993; The Bible and Culture Collective forthcoming; Detweiler 1989; Fewell and Gunn 1993; Moore 1989, 1992, 1994; Phillips 1990c, 1994; Prickett 1991; for the negative reception see Jacobs 1991; Jeanrood 1988; Klein, Blomberg and Hubbard 1993; Morgan and Barton 1989.

2.  However cf. Derrida 1988b: 141; Norris 1989: 197.

part of readers to the Bible and enables a critical, destabilizing intervention within dominant critical practices, disciplines, interpretative traditions and institutions. Deconstruction marks a moment in the reading of
the biblical text in which the metaphysical foundations and masculinist
practices of a Western culture that longs to discover the pure presence
of meaning and truth are *altered* (cf. esp. Grosz 1990: 148-53).

Far from abandoning ethical concerns, deconstruction invigorates the
ethical question *in a certain way*.[3] Deconstruction does this by searching
for a subtler understanding of the ways texts refer, represent and bring
about a different opening onto the world; by seeking a subtler understanding of the relations of speech, thought and reality; by seeking a
subtler understanding of the 'originary' conditions that prevail among
text, critique, reader and context.[4] Key to this effort is the recognition
that readers are fundamentally indebted to texts and that texts preserve
an independence over against readers and any interests they may bring
to their reading. This is not to be confused with the familiar 'subject–
object' relationship characteristic of positivist criticism. For Derrida, the
particular, concrete text

> always reserves a surprise for the anatomy or physiology of a critique
> which might think it had mastered its game, surveying all its threads at
> once, thus deceiving itself into wishing to look at the text without touching
> it, without putting its hand to the 'object', without venturing to add to it
> (1972b: 71).

Deconstructive criticism calls for a hands-on, face-to-face encounter with
the text precisely because the text stands as *other* to the reader and her
interests. Readers show respect for the alterity of the text by writing
upon it, by applying a 'counter-signature' to the text. In this way
readers supplement and thereby affirm their indebtedness as well as the
independence of the text each time they 'sign-on'.[5]

---

3.    For a different understanding of the 'ethics of reading', see Miller 1987, 1989
and Siebers 1988. Derrida challenges the Kantian formulation of the ethical problem
by following both Nietzsche and Levinas. See esp. Critchley 1988.

4.    The text always *affirms* the outside-the-text. See Derrida 1967a: 14. To
deconstruct philosophy, for example, is to think 'in the most faithful, interior way'
about the history of philosophy (Derrida 1972b: 6).

5.    Critics of deconstruction might argue that 'counter-signatures' to the text are
really no more than 'counterfeits' of the original. Presupposed here is a view of text
and reading that radically distinguishes one from the other.

Reading, deconstruction reminds us, is always invested;[6] it is the exercise of a fundamental obligation. Because of the hold a text maintains on its readers, critical reading can never keep us at a safe distance from the text, untouching and untouched. This means that whenever we read we necessarily mark up the text and are in turn marked by it. Critics often object that deconstruction fails to maintain a proper distance from the text: it plays fast and loose with the text by marking up its lines; filling the margins with inappropriate personal jottings, musings and doodles; even reconfiguring the text in different graphic forms with little apparent regard for chronology, authorial intent or disciplinary boundaries (cf. Derrida 1986b). Derrida counters that it is only by (re)marking up(on) the text that readers in fact *take responsibility for the text* and make good on the debt they carry as respectful readers. Furthermore, our debt is not limited strictly to the 'text'—as if it were possible somehow to draw a clear line demarcating text from its history of readings. Every reading is necessarily dependent upon prior signatures and, conversely, every past signature counts upon and is indebted to future readings. Our relationship as readers indebted to one another thus extends backward and forward over time.

In sharp contrast to historical-critical and new literary-critical methods, deconstruction operates with a very specific understanding of text and critical reading. Literary texts work at the limits of logical concepts; they are texts 'which make the limits of our language tremble' (Derrida 1984: 112). Literature, then, is not static but in motion, and critical reading not a steadying but a destabilizing event (cf. Bible and Culture Collective, ch. 2; Moore 1992: 3-11; Moore 1994: 13-41). Far from being an undisciplined, *irresponsible* act of 'free play' that does willynilly whatever the clever reader desires, deconstructive reading is orderly and structured. It is a highly regulated event governed by rules of intelligibility; it is deeply respectful of the text and reader and location within history (cf. esp. Norris 1989: 197-200).[7]

Deconstruction announces a philosophical and literary intervention within the field of biblical studies that seeks to respond to the Other that

6.    This is the point Bultmann insisted biblical exegetes acknowledge about all criticism and interpretation (1966: 291).

7.    From one perspective *all* of Derrida's readings are extended reflections set within a surrounding historical reflection (e.g. 1967a). According to Bennington and Derrida, this constitutes the movement of deconstruction itself (1993: 125); see Attridge 1992: 54.

lies beyond the Bible. Deconstructive reading of the Bible takes the form of a double-handed engagement that is both affirming and analytic.[8] By responding critically and openly with a 'yes' to both text and context, deconstruction discloses not only what the biblical text says (i.e. its common-sense nature as a sign-signal, its reference to the world) but also a secondarity or alterity in relation to the Bible. It is this 'alterity' or 'wholly other' that makes the biblical text and meaning 'absolutely irreducible' (Derrida 1986a: 9) and reading ever unfinished business.[9] Following in the steps of Nietzsche, Heidegger, Blanchot and Levinas, Derrida remind us of the Western metaphysical tradition's habit of forgetting the Other. Deconstruction is concerned with the 'alterity' of the Bible that the logocentric tradition cannot adequately conceptualize or control. Derrida shares with Levinas the view that the Bible, arguably the most important sub-text of Western culture, is a major well-spring for encounter with the Other (cf. Levinas 1994: 126-30).

What is the 'Other' of the Bible with which deconstruction is concerned and to which it responds? In general, the Other 'names the event in poetry, meaning and inscription which escapes human control, grounding or anticipation' (Clark 1992: 110; Derrida 1978: 11). Deconstructive reading is a 'reciprocal indebting or alliance' with this 'Other' (Bennington and Derrida 1993: 187; Derrida, 1986a: 42). A moment's reflection on the way literary texts seemingly yield an unlimited number of readings suggests that one of the fundamental features of texts is that they are more than the sum total of their readings; there is always a 'more', a further reading, that is possible. Reading 'carries with it, and must do so, an essential excessiveness' (Derrida 1991a: 108) but one that is linked always and 'in a certain way' to the meaning of the text. The Other of the text is not inert; it interrupts the critical effort to limit the potential of texts to mean in different ways. But the Other is never *reducible to* a particular meaning. Deconstructive

---

8.    The deconstructive enterprise is 'a double gesture, a double science, a double writing' (Derrida 1977: 195; Derrida 1972b: 41, 100, n. 8). See Derrida 1988b: 152: '…I speak of deconstruction and the "yes"'.

9.    Derrida is dependent in an important way upon Levinas for his conceptualization of the 'Other'. At the same time Derrida criticises the category of the Other and Levinas's construction of an ethics of the face-to-face in a fashion that seeks to push ethical responsibility 'further back' even before the face. See Derrida's important treatment especially in 'Violence and Metaphysics: An Essay on the Thought of Emmanuel Levinas', in 1978: 79-153 and 1992: 11-50. Also cf. Caputo (1993), who pushes the ethical question beyond that of obligation.

reading points to the rigorous encounter with the Other that somehow 'precedes', 'lies beyond' or 'intersects' the text and the signification it produces.

Deconstruction reads for the Other. It takes up the challenge and responsibility of identifying signs (or 'traces') of the Other that break through the biblical text and encourage destabilization and trembling. Following Levinas' phenomenological lead, Derrida regards these traces as marking an originary disruption or trauma by which the Other breaks in and through life itself (cf. Levinas 1985: 21-22 where the Other serves as another way of speaking about 'ethics'). A deconstructive reading marks, initials and records these traces for later analysis. But even the most meticulous deconstructive reading cannot gain an exhaustive hold on this Other. To use a medical analogy, deconstruction is not a surgical procedure designed to cut, suture and heal a textual gap or problem. Nor is it a coroner's examination of some lifeless textual body that inventories its pathologies.[10] Deconstruction is neither corrective surgery carried out on a diseased text nor autopsy performed on a deceased text. Rather, it is active engagement—an ethical engagement, a signing on— by the reader *with* a living text and the Other that comes to the reader as a gift and a challenge; this is why for Derrida all critical reading at root carries an ethical force. On this view deconstruction is a critical reminder of the obligation literary texts impose upon readers to respond to the Other through a hands-on engagement with the particular text. Every time we read we unavoidably leave our mark on the text just as it leaves its mark upon us. Deconstruction's special mark takes the form of a chiastic double reading. It marks receipt of the text, a text that has been signed for many, many times before. As for the mark left upon the reader, it is the obligation to respond to the Other.

For this reason, deconstruction should not be mistaken for some literary or philosophical 'method' for reading texts. Derrida argues repeatedly and forcefully that deconstruction cannot be passed off (or over) as a 'critical method', or 'critique' (understood in the traditional Kantian sense of *krinein*) even though advocates and detractors of

10. Consider the force of effort employed by traditional biblical scholarship to 'correct' the text so that it can be read in a certain fashion. The ingenuity and literary sensitivity required to reconfigure a text in order to make it understandable is precisely the counter-signature that Derrida talks about. Traditional historical-critical readers sign-off on the text, too, but rarely do they acknowledge or take responsibility for their reading as a rewriting.

deconstruction wish to portray it reductively as such.[11] 'To present "deconstruction"', Christopher Norris says, 'as if it were a method, a system or a settled body of ideas would be to falsify its nature and lay oneself open to charges of reductive misunderstanding' (1982: 1). 'Methodological reading', no matter how sophisticated or sensitive, proves 'incapable of getting the measure of what happens in the event and in the signature of the text' (Derrida in Attridge 1992: 51). For this reason critical methods prove incapable of doing justice to the text because they miss something fundamental about the *event* of the biblical text as an encounter with the Other. Method is insufficient *in this respect* for complex reasons that have to do with the ways the metaphysical tradition binds our language and shapes our comprehension of the textuality of the text in terms of the full presence of meaning.[12] In the relentless drive toward universality and generalizability, method has a difficult time accounting for the particularity of the text and the obligation to read for the Other.

Derrida's way of explaining deconstruction is to focus on the *place* and the *how* of his reading (Derrida 1988b: 141; Critchley 1992: 22); deconstruction, in his words, is less a technique than an *event* in which something 'takes place'.[13] To begin with, deconstruction is always found in relation to a specific text: Derrida calls this *the* 'task of reading' (1967a: 158). For once divorced from an actual reading process,

11. Deconstruction does its work at the heart of cultural or socio-institutional realities. Deconstruction is engaged in revealing and transforming these conditions (see Derrida 1988b: 147). However, Derrida speaks elsewhere about deconstruction in ways that have encouraged readers to reduce deconstruction to the status of a method (Derrida 1977: 75, cited in Reed 1986: 73). Cf. Mark C. Taylor (1982: xx), who says 'Deconstruction is postmodernism raised to method'.

12. By 'metaphysical tradition' Heidegger means 'the deployment of the Greek problematic of the Being of what-is, a question which has never ceased to haunt Western philosophers' (O'Leary 1985: 11). Methodology, according to Levinas, is essentially the quest for transparency about the foundations of thinking. In this respect it must assume the strict and formal repeatability of certain processes and procedures. Methodology is what makes science science. For more, see Reed 1986: 74-80.

13. Derrida 1988a: 'Deconstruction takes place, it is an event that does not await the deliberation, consciousness, or organization of a subject, or even of modernity'. '...deconstruction takes place everywhere' 'where there is something (and is not therefore limited to meaning or to the text in the current and bookish sense of the word)...' (p. 4). Derrida ends with the most elliptical of expressions: 'What deconstruction is not? everything of course? What is deconstruction? nothing of course' (p. 5).

deconstruction's 'principles of reading' look very anemic indeed. It pursues a certain kind of two-stage reading process: a 'dominant interpretation' is offered up in the guise of a commentary upon the text, which is immediately followed by an opening up of the commentary and text to the blind spots that dominant readings overlook or push aside. The first reading relies necessarily upon traditional, critical commentary ('an indispensable guard rail' or 'safeguard' [1988b: 141], Derrida calls it) that reflects the minimal consensus that a community of readers reaches about its texts, a consensus that serious, conscientious reading must never ignore. 'Critical reading' in the traditional sense is absolutely necessary for deconstruction to take place:

> to recognize and respect all its classical exigencies is not easy and requires all the instruments of traditional criticism. Without this recognition and this respect, critical production would risk developing in any direction at all and authorize itself to say almost anything (1967a: 158).

For biblical scholars this means an embracing—not rejection—of historical-critical and traditional literary readings. The deconstructive reader must be competent in recovering these dominant interpretations; otherwise, one could indeed say 'just anything at all' (1988b: 144-45, cited in Critchley 1992: 24).

The second reading or moment, however, does not duplicate the critical commentary in the form of a 'doubling' or redundant commentary. The first reading must be recognized and respected, but it serves finally as the 'host' for a second 'invasive' reading that does something more. From Derrida's perspective, traditional commentary is deficient because it always 'doubles the reading'; it 'has always only *protected...never opened*, a reading' (1967a: 158). In other words, commentary inhibits the recognition of and intervention by the Other; commentary suppresses readers' response. Derrida reasons that traditional commentary, ironically, turns away from the text in favor of some final referent or transcendental signified that lies beyond the text. Commentary desires a point of mastery in order to control and anchor the text, its reading and its readers. Logocentric commentary—the preferred reading style of the West—is docetic; it favors the spirit at the expense of the body of the text. It abandons its responsibility to the physical text (p. 159).[14] Biblical commentary from this perspective is exegesis gone ek-static.

---

14. Derrida clarifies what he means by 'transcend' in the interview with Attridge:

The signifying structure that deconstructive reading *should* produce is one that would put the search for this 'transcendental reading' *in question*, 'not to annul it but to understand it within a system to which such a reading is blind' (p. 160). Rather than escape textuality or double it, critical reading should interrupt the original text in an aggressive way; critical reading becomes the place where the Other is encountered. One of the values of deconstruction for reading the Bible is that it wedges open established reading practices that close down the text and dry up its excess. For Derrida, textuality is 'an irreducible process of opening/ closing that reforms itself without let-up' (1972a: 337). The text is always open, its future always coming because in an odd sense it has yet to arrive.

In the deconstructive encounter with the Johannine text we come face-to-face with a complex, ironic text that features a woman who by all religious, cultural and sexual standards is Other. It is a text that concerns itself with the responsibility for giving and receiving. It is also a text concerned with signs, markers and traces of what is present and absent, seen and not seen, understood and misunderstood. Finally, it is a text intent upon telling us something about reading and resisting the closure of Scripture. At bottom the encounter with the Samaritan woman in John 4 is a face-to-face challenge to read responsibly by responding to this particular text and to the Other that interrupts the Gospel in ways I as critical reader cannot control. In the encounter between the Samaritan woman and Derrida in the well-text we experience first-hand what it means to read for more in multiple, metaphorical ways and to leave behind a formal mark—our chiastic χ, our Johannine Hancock—as a sign and deposit of our willingness to accept responsibility to read for the Other.

### Gaining a Measure of the Event of the Samaritan Text

Derrida reminds us repeatedly that deconstruction is an *event*, not a method for reading the Bible. It is helpful to see deconstruction as a two-stage or double-handed reading process that moves chiastically (cf.

---

' "Transcend" here means going beyond the interest for the signifier, the form, the language (note that I do not say "text") in the direction of the meaning or referent' (Attridge 1992: 45). Deconstructive reading is not a matter of negating the transcendent reading *but working with it*. Cf. Derrida 1967a: 49-50.

1972b; 1988b). The first step demands a careful attention to traditional critical readings; the second reads back through and over against the standard readings in search of what else the text has to say, to open up the reading and text to enable the Other to have its say. The readings of Olsson 1974, O'Day 1980 and 1992, Boers 1988, Culpepper 1983, Schüssler Fiorenza 1983, and Joplin 1992 form a solid guard rail to my reading of John 4. In addition, modern source-, form-, composition- and redaction-critical readings—which give support to modern literary (in particular, narrative and narratological) readings of John—undergird the Gospel text as it is received and read today. In their own ways traditional historical and contemporary literary critics attempt to take seriously the biblical text, but they can not do justice to the *textuality* and *otherness* of John's narrative.[15] We run up against the limits of method at this point. In Levinas's words, method—historical, literary, indeed any methodological approach—fails to account for the particular *mode of being* of Scripture.[16]

Among the Fourth Gospel's many memorable passages, the account of the Samaritan woman's encounter with Jesus at the well stands out by virtue of its textual difficulties, its narrative and discursive complexity,

15. Olsson is very explicit about the linguistic and literary approach he takes. He calls it a 'textual exegetics' (1974: 14). It is an approach that seeks to account for the relationship between text construction (*Textkonstitution*) and text reception (*Textrezeption*). He sees his work as falling in the 'no-man's-land between exegesis and linguistics' (p. 7); although, in contrast to Boers, the relationship between the two is osmotic and co-dependent. O'Day's approach features a 'rhetorical poetics' of the text that seeks to explain 'how' the text works to produce the meaning it does. She is mainly concerned with identifying narrative mechanisms (e.g. irony) employed by text to engage the reader both in the production of meaning as well as in the process of revelation. She is interested, too, in engaging in the critique of the philosophical influence enjoyed by Bultmann's distinction between 'Dass' and 'Was' and the way that a conceptual diad has constrained the reading of John 4. Boers depends heavily upon a Greimasian structuralist model to establish the basis for a reading that moves, like Olsson's, 'between' structural and traditional 'historical' analysis, but it is quite clear that the center of gravity for Boers lies with the structural linguistic, synchronic side of the text.

16. See 1994: 126-27. Levinas says apropos the 'unsettling effect' of critical exegesis: 'It is not because of scientific rationalism's penetrating Scripture that men have ceased hearing the Word; perhaps quite to the contrary, biblical criticism is gaining possession of the texts because of a listening that is incapable of perceiving the divine resonance of the Word, which, thus reduced to a linguistic fabric, itself requires the precautions of a science' (p. 126).

and its interpretative ambiguities and richness. Traditional historical, literary-critical, feminist and deconstructive readers find common ground on this point. John 4 is typical in many respects of the evangelist's grammatical, narrative and theological style and its deeply ironic texture.[17] The passage is filled to overflowing with christological statements and designations about Jesus' identity—Lord (v. 11), greater than our father Jacob (v. 12), prophet (v. 19), Messiah (v. 25), 'I am' (v. 26), Christos (vv. 25, 29), savior of the world (v. 42)—that build in ironic fashion toward and climax in an identification of Jesus as the Revealer, the Sign-maker par excellence. In the swirl of narrative discourse and action two pivotal metaphors surface: 'living water' (*hudōr*) and 'the gift from God' (*tēn dōrean tou theou*) (cf. Schüssler Fiorenza 1983: 328). These two metaphors are the vortices for the extensive textual irony that attracts different reader responses. Haenchen's assessment rings true: 'This pericopae is a veritable tangle of difficulties' (1984: 217) that defies every historical, literary and theological solution. It is precisely in the ironic tension and textual ambiguities of John 4, however, that deconstruction finds its place to work.

### A Jarring Woman in a Jarring Text

From a compositional standpoint, John 4 presents, as Bultmann argues, a 'complex edifice created by the Evangelist' (1971: 176); 'the story is neatly contrived dramatically', Barrett concurs (1978: 232).[18] But such

---

17. Whether the Fourth Evangelist makes use of a special Signs Source or constructs the text out of a variety of traditions and texts does not affect directly the question about the overall effect achieved by the narrative with all of its 'entanglements' and 'inconsistencies'. The text is still read as a totality (Olsson 1974). Textual difficulties are 'framed' in specific ways when the text is read as a whole, for example, as awkward moments within the flow of the narrative.

18. The exchange with the Samaritan woman follows upon a briefer exchange with Nicodemus where the issue of water (Barrett 1978: 228) and of women enter in the dialogue only to be picked up in ch. 4. This linkage is suggestive of a set of antinomies that sets male over against other than male, Jew over against other than Jew (a 'we–you' contrast from v. 9 onwards; Barrett 1978: 237); 'real' water over against other than water ('living water'), etc. These polarities inform the Gospel narrative deeply throughout and are brought forward to center stage in this stretch of text that forms a narrow causeway skirting the deep (*bathu*) water on all sides and linking the first and second signs. Given the thematic and narrative placement of the exchange with the Samaritan woman, if the Samaritan woman is a 'minor' character, then it is hard to imagine what a 'major' character would be.

statements of literary or aesthetic appreciation hardly do justice to the legion of textual aporias and narrative rough spots (Olsson 1974: 20) that surface in a careful reading: for example, the disputed opening transitional verses,[19] the nameless Samaritan woman's aggressive ('feisty' is the term Boers uses) behavior, the unexpected response to Jesus' request for a drink of water, her left-behind jar (*tēn hudrian autēs*), the mysterious and often untranslated 'bucket' (*antlēma*), the ambiguous intertextual function of women-at-the-well scenes (cf. Olsson 1974: 162-73), the Samaritan woman's relationship to 'others' (*alloi*) in v. 38,[20] the heavy interpretative hand of the narrator, the imbrication of multiple layers of irony, and more. The text is replete with textual problems that focus attention on the woman's attitude, her relationship to Jesus, to the disciples and to the Samaritan townsfolk, the linkage to Jesus' healing of the official's son (vv. 49-54), the use of irony to affect the way readers read the text and relate to its argument, and the relationship to Jesus' second sign (*deuteron sēmeion*). The widespread and conflicting readings of this passage suggest something important about the way this text resists any confident critical handling and closure. Indeed, John 4 invites us back repeatedly to wrestle with its aporias, tensions and points of textual undecidability.[21] Like the well itself, the text draws readers back again for further reading.

The author is 'an adroit story teller *who endeavors to report a coherent story*'; 'the narrator...knew how to write' (Haenchen 1984: 231; italics mine). Haenchen can hardly hide his mixed assessment of the storyteller who tries—unsuccessfully—to give the reader a coherent story. Moreover, Haenchen's frustration with this text is a sign that John's narrative resists being swept clean methodologically. Given the difficulties of this text, we might see Haenchen's reaction as a fundamental uneasiness with more than just the narrative style and substance

19. Bowman describes the absence of temporal markers here as 'the one real gap in the temporal indications of the Fourth Gospel' (1975: 113).

20. The verse invites a measure of allegorical interpretation, I...you...you... others. 'It is however impossible to give a simple and precise interpretation, not because there are no allusions but because there are several' (Barrett 1978: 243).

21. When Derrida speaks of the 'undecidability of a text' he is referring to the structural capacity of all texts to generate more than one meaning.'...undecidability is always a determinate oscillation between possibilities (for example, of meaning, but also of acts)' [1988b: 148]. The concept is used by Derrida to speak of relations of force in writing, which means that every act of writing is located within a specific historical setting even as writing works to destabilize the situation.

of John 4; following Derrida, I suggest that it is an uneasiness with Johannine *textuality* as such that resists being reduced and explained away methodologically. For that reason, it is tempting to find in the disciples' confusion and displeasure over the Samaritan woman's encounter with Jesus (vv. 27-30) a reflection of the critics' own reaction to this text. Such a narrative identification would begin to account for the strong negative reactions that the Samaritan woman often elicits from male critics (see Schüssler Fiorenza 1992; Moore 1994: 47) who, reflecting an engendered identification with the disciples in v. 27, marvel disapprovingly at Jesus' engagement with a woman who violates cultural norms.

Cast in de Manian terms, we have in the narrative of the Samaritan woman an allegory of the difficulty of reading this text and a clue to its own deconstruction. The narrative captures here a much deeper tension and discomfort, a discomfort with what is Other—the Samaritan tradition, the woman and the text. This tension surfaces in the difficulty the narrator has narrating a smooth and confident portrayal of Jesus both as the embodied Logos (1.14) and as a sign-making pleromatic force. This is a tension Werner Kelber identifies with the Gospel's intense struggle to say at one and the same time 'the Word became flesh' and 'we beheld his glory'—the tension between what is traditionally characterized in the Fourth Gospel as an 'incarnational versus epiphantic Christology'.[22] The narrator draws readers' attention to numerous tensions (textual, theological, metaphysical, etc.) that flow throughout the Gospel, including especially John 4, tensions over the Samaritan woman's resistance to Jesus and the disciples' negative response to her. In so doing, the narrative discloses something about its own textuality and readability that revolves in some fashion around the unsuccessful attempt to avoid encounter with the Other, on the one hand, and to read oneself allegorically into the text on the other. The narrative poses to its readers, sometimes rhetorically in the structural form of irony, sometimes narratively in the discourse between characters, those hypothetical questions that *should be asked* by real readers of the text (e.g. those

---

22. 'The very narrative which thrives on the erasure of the transcendental *arché* cultivates a signs language which aspires pleromatic presence' (Kelber 1990: 93). The extent to which textual and narrative tensions like these prompt source-critical distinctions such as Bultmann makes between independent Signs and Discourse traditions, is a problem to be pursued. It is to traditional 'guard rail' questions that deconstruction must in some way answer.

attributed to the disciples: *oudeis mentoi eipen, ti zēteis ē ti laleis met' autēs?*, 'yet no one said, "what are you after?" or "why are you talking with her?"'). Does the Johannine text deliberately call its readers to a textual awareness designed to make us 'uncomfortable' not only with the Samaritan woman but with Gospel text as Other?[23]

The recent excursion in narratological criticism offers one path critics have followed in dealing with the textual tensions and ambiguities that abound in this passage. In Culpepper's impressive effort, he pays careful attention to the various narrative roles played by women and culturally marginalized characters throughout the Gospel. He describes the Samaritan woman as a 'minor' character, from his point of view an apt description in light of a certain narratological logic and model of characterization. Olsson takes a different tack. From the point of view of the pericope's overall narrative and discursive structure, the Samaritan woman plays a 'major' or pivotal role, for example, by virtue of her words and actions she links the two major scenes of the story (Jesus in dialogue with the Samaritan woman, vv. 7-26, and Jesus in dialogue with the disciples, vv. 27-38, with vv. 39-42 serving as the pericope's 'remarkable' conclusion). The Samaritan woman's 'work' not only holds vv. 8-27 together; it serves as a linchpin linking the exchange with the disciples and the testimony of the townsfolk (Olsson 1974: 148).

Furthermore, from the point of view of discourse structure, the exchange between Jesus and the Samaritan woman spotlights her at the center of one of the longest, sustained dialogues in all of John's Gospel (p. 115).[24] Along with Martha, the Samaritan woman captures the narrator's and reader's attention.[25] To say that the Samaritan woman is 'minor' or 'major' effectively frames her and the text methodologically

23. See Schüssler Fiorenza 1983: 326, who reads the shock of the disciples as reflecting the consternation among Christians in the Evangelist's community over the role played by women. I want to suggest that the contemporary critic may share some of that same 'consternation'.

24. 'Dialogue rather than action carries the scene', according to Culpepper (1983: 136).

25. On Martha see Schüssler Fiorenza 1983: 329. On the central role of women in general in the Fourth Gospel see Brown 1975 and Schneiders 1982. So also Talbert 1992: 114-15, who sees the narrative organization falling into a double-scene structure: Introduction (4.4-7a), Scene One (vv. 7-26) and Scene Two (vv. 27-44). Scene One concentrates attention on the Samaritan woman and falls into two parts structured on the basis of the two imperatives, 'Give me' (vv. 7b-15) and 'Go, call, come' (vv. 16-26).

according to a particular narrative theory of characterization or action that succeeds in blocking us from seeing this woman in ways that exceed narratological norms: in doing so we miss her face. From a deconstructive perspective, the desire for a narratological (or any) method to resolve textual tensions comes with a price. Not only does it create a false confidence that critique can eventually master the text and what is other about it, it also protects us as readers from staying critically alert to the engendered and vested nature of our critical language and models and the potentially negative impact these methods have upon real readers (cf. Levinas 1994: 126-27).[26]

Schüssler Fiorenza presents a different strategy. Her feminist critique challenges us to see the Samaritan woman as part of a cohort of women in John's Gospel who occupy an important narrative spotlight. In Schüssler Fiorenza's view women function as a paradigm of both 'women's apostolic discipleship' and 'leadership in the Johannine communities' (1983: 333). Mary of Magdala, in particular, is identified as 'the apostle of the apostles'. Martha fulfils a comparable if not contrastive role in ch. 11 (although compare the adulterous woman in 7.53–8.11). Schüssler Fiorenza makes much of Martha's role. By narrative's end Martha turns out to be the 'spokesperson for the messianic faith of the community' (p. 329) whose confession of faith is taken up again and repeated by the narrator in 20.31. On Schüssler Fiorenza's reading women occupy important narrative and writerly roles throughout the text in ways that serve to challenge and undermine traditional, mainstream readings of John's text in which women are subordinated or removed. Her strong feminist critique makes us aware of the *en/gendered consciousness* of the men and women who *read* the text— both in the Evangelist's day and in our own.[27] It enables us to see how

26. Levinas is criticized by a number of feminist critics for his masculinist treatment of the feminine. See Chalier 1991; Ziarek 1993; Irigaray 1991; and of course Derrida 1992. On the diversity of feminist positions regarding the feminine see Rowley and Grosz 1990: 175-204.

27. See Joplin on the woman taken in adultery as a mild example of a deconstructive reading. She examines the way biblical commentators uphold distinctions that the Gospel text seeks to undermine (1992: 234). See Moore 1994: 43-64 for a deconstructive feminist-psychoanalytic reading of John 4. What distinguishes Moore's reading is his effort to show how the text subverts the fundamental male-female binary opposition, which he regards as 'a gigantic pavilion whose stakes extend very deep into the world indeed' (p. 46). However, what remains unclear after Moore's powerful analysis is precisely what is meant by 'into the world'. The

the Gospel text invites us to emulate Martha and Mary, to 'read like a woman', as Jonathan Culler might say (Culler 1992: 43-63).

Curiously, not just any woman appears to be an appropriate reading model. According to Schüssler Fiorenza, Martha is the woman that the text lifts up as the acceptable role model, not the Samaritan woman who resists Jesus and pursues her own agenda, which includes a personal life taken by male critics as a sign of weakness and failure in contrast to Jesus' second sign that marks strength and success. But why does the Samaritan woman not serve as a role model? If the woman at the well had been a more traditional woman like Rebecca or Sarah we could imagine a very different reading effect. It is not just that it is 'woman', because the well–screen leads us to expect a woman. Johannine irony demands an otherness that exceeds gender, and the Samaritan woman in all of her religious and cultural otherness provides that alter-image. Because the Samaritan woman's otherness facilitates textual irony, traditional biblical readers busily dismiss or gloss over her otherness (including her gender) in order to arrive at some narrative, ideological (including feminist) or theological point. John's ironic narrative works as well as it does because the text relies on an otherness about the text that is not easily domesticated. While Schüssler Fiorenza's feminist reading strategy draws attention to the gender determinants in reading the Gospel, her theological interests domesticate the Samaritan woman *text* in ways that subordinate women in a different way—in this case to a particular liberative theological hermeneutic.

Gail O'Day's (1986) rhetorical reading of the irony in the depiction of the Samaritan woman illustrates one way the otherness of Johannine textuality—not unlike the woman herself narratively—functions in service of a theological purpose. According to O'Day, the heavily ironic structure of the narrative effectively places the reader in a position to 'read over' the Samaritan woman's shoulder. From the Evangelist's point of view, irony enables the Evangelist to create and recreate the dynamics of revelation. By playing off the tension between surface and

political and institutional implications of his style of feminist reading are left unexplored. In other words, it is not clear in what sense for Moore deconstruction is a political intervention within the world's institutional structures and practices. It is also not clear whether Moore would agree with Nancy Hartsock's (1981: 36) statement that 'at bottom feminism is a mode of analysis, a method of approaching life and politics, rather than a set of political conclusions about the oppression of women'.

depth, apparent and the real, intended and unintended, irony calls for the reader not merely to substitute the

> 'correct' intended meaning for the incorrect surface meaning of the ironic expression, but rather [the reader] is asked to hold the two meanings in tension and, as a result of moving through that tension, to arrive at what the author intends to express (1986: 663).

The structure of this ironic movement is suspiciously binary and hierarchical: the two meanings are paired, with one subordinated to the other as part of the overall drive to resolve *the ironic tension itself* toward the goal of determining what the author meant.[28]

O'Day's theological resolution of textual irony and narrative rough spots is conspicuously—and suspiciously—neat and clean. The Samaritan woman's 'work', or *ergon*, to use Olsson's term, is a struggle to make sense. In one sense the text is about the semiotic problem of finding the proper referent and locating the sense of words and deeds. Both reader and woman struggle to make sense of the meaning of signs. Narratively speaking the Samaritan woman's relationship to the sign-maker/'gift of God' (*tēn dōrean tou theou*) is neither simple nor easy, nor is it a reciprocal relationship from the narrator's point of view: it is Jesus who utters the word-sign and performs the deed-signs. Jesus uses the word-sign one way but the Samaritan woman takes it in a different direction; Jesus seeks to give the 'gift' as the real sign but she does not accept it. Perched on the Samaritan woman's shoulder, the reader knows who Jesus is by virtue of having the advantage of watching the Samaritan woman struggle, come to some unacknowledged level of self-under-standing and eventually disappear from the text, but not before the narrator puts her to use by bringing 'others' to believe. Her struggle serves didactically as a negative *typos* of the way the reader comes to an understanding of who Jesus is: the Samaritan woman's work (*panta hosa epoiēsa*, 'all that I ever did', v. 29) amounts to a negative invest-ment in the reader's understanding. As the Samaritan woman's *ergon* is put to the service of bringing the townsfolk to knowledge (v. 42), so too the narrative is put in service of the reader's desire and need to know.

---

28. O'Day's treatment of this passage in *The Women's Bible Commentary* focuses less on the rhetorical issues of the text and more on the undermining effect the passage has upon male–female boundaries issues in the Gospel as a whole. O'Day also discusses the masculinist character of the commentary tradition that imports sexist judgments about the woman in the text, thereby 'skewing a faithful reading of the text' (1992: 296).

Within this hierarchical theological structure the Samaritan woman's *ergon* is to be frustrated, to fail (to draw water, to receive the living water, to confess Jesus unambiguously as Messiah, etc.) and eventually to disappear; ironically, in so doing she leads others—Samaritans and readers alike—to faith (v. 39), which means acceptance of the gift of God. The gift she does not receive others come to possess. But there is an unsettling remainder after all is said and done both by the narrator and O'Day. Reading O'Day's own question back against herself, we ask if this moment of irony for the reader is 'as simple as it appears' (p. 665)? Or, put another way, can the generative power and undecidability of textual irony and the alterity of this particular text be so easily tamed by invoking the Samaritan woman's experience of misunderstanding itself as an exhaustive allegory (a signifier)—with a positive benefit for the reader, of course—of what takes place on the reader's part (the signified) when encountering the Johannine text?

O'Day is certainly correct to underscore the ironic features of the Gospel narrative as many traditional critics have done and to locate within the text those places where irony is at work creating a high degree of tension. But by gathering up the ironic force or power of the *text itself* and attributing it to the Evangelist, she subordinates text to reader. Theology and allegory combine to produce a 'theoallegorical' discourse that places control of John's text in the hands of a certain kind of *reader* and institution that regulate the text (cf. Kelber 1990, who finds this tension written into the Gospel text itself). Speaking for these authorities, O'Day quiets the intervention of the alterity of the text by explaining away the text's trembling and strangeness in ways that calm the text down and make it safe for theological commentary and critique. O'Day reads in a way that silences the text and constrains its semiosis, not unlike the way the narrator seeks to silence the Samaritan woman and diminish what is Other by making her go quietly away. Fortunately for us, both text and Samaritan woman resist. The Other persists in being disruptive.

Is it possible to imagine that textual irony *exceeds* the narrator's purpose and the reader's theological control, that textual irony works semiotically as a disruptive force to *proliferate*, not *restrict* readings? In this watery text does irony disseminate or desiccate readings? Why are contemporary critical readers so bent on making the *reader's experience* the interpretative focus, if it is not in some fashion part of a stronger need to constrain the inherent undecidability of the Johannine text? We resort to making the reader central (as traditional historical- and literary-critical methods do), because to do otherwise—to displace the reading self from center as poststructuralist and postmodern critique argues has happened—means we must recognize that the text preserves a certain independence over against every reader and every desire to place the text under tight methodological control. John 4 in this respect proves as hard to tame textually as the Samaritan woman herself narratively! By virtue of its ironic troping we are constantly faced with the prospect that textual undecidability makes room for more meaning; it is possible always to add one more signature to the text—indeed textual irony invites it. Deconstructive reading works in the text to keep difference resonating and meaning proliferating. It works to disrupt the smooth flow of methodological reading that has difficulty making sense of the Samaritan woman's left-behind jar.

Irony opens up more than one response or reading. In classical terms, it is a trope of non-closure rather than closure, always pointing to the difference between what the text says and what it means, between the narrative signifier and its signified. Irony therefore calls closure of every sort into question, whether it be feminist, formalist, historicist, ideological, narratological, poststructuralist, semiotic, structuralist, or whatever. Insofar as irony works to keep our attention fixed on *difference* between text and meaning, between narrative characters and reader, irony—to follow De Man's lead—proves to be the very 'condition for the possibility for all tropes and the condition of impossibility for a cognition which is not conditioned by tropes' (Hart 1989: 158-59; see De Man 1979: 301). In other words, irony works in the Johannine text as a trope of its own undecidability or as a sign of its semiotic effervescence; irony here is the very source of the textual 'spring of water welling up (*hallomenon*) to eternal life'. To see the Johannine text and the Samaritan woman's exchange with Jesus as deeply ironic, therefore, is to recognize that we are face-to-face with Johannine *textuality* which is not reducible to redactional or narrative intention. Irony keeps meaning and readings flowing, even though pressure builds as the narrator struggles to contain the unruly, semiotically unstable text and make it theologically safe.

Where O'Day's and other literary readings of Johannine irony miss the mark is in failing to perceive irony as a deep constitutive element of Johannine *textuality* itself. Theoallegorical (be it narratological, feminist, theological) reading prematurely shuts down the generative power of the

text long before it is ready—indeed if it ever is—in an effort to name
and tame the text and its Other, to wrestle it into some acceptable conceptual order, to assign it a narrative name and purpose (*Logos*, or, as
the narrator says parenthetically in v. 2, *ho legomenos christos*) to apply
a final signature to the pericope (*deuteron sēmeion*), and to possess the
gift once and for all. The deep irony here is that this story, which is
narratively resolved under the sign of Jesus' 'second sign' (*deuteron
sēmeion*), stands on shaky textual grounds (cf. Kelber 1990: 93). The
alterity of the Johannine text reserves to itself the potential to keep
readers reading and signing on in new and different ways by intervening
in the text in an unpredictable manner. Irony makes the difference
between text and reader unstable and subject to countless readings that
defeat closure. Irony keeps the text ajar. The irony of the Johannine text
presents us as readers with an ethical challenge—to read for what makes
multiple levels of meaning possible, namely the potential of this and
every text to proliferate readings without regard to what readers may or
may not like—to read for alterity. The alterity of the Johannine text, like
the Samaritan woman herself, comes to us without much forewarning.
Indeed, from a deconstructive perspective, like the Samaritan woman's
reaction to Jesus' request for a drink, the text appears to show little
regard for cultural or critical custom. Like the text, the Samaritan
woman is a trembling, unstable presence that in some ways could care
less what we think theoallegorically.

### Jarring the Text Loose

Let us now return to the text for a second reading for the Other. This
amounts to the second half of the deconstructive movement—to complete the chiastic stroke that marks our taking responsibility for the text.
As we have suggested, the narrative of John 4 has long served as a deep
textual well to which theologians and exegetes come repeatedly to slake
their thirst for a clearer understanding of Jesus' identity. We have
suggested that textual meaning springs from irony. There is no little
irony in the fact that textual waters run deep in spite of repeated critical
efforts to draw off the plenitude of meaning. Issues of irony, misunderstanding and awakened self-understanding are the focus of the
Samaritan woman's encounter with Jesus: she frequently serves the very
useful subordinate theological purpose of being the woman who
misunderstands Jesus' identity in profound ways, ways that the narrator

ironizes for the benefit of the reader (so O'Day 1986) and masculinist
interpreters use to '[reflect] their own own prejudices against women'
(O'Day 1992: 296). Much of the commentary tradition centers attention
upon Jesus as the metaphorical bread and water at the woman's
expense. But if we deliberately recalibrate our reading and attend to
Johannine *textuality*, can we discover anything different about the
narrative identity of the Samaritan woman who is so often cast in a subordinating role to Jesus? How does our reading change things when we
ask first about *this* woman's name, her body, her property, her hunger,
her thirst, her identity—her *face* in this text (see esp. Joplin 1992)—that
escape easy methodological accounting?

Jesus' somatic needs precipitate the dialogue with the Samaritan
woman. He makes the first overture—'Give me something to drink'
(*dos moi pein*), he says. We know from structuralist and folklorist studies
that the central narrative logic of a story typically establishes a lack that
is to be overcome by the central character, with the help or hindrance of
subordinate characters (cf. Boers 1988; Culpepper 1983). What is the
narrative lack to be answered here? Jesus arrives first at the well (v. 6);
he has the somatic first and semiotic last word in this chapter (vv. 7, 53).
Sandwiched in between is a narrative account of a Samaritan woman
who is engaged with Jesus, the disciples, and the Samaritan townspeople
over matters of signs, bodies, food, drink and words. The text notes that
the geographic spot where the encounter takes place belongs to the
Samaritans: the field had been given to them by Jacob (*hos edōken
humin to phrear*, v. 12). The Samaritan woman's 'showing up' allows
for the possibility that her drawing of water is part of a routine that
Jesus has interrupted and now controls. The narrative action invites the
broad critical commentary tradition to subordinate the Samaritan
woman's *ergon* to Jesus' somatic and semiotic needs (cf. v. 54).
Certainly the traditional masculinist view of the woman (e.g. her many
'failed' marriages) is reinforced by the perception of a woman and
narrative action taken over by Jesus. This creates a tension and point of
interpretative conflict especially for feminist readers since the Samaritan
woman and her actions are fairly regarded as the epicenter of both
dialogue and narrative action as seen within the wider narrative (Olsson
1974). The relationship of Jesus to this woman underscores a tension in
the hierarchy of values (male–female) within both the text and the reception history of the Gospel that deconstruction exploits—and ultimately
subverts. For a text taken as providing clear theological clues as to

Jesus' nature, the same narrative also preserves substantial tensions and conflicts, one of which concerns whose body and words—Jesus' or the Samaritan woman's—are foregrounded by the text.

The eventual departure of the difficult woman from the narrative (to be replaced by the more agreeable 'believing' Samaritan townsfolk, v. 42) is typically viewed as a positive narrative and theological turn of events: in spite of initial difficulties with the Samaritan woman all turns out positively in the end. But in this narrative which ends on a note about Jesus' signs we record a number of other signs which indicate that the Samaritan woman's relationship with Jesus and her role in the text is far more ambiguous than traditional ironic, theoallegorical or masculinist readings may have allowed. Out of haste to drive off a resistant, obstreperous woman and to resolve the textual tensions as a Jesus success story in which 'other' Samaritans come and believe, critics read past this woman's body and words. In haste to get to Jesus' healing sign at the pericope's end interpreters overlook signs that the Samaritan woman leaves behind in the text. In the drive to achieve interpretative (i.e. theological) closure, critics treat lightly the textuality of a Gospel narrative about food and drink that itself resists being consumed and digested. Could this be in part why the Samaritan woman refuses to give Jesus drink even upon command? Does the Johannine text resist giving itself up completely to any reader for critical consumption and digestion?

As for the Samaritan woman, the narrative initially presents her engaged directly with Jesus in conversation: his demand for a drink prompts an immediate counter-question that establishes her in a resistant position over against him. From what the disciples say and from what would be expected, she does not display the requisite deference toward Jesus as a Jew, a male or a sojourner. Against the backdrop of the traditional women-at-the-well screen the Samaritan woman's actions are disturbingly different. Compared to Rebecca's response when she gives water to Eliezer (Gen. 24.18) or Hagar's fetching of water (Gen. 21.18; cf. *hudatos zōntos*), for example, she is not responsive to the request of a stranger in need, as would have been expected in women-at-the-well scenes in Jewish tradition (see esp. Olsson 1974: 162-70). In fact, the literal statement in v. 11 indicates she has already made a judgment about Jesus' ability to draw 'living water', even though at one level the narrator's irony seeks to erode confidence in *her* own ability to comprehend fully her own somatic and semiotic needs. What do we make of this dissonance? Olsson argues persuasively that what we have is a 'strongly screened text' with the well-screen serving to encourage the reader to forge important intertextual links between Genesis 21, 24, 29, Exodus 2 and John 4. But what sense are we to make of the *differences* (Olsson 1974: 257)?[29] Olsson and other commentators are not so helpful here. From a deconstructive point of view these dissonances serve as occasions for the text's *ergon* in pressuring the reader to make sense of what is somatically and semiotically 'other' about the text.

The Samaritan woman departs the narrative in v. 28 without complying directly with Jesus' request. Notably she leaves behind her water jar (*aphēken oun tēn hudrian autēs hē gunē*; cf. Gen. 24.43, *tēs hudrias sou*), a point that the narrative underscores. She leaves behind something else, namely, a lasting impression about who she is. More than any other woman or man in the Johannine narrative, the Samaritan woman makes a mark with her 'attitude'. It is her directness and bearing toward Jesus that the disciples marvel over and that Giovanni Francesco Barbieri Guercino has captured in his portrait of the Samaritan woman in his *Christ and the Samaritan Woman*. The woman appears fully engaged with Jesus: her eye contact is direct, her head is held high, her posture is forceful, her grasp is firmly upon the bucket (cf. Boers 1988). Far from the narrative-theological presentation of a subordinate, dense, personally failed woman, Guercino's Samaritan woman has bearing and presence. She faces up to Jesus' questions and gifts and does not wilt. Has Guercino captured something of the textual Samaritan woman not seen by the theoallegorical commentary screen? Simply from the point of view of discursive exchange she holds her own compared with Nicodemus in the preceding chapter. And she holds her own with Jesus through v. 15; at which point she reverses roles and demands of Jesus the 'water that slakes all thirst' (*dos moi touto to hudōr, hina mē dipsō mēde dierxōmai enthade antlein*). The Samaritan woman's persistence in resisting Jesus' initial request for water and the gift of Jesus' living water is *her* sign and signature in this narrative that competes with Jesus' second sign at chapter's end (v. 54).

What happens narratively to the Samaritan woman? She makes no subsequent bodily reappearance, only an indirect discursive sign remains in the reported discourse attributed to the Samaritans from the city (v. 39). (Is there a great surprise that a masculinist interpretative tradition

---

29. Boismard (1973: 225) identifies a strong intertextual relationship between John 4 and Genesis 24.

dominates in light of what the narrator does to the woman?) Her somatic departure in v. 28 is abrupt and final; her words linger, however, on the lips of others but eventually these linguistic signs disappear too. The narrative tension expressed in the opposition between Jesus' *sōma* and his *logoi* spills over onto the Samaritan woman. After she disappears and her words ebb away, what remains in the text is that empty water jar and her words. Her work (*ergon*) of drawing water is left incomplete just as her acknowledgment of Jesus and acceptance of his gift falls way short of completion. She does not explicitly identify Jesus as Messiah as Martha does in 11.27; Jesus must do that himself in v. 26 (*egō eimi, ho lalōn soi*), to which the narrator adds 'his' voice in v. 25 (*ho legomenos christos*). And it is a disclosure that the Samaritan woman does not accept (cf. v. 29). The Samaritan woman's presence in the narrative in body, word and deed is an interruption—of Jesus' word and deed. She disappears from the text, displaced narratively by 'others' (Samaritans) who first come to believe on account of her testimony (v. 39), but eventually even her words (*ouketi dia tēn sēn lalian*, v. 42) are no longer needed. They are prepared to receive the gift that Jesus offers, but she does not accept. Curiously, their belief is directly attributed to this woman (v. 39), but is there no little irony in the fact that their belief results from a narrative interruption, a non-responsiveness, non-acknowledgment and resistance on her part?

Wanting to make the best of an apparently awkward narrative situation, commentators like to turn the Samaritan woman into a positive *typos* of faith herself, a symbol of the missionizing disciple (Schüssler Fiorenza 1983; Boers 1988) to the retrograde Samaritans. But to generalize her character in this way risks enlisting the woman once again in a triumphalizing theology and ideology that ignores who she is in the particular, to erase the face of a woman who engages Jesus face-to-face in dialogue and demands sustenance from *him*. It is that particular face that the *narrative* partially discloses, hides and eventually removes; but it is the *textuality* of John's narrative that invites us as readers to read otherwise for the face of the particular, other woman who stands up to and over against Jesus, the particular man and Jew. It is a textuality that challenges us to read actively within and against a commentary tradition that finds it methodologically normative to write her right out of the story, to quiet her, to relegate her to the status of a minor character or a theological *typos*, to subordinate her as 'woman' or 'other' ultimately for a theoallegorical purpose. It takes care of everything except for her jar that remains as a sign of her absence. The *text* challenges us to confront the alterity of John's Gospel—to make sense narratively and ideologically of the tendency on the part of commentators to treat her typologically at the expense of her singularity, her face. This is what methodology does so well, namely, deal with the general and not the particular. What are the consequences for our reading of the text if she remains undigested by the narrative as the theological main course? Is she not the textual ort to Jesus' narrative food? Deconstruction wants to know. At the end of the chapter the narrator moves to tie up loose ends by turning to the healing of the official's son, followed by a capstone assessment of Jesus' many signs (v. 54). This is a further effort to distance Jesus and the reader from the concreteness of the exchange and specificity of this woman. After all, that is how generalizing, summative statements work.

However, the Samaritan woman is not so easily generalized or erased from the text. Just as she does not go away quickly or easily in the narrative, she is even more difficult to get rid of textually without expending enormous methodological effort to ignore or to deny the marks she has left upon text and reader alike. Traces of her otherness remain in the text in the specific form of that water jar (Barrett 1978: 240; Boers 1988: 182). The jar sits at the well lip of the text as the sign of a woman who is not yet completely eliminated, digested or subjugated by the narrator or a certain critical reading tradition that wants to interpret her and the text finally in masculinist, theoallegorical terms. Her narrative signature in the text cannot be so easily erased, just as the signs of the 'well-screen' cannot be ignored from an intertextual point of view. Indeed, just as the well-screen is needed to make intertextual sense of the action, so too her jar is needed to make sense of the otherness of this text: it is a sign as enduring as that of Jesus' healing. The jar continues to sit in the well text as a reminder to the reader of a woman who is *other* to Jesus—and as a textual figure who is *other* to the male disciples and to the text's readers too—a face that cannot be completely effaced from the text. In spite of the substantial narrative effort to discount this Other—this is the theologocentric move par excellence—to contain and eventually to displace the Samaritan woman, she and the text resist and the jar marks her spot: it is a sign not of the text's closure and univocity (cf. v. 54) but of the incompleteness and undecidability that serves as the wellspring that nourishes readers so that they return to the well text to read (cf. Kelber 1990). The jar and the Samaritan woman herself are textual signs that bring us back again and again to the Gospel well text for that refreshing read. Ironically, in spite of the narrator's not insubstantial efforts to resolve her out of the narrative, the text retains her sign and signature to generate further readings.

The Samaritan woman is encrypted in the text with the water jar as her head stone very near the spot, tradition has it, where Jacob's body lay buried.[30] We ask, Is she the matriarch of that other, displaced religious tradition that worships what it doesn't know or see on the mountain (vv. 21-22)? John 4 serves as her textual burial place (not only for Jacob and Jesus but for woman too) to which readers return time and time again for a different kind of sustenance and homage (cf. the women at the tomb in John 20). The Samaritan text signals an *other* water and bread of life that is neither the literal water of the Samaritan well nor the figurative 'water' that Jesus proposes. The Samaritan woman's jar is a sign of that other textual 'living water' that displaces Jesus' very *logoi* and *sōma* (cf. Kelber 1990: 93).

From a deconstructive perspective the Samaritan woman text en/genders questions about the Johannine text and our fundamental relationship to it as readers. By not removing the water jar, the narrator has failed to wipe the text clean of all traces of this woman's identity and presence and all traces of that other religious tradition she represents.[31] The text keeps alive the gender question. This is odd, given the narrator's preoccupation with signs all throughout the Gospel, especially as they relate to Jesus' presence and absence. How could the narrator have overlooked this woman's mark, trace, signature? Like the water jar in the story, ready to be retrieved at a moment's notice by the next woman coming to fetch water, the jar marks a textual aporia sitting there waiting to be discovered by the next reader who comes to the text looking for sustenance. One of the responsibilities deconstruction has as a reading practice is to be on the lookout for those overlooked signs of Otherness, those places where the textuality of the Gospel continues to capture readers' attention. The deconstructive reader seats herself by the narrative well and makes use of that jar to dip into the text, to draw new meaning and to challenge masculinist reading practices and institutional

30. Note the suggestive intertextual play on tomb and well imagery through the use of *ton lithon* in Gen. 29.3 and Jn 20.1.

31. If the woman is 'dirty', that 'contamination' extends to the vessel, and it too is unclean. Is this the reason the jar is left behind? Is the jar the unclean gift? See Daube 1956; Barrett 1978: 232.

structures. Of course the great irony in this heavily ironic text is that with a little deconstructive push the jar can be made to fall into the deep well of the text. Meaning splashes out over top and douses those exegetes who peer down into the text from their safe theological dry places. However, more than the reader gets wet. The jar is a rem(a)inder that the text, as Derrida points out, always retains a surprise for those institutions responsible for making certain readings possible.

For all its supposed theoallegorical clarity John 4 remains finally an opaque and disconcerting text with many fissures and unresolvable tensions, some great and others small, with uncooperative characters and indelible signs that mark presences and absences. The jar is one such spot that draws attention to the male–female hierarchy within the text and the interpretative tradition. John 4 is an edgy text long in dialogue, irony and tension, short in metaphorical and narrative resolutions.[32] The Johannine text presents a series of difficulties that traditional historical and literary approaches have not been able satisfactorily to resolve in spite of substantial methodological and theological effort. This has prompted some critics to write off these 'aporias'.[33] But it is precisely with such difficulties, Derrida suggests, that more is revealed about the text—and about its meanings, history, readers and institutional practices, about its impracticalities and impossibilities—than necessarily meets the methodological eye. The event of the text is measured deconstructively, we might say, by the difficulties that linger narratively, rhetorically, institutionally and philosophically and the ethical call that goes out to readers to take Johannine textuality seriously, literally, historically. This is one way a deconstructive reading responds to the Other; it is one way of being responsible for otherness and being responsible to act. It is in this

---

32. The critical view that would see the narrative as essentially historical runs into trouble as the reader progresses through the passage. The realistic character of the initial dialgue fades as the narrative action unfolds. See Olssen 1974: 129.

33. Olsson says of vv. 1-6 that 'This section is one of the less coherent scenes in the Gospel' (1974: 135). He goes on to speak of these 'aporias' as 'inconsistencies and contradictions' that threaten the compositional literary unity of Jn 4 (p. 116). Fortna (1970: 189-191) also attempts to explain these 'contradictions'. However, the sense of *aporias* used by these textual critics contrasts markedly with Derrida's sense of aporia, which he draws from Aristotle as the impossible or impracticable meant in philosophical and logical terms (cf. 1993: 12-42). For Derrida, *aporia* signifies the fundamental experience of the Other. See Moore 1994: 69-72 for further discussion of the different senses of *aporia*.

way that deconstructive reading meets its ethical obligation to the woman at the well.

## The Gift of Johannine Textuality

Traditional exegetes and commentators agree that John 4 is a narrative concerned primarily with the giving and receiving of signs and gifts. But what kind of gift-sign does the Johannine text itself make to its deconstructive readers? We have already said that the text makes the tropes of 'the gift of God' (*tēn dōrean tou theou*) and the 'living water' (*hudōr zōn*) the pivotal metaphors in the text. As Olsson points out, the most important semantic areas in John's text are marked by the words 'water' and 'give'. Their rich association in Judaism with Torah and in Hellenism with Wisdom suggests that *tēn dōrean tou theou* and *hudōr zōn* serve as the metaphorical intersecting points of Greek and Hebrew semantic fields, intertextual traditions and cultures; 'Jewgreek is greekjew: extremes meet', says Derrida (1978: 153). It is the place where what is other is encountered. Because of the very wide range of allusions and connotations (see Barrett 1978: 233),[34] it is perhaps not surprising that the narrator exploits the fecundity of these metaphors and ends up narrating a story about the otherness of a Samaritan woman and men, about people who receive the gift of God and others who apparently miss the point about the gift in a number of ways in the process. All this draws attention to the otherness of the text.

We have already suggested how the watery well works as a liquid metaphor for a text that refreshes its readers. The metaphor of gift (*tēn dōrean*) is another metaphor for Johannine textuality itself that gives us a clue about what it means to be readers responsible to the text. For this reason Derrida's comments about the structural character of the 'gift' are helpful for explaining what is at stake when we begin to think about the way in which John's text itself presents the narrative of the 'gift of God' and the way the text itself functions as the *event of giving* to its readers as an allegory of its own deconstruction.

By definition, giving is a non-reciprocal event. It is an unconditional act that carries with it no expectation of response or reaction. Were a

---

34. Barrett explains that 'John uses the expression no doubt because it aptly conveys what he wishes to say, partly because of its twofold, Jewish and Greek, background, and partly because its double meaning conformed to his ironical style' (1978: 233; cf. 3.5, 7.38, and 19.34).

response imagined—say, a thank you, an acceptance, a return gift (Derrida 1991: 91-92)—the gift would cease being a gift and become instead an object of exchange. An 'exchange of gifts', by this definition, is an oxymoron. The non-reciprocal, unidirectional flow of the gift means that it comes with no strings attached from some other place,[35] from a beyond, with no calculation of an acceptance, although it does call for a response; there is never a 'reason' per se to be offered for a gift because that would require a prior logic, subjectivity and intentionality. The moment the gift enters the circle of exchange it is annulled. The structure of the gift is such that it is not the subject who makes the giving possible but the gift that makes the subject subject in relation to it in the first place: the gift always precedes. Therefore, the gift does not rest upon my *being* a subject prior to its sending but is an invitation and a calling to acknowledge a fundamental dependency upon what is other, as Levinas would say, a resting on the face-to-face relationship that precedes my being either a sender or a receiver. The gift makes me *me* in the particular. It makes me responsible to respond and to receive.

John's narrative irony works so as to make the text a gift in just this way. On the narrative surface the text is about the repeated and stymied efforts on Jesus' part to maneuver the Samaritan woman into drawing water for him and the ineffective effort on his part to get the Samaritan woman to acquire an understanding of what the real gift of the living water (*hudōr zōn*) of God is and to receive it. As the text stands, she perceives Jesus as a prophet (v. 19) but her confession to the disciples in v. 29—'Can this be the Christ?'—is less than enthusiastic or unambiguous. The Samaritan woman appeals unsuccessfully to Jesus to give her this 'spring of water' (*pēgē hudatos hallomenou eis zōēn aiōnion*), but there is effectively no exchange between them. The narrative strategy of ironic misunderstanding on the woman's part draws attention, if not to the outright rejection of Jesus' gift, at least to its non-acceptance.

With regard to the 'others' (explicitly identified as the Samaritan townsfolk), Jesus' gift is linked narratively to a process of *exchange* of information; in v. 42 they hear for themselves. However, with respect to the Samaritan woman that mode of gift-giving never materializes because she resists. Although it is precisely an exchange relationship that

---

35. Cf. Heidegger's notion of 'Sending' discussed in Derrida 1991b. Also see Heidegger's intriguing essay on the 'Thing' with its attention on the 'jug' (1971). In this essay the jug serves as the focus for Heidegger's analysis of Being and being. It is particularly suggestive for our reading of otherness in Jn 4.

leads the other Samaritans first to 'receive' her 'testimony' (*dia ton logon*), to believe and then to go seek out Jesus, for the Samaritan woman there is no acceptance, no structure or cycle of exchange. The chapter ends with Jesus saying to the official, unless he sees 'signs and wonders'—unless he accepts—he will not believe (v. 48). 'Successful' belief throughout this chapter is tied up narratively with an understanding and *acceptance* of the gift of God presented precisely in terms of exchange.

At the same time there is another sense of gift in circulation here. From the *narrative* point of view the gift of God is ¢aught up in terms of exchange, which means that the Samaritan woman's rejection of this relationship is positively presented as a deficiency or inadequacy that the narrator underscores with pointed comments in the disciples' judgmental statements about her discourse with Jesus. However, 'others' *do* accept her testimony and come to believe, but what exactly do they accept and on what grounds? This apparently happens as a result of *noncooperation* if not outright *resistance*. From a theological perspective, the narrative succeeds in achieving a certain kind of closure. Nonetheless, the presence of a theological reading relies upon the ironic openness and ambiguity of the Samaritan woman's response and her absence from the text; narrative meaning is grounded finally in textual *difference* that is too often overlooked by fixating upon a successful narrative pattern of exchange at the expense of what is other, of what is *not* exchanged. The Samaritan woman's non-giving and non-receiving is a narrative sign that the narrative-theological gift-giving and reception can not take place without her. Ironically, and this is the deconstructive point, she is *textually* central and necessary for the success of the narrative and its theological reading because she is Other—outside of normal culture, outside of typical patterns of giving and taking, outside of women-at-the-well scenes. It is the Samaritan woman as Other that enables belief, reading and meaning to happen.

In this textual view the Samaritan woman works narratively as a model for missionizing but in a very different way than Schüssler Fiorenza or O'Day might imagine. From this point of view her 'non-testimony' has a different kind of potency. She serves allegorically as a model for reading the text as text that is different from the passive response posited for the safe exchange-minded ironic readers of John's narrative. What is often regarded as the Samaritan woman's 'weakness' as a model of how not to respond to the giving of the gift of *pēgē hudatos hallomenou eis zōēn aiōnion* may in fact be just the opposite. Her refusal to receive draws attention even more to the gift-like character of the text that does not demand reciprocity but perhaps invites the resistance that comes with speaking face-to-face. In one sense the gift of the text—like the Samaritan woman herself—carries no reciprocal response, offers no thank you, may even entail opposition on the part of its reader.

Deconstructive reading is attuned to what is fundamentally and necessarily gift-like, defined here as what is *other* about the text. The text presents the feisty Samaritan woman's refusal to engage Jesus in an exchange relationship (in contrast to the normative Rebecca and Hagar)—as a sign of *another way* to engage the otherness of the gift of life and the otherness of the text itself that the text narrates theoallegorically (cf. Taylor 1984). Attention to the Gospel narrative's ironic character opens up the possibility for the reader of locating in the Samaritan woman's interaction with Jesus *another way* to be a responsive disciple and a responsible reader whose resistance and non-compliance reaffirms the alterity of the gift of God that lies outside of all theological categories. The ethical point to be drawn here is that just as Jesus cannot do without the Samaritan woman, the Johannine narrative text cannot do with the water jar, theological reading cannot do without atheological reading, historical biblical exegesis cannot do without deconstructive reading as the Other to its traditional methodological practices; masculinist readings depend upon feminist constructions. The event of reading John 4 deconstructively causes text and institutional reading practices to tremble. The consequence is not the dulling of the Johannine narrative or reading but a re-enchantment of Johannine textuality and with it an intensification of the ethical demand placed upon its readers.

## Conclusion

Standing back for a moment from the text, one way to make sense of deconstruction's intervention within biblical studies is to see it as a response to a widespread postmodern crisis.[36] Deconstruction challenges contemporary biblical criticism to a different kind of engagement with a world undergoing rapid and fundamental change.[37] In this sense it has

36. See Bennington's caution, however, against reducing Derrida to the status of a postmodern thinker (Bennington and Derrida 1993: 287-91); also Norris 1989: 188.

37. Strongly reminiscent of Bultmann's effort to link Heidegger's existential

profound ethical and political implications. Deeply rooted in the cognitive and cultural transformation of modernity, Derridian deconstruction is a form of oppositional thought and writing that is concerned with the modern relationship between human beings and the world. In the crosshairs of its sights is the unlimited role that Reason, hypostatized within the metaphysical tradition, enjoys in providing a rational account of every aspect of modern life (Derrida 1983: 7). Biblical criticism is the quintessential modern methodological project designed to give a full rational accounting of the biblical text—usually in masculinist terms.[38]

Deconstruction locates itself more specifically within the circle of poststructuralist criticism and close to feminist criticism, targeting the 'master masculinist narratives' that have shaped the relationship of the academy, including biblical studies, to the modern social world and left it, in Max Weber's words, 'disenchanted'. Although neither deconstructive nor feminist, Weber's assessment of modernity anticipated the critique of the postmodern condition identified with Lyotard (1984). Weber succeeded in focusing attention upon the interrelated practices and beliefs and 'those foundational interpretive schemes that have

analysis to historical method, deconstruction locates some of its roots as well in the Heideggerian effort to analyse the relationship of human being to world. Deconstruction seeks overall to disclose 'the *metaphysical* concept of history...the concept of history as the history of meaning' (Derrida 1972b: 56, emphasis mine) that reigns in and regulates Western culture (including Heidegger's own 'destructive' writings) as Law. For biblical interpreters deconstruction should mark at once a certain 'repeat' of an earlier philosophical intervention and at the same time a 'going beyond' Bultmann's existential phenomenology toward what Derrida calls 'a new conception of history—a 'monumental history'—with its different understanding of text, reading and writing, and the relationship of texts to the world. One important difference from Bultmann's effort is that deconstruction's critique extends to the *theological* heart of modern biblical studies itself. Deconstruction holds enormous potential for undermining much of what modern critics accept as self-evidently true and for transforming the ways biblical exegetes in different historical settings today can make sense of the biblical text, the history of interpretation of the Bible, the relationship of biblical interpretation to society, and the nature of criticism as an ethical act meant to transform the postmodern world in which they live (Derrida 1972b: 58-59; also see G. West 1992; Schneidau 1982).

38. For a succinct treatment of the 'problematic of postmodernity' in general as it relates to biblical studies see the Bible and Culture Collective forthcoming, esp. ch. 1. Also helpful on the relationship of politics to postmodernism is White 1991: 13-30. White sets up a useful distinction between 'oppositional' and 'non-oppositional' positions to sort out different types of postmodern thought and action.

constituted the ultimate and unquestioned sources for the justification of scientific-technological and political projects in the modern world' (White 1991: 4; cf. Lyotard 1984: xxiv; Cascardi 1992: 16-71). In reaction to the ubiquitous logic and processes of rationalization and the deeply-rooted modern quest for clarity, closure and consensus, deconstruction draws attention to an originary responsibility for the Other that Reason has 'pushed aside, marginalized, forcibly homogenized and devalued' (White 1991: 19). For its part deconstruction is not keen to promote an alternative foundation, conceptual scheme or method; and it is important to see that its concerns overlap a certain practice of 'feminism as construct' that 'attempt[s] to move feminist knowledge beyond the stage of being an oppositional critique of existing male-defined knowing, knowledge, and theory' (Gunew 1990: 25). For its part, deconstruction seeks to leverage[39] a fundamental rethinking of the place of Enlightenment Reason and the nature of our ethical responsibility as critics of the Bible in the postmodern world in relation to what is other. Echoing and radicalizing Schüssler Fiorenza's appeal (1988), deconstruction calls for us to face up to the crisis of 'ethico-political responsibility' confronting us as critical readers of the Bible today (cf. Derrida 1988b: 111-54).[40]

Deconstruction challenges biblical scholars to rethink in a certain way the nature of the Bible as a particular text, the event of reading and writing, the nature of our disciplinary practices, and the ethical responsibilities we face as readers of texts and as intellectuals in today's society (cf. C. West 1993: 87-188). Given the wider cultural and institutional stakes of deconstruction, traditional biblical critics have reason to be wary. Operating against the grain of a pervasive masculinist metaphysical tradition that has shaped our modern presuppositions, practices and privileges, deconstruction vies for an alternative understanding and critical practice. More than the biblical text, deconstruction reads the 'general text' for those practices of modern biblical studies that privilege the

39. The 'lever' (*mochlos*) is an important concept for Derrida in discussing what is needed to move from a certain kind of foundationalist ethical thinking to an alternative way of regarding ethico-political responsibility. The alternative account of ethical responsibility is arrived at not by 'leaping' from one foundation spot to another but by prying up ethico-political discourse from its old modern foundation for a different configuration. See White 1991: 79-81. Also Caputo 1993: ch. 1.

40. For an assessment of Derrida on this score see Critchley 1992; Norris 1983; White 1991: 76-94.

*hierarchy* of oppositions like presence–absence, history–myth, speaking–writing, text–context, male–female, exegesis–eisegesis, explanation–interpretation, and the *force* that maintains a certain relationship to text and context characteristic of our modern metaphysical way of thinking.[41] But reading and writing toward what practical end? Is it to invert these metaphysical oppositions? Is it to replace one social construction with another? Is it to affirm a postmodern condition that has eclipsed modernity? What different world does deconstruction imagine? First and foremost, it is a modern world in which we are positioned differently. I have suggested that deconstruction seeks a different kind of response to and responsibility for text and context. To gain a measure of the text is to recognize from the inside the power of the metaphysical tradition to instantiate these oppositions and a certain structure of force in our institutional practices, which is expressed in the drive toward methodological mastery. In addition, it is to recognize from the outside the failure of every critical strategy to exhaust the meaning of the text and to restrain the reading process. By underscoring the radical 'otherness' of the Bible—marked in various ways by alternative meanings, readers, interpretative traditions, communities, practices, and so on—deconstruction works prophetically for a different kind of reading and writing *position* in the world. It does so by embracing the twin ethical aim characterized as a *responsibility to otherness* and a *responsibility to act*.[42]

Furthermore, deconstructive criticism calls for a different grasp of the history of the text. It calls for room to be given to alternative conceptions of the other of history and the history of the text no longer expressed in standard metaphysical terms as the 'history of the Bible's

41. O'Leary summarizes the relationship of deconstruction to metaphysics nicely: 'Deconstruction is not the reduction of meaning to a mere nothingness, or to the empty space lit up by the play of signifiers. It is a wrestling with the metaphysical tradition of meaning which, to use Heidegger's terms, it appropriates in a more originary way, by bringing to light the play of dissemination which the stable hierarchies of metaphysics occlude' (1985: 44).

42. White (1991: 76-94) argues that to date deconstruction has been more successful in making clear what he calls a 'responsibility of otherness' than a 'responsibility of action'. I agree in part, although we must be careful when making these 'practical' judgments to situate the specific critique. For example, a number of feminist critics successfully employ deconstruction in quite specific, political ways. Blanket assertions must be guarded against. Cf. Weedon 1987: 136-75; Welch 1990: 103-53. On the relationship of feminism and deconstruction in biblical studies see Jobling 1990.

meaning' but as 'monumental history', a history of discrete events of writing and rewriting and rerewriting, a history of the event of the Bible as Text that refuses to hypostatize text or extract it from its many potential contexts. Deconstruction calls for alternative institutional reading practices that do justice to the text. For this reason it is simply wrong to regard deconstruction as a relativistic, non-political philosophical or literary gesture designed to fix (in the senses of 'stilling' and 'repairing') the text (cf. Norris 1989: 187-96); deconstruction is not interested in reducing texts to enactments of methods, techniques, ideologies or theories of reading or in promoting an alternative metanarrative that in its own right accounts for everything. It has other aims; it aims for the Other. What sets deconstruction apart is its response to what is other about the text by orienting a way of thinking, of writing and reading in relation to this Other that demands we face up to institutional configurations of power, gender and ideology. In short, deconstruction calls for a way of living with the Bible in a postmodern world today that reinscribes biblical studies in a certain responsible way within the culture of criticism and the criticism of culture.[43] Deconstruction attempts to hold biblical studies accountable for its involvement in this 'disenchanted world'.

I realize that my particular reading of John 4 may not have slaked the powerful methodological thirst for closure and aesthetic pleasure (cf. Alter 1989). But this result is, I would claim, consistent with the character of the Johannine text and with a postmodern context deeply suspicious of comprehensive readings and closure. In this respect deconstruction's 'agenda' clashes smartly with the modern methodological need to achieve a point of exteriority from which to make an independent and totalizing assessment of texts and readings.[44] The effort to read John 4 deconstructively not only has put me at odds (like the Samaritan woman) with the narrative and made me responsible to a textuality which I cannot reduce finally to a particular set of interests and concerns

43. See Gerald West (1992) and Cornel West (1993) for two different 'contextualized' deconstructive approaches, the first for a South African, the other for a North American audience. The expression 'culture of criticism and the criticism of culture' is borrowed from Giles Gunn (1987).

44. Levinas characterizes the aspiration to radical exteriority as the metaphyscial gesture *par excellence*. In the Western philosophical tradition it is 'radical exteriority which, above all,...constitutes truth' (1969: 29). We must 'let be' this aspiration, finally, but it is not the final word.

(be they theological, methodological, aesthetic, ideological, etc.), but it has also called me to contest institutional expectations to produce, authorize and legitimate a much-desired panoptic view that privileges what we might call a generalizable, 'transcendent reading' of the Bible. More particularly, reading John 4 deconstructively encourages me to read for and with the *text* of the Samaritan woman and against a dominant critical and narrative theological tradition that regards her negatively as culturally, religiously and sexually other, as Samaritan Woman. It invites me to regard the text and the otherness marked here as more than I dare imagine, more than I can exhaustively explain even with allegory as a helper. Whereas Haenchen and others might see otherness, openness, undecidability and woman as a textual problem waiting to be resolved, it is my responsibility to stay with Johannine textuality, which means attending to the face of that woman/other traced within it and to read self-reflexively for my face reflected as well in the text (cf. Bultmann 1960: 290). It calls me to be on guard against reinscribing the other in my image for my purposes.

Reading John 4 responsibly, deconstructively, in Derrida's words 'carries with it, and must do so, an essential excessiveness' (1991a: 108), but one that is linked always and 'in a certain way' to the meaning of the text.[45] That linkage must always be concrete, specific and local—facial, to use Levinas' image. To make deconstructive reading part of some general system or methodological program is to lose sight of the specific face of the text, which means its institutional context, its reception history, its flesh and blood readers. Because deconstructive reading is 'an interruption of the other' (Derrida 1986: 24), its outcome is not calculable in advance; it is reading that demands we give the other a 'chance', which means taking a chance. This is a kind of reading that is ultimately not methodologically safe and not easily predictable. Modern biblical scholars should hear an echo of Bultmann's warning that a reading of the Bible must not presuppose its results in advance (Bultmann 1966).[46] We read at our own risk.

45. '[T]he meaning [of a text] has to link in a certain way with that which exceeds it' (Derrida, 1989: 846).

46. Compare Bultmann and Derrida on the point of calculation: 'The question whether exegesis without presuppositions is possible must be answered affirmatively if "without presuppositions" means "without presupposing the results of the exegesis". In this sense, exegesis without presuppositions is not only possible but demanded' (Bultmann 1960: 289). Derrida says: 'When I try to decipher a text I do

To read deconstructively in this fashion has far-ranging institutional and disciplinary implications: it is to resist any personal or disciplinary effort to complete the text and to sign off with that Final Sign and signature, to engage in a summative semiotic effort that even the Johannine narrator concedes not even the world could contain (cf. 20.30; 21.25). To read responsibly means being prepared to see the narrative as essentially ajar; it means rejecting the narrative as a traditional theological gift that wraps up meaning or as a watering hole that runs dry. It means, in terms of the Samaritan woman, aligning our interests with her by being uncharitable and getting in Jesus' face, the face of a Jeṣus constructed by a narrator and a commentary tradition that effaces *her* for the theological sake of *him*. In this respect the feminist critic and Derrida can stand together and demand an accounting of the Samaritan woman's treatment at the hands of John's Gospel by reading against the grain of a commentary tradition that aims to safeguard masculinist reading strategies, to close down textuality and to reinforce patriarchal prerogatives.

Deconstructive reading strategies confer a different kind of status upon the reader, the activity of reading, and the readability of the biblical text. It is not 'natural' to be a deconstructive reader, but then that can be said of *every* reader and *every kind* of reading, including modern critical reading. To read deconstructively you must be '"formed", "trained", instructed, constructed, even engendered, let's say *invented* by the work' (Derrida in Attridge 1992: 74, emphasis his). Put another way, deconstruction underscores the unfinished nature of *reading* and the *reader* by attending carefully to the concrete, particular, historical text and the face of the specific other that erupts in it. Once under way, deconstruction moves to query the presumptive understandings of text and context by doubling back like a stranger upon its signifying institutional ground. If it is 'good' deconstruction, it surprises the logic and flow not only of the Johannine but also of the general text that shapes our masculinist institutional discourse and reinforces the disenchanted modern world in which biblical studies currently finds itself mired. When deconstruction succeeds, it does so by rejecting invitations to drink or to give drink in order to act differently. Like the Samaritan woman it intervenes, it deconstructs, it re-enchants.

not constantly ask myself if I will finish by answering *yes* or *no*, as happens in France at determined periods of history, and generally on Sunday' (1972b: 32).

## BIBLIOGRAPHY

Abrams, M.H.
1991        *Doing Things with Texts: Essays in Criticism and Critical Theory* (ed. Michael Fisher; New York: Norton).
Adorno, Theodor
1983        *Against Epistemology: A Metacritique: Studies in Husserl and the Phenomenological Antinomies* (trans. Willis Domingo; Cambridge, MA: MIT Press).
Alter, Robert
1989        *The Pleasures of Reading in an Ideological Age* (New York: Simon & Schuster).
Attridge, Derek (ed.) and Jacques Derrida
1992        *Acts of Literature* (New York: Routledge & Kegan Paul).
Barrett, Charles Kingsley
1978        *The Gospel according to St John* (Philadelphia: Westminster Press, 2nd edn).
Beardslee, William
1993        'Poststructuralist Criticism', in McKenvie and Haynes 1993: 221-36.
Bennington, Geoffrey and Jacques Derrida
1993        *Jacques Derrida* (trans. Geoffrey Bennington; Religion and Postmodernism; Chicago: University of Chicago Press).
Bernasconi, Robert and Simon Critchley (eds.)
1991        *Re-Reading Levinas* (Studies in Continental Thought; Bloomington: Indiana University Press).
The Bible and Culture Collective [Elizabeth Castelli, Stephen Moore, Gary Phillips and Regina Schwartz] (eds.)
Forthcoming    *The Postmodern Bible* (New Haven: Yale University Press).
Boers, Hendrikus
1988        *Neither on this Mountain nor in Jerusalem* (SBLMS, 35; Atlanta: Scholars Press).
Boismard, M.E.
1973        'Aenon, près de Salem (Jean III, 23)', *RB* 80: 218-29.
Bowman, John
1975        *The Fourth Gospel and the Jews: A Study in R. Akiba, Esther and the Gospel of John* (Pittsburgh: Pickwick Press).
Brown, Raymond
1966        *The Gospel according to John (i–xii)* (Garden City, NY: Doubleday).
Bultmann, Rudolf
1960        'Is Exegesis without Presuppositions Possible?', in *Existence and Faith: Shorter Writings of Rudolf Bultmann* (trans. Shubert M. Ogden; New York: World Publishing): 289-96, 314-15.
1971        *The Gospel of John: A Commentary* (trans. and ed. G.R. Beasley-Murray *et al.*; Philadelphia: Fortress Press).
Cascardi, Anthoni
1992        *The Subject of Modernity* (Literature, Culture, Theory; Cambridge: Cambridge University Press).

Caputo, John
1993         *Against Ethics: Contributions to a Poetic of Obligation with Constant Reference to Deconstruction* (Bloomington: Indiana University Press).

Chalier, Catherine
1991         'Ethics and the Feminine', in Bernasconi and Critchley 1991: 119-29.

Ciaramelli, Fabio
1991         'Levinas's Ethical Discourse. Between Individuation and Universality', in Bernasconi and Critchley 1991: 83-105.

Clark, Timothy
1992         *Derrida, Heidegger, Blanchot: Sources of Derrida's Notion and Practice of Literature* (Cambridge: Cambridge University Press).

Cohen, Richard A. (ed.)
1986         *Face-to-Face with Levinas* (Albany: State University of New York Press).

Critchley, Simon
1992         *The Ethics of Deconstruction: Derrida and Levinas* (Cambridge: Basil Blackwell).

Culler, Jonathan
1982         *On Deconstruction: Theory and Criticism after Structuralism* (Ithaca, NY: Cornell University Press).

Culpepper, Alan
1983         *Anatomy of the Fourth Gospel: A Study in Literary Design* (Philadelphia: Fortress Press).

Daube, David
1956         'Samaritan Woman', in *The New Testament and Rabbinic Judaism* (London: Athlone Press): 373-82.

De Man, Paul
1979         *Allegories of Reading: Figural Language in Rousseau, Nietzsche, Rilke, and Proust* (New Haven: Yale University Press).

Derrida, Jacques
1964         'Violence et Métaphysique, essai sur la pensée d'Emmanuel Levinas', *Revue de Métaphysique et de Morale* 69: 322-54, 425-73.
1967a        *Of Grammatology* (trans. G.C. Spivak; Baltimore: Johns Hopkins University Press).
1967b        *Speech and Phenomena, and other Essays on Husserl's Theory of Signs* (trans. David B. Allison; Evanston, IL: Northwestern University Press).
1972a        *Dissemination* (trans. B. Johnson; Chicago: University of Chicago Press).
1972b        *Positions* (trans. Alan Bass; Chicago: University of Chicago Press).
1977         'Signature Event Context', *Glyph* 1: 172-97.
1978         *Writing and Difference* (trans. Alan Bass; Chicago: University of Chicago Press).
1982         *Margins of Philosophy* (trans. Alan Bass; Chicago: University of Chicago Press).
1983         'The Principle of Reason: The University in the Eyes of its Pupils', *Diacritics* 13: 3-20.
1984         'Deconstruction and the Other', in Richard Kearney (ed.), *Dialogues*

| | *with Contemporary Continental Thinkers* (Manchester: University of Manchester Press): 105-26. |
|---|---|
| 1986a | *Altérités* (with Pierre-Jean Labarriare; Paris: Osiris). |
| 1986b | *Glas* (trans. John P. Leavey and R. Rand; Lincoln: University of Nebraska Press). |
| 1988a | 'Letter to a Japanese Friend', in David Wood and Robert Bernasconi (eds.), *Derrida and Différance* (Evanston, IL: Northwestern University Press): 1-5. |
| 1988b | *Limited Inc* (ed. Gerald Graff; trans. Samuel Weber and Jeffrey Mehlman; Evanston, IL: Northwestern University Press). |
| 1989 | 'Biodegradables: Seven Diary Fragments', *Critical Inquiry* 15: 812-73. |
| 1991a | ' "Eating Well", or the Calculation of the Subject: An Interview with Jacques Derrida', in Eduardo Cadava, Peter Connor and Jean-Luc Nancy (eds.), *Who Comes after the Subject* (London: Routledge & Kegan Paul): 96-119. |
| 1991b | *Given Time: Counterfeit Money* (trans. Peggy Kamuf; Chicago: University of Chicago Press). |
| 1992 | 'At This Very Moment in This Work Here I Am', in Bernasconi and Critchley 1991: 11-50. |
| 1993 | *Aporias: Dying-Awaiting (One Another at) the 'Limits of Truth'* (trans. Thomas Dutoit; Meridian; Stanford: Stanford University Press). |

Detweiler, Robert
| 1989 | *Breaking the Fall: Religious Readings of Contemporary Fiction* (Studies in Literature and Religion; London: Macmillan). |

Feyerabend, Paul
| 1975 | *Against Method: Outline of an Anarchistic Theory of Knowledge* (London: Verso). |

Fewell, Danna Nolan and David M. Gunn
| 1993 | *Gender, Power and Promise: The Subject of the Bible's First Story* (Nashville: Abingdon Press). |

Fortna, Robert
| 1970 | *The Gospel of Signs: A Reconstruction of the Narrative Source Underlying the Fourth Gospel* (Cambridge: Cambridge University Press. |

Gasché, Rodolphe
| 1986 | *The Tain of the Mirror: Derrida and the Philosophy of Reflection* (Cambridge, MA: Harvard University Press). |

Grosz, Elizabeth
| 1990 | 'Philosophy', in Gunew 1990: 147-74. |

Gunew, Sneja (ed.)
| 1990 | *Feminist Knowledge: Critique and Construct* (New York: Routledge). |

Gunn, Giles
| 1987 | *The Culture of Criticism and the Criticism of Culture* (New York: Oxford University Press). |

Hart, Kevin
| 1989 | *The Trespass of the Sign: Deconstruction, Theology and Philosophy* (Cambridge: Cambridge University Press). |

Hartsock, Nancy
    1981            'Fundamental Feminism: Process and Perspective', in C. Bunch *et al.*
                    (eds.); *Building Feminist Theory: Essays from Quest, A Feminist
                    Quarterly* (New York: Longman).
Haenchen, Ernst
    1984            *John. I. A Commentary on the Gospel of John: Chapters 1–6* (trans.
                    and ed. Robert Funk; Hermeneia; Philadelphia: Fortress Press).
Heidegger, Martin
    1971            'The Thing', in *Poetry, Language, Thought* (trans. Albert Hofstadter;
                    New York: Harper & Row): 163-87.
Irigaray, Luce
    1991            'Questions to Emmanuel Levinas: On the Divinity of Love', in
                    Bernasconi and Critchley 1991: 109-18.
Jacobs, Alan
    1991            'Deconstruction', in Clarence Walhout and Leland Ryken (eds.),
                    *Contemporary Literary Theory: A Christian Appraisal* (Grand Rapids:
                    Eerdmans): 172-98.
Jeanrond, Werner R.
    1988            *Text and Interpretation as Categories of Theological Thinking* (trans.
                    Thomas J. Wilson; New York: Crossroad).
Jobling, David
    1990            'Writing the Wrongs of the World: The Deconstruction of the Biblical
                    Text in the Context of Liberation Theologies', *Semeia* 51: 81-118.
Joplin, Patricia Klindiest
    1992            'Intolerable Language: Jesus and the Woman Taken in Adultery', in
                    Philippa Berry and Andrew Wernick (eds.), *Shadow of Spirit:
                    Postmodernism and Religion* (New York: Routledge & Kegan Paul):
                    226-37.
Kelber, Werner
    1990            'In the Beginning were the Words: The Apotheosis and Narrative
                    Displacement of the Logos', *JAAR* 58/1: 69-98.
Klein, William, Craig Bromberg and Robert Hubbard
    1993            *Introduction to Biblical Interpretation* (Dallas: Word Books).
Leavey, John
    1987            'Four Protocols: Derrida, his Deconstruction', *Semeia* 23:43-53.
Levinas, Emmanuel
    1969            *Totality and Infinity* (trans. Alphonso Lingis; Pittsburgh: Duquesne
                    University Press).
    1976            'Sécularization et faim', in E. Castelli (ed.); *Herméneutique de la
                    sécularisation* (Paris: Aubier–Montaigne): 101-109.
    1978            *Existence and Existents* (trans. Alphonso Lingis; The Hague: Martinus
                    Nijhoff).
    1981            *Otherwise than Being or beyond Essence* (trans. Alphonso Lingis; The
                    Hague: Martinus Nijhoff).
    1985            *Ethics and Infinity* (trans. Richard Cohen; Pittsburgh: Duquesne
                    University Press).
    1990a           *Difficult Freedom: Essays on Judaism* (trans. Seán Hand; Baltimore:
                    Johns Hopkins University Press).

| 1990b | *Nine Talmudic Readings* (trans. Annette Aronowicz; Bloomington: Indiana University Press). |

1991b     'Wholly Otherwise', in Bernasconi and Critchley 1991: 3-10.

1994      'The Strings and the Wood: On the Jewish Reading of the Bible', in *Outside the Subject* (trans. Michael Smith; Stanford: Stanford University Press): 126-34.

Levinas, Emmanuel and Richard Kearney

1986      'Dialogue with Emmanuel Levinas', in Cohen 1986: 13-34.

McKenzie, Steven L. and Stephen R. Haynes (eds.)

1993      *To Each its own Meaning: An Introduction to Biblical Criticisms and their Application* (Louisville: Westminster/John Knox).

McKnight, Edgar V.

1978      *Meaning in Texts: The Historical Shaping of a Narrative Hermeneutics* (Philadelphia: Fortress Press).

Miller, David L.

1987      'The Question of the Book: Religion as Texture', *Semeia* 40: 53-64.

Miller, J. Hillis

1987      *The Ethics of Reading* (New York: Columbia University Press).

1989      'Is There an Ethics of Reading?', in J. Phelan (ed.), *Reading Narrative: Form, Ethics, Ideology* (Columbus: Ohio State University Press): 79-101.

Miller, Nancy

1986      *Subject to Change: Reading Feminist Writing* (New York: Columbia University Press).

Moi, Toril

1985      *Sexual/Textual Politics: Feminist Literary Theory* (New Accents; London: Routledge & Kegan Paul).

Moore, Stephen D.

1989      *Literary Criticism and the Gospels: The Theoretical Challenge* (New Haven: Yale University Press).

1992      *Mark and Luke in Poststructuralist Perspectives: Jesus Begins to Write* (New Haven: Yale University Press).

1994      *Poststructuralism and the New Testament: Derrida and Foucault at the Foot of the Cross* (Minneapolis: Augsburg/Fortress Press).

Morgan, Robert with John Barton

1989      *Biblical Interpretation* (New York: Oxford University Press).

Newsom, Carole A. and Sharon H. Ringe (eds.)

1992      *The Women's Bible Commentary* (Louisville: Westminster/John Knox).

Norris, Christopher

1982      *Deconstruction: Theory and Practice* (New Accents; New York: Methuen).

1983      *The Deconstructive Turn: Essays in the Rhetoric of Philosophy* (New York: Methuen).

1989      *Deconstruction and the Interests of Theory* (Oklahoma Project for Discourse and Theory, 4; Norman: Oklahoma University Press).

O'Day, Gail

1986      'Narrative Mode and Theological Claim: A Study in the Fourth Gospel', *JBL* 105/4: 657-68.

1992        'John', in Newsom and Ringe 1992: 293-304.

O'Leary, Joseph S.
1985        *Questioning Back: The Overcoming of Metaphysics in Christian Tradition* (Minneapolis: Winston Press).

Oliver, Kelly (ed.)
1993        *Ethics, Politics, and Difference in Julia Kristeva's Writings* (New York: Routledge & Kegan Paul).

Olson, Alan
1990        'Postmodernity and Faith', *JAAR* 58/1: 37-53.

Olsson, Birger
1974        *Structure and Meaning in the Fourth Gospel: A Text-Linguistic Analysis of John 2.1-11 and 4.1-42* (Uppsala: Gleerup).

Phillips, Gary
1990a       'Thinking the Place of Biblical Studies: Some Questions', in Burke O. Long (ed.), *Rethinking the Place of Biblical Studies in the Academy* (Brunswick: Bowdoin College Press): 29-48.
1990b       'Toward a Philosophical Biblical Criticism: Cutting the Umbi(b)lical Cord: A Review of Stephen Moore's *Literary Criticism and the Gospels: The Theoretical Challenge*', paper presented to the Literary Aspects of the Gospels and Acts Group, Annual Meeting of the Society of Biblical Literature/American Academy of Religion, New Orleans, LA, November 13–16.
1990c       'Exegesis as Critical Praxis: Reclaiming History and Text from a Postmodern Perspective', *Semeia* 51: 7-50.
1994        'Drawing the Other: The Postmodern and Reading the Bible Imaginatively', in D. Jasper and M. Ledbetter (eds.), *In Good Company: Essays in Honor of Robert Detweiler* (Atlanta: Scholars Press): 447-82.

Prickett, Stephen (ed.)
1991        *Reading the Text: Biblical Criticism and Literary Theory* (Oxford: Basil Blackwell).

Raschke, Carl
1987        'From Textuality to Scripture: The End of Theology as Writing', *Semeia* 40: 39-52.

Reed, Charles William
1986        'Levinas' Question', in Cohen 1986: 73-82.

Rorty, Richard
1984        'Deconstruction and Circumvention', *Critical Inquiry* 11: 1-23.

Rowley, Hazel and Elizabeth Grosz
1990        'Psychoanalysis and Feminism', in Gunew 1990: 59-120.

Schneidau, Herbert
1982        'The Word against the Word: Derrida on Textuality', *Semeia* 23: 5-28.

Schneiders, Sandra
1982        'Women in the Fourth Gospel and the Role of Women in the Contemporary Church', *BTB* 12: 35-45.

Schüssler Fiorenza, Elisabeth
1983        *In Memory of Her: A Feminist Theological Reconstruction of Christian Origins* (New York: Crossroad).

1988       'The Ethics of Biblical Interpretation: Decentering Biblical Scholarship', *JBL* 107: 3-17.

1992       *But She Said: Feminist Practices of Biblical Interpretation* (Boston: Beacon Press).

Siebers, Tobin
1988       *The Ethics of Criticism* (Ithaca: Cornell University Press).

Talbert, Charles H.
1992       *Reading John: A Literary and Theological Commentary on the Fourth Gospel and the Johannine Epistles* (Reading the New Testament Series; New York: Crossroad).

Taylor, Mark C.
1982       *Deconstructing Theology* (Atlanta: Scholars Press).
1984       *Erring: A Postmodern A/theology* (Chicago: University of Chicago Press).

Watson, Stephen
1988       'Levinas, the Ethics of Deconstruction, and the Remainder of the Sublime', *Man and World* 21: 35-64.

Weedon, Chris
1987       *Feminist Practice and Poststructuralist Theory* (Oxford: Basil Blackwell).

Welch, Sharon
1990       *A Feminist Ethics of Risk* (Minneapolis: Fortress Press).

West, Cornel
1993       *Prophetic Thought in Postmodern Times* (Beyond Eurocentrism and Multiculturalism, 1; Monroe, ME: Common Courage Press).

West, Gerald
1992       'Power and Pedagogy in Biblical Studies in a South African Context: Problematizing Biblical Studies Pedagogy', paper presented to the Conference on Critical Thinking in the Teaching of Biblical Studies, a presession of the Annual Meeting of the Society of Biblical Literature, San Francisco, CA, November 21–24.

White, Stephen
1991       *Political Theory and Postmodernism* (Modern European Philosophy; Cambridge: Cambridge University Press).

Ziarek, Ewa
1993       'Kristeva and Levinas: Mourning, Ethics, and the Feminine', in Oliver 1993: 62-78.

# A SHEEP IN WOLF'S CLOTHING:
## AN OPTION IN CONTEMPORARY NEW TESTAMENT HERMENEUTICS

### Edgar V. McKnight

### *Introduction*

Literary approaches to the New Testament function within the context of different agendas and disciplines and respond to the different constraints and needs of those agendas. As a movement related to historical criticism, literary criticism coordinates linguistic and literary data with the historically determined intention of the author and situation of original readers. A more literary flavor results from attention to 'implied authors' and 'implied readers'. As a movement within the field of literature itself, literary criticism of the New Testament may give attention to any of the variety of literary themes and approaches, from the mimetic concerns of Plato and Aristotle to the deconstruction of Derrida. As a movement related to the hermeneutical tradition of Schleiermacher and Bultmann, literary criticism may be used for the prolongation of the text in the life of contemporary readers.

Historical, literary, hermeneutical and other agendas cooperate and conflict in the study of the New Testament. In a gracious review of my *Postmodern Use of the New Testament*, A.K.M. Adam warns readers that my work could be seen by radical postmodernists as a 'sheep in wolf's clothing' because I utilize literary criticism, including the strategies developed with the close-reading of New Criticism, for constructive purposes (Adam 1990). I am interested in the meaning of the constructive moment even though it is local, ad hoc and provisional—and thus can be deconstructed in its turn. This essay is designed to explore the hermeneutical use of literary insights in a postmodern mode. Since my own entry into literary study of the New Testament helps to explain my concern with the hermeneutical agenda, the first part of the essay will be autobiographical. Important philosophical and political differences in the total enterprise of New Testament studies will be disclosed in my experience. A second part will situate postmodern literary study in the hermeneutical tradition and delineate the dissatisfaction not only of severe postmodern critics but also of anti-postmodernists in the hermeneutical tradition. A final major section will compare and contrast the agendas and approaches of the Radical Reformation and contemporary feminists to show how a contemporary approach may be fashioned to do justice to postmodern anti-foundational insights and to the need for critical criteria for reading and interpretation.

### Autobiographical: Entry into the Literary World

In the early 1970s I began investigating the potential of reader-oriented literary approaches for the rehabilitation of hermeneutics in the Schleiermacher–Bultmann tradition, giving attention to meaning for the ever-contemporary reader. The beginning was a simple proposal for a dissertation at Oxford University during my first sabbatical from college teaching, an investigation into the relationship between diachronic historical approaches using historical linguistics as a model and synchronic literary approaches using structural linguistics as a model. In 1972, I had been asked by the book review editor of the *Journal of Biblical Literature* to review for American readers a book by Erhardt Güttgemanns that had caused some stir in German New Testament circles (McKnight 1972). The book was entitled *Offene Fragen zur Formgeschichte des Evangeliums* (1970); but it was much more than a series of 'Offene Fragen' (Candid Questions); it was a declaration that the whole tradition of New Testament scholarship has to be shelved. Historical criticism had to be replaced by a linguistic exegesis based on the principles of structural linguistics. Form criticism was the first opponent to be demolished in Güttgemanns' work, for (according to him) history and the sociological situation of the early church had nothing to do with the essence of the self-contained small units or forms of the synoptic Gospels. The forms on a deep level grow out of nonhistorical anthropomorphic and linguistic factors. The review of the book caused me to rethink the whole set of assumptions and practices of historical criticism. Is the form and meaning of the text the result of historical and cultural factors or of nonhistorical, transhistorical factors that might even govern the perception of history and culture?

As I proceeded in my research under the tutelage of Professor John Macquarrie (the dissertation was in philosophical theology rather than biblical studies because of the orientation of the faculty in biblical studies), I discovered a structuralism earlier than that of the French 'narratologists' who influenced the work of Erhardt Güttgemanns. East European structuralism or formalism provided theoretical and practical resources for development and use of a view of textual unity or structure that is energetic and dynamic and capable of responding to cultural and individual development and valuation. Non-literary factors influence literature not in a direct way or in a way to change the nature of literature and the literary work as a nexus of relationships. Literary structure is dynamic and not static, capable of responding to its different contexts and maintaining the nexus of internal relationships. The 'determinate' structure of meaning is not a static 'summative whole', but it exists in a ceaseless stage of movement.

My dissertation, 'The Significance of the Structural Study of Narrative for New Testament Hermeneutics', introduced me to all sorts of questions: the different levels and kinds of literary structures, the dynamic relationship between the nexus of literary factors and the reader, the dynamic relationship between the reader and the community, and the dynamic structure of readers themselves.

Conversation with my two examiners upon the completion of my dissertation made me realize that I had moved far away from foundationalist historical-critical assumptions that were accepted by many (at least at Oxford in the 1970s) as facts instead of hypotheses. The examiners were an English tutor and an Old Testament professor. The major objection of both examiners was the very orientation of my study, the hermeneutical context. I assumed the validity of hermeneutics, and (in order to carry out my more ultimate goal) I attempted to show the importance of a synchronic as well as a diachronic perspective and the interdependence of elements not only within the text but also outside of the text, including the reader and the reader's culture. I was proposing an open, corrigible structure, not the timeless a-historical structure of structural*ism* but one that is understood and informed by hermeneutical insights and decisions.

I was working on a meta-critical level, submitting both the structuralist and hermeneutical critical agendas to a yet higher level of critical evaluation. My examiners were situated at the critical level, which requires a basis of comparison accepted as a given, a foundation from which secure results follow. At the critical level, critics assume that they are employing criteria that are foundational in some final sense. In fact, they are employing criteria that are accepted as foundational because of the influence of their academic communities. The metacritical level of evaluation moves away from secure foundations. There seem to be no objective criteria independent of the aims and interests of those involved in the process of reading and interpretation.

My examiners represented historical linguistics and the historical approach and wanted me to 'reduce' my study to such a model. The English tutor suggested that I adopt the view of E.D. Hirsch, Jr and make a distinction between the meaning of the text, which can be detected by historical approaches, and the application of that meaning, which is not subject to historical-critical strictures. The Old Testament professor suggested that I should begin with the historically-oriented biblical studies of C.H. Dodd—rather than the theologically-oriented New Testament hermeneutics of Rudolf Bultmann.[1]

## Postmodern Literary Study
## from Hermeneutical and Metacritical Perspectives

For conventional historical-critical critics, a New Testament hermeneutics informed by non-foundationalist reader-oriented literary approaches is suspect because it problematizes the firm mooring of history. For the postmodern literary critic, however, a reader-oriented hermeneutical approach to biblical literature is a sheep in wolf's clothing. The wolf's clothing is a result of postmodern questioning of assumptions of conventional critical approaches (such as the independence of fact and meaning from value and interpretation, the stability of texts and even the autonomy of the self and the nature of reality). The sheep-like quality? The refusal to acknowledge that the questioning of such assumptions must conclude with a nihilistic skepticism. This refusal may be rationalized since it is situated in the literary and hermeneutical traditions.

Before the mid-twentieth century, literary studies moved from

---

1. The dissertation, essentially as it was deposited in the Bodleian Library at Oxford, was published by Fortress Press in 1978 with the title *Meaning in Texts: The Historical Shaping of a Narrative Hemeneutics*. The book received an award in 1978 at the annual meeting of the Modern Language Association of America from the Conference on Christianity and Literature for furthering the dialogue between Christianity and literature. The difference in the reception by my examiners and members of the Conference on Christianity and Literature may well represent the difference between British and American attitudes in the 1970s toward Continental modes of literary analysis.

historical domestication of the text to new-critical formalist analysis, and then to rehabilitation of historical, social and psychological factors (not as extrinsic, but as intrinsic factors), and more recently to a radical theoretical and practical decontextualizing and deconstruction. Developments in structural semiotics, poststructuralism and deconstruction associated with scholars such as Roland Barthes, Umberto Eco and Jacques Derrida became important. Barthes sees the structure of a text as dynamic and involving the reader in a process of analysis without a final synthesis or end (Barthes 1975). Eco sees the process of reading as involving moves both within the text (intensional) and outside the text (extensional). The various levels and sublevels of textual and extra-textual realities are interconnected, and the reader moves back and forth within and without the text to produce meaning (Eco 1979). Derrida sets knowledge, language, meaning and interpretation not simply within a dynamic cultural context but within a larger context of power and authority. Derrida's deconstructive approach to literature is concerned with the examination of the desire for mastery—the mastery of knowledge through language and the mastery of meaning through interpretation—and the subversion of that desire through the very nature of language itself. The language and logic that form the resources of an author cannot be dominated absolutely by an author. The author uses them by being governed by them. A deconstructive reader seeks to discover relationships between what the author commands and what the author does not command of the patterns of the language used by the author (Derrida 1976: 158). Reading in the conventional mode is a synthesizing process with the subject/reader being governed (as the subject/author is) by language. But a deconstructive reading gives *conscious* attention to the impulse toward and result of the synthesizing of the conventional reading process in order to break its 'domination'.

The positive and negative reactions to semiotics, poststructuralism and deconstruction in America may be explained in part by the fact that the dominant American brand of deconstruction is a result of a by-passing of the hermeneutical tradition of Schleiermacher, Dilthey, Heidegger and Gadamer. The deconstructionist critic is then merely a distanced observer of the 'scene of textuality' who refines all writing into 'free-floating' texts. The continually unsituated deconstructionist critic is characterized by a forever new or unmastered irony. A mastered irony does not ignore the valid insight of deconstruction but does not remain forever unsituated. (See Kierkegaard 1968 for a discussion of 'mastered' and 'unmastered' irony that has influenced the hermeneutical tradition). When reader-oriented interpretation comes to biblical texts through the hermeneutical tradition, it seeks to situate possibility in an actual worldly relation; it is a sheep in wolf's clothing.

Theoretical and practical resources are available to provide a post-modern or a postcritical rationale for and program of hermeneutics, but the 'modern' Enlightenment quest for intellectual certainty and concentration on empirical data continues to influence us, as does Immanuel Kant's attempt to transcend the level of empirical data by a metacritical elucidation of forms and categories making possible the cognitive activities of the human subject. The history of the Enlightenment is the history of shifts back and forth between epistemological idealism and realism, but Kant shifted the center of philosophical inquiry to an examination of the concepts and categories in terms of which we think and reason. Kant disagreed with a severe empiricism by holding that there are *a priori* elements in cognition. These *a priori* concepts are indispensable for knowledge of objects (Kant 1952).

Kant made a basic epistemological distinction between knowledge of phenomena (empirical data) and understanding of transcendental noumenal realities. Kant's was an epistemological dualism, not an ontological dualism. This epistemological distinction, however, became an ontological dualism. Phenomenal reality became distinct from noumenal reality. Developments after Kant may be seen first (in the 'modern' phase) as the inability to accommodate transcendence in any traditional sense whatsoever and then (in a 'postmodern' phase) as the inability to achieve the desired certainty in dealing with the natural world.

Attempts to maintain a 'modern' Enlightenment rationality and raise it to a metacritical level to serve as a foundation constitutes a recapitulation of Kantian thought—albeit a reversal in that a foundation for the knowledge of phenomena (empirical data) as well as (or instead of) a foundation for understanding of transcendental noumenal realities is sought. Attempts to rehabilitate rationalism do not have the goal of a complete and coherent theoretical absolute that can be articulated fully either deductively or inductively. Enlightenment rationalism has been judged universally to be instrumental, always operating upon subordinate levels from within superior levels that the given rationalism is unable to reach. Acknowledgment of the limits of Enlightenment rationality, however, does not mean devolution into irrationalism.

Hans-Georg Gadamer is the scholar claimed not only by postmodernism but also by a revitalized, albeit relativized, modernism. Gadamer's acceptance of Wilhelm von Humboldt's view of language as an unbordered creative power of thought and speech making unlimited use of limited materials allows both moves. Gadamer developed a hermeneutics giving attention to historical consciousness and expanding hermeneutical options beyond the Romanticism of Schleiermacher and Dilthey and the existentialism of Heidegger and his heirs. We do not simply question the work with our scientific methods *or* simply see in the work what we bring; we come to the work participating in the same structure of being that is the basis for our understanding of what was intended in the work.

Gadamer finds mediation of the two poles—tradition and the 'I'—in language. Tradition brings itself to language and human consciousness is linguistic. In this mediation, human consciousness is not dissolved. Indeed, Gadamer emphasizes that

> there is no possible consciousness...in which the 'object' that is handed down would appear in the light of eternity. Every assimilation of tradition is historically different: which does not mean that every one represents only an imperfect understanding of it. Rather, every one is the experience of a 'view' of the object itself (Gadamer 1975: 430).

Gadamer's view of the historically-constrained and finite nature of the hermeneutical actualization of texts and traditions may be emphasized. But his indication of the universality of language may also be emphasized; and within the hermeneutic tradition a broader base than Enlightenment rationality is sought by such scholars as Jürgen Habermas and Karl-Otto Apel. They do not deny that truth always and of necessity exceeds method (a fact emphasized by Gadamer), but they posit some kind of provisional notion of the universal, which is then used as basis for a metacriticism that is able to acknowledge and contain the relativity of Enlightenment rationalism. Habermas and Apel seek to expand and not to undermine traditional epistemology. The actual pragmatic function of tradition and communities of interpreters is not denied; what is denied is the conclusion that a particular tradition and community of interpreters is unrelated to universal norms. They seek a transcendental dimension that is not merely contextually internal to particular societies but that will allow a critique of particular societies. Apel depends upon a hypothesis of universal commensurability whereby languages are intertranslatable and 'language games' overlap, merge, fall apart and reintegrate. The historically constituted life form of a given society (language) is

> not only the normatively binding 'institution of institutions'...it is also the 'meta-institution' of all dogmatically established institutions. As a meta-institution, it represents the instance of criticism for all unreflected social norms, and...it does not abandon the individual persons to their merely subjective reasoning (Apel 1980: 119).

The modern mentality that cannot abide skepticism and that searches for new foundations is the result of a certain telling of the story of the Enlightenment. In that telling, according to Stephen Toulmin, humanity in the seventeenth century

> set aside all doubts and ambiguities about its capacity to achieve its goals here on Earth, and in historical time, rather than deferring human fulfillment to an Afterlife in Eternity—that was what made the project of Modernity 'rational'—and this optimism led to major advances not just in natural science but in moral, political, and social thought as well (Toulmin 1990: ix).

The story as seen from the 1990s is more ambiguous. Toulmin declares that

> in choosing as the goals of Modernity an intellectual and practical agenda that set aside the tolerant, skeptical attitude of the 16th-century humanists, and focused on the 17th-century pursuit of mathematical exactitude and logical rigor, intellectual certainty and moral purity, Europe set itself on a cultural and political road that has led both to its most striking technical successes and to its deepest human failures (1990: x).

Important heroes in the postmodern retelling of the story are the early humanists who were content with a lack of certainty. Acknowledgment of the impossibility of the ideal of Enlightenment certainty may then result in a positive (instead of a nihilistic) 'skepticism'. This sort of skepticism would acknowledge that questions are always asked and answered in terms dependent upon historical and social contexts. It would have a toleration for other contexts with their questions and answers. It would even question the level of validity of one's own answers in one's own context and not be disabled by such questioning.

### *Hermeneutics, the Radical Reformation and Contemporary Feminists*

In this final section I will use the experiences and approaches of the Radical Reformation and contemporary feminists to reformulate a hermeneutics that utilizes and matches postmodern philosophical and literary insights. I will first suggest a reformulated hermeneutics with these two groups in mind. Then I will examine the agendas of these two groups and correlate them with the hermeneutical tradition.

*Reformulation of Hermeneutics*

In a reformulated hermeneutical approach, the importance of texts and the assumption that readers can make sense of texts are significant. The problematizing of 'texts', 'readers' and 'sense' in the post-modern epoch is taken seriously but not allowed to disable the hermeneutical drive for meaning. All of the resources of linguistics, the natural language of texts and the languages of literature are utilized. Extrinsic approaches such as history, sociology, psychology and anthropology provide an understanding of the originating circumstances (personal, social, historical and so on) for the hermeneutical approach. A hermeneutical concern for present meaning cannot reduce meaning to some ostensible original historical meaning or to other extrinsic causes. The view of the text as a scientific object *as such* precludes achievement of meaning-for-the-reader.

The hermeneutical approach posits a meaning beyond the meanings of words and sentences, a meaning that does not simply derive from the words and sentences. It posits a meaning that is not obtained from a simple recovery of the originating circumstances. The knowledge sought in hermeneutics is as complicated as the knowledge of other persons— and the procedure just as complicated. Schleiermacher's system of hermeneutics involves a dynamic procedure allowing the achievement of the desired sort of meaning by the coordination of a series of polarities or contrasts. The dynamic procedure whereby these polarities are coordinated and the series of polarities harmonized calls upon imagination (divination) as well as criticism (comparison). The relationship between parts and wholes (with the parts determined by the whole and the whole determined by its parts) is one polarity; and the same sort of relationship exists between individual thinking and social speaking, language as a general system and language in particular use, and grammatical interpretation involving language and psychological interpretation involving human beings and their expressions of thought.

The interest or focus of interpretation has changed in the history of hermeneutics from Schleiermacher's feeling for the infinite to Dilthey's life, Heidegger's being, Bultmann's possibilities of human existence, the

New Hermeneutic's language event and so on. In order to achieve the level and sort of interest seen as appropriate, hermeneutics had made a distinction between a surface level (what the text says) and a deeper level of intention, but in his treatment of myth Bultmann came to see the radical relativity of language as an objectifying of understanding, the objectification in myth being contrary to the understanding seeking expression in it. Bultmann, on the basis of his conclusion as to the subject matter of Scripture, finds that myth, instead of really intending to give an objective world-view or to tell of divine powers, expresses the way humans understand themselves in their world. With Bultmann, a process of demythologizing was proposed in order to arrive at the genuine subject matter of the text. With the New Hermeneutic, the dialectic changed from myth versus understanding of existence to language versus language-event. The issuing of the utterance is the performing of an action.

The hermeneutic tradition of Bultmann and the New Hermeneutic stagnated because the resources of the hermeneutical tradition of Heidegger were unable to provide the means of achieving the interests and goals involved. The present task may be envisioned as the revitalization of the hermeneutic tradition by means of resources in the European hermeneutic tradition and American literary studies. Particular hermeneutical interests will (as they always have) direct the utilization of these resources. The process of deconstruction, for example (as suggested earlier), will be accommodated to the hermeneutical agenda. Deconstruction is comparable to the demythologizing of Bultmann. It is capable of allowing readers to move beyond readings that have become dogmatized and that do not speak to those readers. Demythologizing as a hermeneutical strategy, however, has an ultimately positive presupposition about the possibility of meaning and significance. Deconstruction's position about textual meaning is more problematic. So a hermeneutical approach will utilize strategies of deconstruction with assumptions somewhat in tension with the philosophy of deconstruction. But only somewhat in tension, for a postmodern hermeneutical approach will continue to be skeptical while benefiting from the local, ad hoc and provisional meaning that is found.

The same sort of system of polarities and contrasts that we find in Schleiermacher are appropriate for a postmodern hermeneutical approach. Some of these polarities include:

1.  modernism versus postmodernism—with the postmodern being defined in relation to the modern and remaining related to the modern in a dialectical fashion;
2.  historical criticism (and other critical approaches) as foundational versus historical criticism (and other critical approaches) as instrumental;
3.  the text as a historical artifact to be distanced for scientific study versus the text as a literary source of meaning and significance with which rapport is sought;
4.  the intention of the author versus the intention of readers;
5.  logic versus the imagination;
6.  intellectual certainty involving the universal, general and timeless that can be established with mathematical exactitude and logical rigor versus a benign skepticism concerned with truthfulness related to the particular, local and timely.

## The Radical Reformation and Feminists

The Radical Reformers and their descendants have found a positive skepticism to be necessary and satisfying. Contemporary feminism will benefit from a view of interpretation *and* humankind implied in such a positive skepticism. The Radical Reformers and their descendants may be compared and contrasted with the Catholic and Protestant scholasticism and rationalism prevailing in their origin and history. In overly simplistic terms, the Catholic reading of the Bible was constrained by the church as a known extrinsic institution. The church was a foundational beginning and ending point. The Protestant reading was constrained by doctrine—an extrinsic principle such as *sola fide*—again, a foundational beginning and ending point. (The existential philosophy and categories that served Rudolf Bultmann are comparable to these churchly foundations.) The Radical Reformers were concerned with both church and doctrine, but the way they saw themselves as church influenced their reading of the Bible and their concern for doctrine. They existed as church in the present. But that present Christian community was aware of itself as the primitive and the eschatological community. The Bible, then, had contemporary and not mere antiquarian relevance. The Radical Reformers were like the Qumran community in that they read the Bible as referring to them and their lives in the present. They were like the Jesus of Luke's Gospel who indicated that the Scripture he had just read in the synagogue in Nazareth 'has been fulfilled in your hearing' (Lk. 4.21).

Doctrine was important to the Radical Reformation, but doctrine stood in relation to the life and practice of the church as primitive and eschatological community. A dialectical relationship existed between doctrine and practice, which means that a doctrine satisfying at one time was unsatisfying at another. James William McClendon, Jr and James M. Smith have explicated a 'principle of fallibility' that was characteristic of the Radical Reformers: 'Even one's most cherished and tenaciously held convictions might be false and are in principle always subject to rejection, reformulation, improvement, or reformation' (McClendon and Smith 1975: 118).

The effort at this point is to gain from the Radical Reformation a key to a postmodern reading of the Bible that is properly skeptical but not nihilistic. The importance of ideological 'location' is obvious, with earlier interpretations and formulations always subject to reformulation, not through the securing of better information or the devising of a more effective way of reasoning, but through the dynamics of life itself. With the Enlightenment ideal of certainty (as Toulmin stressed), the particular gave way to the universal, the local to the general, the timely to the timeless. The rhetorical context of arguments did not matter—only the rational. In our retelling of the story of the Enlightenment, we evaluate skepticism in an unconventionally positive fashion:

> In theology or philosophy, you may (with due intellectual modesty) adopt as personal working positions the ideas of your inherited culture; but you cannot deny others the right to adopt different working positions for themselves, let alone pretend that your experience 'proves' the truth of one such set of opinions, and the necessary falsity of all the others (Toulmin 1990: 29).

With the Radical Reformers, the religious context was most important, and this context was most frequently some dominant state and/or churchly power to which the Radical Reformers were reacting. For descendants of the Radical Reformers, the context is often social. As James William McClendon, Jr points out, with the Swiss brethren in the sixteenth century, it was Catholic views of sacrament and society and Zwinglian Evangelicalism. With Roger Williams in the seventeenth century, it was Puritan models and assumptions. With Issac Backus in the eighteenth century, it was New England's struggle for religious liberty. With Thomas and Alexander Campbell in the nineteenth century, it was Locke, the Scottish Enlightenment, and the American frontier. With Walter Rauschenbusch in the twentieth century, it was urban industrialization and poverty (McClendon 1986: 37).

In the face of a dominant political, religious and/or social 'establishment' with its reading (or domestication) of the Bible, the Radical Reformation carried out a counter-ideological reading. First, however, came the prevailing reading. This reading was necessary so as to 'try' the conventional position. This attempt to naturalize or make their own the sense made of the Bible by others is cited by McClendon as a principle paralleling the principle of fallibility. It is the principle stated by Roger Williams:

> It is the command of Christ Jesus to his scholars [a title Williams felt belonged to all believers] to try all things: and liberty of trying what a friend, yea what an (esteemed) enemy presents hath ever (in point of Christianity) proved one especial means of attaining to the truth of Christ (Williams 1963: 29).

The trying of the prevailing reading was, of course, in light of the reformers' perception of themselves as the primitive and eschatological community. And this was the norm for their counter-reading.

The agenda of the Radical Reformers and their strategy of reading are not as obvious today as in earlier epochs because their descendants have become the victims of others' agendas and have not been faithful to their own guiding vision. In this last decade of the twentieth century, feminist criticism may provide more persuasive patterns for interpretation that give conscious attention to general cultural norms and ideologies at odds with ideological perspectives and goals of interpreters.[2] The continuing dynamic relationship between extraliterary life and the literary text and its interpretation is not yet appreciated fully by feminists because they (we) are in the midst of a particular struggle against general cultural norms and ideologies and find it difficult to affirm the principle of fallibility of the Radical Reformers for themselves. Feminists are caught up in the Enlightenment ideal of certainty—at least as a strategy in their struggle. I begin, then, with an illustration from experiences of Jean E. Kennard of the way that changes in extraliterary life affect literary life and conventions; this illustration will provide opportunity for

---

2.    For various perspectives on the relationship of feminism to postmodernism, see Nicholson 1990. Anderson 1991 surveys recent feminist biblical criticism. I am indebted in this section especially to Schweickart 1989.

highlighting some factors in feminist interpretation and imply the challenge of seeing feminist criticism in dynamic terms.

Kennard cites a section from Northrop Frye's *Anatomy of Criticism*:

> All humor demands agreement that certain things, such as a picture of a wife beating her husband in a comic strip, are conventionally funny. To introduce a comic strip in which a husband beats his wife would distress the reader, because it would mean learning a new convention (Frye 1957: 225).

Kennard acknowledges that she first read the book fifteen years earlier and had reread the book several times. Only in the late 1970s and early 80s did the sentences become objectionable. Her objection was not with a concept of 'a convention as an agreement which allows art to communicate'. Rather it was in Frye's choice of an example.

> For me, obviously, a convention had changed, and some of the reasons at least seemed apparent. Such extraliterary experiences as talking with friends who worked with battered women, an increased awareness of violence in every city I visited, together with reading feminist scholarship, had led me to formulate values which resisted the convention Frye named. I no longer agreed to find it funny (Kennard 1981: 69).

Before Kennard experienced resistance to Frye's example, she experienced an appreciation of texts in general and the text of Frye in particular. She assumed that something could be gained from reading and interpretation. An early conventional processing of the text was made possible, then, by a language and world-view shared by author and reader. Had Kennard first come to the text in the 1990s with convictions of the 1990s she might have been forced to reconstruct the world-view of Frye in order to appreciate how the text would have been processed originally.

A feminist reading will begin by following conventional approaches, uncritically synthesizing the text as it unfolds and/or critically seeking the 'intention' of the author. But this is a beginning and a strategy. The goal of feminism precludes this as the final aim! The meaning obtained in an initial reading is relativized from a metacritical perspective in at least two ways. It is relativized because it is seen as a *representation* created by a reader. It is also relativized because it is represented or actualized in terms of what the author may have meant to a reader at a particular time. This representation or 'meaning' is not one that is normative for all time. A metacritical perspective allows a reader to free herself from the power of what may be taken to be the 'obvious' meaning. Beyond this initial interaction with the text are further positive and negative moves dependent not only upon the power assumed by the reader vis-à-vis the text but also upon the feminist location. The text has the power to structure the experience of the reader, and the female reader may simply accept the values implicit in the text—values that must be observed and assumed provisionally in an initial uncritical reading or in a critical reading directed to the author's intention. But the reader may become conscious of what is happening in the reading and recognize that the power of the text is matched by the essential role of the reader and the process of reading. To read in light of feminist perspectives and goals the reader must learn to resist any androcentric bias of the text, the literary canon and traditional critical approaches. For a feminist, according to Patrocinio Schweickart, androcentricity is 'a sufficient condition for the process of emasculation' (Schweickart 1989: 26). A text that serves the male reader positively as 'the meeting ground of the personal and the universal' (*ibid.*) becomes oppressive to the woman reader. (Recall the experience of Jean Kennard). Schweickart suggests the negative hermeneutic of 'ideological unmasking'. 'The reader recalls and examines how she would "naturally" read a male text in order to understand and therefore undermine the subjective predispositions that had rendered her vulnerable to its designs' (p. 34).

The negative hermeneutic is possible only because of the possibility of a positive hermeneutic 'whose aim is the recovery and cultivation of women's culture' (p. 35). The normative dimension of the feminist story makes visible and pushes beyond the reading that denies women's culture (perhaps only implicitly and unconsciously, but thereby more powerfully). Just as the Radical Reformers and their descendants interpreted the Bible against the horizon of a dominant church, state and society, feminist critics interpret literature against the horizon of a male-oriented context of writers and interpreters. If they wish the text to serve as the meeting ground for the personal and universal for themselves, feminists must go beyond contemporary male-oriented interpretation, beyond the text, but by means of the text. Theory and strategy are devised and followed in view of a more comprehensive praxis. 'Feminist criticism...is a mode of *praxis*. The point is not merely to interpret literature in various ways; the point is to *change the world*' (p. 24). Schweikart indicates that this involves the producing of 'a community of feminist readers and writers' with the hope that ultimately 'this community will expand to include everyone' (p. 39).

The 'evangelistic' goal of feminism requires theory and strategy that has a validity beyond feminism. What is desired is a concept of validity comparable in power to that which has supported male academic assertions of validity that have excluded women. In the view of some feminists (operating from a 'modernist' perspective), feminist criticism benefits from the Enlightenment view of certainty that has supported male agendas. In their view, it is only from such a perspective that the feminist agenda can be validated and carried out effectively. Christine DiStefano asks if postmodernism may not be a theory whose time has come for men but not for women. Since men have had their Enlightenment, they can afford the claims of postmodernism. But women cannot afford a sense of humbleness regarding the coherence and truth of their claims (DiStefano 1990).

Feminist criticism, then, is thrust squarely into the contemporary hermeneutical debate between scholars such as Habermas and Apel and scholars such as Stanley Fish and Richard Rorty. Schweikart offers a criterion that is helpful to feminist biblical scholars, the criterion of an expanding community and continuing dialogue (she is using Habermas's idea that consensus obtained through domination-free discourse is the warrant for truth; see Habermas 1973: 211-65). But this criterion cannot simply be pronounced; it must be situated in terms of existing criteria. Historically-oriented biblical scholars have absorbed a foundationalist approach, and they are able to operate effectively within historical criticism by reconstructing the life worlds behind biblical texts in a way to rehabilitate biblical texts for the feminist agenda. Phyllis Trible and Elizabeth Schüssler Fiorenza, in particular; have done a remarkable job of placing feminist biblical interpretation at the bar of conventional historical critical norms. Some critics, however, have noted that this historical critical scholarship is not 'objective', that social and hermeneutical interests determine the weighing of hypotheses and even the selection of hypotheses to be considered (see Thiselton 1992: 439-52).

Mary Ann Tolbert is more comfortable than Trible and Schüssler Fiorenza with the functional or instrumental use of criticism. She is fully aware that reason functions within a community's advocacy of its agenda.

> To assert that all scholarship is advocacy is not...to chart new ground and invite anarchy. It is only to admit honestly what the case has been and still is. The criteria of public evidence, logical argument, reasonable hypotheses, and intellectual sophistication still adjudicate acceptable and unacceptable positions (Tolbert 1983: 118).

It is these criteria themselves that raise additional problems. 'The "public" who determines what is reasonable, who form a "consensus view" are special interest groups with different cannons of validity... No value neutral position exists nor ever has' (*ibid.*).

With Tolbert we find satisfaction with an instrumental rationality constrained by interest groups. Rationality is not denied; it is located. Can feminists save themselves from the charge of simply being constrained by one interest while male scholars are constrained by another, with no basis for adjudication? The goal of feminist criticism requires a particular location, but in order to maintain validity that location must be at least theoretically expanded beyond that location. In feminist interpretation, then, the end that justifies and guides interpretation is not a self-serving parochial agenda but one that extends beyond feminism. I would suggest that it involves at the same time a redefinition of what it means to make sense of texts and what it means to be human.

In both the hermeneutical tradition and in postmodernism we find implicit and explicit challenges to prevailing notions of interpretation that are related to the question of what it means to be a human being. Schleiermacher and the Romantics shared a distrust of what could be achieved by rational argument alone and emphasized feeling, life, imagination and the sense of the infinite. Schleiermacher emphasized 'divination' (imagination) and indicated that this must interact with comparison (criticism). The creative, intuitive capacity is associated with the feminine and the comparative with the masculine.

> Divinatory knowledge is the feminine strength in knowing people: comparative knowledge, the masculine...the divinatory is based on the assumption that each person is not only a unique individual in his own right, but that he has a receptivity to the uniqueness of every other person (Schleiermacher 1977: 150).

In the post-modern epoch, there is a distrust of rational argumentation akin to the Romantics' distrust and an attempt to relate the affective (feminine) and cognitive (masculine). Geoffrey Hartman proposes a role for literary study in the deconstructionist or postmodern mode: 'to word a wound words have made'. Hartman's proposal maintains a polarity between the modern and the postmodern. Anti-representational modes of questioning deconstruct the illusion that particular texts 'have a direct, even original, relation to what they represent'. What seems to be a cause (reality, presence) is in fact an effect, an illusion of depth. Hartman, however, sees that there is 'a reality of the effect' that is inseparable from the 'reality of words'. The movement of liberation of language from representational concepts 'should not cheapen the mimetic and affectional power of words, their interpersonal impact'. The wounding results from the equivocal nature of words and the lack of satisfaction of demands of the psyche that a self be defined or constituted by words. But literature has a 'medicinal function', which is 'to word a wound words have made'. Words themselves help us tolerate the normal conditions of 'partial knowledge', which is the condition of living in the context of words (Hartman 1981: 121, 131, 133, 137).

Hartman contrasts the cognitive function and the 'recognitive' function. The cognitive has to do with truth and evidence. A true statement is something that we know or do not know. This is the arena of instrumental rationality. A truthful statement is validated by different criteria than a true statement. A truthful statement is one that we can acknowledge or fail to acknowledge. For Hartman, acknowledgment is the 'recognition' that is beyond cognition and that brings closure and the healing of the wounded spirit (p. 155).

James S. Hans suggests that the new way of conceiving of language is in reality a new concept of humankind. Hans, too, maintains a dialectical relationship between the modern and the postmodern. After a lengthy history of trying to subjugate the world by means of language and to subjugate language itself, 'we have arrived at the point where we should be capable of listening to language and allowing ourselves to be played by it' (Hans 1981: 104). When we speak of the end of humankind, it is not

> to deny the human or to act as if it doesn't exist: it is simply a way to reenregister our views of the activities in which we participate in a way which places the human in a more modest, though still important, place. Our location is never central because there never is a central location (Hans 1981: 198).

In this sense the end of humankind is really a beginning of a different kind of human. The play of language from this perspective is inaugurated by the orientation of readers. Language is an instrument in the same sense that feet are instruments: 'Our language takes us where we want to go, but we often don't know precisely where we want to go, so, given a general direction, we follow the play of language that is inaugurated by our orientation' (Hans 1981: 105).

That language 'takes us down paths we hadn't originally foreseen' is true, but true also is the fact that 'we have provided the general direction ourselves'. When the play of language takes over, it places our specific purposes into the larger perspective of its own play. This play of language, then, 'is one of the chief ways through which we confirm or deny the value of specific propositions for which we are using language at any particular time' (*ibid.*). The readers' instrumental approach to language allows the play within the field of language. This play of language then doubles back to the instrumental use. In the process, conventions of perception and orientation are generated, but those conventions are constantly changed through interaction with other fields. We do not arrive at some foundation outside of life, for this more comprehensive play is one that is activated by the orientation humans apply, through language, to the situations that confront them.

The insights of Hartman and Hans concerning the nature of literature and the human in the new context are especially important for feminist criticism. In the functioning of language in a postmodern mode, historical-critical theory and practice (and other particular critical tools) must be seen as instrumental, penultimate not ultimate. To capitulate to modern Enlightenment critical ideas for temporary strategic advantage is not only to retreat from our contemporary world-view but it is to deny the genuine basis for validity. There is a contemporary yearning for validity, then, but when the Enlightenment view of validity is evaluated from postmodern and feminist perspectives, that view becomes suspect. Yet, a validity is possible. This validity is a result of the reading's connecting not with the author of the original text but with a community of readers. To the extent that that connection is made by a feminist, according to Schweikart, and 'to the extent that the community is potentially all embracing, her interpretation has that degree of validity' (Schweickart 1989: 39).

A challenge for feminist critics is to operate in their local context but to see that context as embracing more than the local. To whatever extent the universal is to be seen, it is seen in the local. In the midst of conflict, the community assuring validity may have a distorted vision; it may be a limited and limiting community. It is that sort of limited community and that sort of limiting validation that Anthony C. Thiselton has in mind when he challenges the socio-pragmatic approaches of Stanley Fish and Richard Rorty:

> If there can be no critique from *outside* of a community, hermeneutics *serves only to affirm its corporate self, its structures, and its corporate values. It can use texts only by the same ploy as that which oppressors and oppressive power-structures use, namely in the service of its own interests* (Thiselton 1992: 7, italics in original).

This clear danger is avoided by maintaining the same sort of suspicion vis-à-vis the reading of the community as is maintained vis-à-vis oppressive readings. We are back to the principle of fallibility of the Radical Reformers.

## *Conclusion*

The reading of the Bible by the Radical Reformers and their descendants and the reading of literature (including biblical literature) by feminists, then, are similar at the formal level. Both take the text seriously. Although feminists are not content to deal with 'male' texts at a superficial level of the author's intention, they acknowledge that male texts play upon authentic liberatory aspirations. Community is important, a community defined in part over against a dominant group and/or ideology. Both are consciously concerned with texts for ideological reasons related to the praxis of the group. In order to obtain the appropriate reading, both must read against the grain of the dominant reading—against the grain of what has become the 'obvious' reading. Both must move beyond the superficial level to a level that informs their life and practice. Both are 'evangelistic' in that they have a utopian dream that their community will expand to include everyone. The reorientation of hermeneutics in general may be informed, then, by the reading of the Radical Reformers and their descendants and by contemporary feminists.

Finality in terms of meaning is not claimed. The meaning achieved, limited and ad hoc as it is, provides satisfaction in terms of criteria of praxis, openness and continuing communication.

## BIBLIOGRAPHY

Adam, A.K.M.
1990        Review of *Postmodern Use of the Bible*, by Edgar V. McKnight, *CBQ* 52: 758-59.

Anderson, Janice Capel
1991        'Mapping Feminist Biblical Criticism: The American Scene, 1983–1990', *CR*: 21-44.

Apel, Karl-Otto
1980        *Toward a Transformation of Philosophy* (London: Routledge & Kegan Paul).

Barthes, Roland
1975        *S/Z* (trans. Richard Miller; London: Jonathan Cape).

Derrida, Jacques
1976        *Of Grammatology* (trans. G.C. Spivak; Baltimore: The Johns Hopkins University Press).

DiStefano, Christine
  1990        'Dilemmas of Difference: Feminism, Modernity, and Postmodernism',
             in Nicholson 1990: 63-82.
Eco, Umberto
  1979        *The Role of the Reader: Explorations in the Semiotics of Texts*
             (Bloomington: Indiana University Press).
Frye, Northrop
  1957        *Anatomy of Criticism: Four Essays* (Princeton, NJ: Princeton
             University Press).
Gadamer, Hans-Georg
  1975        *Truth and Method* (New York: Seabury).
Güttgemanns, Erhardt
  1970        *Offene Fragen zur Formgeschichte des Evangeliums: Eine methodische
             Skizze der Grundlagenproblematik der Form- und Redaktions-
             geschichte* (BEvT, 54; Munich: Chr. Kaiser Verlag [ET: *Candid
             Questions Concerning Gospel Form Criticism: A Methodological
             Sketch* (trans. W.G. Doty; PTMS, 26; Pittsburg: Pickwick Press, 1979)]).
Habermas, Jürgen
  1973        'Wahrheitstheorien', in H. Fahrenbach (ed.), *Wirklichkeit und
             Reflexion* (Pfullingen: Nesge).
Hans, James S.
  1981        *The Play of the World* (Amherst, MA: University of Massachusetts
             Press).
Hartman, Geoffrey H.
  1981        *Saving the Text* (Baltimore: The Johns Hopkins University Press).
Kant, Immanuel
  1952        'Transcendental Deduction of the Categories', in *Critique of Pure
             Reason* (trans. J.M.D. Meiklejohn; Great Books of the Western World,
             42; Chicago: Encyclopedia Brittanica).
Kennard, Jean E.
  1981        'Convention Coverage or How to Read Your Own Life', *New Literary
             History* 18: 69-88.
Kierkegaard, Soren
  1968        *The Concept of Irony* (Bloomington: Indiana University Press).
McClendon, James William, Jr
  1986        *Systematic Theology*. I. *Ethics* (Nashville: Abingdon Press).
McClendon, James William, Jr and James M. Smith
  1975        *Understanding Religious Convictions* (Notre Dame: University of
             Notre Dame Press).
McKnight, Edgar V.
  1972        Review of *Offene Fragen zur Formgeschichte des Evangeliums*, by
             E. Güttgemanns, *JBL* 91: 554-57.
  1978        *Meaning in Texts: The Historical Shaping of a Narrative Hermeneutics*
             (Philadelphia: Fortress Press).
  1988        *Postmodern Use of the Bible: The Emergence of Reader-Oriented
             Criticism* (Nashville: Abingdon Press).
Nicholson, Linda J. (ed.)
  1990        *Feminism/Postmodernism* (London: Routledge & Kegan Paul).

Schleiermacher, Friedrich
1977        *Hermeneutics: The Handwritten Manuscripts* (ed. H. Kimmerle; trans.
            J. Duke and J. Forstman; Missoula, MT: Scholars Press).
Schüssler Fiorenza, Elisabeth
1983        *In Memory of Her: A Feminist Theological Reconstruction of Christian
            Origins* (New York: Crossroad; London: SCM Press).
Schweickart, Patrocinio P.
1989        'Reading Ourselves: Toward a Feminist Theory of Reading', in
            E. Showalter (ed.), *Speaking of Gender* (London: Routledge & Kegan
            Paul): 17-44.
Thiselton, Antony C.
1992        *New Horizons in Hermeneutics* (Grand Rapids: Zondervan).
Tolbert, Mary Ann
1983        'Defining the Problem: The Bible and Feminist Hermeneutics', *Semeia*
            28: 113-26.
Toulmin, Stephen Edelston
1990        *Cosmopolis: The Hidden Agenda of Modernity* (New York: The Free
            Press).
Trible, Phyllis
1984        *Texts of Terror: Literary-Feminist Readings of Biblical Narratives*
            (Philadelphia: Fortress Press).
Williams, Roger
1963 [1652] *The Hireling Ministry None of Christ's* (in *Complete Writings*, 7; New
            York: Russell & Russell).

# MATTHEW'S DARK LIGHT AND THE HUMAN CONDITION

## Dan O. Via

### *Introduction*

In this paper I am examining a text that has long intrigued and puzzled me, a short text from the sixth chapter of Matthew: 'The eye is the lamp of the body'. Since the essay proceeds as a rather close reading it will be well to have the text before you. I quote Mt. 6.22-23 from the NRSV.

> The eye is the lamp of the body. So, if your eye is
> healthy, your whole body will be full of light; but if
> your eye is unhealthy, your whole body will be full of
> darkness. If then the light in you is darkness, how
> great is the darkness!

Now let me make a longer, rather paraphrastic translation:

> The eye is the lamp of the body. If then your eye should
> be whole—and it *might be*—your whole body will be in the
> light. But if your eye should be evil—and that also
> *might be*—your whole body will be in the dark. If then
> the light in you *is* darkness—and that in fact *is* the
> case—how great the darkness is!

It is this paraphrase that I hope to interpret and to justify in the article. The paraphrase makes explicit certain anthropological aspects of the text, for my interpretation is generated by an anthropological question: what does the darkened light of Mt. 6.22-23 tell us about human being in principle (the ontological) and about the actual human condition (the ontic). Human beings in principle have the capacity for a true vision of reality, but in actual fact the light of understanding is darkness.

In an essay on Mt. 6.22-23 a few years ago, Hans Dieter Betz stated that this passage had never been satisfactorily explained (1985: 71). As illuminating and provocative as his discussion of it was, after reading it several times I decided that the text still had not yet been satisfactorily explained. Whether that will be the case after my effort is for the reader to decide.

Our saying appears also in Lk. 11.34-36 and, therefore, must have been in Q, but Luke does not include it in his sermon on the plain. Matthew does place it in the long middle section of his sermon on the mount in which he reinterprets the Law and the Prophets (5.17; 7.12). Perhaps Matthew includes it in the sermon on the mount because of the broad ethical connotation of the sound eye. More particularly it may follow 6.19-21 because the latter ends with a reference to the heart: 'There [where your treasure is] will be your heart also'. Because Mt. 6.22-23 portrays the eye as an image of the interior person—the heart— it was natural to place side by side these two sayings that speak respectively of the heart and the eye. This connection was also natural in the Jewish background of Matthew and his community. Deut. 15.9, for example, places in parallel the base thought in the *heart* and the hostile *eye*.

My approach will be to move through the text three times, from three different angles or at three different levels of explicitness. I will call these three hermeneutical vantage points: (1) the grammatical–logical–philoso-phical structure; (2) the metaphorical structure; (3) the narrative structure.

*The Grammatical–Logical–Philosophical Structure*

The passage has a threefold structure.[1] (1) There is a thesis or theme sentence that states a possibility: 'The eye is the lamp of the body'. (2) Then follows a commentary on this thesis formed as a balanced antithetical parallelism: '...if your eye is healthy...if your eye is evil'. (3) A conclusion is drawn about which of these possibilities is actualized: '...the light in you is darkness'.

Let me give a bit more substance to this structure.

1.    The *thesis* that the eye is the lamp of the body states an ontological possibility or possibility in principle that may or may not be a possibility in fact. But the sentence is a declarative sentence in the indicative mood. Why then do I say that it does not state a fact but only a possibility, and a possibility in principle at that?

2.    The *commentary* turns what appears to be a fact into an uncertain possibility. 'If your eye be sound, your body will be

---

1.    This will be a modification of the outline offered by Betz (1985: 73-74).

illuminated. If your eye be evil, your body will be in the dark.'
These are, grammatically speaking, third class conditional
sentences. They state two ways in which the eye may function
qualitatively, and they state these in a very contingent fashion.
The conditions are expressed in the subjunctive mood and thus
state conditions that are undetermined or uncertain. They may
or may not be fulfilled. The eye is the lamp of the body, but it
is undetermined how it will function. It may be sound and
produce light. But it may be evil and produce darkness. Since
the eye is a lamp that may produce darkness, the eye is not a
lamp in fact but only a lamp as a possibility in principle. That
we are talking here about a possibility in principle is also underscored by the fact that Matthew speaks in general or abstract
terms about 'the' eye rather than using the more concrete
'your' eye, which we have in Lk. 11.34.

3.     The *conclusion* is actually a further commentary on the original thesis, a conclusion about which of the eye's two possible
ways of functioning is actually realized. Here we have a first
class condition in the indicative mood, a condition determined
as true. 'If your eye—or the light in you—is darkness (and it
is), then how great is the darkness.' So we learn in the conclusion that the negative possibility in principle is the actual state
of affairs. The body in principle has an eye, a lamp, a source of
light, but in actuality the light is darkness—an oxymoron, the
combination of opposites.

I have been assuming that the eye as the lamp of the body in 6.22 is
the same as the light in you in 6.23b, and I believe that in part that is
true. But the identification of the one with the other requires some
defense. It also needs to be pointed out that in some part the eye is not
absolutely identical with the light in you, and that will be taken up in the
discussion of the metaphorical structure.

My contention here is that if the eye is the lamp of the body, then the
eye is also the light in you. That is so because of the obvious inherent
similarity of the lamp (*luchnos*) and light (*phōs*) images. Both phenomena radiate. Moreover, Matthew uses the same two terms together and
synonymously in 5.14-15. You are the *light* of the world. A *lamp* is not
put under a bushel but on a lamp stand where it gives light.

Another argument in favor of identifying the eye as a lamp and the
light is that both lamp and light are attached to the person, the personal

self. The light is explicitly the light *in you*. And the lamp is the lamp *of the body*. The personal pronoun 'you' represents the person or self, and so does the body. I shall argue the latter point in a moment. Thus both lamp and light signify the self's capacity to see, and for Matthew seeing is a symbol for understanding (13.14-15).

The synonymity of the lamp of the body and the light in you is supported in the third place by the fact that this saying presents itself as a connected, logical whole. The 'therefore' (*oun*) or 'then' that introduces the clause about the light in you ties this conclusion firmly to what has just been said in assessing the eye as the lamp of the body. The two expressions belong to one connected thought. If they did not mean the same thing, the light in you statement could be the conclusion to some other analysis but not to this one.

I turn now to my claim that in this text the body is the self. In biblical thinking the term 'body' can refer to one's physical presence in the world, one's physical body, or it can be a metaphor for the whole self (Via 1990: 68-70). I argue that in our text it is a metaphor for the self. One argument for this is that it is parallel to the personal pronoun 'you'. Beyond that the adjectives that are predicated of the body suggest the cognitive-subjective rather than the physical. The body will be illuminated, that is, in the light (*phōteinon*), or in the dark (*skoteinon*). The connotation of the physical that attaches to the body inevitably plays upon the choice of words here. That is in fact what creates the semantic tension from which the metaphor results. To speak of the physical body as illuminated or enlightened or, on the other hand, as in the dark is puzzling because it is literally pointless. Thus the relationship between the noun and the adjectives predicated of it is tensive and thereby suggests a non-literal level of meaning. The knowing self and not the physical body is in view.

Notice the emphasis on the wholeness of the body. The adjective whole (*holon*) modifies body both times it is used. This makes the eye distinctly a part of the body, something distinguished from the whole. The whole self sees or fails to see, has a true or false understanding, exists in the light or in the darkness, depending on whether the part, the eye, the source of light, is sound or evil.

That a person sees with her eye is a truism to which it would not be worth calling our attention if it were meant in a conventional sense. But that it is not meant in a conventional sense is seen in the metaphorical description of the body, in the foregrounding of the whole–part opposition and in the oxymoron dark light. The self sees or fails to see, but it sees with the eye that as part both belongs to the whole self and is distinguished from it. What is the seeing of the eye that is both the whole self's seeing and not the whole self's seeing? In what perspective would it make sense to say that one's vision or understanding, which is only a partial understanding, can give either total clarity or total obscurity?

That claim would make sense if the partial or limited understanding—the eye as lamp—were understood as the angle or vantage point from which one sees, one's presuppositional starting point. As the point from which one sees, one's presupposition or preunderstanding, the light of the eye is not the totality of what one understands. But as the vantage point it is fused with the total vision and shapes it to some degree. Thus the sound and evil eye are two kinds of pre-understanding. In principle either is possible. But in actuality the human condition is that the angle of vision is so deformed—so much in the darkness—that nothing whatsoever is seen; only darkness obtains.

I have been interpreting this text at the level of ontological–epistemo-logical–hermeneutical discourse. I take it that the text refers to how one comes to understanding or how one fails to understand. Is that correct? Or is that even one legitimate level of interpretation among others? If Ulrich Luz is right, I have been on the wrong track, for he states that the text is not concerned with the nature of human beings but with their action (Luz 1989: 397-98). I think that he is right in what he affirms and wrong in what he denies. The adjective 'sound' (*haplous*), which modifies eye, can mean healthy, especially in light of its association with the Hebrew root *tam* (Luz 1989: 396). Thus when modifying 'the eye' understood metaphorically, as in our text, it can mean 'illuminating'. The adjective 'sound' can also, however, have an ethical connotation (Prov. 11.25; 2 Cor. 8.2; Jas 1.5) (Guelich 1985: 329-30), suggesting uprightness, sincerity and generosity. In like manner the adjective 'evil' (*ponēros*) can mean unhealthy (Luz 1989: 396; Guelich 1985: 331). Thus, when modifying 'the eye' understood metaphorically, evil can mean 'obscuring'. But obviously 'evil' also has an ethical meaning (Guelich 1985: 330). Many scholars have interpreted the sound eye and evil eye in terms of generosity and liberality versus stinginess and acquisitiveness (Davies and Allison 1988: 640; Gundry 1982: 113; Beare 1981: 182; Hill 1972: 142; Betz 1985: 85).

John Elliott has set our passage in the context of the evil eye belief of the Mediterranean world generally. The essence of the belief was that certain individuals, animals, demons or gods have the power to cast a spell or produce a malignant effect upon every object on which their eye or glance might fall. The power of the evil eye can destroy life and health. This belief was especially fostered in societies that perceived goods to be in short supply and life to be essentially competitive and conflictive. The evil eye is an oppressive weapon in this conflictive world (Elliott 1988: 46, 52), a means of acquisition at the expense of others.

In addition to the word for evil that is used in the Matthew text, the evil eye phenomenon was also expressed by the terms *basanos* (one who possesses and injures with the evil eye; Prov. 23.6; Sir. 14.3), *baskanein* (to begrudge or afflict with the evil eye; Deut. 28.54; Sir. 14.6, 8; Gal. 3.1), and *baskania* (fascination or acquisitiveness; Wis. 4.12) (Elliott 1988: 55-56). Elliott observes (pp. 54-59) that in Jewish writings prior to the New Testament period the evil eye was understood increasingly in moral terms (Sir. 18.18; 14.3-10; Tob. 4.5-17; 4 Macc. 1.26).

With regard to our text Elliott believes that the larger cultural context as well as the immediate literary context (Mt. 6.19-21, 24) confer the moral sense of acquisitiveness on the evil eye in Mt. 6.22-23. At the same time the contrast with 'sound' (*haplous*) eye and the theological element in 6.24, 25-34 give the added sense of disloyalty to God (p. 61).

I have no doubt that the ethical dimension of meaning belongs to this text. Yet there is a discernible difference between the evil eye belief as generally understood in the broad culture and Matthew's employment of it. For Mediterranean culture the evil eye is a negative power by which people inflict injury on others. In Mt. 6.22-23, however, the evil eye is a condition through which one injures oneself. That points us back to the ontological-hermeneutical level of meaning.

The hermeneutical and ethical levels of meaning complement and, in fact, interpenetrate each other. The saying itself may be more strongly hermeneutical, but the ethical is not absent, and the context is distinctly ethical. The ethical dimension materially affects the hermeneutical claims, the claims about how one comes to understanding or its opposite. The most immediate context (6.19-21, 24) suggests that the sound eye is the recognition of the untrustworthiness of earthly treasure or money. The heart directed toward material wealth, on the other hand, will have a distorted picture of reality. If we broaden the context somewhat we find that the evil eye is a pre-understanding that does not see the truth about oneself, specifically one's own moral flaws (7.3-4), and thus does not have the right vision of reality more broadly (7.3-5). The evil eye that darkens the total vision of the self is a blindness to the impurity and rebellion on the inside of oneself (23.26-28).

### The Metaphorical Structure

The logical-philosophical structure and the metaphorical structure interpenetrate each other and cannot be neatly separated. Therefore, some metaphorical relationships have already been considered. Seeing is a symbol for understanding in 6.22-23 (cf. 13.14-15, where understanding stands in a metaphorical relationship with seeing and hearing). This symbolic meaning of seeing is reinforced by the metaphorical connection between the noun 'body' and the adjectives 'in the light' and 'in the dark'. This tensive relationship between the noun (physical) 'body' and adjectives that pertain to cognition shows that the body means, not the physical body, but the knowing self. Now there are two additional metaphorical—or possibly metaphorical—structures that I want to inquire into. The first is the connection between the eye and the lamp, and the second is the relationship between the eye and the light in you.

Perhaps at this point I should be a bit more specific about the understanding of metaphor that I have been assuming. Metaphor is not mere ornamentation but is a redescription of reality. Moreover, metaphor is not primarily a transfer of meaning from one noun to another. Rather metaphor is an utterance in which meaning is transferred from one semantic field to another semantic field that had hitherto been separated from the first. A meaning is wrenched from its normal context and placed in another. A meaning is predicated of something to which it seems not to belong. In view of the factors of identification and predication the logical, if not the syntactic, model for a metaphor is the sentence. Metaphor then is tensive language, is primarily an affair of semantic tension. The tension is not between the new meaning (created by seeing something as something else) and some alleged original or primitive meaning. It is rather a tension between the new meaning and meaning that is established by ordinary usage and found in the dictionary. The metaphorical meaning puts a strain on conventional wisdom (Ricoeur 1976: 37, 47, 49-50, 68; Ricoeur 1984: 14, 15, 20, 44, 48, 98, 229, 230, 231, 290-91, 299; Soskice 1985: 19, 21-23; Wheelwright 1954: 25-26; Wheelwright 1962: 42-44, 46-50, 53-55, 70-74, 78-80, 86).

## The Eye is the Lamp

The thesis of our text is: 'The eye is the lamp of the body'. Is this sentence a metaphor? In order to answer that question we must first consider more carefully what the sentence actually seems to say. The eye is a lamp, and for Matthew a lamp shines, radiates, emits light onto objects (5.15). Thus in 6.22 light goes out from the eye.

This seems to bring the thought of the sentence into line with the understanding of vision that is found in the Hebrew Bible and Jewish sources. According to Davies and Allison (1988: 635-36) pre-modern people, including the Jews, believed that the eye contains a light or fire that makes sight possible (Prov. 15.30; Lam. 5.17; Dan. 10.6; Sir. 23.19; *T. Job* 18.3). The *Testament of Job* reference is particularly revealing: *hoi emoi ophtalmoi tous luchnous poiountes eblepon*, 'My eyes acting like lamps were seeing' (or 'searching out') (Kraft 1974 on *T. Job* 18.3). A lamp is its own source of light, not a channel for light from elsewhere. Davies and Allison state that only since about 1500 in the West has the intromission theory of vision been universally adopted. The ancients held an extramission theory. Thus it is anachronistic for modern commentators to interpret our text as if the eye were a window through which light entered the body from outside rather than the source of its own light (Davies and Allison 1988: 635-36). In the understanding of Jewish culture, the movement of vision is from inside to outside.

What about Hellenistic culture? I will consider both the Platonic and the Aristotelian traditions. According to Betz, Plato, along with Empedocles, assumed that the agent of cognition is located within human beings and that cognition, especially vision, occurs by an effluence or emission from within the body toward the outside. Light flows out from the eye. Matthew and the Jewish understanding are basically in agreement with Plato (Betz 1985: 78, 79, 83).

Plato seems to me a bit more ambiguous than Betz acknowledges. Plato states that vision is composed of three factors: the visible (color), the faculty of sight and light (*The Republic* 507 B–E). Not only is daylight one of the three necessary elements in vision, but light also defines the eye's faculty of sight. Plato refers to light-bearing eyes (*Timaeus* 45B). The pure fire within us, akin to the light of day, flows through the eyes in a stream. He then seems to say that the stream of fire flowing out from the eyes coalesces with the daylight to which it is so similar and collides with external obstructing objects. This fiery stream then distributes the motions of objects throughout all the body and even into the soul and brings about the sensation we call seeing (*Timaeus* 45B–46A). Evidently Plato's position is that the light from within, having coalesced with the daylight, collides with external objects and then reverses itself and carries the motions of objects back to the soul. But does Plato imply that something comes from the initiative of objects as well? He does speak of the fire of vision coalescing with the fire of reflected faces (*Timaeus* 46B). Evidently the object is not purely passive.

Something like this seems to be the interpretation of Plato in Theophrastus (371–287 BCE), who is our most important source for earlier Greek physiological psychology according to G.M. Stratton (1917: 15).[2] It is Theophrastus's own position that sense perception, like knowledge, is in accord with nature (Stratton 1917: 93, 95). In principle it gives true knowledge and is not falsifying. It is the case, however, that some perceptions are better than others; some are healthy and some are sick (Stratton 1917: 129, 131). Matthew is in agreement with this position. Theophrastus reports on Plato's reflections in *Timaeus* (which I have already discussed) and notes their emphasis on the light in the eye. In Theophrastus's assessment Plato's view is midway between those who say that vision falls upon objects (proceeds from the eye) and those who hold that something is borne from the visible object to the organ of sight (Stratton 1917: 69, 71). This interpretation shows that Theophrastus was aware of two different theories of sight current in his time. For some, vision occurs as an outgoing process from the eye, and for others, it occurs as an incoming process. Theophrastus seems to side with what he takes to be the majority of the scientists of his time, those who hold that the organ of vision is itself a phenomenon of fire, for he rejects the idea that vision is generated by the object's imprinting the air and the air, in turn, the eye (Stratton 1917: 99, 111, 113).

How would the reader who is an heir of the ancient Jewish or Platonic tradition read Matthew's thesis sentence: 'The eye is the lamp of the body'? He would not read it as a metaphor. She would not read it as a semantic tension that effects a redescription of reality. This reader would experience a succinct statement of conventional wisdom, one that accorded in a straightforward way with the current theory of vision. The eye *in fact is* a lamp. This reader would not experience metaphorical

2.    Stratton (1917) has included Theophrastus's writings on this subject in his book on Greek physiological psychology. The following references to Stratton are for the most part references to the text of Theophrastus rather than to Stratton's commentary.

tension until he or she reached the first commentary (6.22b-23a) where the adjectives shift the meaning of the noun 'body' from a physical to a subjective or cognitive level.

The reading experience would have been different for an Aristotelian. According to Aristotle a sense is affected by the thing perceived—color, flavor or sound (*On the Soul* 2.12). How does this work? Aristotle rejected as nonsensical Plato's belief that the eye is of the nature of fire and that sight occurs because light issues from the eye as from a lantern. If that were the case, the light from the eye would not go out in the dark, and vision at night would be possible. The eye consists in fact of water, not fire, and the power of vision resides in the water's transparency, a quality it shares with the air (*On Sense* 2). It is unreasonable, Aristotle continues, to suppose that vision occurs because light is emitted from the eye and coalesces with the daylight or with an object. Vision is impossible without light, but vision is generated because the object perceived causes the sense to operate. The sensible object sets in motion the medium of sensation—whether that medium be light or air—and the motion, received by the eye, is what produces vision (*On Sense* 2).

The Aristotelian reader, assuming that vision proceeds from the object through the watery transparency of the eye, would read Matthew's thesis sentence as a metaphor. She would experience considerable semantic tension in the claim that the eye is a radiating light and would be prompted to look for a non-literal meaning. That effort would be encouraged by the metaphorical expressions in the first commentary— the body in the light or in the dark.

The modern reader would have much the same experience as the Aristotelian. The eye as a radiating light would be experienced as tensive, and a non-literal meaning would be sought. Again the metaphors in the commentary would support this. It is the knowing self and not the physical body that is in view. So the seeing eye must be a way of understanding. But since the eye, as radiating lamp and as *part* of the whole, in some way generates and constitutes a larger understanding, then the eye must be understanding as pre-understanding, as the vantage point for looking. It is the subjective element in understanding, which goes out from the knowing self and fuses with the knowledge that comes from the object and shapes, and thus in part constitutes, that knowledge.

When this point is reached, the metaphorical tensiveness subsides because the idea that our understanding is shaped by the knower's subjective position—the lamp radiating outward—is widespread. Recall the place of pre-understanding in the tradition of Dilthey, Heidegger, Bultmann, Gadamer and Merleau-Ponty; the role of the reader in reader-response criticism; the function of theories and models in the social and natural sciences.

I have obviously been much influenced by this hermeneutical tradition. The meaning of a text is always defined in part by and is relative to the presuppositions of the interpreter, assumptions shaped both by subjective experience and social location. Interpretation in the light of such pre-understanding is inevitable. Interpretation according to presuppositions of which the interpreter is critically aware is fruitful. My conviction that pre-understanding inevitably and—when critical—properly shapes interpretation has undoubtedly influenced my interpretation of Mt. 6.22-23 as dealing with the relationship between pre-understanding and understanding. But I do not believe that my presupposition has led to a deformation of the text. It has rather led me to see *one* level of meaning which lies within the multivalent possibilities that the text offers. It is neither the only nor an exhaustive interpretation of the text, but it is *one* angle on the *truth* of the text, conditioned but not dominated, by the presuppositional starting point. No other interpretation, in principle, can claim any more. My theoretical position here is as much influenced by recent reader-response criticism as by Heidegger and Bultman.

I hope that approaching the metaphorical structure of our saying by asking for whom would the possible metaphor really be a metaphor has illustrated the complementarity of historical and literary criticism. Identifying the historical-cultural context and thus the assumptions of the text and also of the ancient and modern readers—an exercise in historical criticism—has an impact on the question of whether the utterance is metaphorical—an issue of literary criticism. The *literary* or *rhetorical* level of the utterance is seen to be dependent, at least in part, on the cultural posture of text and readers.

### The Light in you is the Eye

I turn now to a briefer discussion of the relationship between the lamp of the body and the light in you. I argued in the first section that the lamp of the body and the light in you are equivalents of each other. If the eye then *is* the lamp of the body (6.22a), it is also the light in you. That conclusion obviously means that we can also say that the light in you is the eye. The text supports that reading. The light in you is exactly the same thing as the eye. My discussion will proceed on the metaphorical level of the text's understanding of the eye and vision—the eye as the presuppositional vantage point for understanding.

Again, within the text the light in you is the eye, but when we consider the intertext composed of Matthew and certain elements in the Greek and Jewish traditions, the picture becomes more complex. Recall that for Plato the eye is not identical with the light but is the opening through which the light flows from within. The light is more than the eye. The Jewish tradition offers similarities, and I choose here to consider two such texts from the LXX that provide an intertext with Mt. 6.22-23. The first of these (Deut. 15.9) expands the meaning of the eye, and the second (Prov. 20.27) enlarges upon the meaning of the light.

In Deut. 15.9 (LXX) the hidden, lawless word in the heart is made parallel to and synonymous with the eye's being evil or stingy (*ponēreuomai*) to the brother. Since in biblical thinking the heart is the center of the whole person, the hidden core and the seat of understanding and will, the synonymous parallelism of eye and heart metaphorically, but not literally, identifies eye and heart, part and whole, external and internal. Thus intertextually the eye in the thesis statement 'the eye is the lamp of the body' means more than the literal eye and more than the eye as *pre*-understanding. The eye is not just a part of the self but is rather the self's organizing center. This has been established by the intertext of Deut. 15.9 and Mt. 6.22-23 before we move to the commentaries of the Matthew text.

In Prov. 20.27 (LXX) the light (*phōs*) is identified with the spirit of humankind that searches out the person's private inner parts. The noun translated spirit here (*pnoē*) ordinarily means breath or wind, but it can shade off into the sense of spirit (*pneuma*), which is surely demanded by the context here. This passage is similar to 1 Cor. 2.10-11 in the function that it assigns to the human spirit. The 1 Corinthians text speaks of the Spirit of God searching out the deep things of God and attributes an analogous function for human beings to the human spirit: it searches out the human depths. Both Prov. 20.27 and 1 Cor. 2.10 use the same verb for 'to search out' (*eraunaō*). Since the light in humankind in Prov. 20.27 is the spirit that has access to the innermost recesses of the self, it is more than the eye of Mt. 6.22a-23a, even when the eye is understood metaphorically as understanding, for the eye in Matthew 6 is understanding as a limited vantage point from which to comprehend. The intertextual connection between Prov. 20.27 and Mt. 6.23b draws the light of the latter into the semantic field of the former—light as the spirit that searches out the inner person. The light, then, expanded intertextually as the spirit that searches out the human depths, is *more* than the eye as the (intratextually) limited pre-understanding. However, the expanded intertextual meaning of light is very nearly the *equivalent* of the expanded intertextual meaning of eye—the eye as a synonym for heart, the self's organizing center.

There is a complication in Prov. 20.27 that should be noted. The searching spirit is not just light but is specifically the light of the *Lord*. Does that mean—contrary to normal Jewish thinking—that the human spirit is metaphysically identical with the divine light? Or does it mean—as the broader Jewish context would suggest—that the human spirit is guided by the divine light?

My conclusion from the foregoing is that the light in you in Mt. 6.22b can shade off into meaning the human spirit in its innermost depth. Therefore, it is not unambiguously identical with the eye of 6.22-23a. The relationship between the eye as lamp and the light in you is tensive and therefore metaphorical. That is to say, that is the case when the eye as lamp is understood as the limited presuppositional vantage point for understanding and the light in you is understood as the searching human spirit that knows the deepest secrets. *Intra*textually the light in you is straightforwardly the eye as lamp. Both mean the same thing: pre-understanding. But *inter*textually the partial vision of pre-understanding (eye) is tensively identified with the much more penetrating vision of the spirit (light in you). *Intra*textually the light in you is the part (the eye). *Inter*textually the light in you is something approaching the whole (the penetration of the spirit). I am taking the far-reaching knowledge of the spirit to be the substantial equivalent of the illumination of the whole self (Mt. 6.22b).

What is the import of this metaphorical connection? The part (eye as lamp) is the whole (light in you). We have already observed that in 6.22b-23a the angle of the eye *affects* the whole understanding of the self. The metaphorical identification of these two elements intensifies that relationship and suggests its reciprocity: not only does the limited angle of vision guide to some significant degree the total understanding of a person, but an enlargement in one's total understanding can reform the vantage point from which one sees. The partial understanding of pre-understanding becomes less and less partial.

In summary, I have been assuming two levels of metaphor in

Matthew's eye–light imagery. *Intra*textually the eye as lamp is literally the same thing as the light in you, but eye = light is a metaphor for pre-understanding or the angle of vision. At the *inter*textual level, however, the eye is not literally identical with the light in you but rather is tensively or metaphorically identical with it. And this metaphorical connection has the effect of drawing the eye = light away from being a metaphor for the partial understanding of the angle of vision and toward being a metaphor for full understanding.

It must be remembered, however, that in our text the actual case for humankind generally is that the light in you is darkness (6.23b). People are blind (7.3; 11.20-24; 23.16, 17, 24, 26). And given the double meaning of the light in you, the angle of vision is too deformed to give true understanding, and whatever understanding one has is too darkened to correct the point from which one understands.

## The Narrative Structure

Matthew 6.22-23 is not a narrative but rather in form-critical terms is a wisdom saying expressing a general truth about humankind. But could it be that it is, nevertheless, an implicit manifestation of an underlying narrative structure? Recall that the saying has three parts: (1) a thesis stating a possibility about seeing (6.22a); (2) a commentary about alternate contingent possibilities that show that the original possibility is only a possibility in principle (6.22b-23a); (3) a concluding commentary stating that the possibility actually realized is the negative one—the bad eye—so that the light is really darkness (6.23bc). These partitions in the grammatical–logical–philosophical structure are based on the shift from a declarative sentence to conditional sentences, changes in the mood of the verbs and semantic factors. The segmentation of the narrative structure that I am about to propose also results from attention to these things, but the three moments of the implied plot in their specifics emerge from confronting the saying deductively with a threefold narrative structure that has its own narrative logic. In this structure the (1) beginning is a moment of possibility that gives way in the (2) middle to some actualization of possibility in a process that in turn leads in the (3) ending to a consequence (Bremond 1970: 247-52; 1978: 33).

This underlying plot structure may be applied to short or long narratives, and I use as an example its manifestation in the Gospel of Matthew as a whole. In the beginning redemptive possibilities are opened up because Jesus is related to God in such a way that he is God with us (1.23) and savior (1.21). The possibility of evil and opposition is suggested by the hostility of Herod, the sin of Israel and Satan's tempting Jesus. In the middle these possibilities are actualized in two processes. In the process of redemption we see the progressive actualization of the Son of God in several roles that he exercises in relation to Israel and the disciples. He is manifested as teacher-judge, archetypal human being, revealer of the knowledge of God, healer and miracle worker. The changes in the historical existence of Israel-church are portrayed in corresponding roles. Disciples merit salvation by their righteousness and entry into the precarious destiny of the Son of Man but also are the graced recipients of healing, faith and knowledge of God. A process of opposition is initiated by Jesus' attackers, but this becomes confluent with the redemptive process, for Jesus finally saves by his suffering and death (16.21; 20.28; 26.28). Jesus must be opposed in order to be who he is. He dies as a new covenant sacrifice, and the disciples in correlation with this are the forgiven community. In the ending Jesus' opponents seem to have achieved their goal in his crucifixion, but life outlasts death. Jesus' death confers forgiveness, and by means of his resurrection and exaltation Jesus is fully constituted as the one who can save Israel because he now has all authority (28.18) and is always present (28.20). And Israel, in the disciples, has its lack of faith and righteousness filled: Jesus is acknowledged in faith as Son (27.54) and worshipped (28.9, 17) and will be obeyed (28.20).

When this narrative logic is applied to Mt. 6.22-23, the three parts of the implicit plot do not correspond to the three parts of the wisdom saying. Yet I do not believe that the narrative structure has been forced on the text. Rather the diction of the latter and the structure fit each other. The implicit plot that emerges from segmenting the text according to the narrative structure unfolds as follows.

The first part of the wisdom saying is the thesis in 6.22a. But the beginning of the plot is comprised of 6.22a-23a. That is because in this stretch of text we remain in the realm of possibility, a possibility with two alternatives. The *beginning* of the *plot* includes the *thesis* and the *first commentary* of the *saying*. Matthew has stated as a declaration that the eye is the lamp of the body, but the commentary tells us that it may produce light or darkness. Since the eye is a lamp that may produce darkness, the eye is not a lamp in fact but only as an uncertain possibility in principle. Here we are still in the mode of 'you might do this' or 'you might do that'. No fate-determining decision has been made. A narrative that fleshed out this motif would portray various possibilities that a protagonist might pursue or perhaps first steps in this or that direction but no move that could not be reversed.

The middle of the plot is composed of 6.23b, the first clause or protasis of a first-class conditional sentence—if the light in you is darkness (and it is). The movement into the middle is signalled by the shift from the subjunctive mood of the previous two sentences to the indicative mood of this clause. Even though 'if the light in you is darkness' is a conditional clause, it suggests by the indicative an actual decision. The possibility of having an evil eye has been realized as the darkening of the source of light. A narrative developing this motif would describe a ruinous decision, or series of such decisions, producing a condition of deformed judgment and understanding from which there could be no turning back, no self-extrication.

The ending of the implied plot is composed of the second clause (or apodosis) of the final conditional sentence (6.23c)—how great is the darkness! The *second commentary* of the *saying* (6.23bc), *short* as it is, *embraces both* the *middle* and *ending* of the narrative's *plot*.

The story, relatively speaking, is long on beginning and short on middle and ending. It wants the reader to be impressed with the possibilities offered—even if the positive possibility turns out not to be actually available. The story gives a relatively extended vision of the possibilities before the negative realities are represented with dramatic brevity.

The exclamatory nature of the 'how great is the darkness' signals that we do have here a result and not simply a continuation of the process generated by the decision in the middle. The 'how great' shows that the decision to turn the potential light into darkness results in a fate from which there is no human escape, a darkness unimaginably great. The ending of a story of this type would narrate the consequence of total not-seeing. The downward turn of this story implied by Mt. 6.22-23 will be reversed only by the upward movement of the larger story in which it is embedded, finally by the resurrection and exaltation of Jesus, which overcome his death.

## Conclusion

I believe that the three structural levels that have been considered—grammatical–logical–philosophical, metaphorical, narrative—complement and reinforce one another, and the resultant picture of the human condition is an obviously pessimistic one. The grammatical–logical–philosophical level affirms that the light of pre-understanding that might give either full illumination or full obscurity has actually given total darkness. The metaphorical level intensifies the circular reciprocity between pre-understanding and understanding: darkness generating darkness. The narrative level dramatically underscores the magnitude of the final darkness.

I have been assuming that there is no cosmos—no ordered reality—apart from language. The world was created by the word (Gen. 1.3, 5, 6, etc.; Jn 1.1, 3). Genesis 1 and John 1 speak in universalizing cosmic terms, but, of course, no person or society actually has a grasp of universal reality as it really is by means of some transcendent language. What we have is a multiplicity of limited life-worlds based on limited and specific linguistic networks. Early Christianity was such a life-world and the Gospel of Matthew, as a whole and in its parts, was a strand in its constitutive linguistic network.

The *kind* of reality one has depends on the specifics of the language. That is to say, the language in its particularity is an interpretation that constitutes reality. One could say that the language is only rhetoric or the expression of an assumption, but there is no reality apart from the confluence of 'stuff' and language. Thus I have taken seriously such things as conditional sentences in their variations. When Matthew says 'if the light in you is darkness—and it *is*' (first class condition), he is giving an interpretation of the human situation. This interpretation is as such a claim about how things are, and it is pessimistic. The reader will decide whether it is true for her or him.

If there is hope for humankind, that will apparently come solely from what God has done as suggested by the movement of the larger gospel narrative. At the same time the very bleakness of the assessment of the actual human condition may prompt us to ask whether there are in the Gospel of Matthew any deconstructive moves that suggest a less dark picture of human being as such. The very fact that Matthew holds open the *possibility* of true understanding might prompt one to look for unexpected realizations of it. Could it be that a brighter representation of the human project, excluded by our text (6.22-23) and pushed to the outside, nevertheless finds its way back inside?

# BIBLIOGRAPHY

Aristotle
  1935        *On Sense and Sensible Objects* (trans. W.S. Hett; LCL; Cambridge: Harvard University Press).
  1935        *On the Soul* (trans. W.S. Hett; LCL; Cambridge: Harvard University Press).
Beare, Francis Wright
  1981        *The Gospel according to Matthew* (San Francisco: Harper & Row).
Betz, H.D.
  1985        *Essays on the Sermon on the Mount* (trans. L.L. Welborn; Philadelphia: Fortress Press).
Bremond, Claude
  1970        'Morphology of the French Folktale', *Semiotica* 2: 247-76.
  1978        'The Narrative Message', *Semeia* 10: 5-55.
Davies, W.D. and Dale C. Allison
  1988        *A Critical and Exegetical Commentary on the Gospel according to Saint Matthew*, I (ICC; Edinburgh: T. & T. Clark).
Elliott, John H.
  1988        'The Fear of the Leer: The Evil Eye from the Bible to Li'l Abner', *Forum* 4: 42-71.
Guelich, Robert A.
  1985        *The Sermon on the Mount* (Waco, TX: Word Books).
Gundry, Robert H.
  1982        *Matthew* (Grand Rapids: Eerdmans).
Hill, David
  1972        *The Gospel of Matthew* (NCB; Grand Rapids: Eerdmans; London: Marshall, Morgan & Scott).
Kraft, Robert A. (ed.)
  1974        *The Testament of Job* (Missoula, MT: Scholars Press).
Luz, Ulrich
  1989        *Matthew 1–7: A Commentary* (trans. W. Linss; Minneapolis: Augsburg).
Plato
  1942        *The Republic* (trans. P. Shorey; LCL; Cambridge: Harvard University Press).
  1942        *Timaeus* (trans. R.G. Bury; LCL; Cambridge: Harvard University Press).
Ricoeur, Paul
  1976        *Interpretation Theory* (Fort Worth: Texas Christian University Press).
  1984        *The Rule of Metaphor* (trans. R. Czerny; Toronto: University of Toronto Press).
Soskice, Janet Martin
  1985        *Metaphor and Religious Language* (Oxford: Clarendon Press).
Stratton, G.M.
  1917        *Theophrastus and Greek Physiological Psychology before Aristotle* (London: George Allen & Unwin; New York: Macmillan).

Via, Dan O.
1990          *Self-Deception and Wholeness in Paul and Matthew* (Minneapolis: Fortress Press).
Wheelwright, Philip
1954          *The Burning Fountain* (Bloomington: Indiana University Press).
1962          *Metaphor and Reality* (Bloomington: Indiana University Press).

# WHAT IS IT ABOUT?
## REFERENCE IN NEW TESTAMENT LITERARY CRITICISM

### William A. Beardslee

We transmit (we hope) fairer things than we can fully grasp.
Archbishop Krüger in Thornton Wilder's *The Eighth Day*

The essential Christian position...is aware of redemptive forces of enormous urgency present through the whole texture of existence.
Amos Niven Wilder, *Spiritual Aspects of the New Poetry*

### *Reference in the History of New Testament Criticism*

The older literary criticism assumed that writing was 'about' something, that it was intelligibly related to a larger world. There was great variety in how the relationship was conceived, and mimetic theories of literary criticism are badly misunderstood if they are reduced to theories of 'copying'— despite the role of the image of the copy already in Plato. (On mimetic theories of literary criticism, see Abrams 1953: esp. 8-14, 30-46[1]). The most discussed difference among mimetic theories has been the difference between 'mimesis' as representational realism and as presentation of a better reality than is available in the empirical world. The relevance of this distinction to studies of the New Testament is clear, for the question whether New Testament books or passages are to be taken as representations of actual states of affairs or as models for transformation (or both, or perhaps, neither) is a lively one.

The intention here is not to discuss the relative strengths of realistic and idealistic representation as approaches to the New Testament. Rather, it is to point out that the older views of the text as representation of reality presupposed that the represented world was a world in which value was intrinsic (this was true at least of the human world). The

---

1. The following discussion is indebted to Abrams both for the history of literary criticism and for the classification of models of interpretation.

modern separation between fact and value had no place in older literary theories of representation, nor in older biblical interpretation. Whether the stress fell on the representation of the broken human condition, as in Romans 7, or on the vision of a transformation of the world, as in 1 Corinthians 15, the assumption of the interpreter was that the values of the presented world were fundamentally woven into the world presented. There was room for debate about the question of truth: does the biblical world present the values of the world as they really are, or are to be? But the modern assumption that the represented world could be viewed neutrally, and that the values seen in it are wholly dependent on the world created by the text, or perhaps even on the point of view of the reader, is foreign to the older interpretations of the text as representation of reality.

In biblical studies, as in literary studies generally, the shift away from mimetic theories of interpretation was first toward a greater interest in the creativity of the author (the expressive theory of interpretation). Nineteenth-century studies of both Jesus and Paul often focused on the creative originality of these biblical figures. This motif is still a lively one in contemporary studies of both Jesus and Paul.

But the picture in biblical studies was different from that in literary studies generally because of the strong historical cast of the discipline as it developed. While literary studies in the nineteenth century often included a strong genetic or historical component—how the text was a product of its background—the historical emphasis was far stronger in biblical studies. Debates about the authority of the Bible as they were cast in this formative period brought the question of reference as reference to factual accuracy into the center of interest in a way quite untypical of literary studies generally.

Thus New Testament scholarship continued, in an historical vein, the long tradition of representational interpretation. Historical study was a principal way in which the New Testament was set in a wider world, the wider world of the ancient Near East, but more deeply, the wider world of the culture of the historians. The effort to define historical occurrence accurately, in the context of a widely-accepted separation between fact and value, led increasingly to a concept of representation as representation of fact. If, nevertheless, values inevitably did inject themselves into the historian's work, the conscious focus was on 'fact' rather than on the values of or in the occurrences. How accurately does the text represent what happened? How does it help the scholar to reconstruct the 'real' events that lay behind the text? Though modern assumptions about what is probable or possible always involved judgments of value, historians attempted to judge about historical probability according to what would have appeared to a 'neutral' observer.

Such historical study has contributed enormously to our understanding of the New Testament. But the larger world in which the New Testament was set was in turn restricted by its often unreflective assumption of modern values, as Albert Schweitzer saw in his *Quest of the Historical Jesus*. For the study of the New Testament, there is no turning back from historical criticism, though there must be continual re-evaluation of it. For our purposes, we note the problematic of the attempted separation of fact and value that is so central to much historical study as it has been practiced in New Testament scholarship. Thoughtful historians today know that such a separation is a methodological fiction.

In literary criticism, the move beyond the interest in the author's creativity and in historical reconstruction was a return to the study of the forms of the text, an element of literary study that has been central since Aristotle and that had been kept alive in various margins of New Testament study during the period of sharp focus on historical reconstruction. The 'New Criticism' was slow to affect New Testament studies, but it has worked a deep transformation in the discipline. No doubt a great part of the appeal of the new literary criticism has been the way in which it liberated the student of the New Testament precisely from the question of the text's accuracy in historical detail. A generation of scholars has produced and is producing rich and varied studies of the New Testament from poetic and rhetorical perspectives that were long neglected. These studies represent a recovery of interest in meaning, but on the whole they have shown little explicit concern with reference. For in their background lies the assumption, drawn from the narrowing of reference in historical study, that reference is correspondence to specific facts in the past.

## A Pragmatic Probe of 1 Corinthians 15

To provide a basis for reflecting about a wider view of reference in interpretation, we shall choose 1 Corinthians 15 as a text to study. Reading this text engages the student in the question of reference in its complexity, as we shall see, and this chapter is chosen for that reason.

Clearly a view of reference different from 'correspondence to historical occurrence' will be required if one is to reflect about the referential dimension of an eschatological text.

Most studies of 1 Corinthians 15 have looked directly at its picture of the expected apocalyptic transformation and at how this is related to the proclamation of Christ's resurrection. These are central and inescapable questions. But we shall approach this text with a different set of questions, drawn from one of the liveliest fields in contemporary literary criticism, the study of the pragmatics of the text, that is, the study of its intended effect on the audience. Questions about the pragmatics of the text inevitably lead to reflection about the world referred to in it, for different perceptions of the world to which the text relates are at the heart of the conflict of interpretation that often comes to light when one reflects about the intended impact of the text. Thus rhetorical criticism has reopened the question of reference, even though this dimension of literary criticism is often only implicit in such studies.

Although much is to be gained by searching out and reconstructing the views of the hearers, and thereby clarifying or criticizing Paul's affirmations (see, for instance, Wire 1990), we shall simply look at the surface indicators of audience effect.

1 Corinthians 15 opens and closes with the theme, 'not in vain' (15.1-2, 58), as Talbert points out (Talbert 1992: 96). Such an *inclusio* was a traditional way of marking the limits of a section of discourse. But this theme is far more than a signal to mark the bounds of the section. What is striking about the chapter is the way in which this figure reappears in virtually every overt reference to the effect on the reader: 15.2, 'unless you have come to believe in vain' (NRSV; so throughout the essay); v. 10, '[God's] grace toward me has not been in vain' (cf. v. 11); v. 14, 'if Christ has not been raised...our proclamation has been in vain and your faith has been in vain'; v. 17, 'If Christ has not been raised your faith is futile...' (cf. other expressions with this tenor in the context); v. 29, 'Otherwise, what will those people do?...'; v. 32, 'what would I have gained by it?' (cf. vv. 32-33 with the quotation from Isa. 22.13, 'Let us eat and drink, for tomorrow we die'); v. 58, '...because you know that in the Lord your labor is not in vain'.

In practical terms the chapter is about survival. Explicitly about survival after death, the actual pragmatic thrust is about the enduring results of actions taken on behalf of the community and thus about the survival of the community. That was the result that was in view. The explicit theme of resurrection is handled very differently from the way in which many modern readers take it. The modern reader who is pre-occupied with the question of individual survival may easily miss the way in which Paul, who undoubtedly believed in individual survival after death, primarily focuses on 'our' destiny, not 'my' destiny, and not only so, but comes to this question not as an isolated one but in relation to the survival in this world of the community. This theme in the chapter draws together the numerous places earlier in the letter where Paul had to deal with the survival of the community. It also links ch. 15 to ch. 13 (a much discussed issue), since the chapter on love is also concerned with survival ('Love never ends', 13.8).

A study of the whole letter would show that the community that Paul was determined would survive was the true community as he under-stood it. It is clear enough in ch. 15 that what is at issue is the survival of a particular kind of community. We may describe it as a community radically open, with no special privilege based on difference. The aim to be a radically open community is the central strand in what Paul says about community, though of course this theme cannot stand alone, and there are other strands, which have often received more attention: it is to be a transformed community (6.11, etc.), and a disciplined community (14.40, etc.). These themes are interwoven with the theme of the open community, yet they are not easy to harmonize with it, and of course in practice Paul only imperfectly saw what a radically open community is. Nonetheless, the direction toward a radically open community remains central, if only imperfectly attained. This is the point of the opposition to 'divisions' in chs. 1–4 and of the affirmation of the diversity of gifts in chs. 12–14, and this theme plays a central role in many of the other specific questions discussed earlier in the letter.

It is the constitution of such an open community that is the 'work' that is not 'in vain'. The acts that create and maintain such a true community are those that the chapter affirms will not be lost, ephemeral and fragile as they appear. The (largely traditional) teaching about the resurrection is offered to provide a wider framework of meaning for the acts that constitute the true community. For such acts to continue, in the sense of continue to happen, to keep on happening, the chapter asserts, one has to believe that they are taken up into a wider world. This issue has appeared earlier in the letter in the discussion of the differential reward for the variety of 'works' (3.5–4.5; cf. 3.13, 'the work of each builder will become visible'). On this see the rhetorical study of Kuck 1992, who concludes that the practical point of differential reward is precisely to encourage diversity in the community: leave to God the final evaluation. The same theme also appears, indirectly, in the suggestion that the 'spirit' of the expelled member may be saved through or by the destruction of his flesh (5.5), even though the immediate thrust of this section is on the expulsion of a member who is held to have acted unacceptably, for the saving of the spirit seems to imply some form of eventual participation in the community.

Evidently the question of the boundary of the community was a matter of vigorous debate in Corinth. Some reconstructions of the discussion see the Pauline pragmatics as restrictive, downplaying the experience of the moment, and establishing a clear act–reward pattern that sorted people out according to what they deserve, and thereby was exclusive rather than inclusive (see Wire 1990). Certainly Paul has often been understood in this way, for instance in the Pastoral Epistles and in much of the popular reading of his letters in the churches through the centuries. But the movement of thought and of rhetorical expression in ch. 15 is in the opposite direction: to emphasize the survival of the whole community in its variety, its lack of elitist distinctions. One point scored by the sharp break between 'flesh and blood' and 'the kingdom of God' (v. 50) is precisely that earthly distinctions do not constitute the true community. Of course it is true that Paul in practice did exclude some types of actions and persons that others believed were proper for the community. He had partially grappled with what it would mean for the community to be open to women; he had not considered that a truly open community would include homosexuals.

Even this brief discussion shows that an emphasis on the pragmatics of the text reopens the range of questions about reference. Rhetorical studies of audience response, however they may be nuanced, inevitably raise the question of reference to a community that existed, or exists, in interaction with the text, and of pressures for change in it—as well as the wider referential question of the grounds for the actions proposed. As one focuses on the values that the text affirms and, in particular, on the value of a truly open community, this reflection cannot go far without thinking about the basis of the values in reality.

## A Note on Rhetoric of Conflict

In concluding this brief probe into the pragmatics of the text, we call attention in passing to a certain tension between the aim of the text as we have discerned it and the rhetorical means of expressing that aim. We focus on the aim of encouraging true, open, varied community, while at the same time recognizing that taken by itself this theme is an abstraction from a more complex image of a community—an open community requires both a transformation of its prospective members and a continuing discipline or maintaining of standards. The complexity of the image of community may in part account for the way in which Paul has used two very adversarial types of rhetoric for the purpose of encouragement of 'true' community. Very conflictual or adversarial language is characteristic both of the apocalyptic literary tradition and of Hellenistic-Roman diatribe style (for instance, 'For he must reign until he has put all his enemies under his feet', v. 25, from apocalyptic language, and 'Fool!', v. 36, from diatribe style). Many of the literary features of ch. 15 are derived from one or the other of these traditions. Does that mean that the language works against the deeper intention of the text? Perhaps to some degree. But note that the apocalyptic language is so shaped that the hearers are included rather than excluded, or at least are invited to be included. The whole chapter deals with the link between Christ and those who belong to Christ, and the traditional note of a final judgment is absent (despite the claim of some to see final judgment in vv. 20-28, if the 'end', *telos*, v. 24, is taken as 'the rest', thereby implying a general resurrection, and thus a judgment). We may note in passing that though Paul strongly believed that people are judged, he seldom employed the image of condemnation at a final judgment.

As for the adversarial cast of the diatribe language, it is worth asking whether this linguistic convention may have been understood somewhat differently in its own time and context from the way in which it appears to modern readers. If both Paul and his hearers understood the exclusionary, condemnatory language of debate as one way of clarifying one's position, a position that in its total setting could be communicated also in more give-and-take fashion, the whole question of Paul and his 'opponents' could be seen freshly. There are hints that this may at least be partly so. The dialogue partners were not only 'fools'; they were also 'brothers and sisters' (literally, of course, 'brothers', 1.10, etc.), and 'my beloved children' (4.14, in the context of some fairly stern advice, admittedly). These, too, are conventional phrases. But we may well have sharpened, in our reading, the thrust of the adversarial language. Here is a theme that merits further study.

The third type of rhetoric that appears in the chapter is the wisdom reasoning by analogy about different kinds of flesh or body. Wisdom rhetoric is also central to ch. 13, where it expresses a most paradoxical wisdom. Here, too, the analogical reasoning that 'not all flesh is alike' (v. 39) is used to express a paradoxical tension of discontinuity and continuity. There is continuity in that it is somehow the same person who is raised, but there are contrasts among different kinds of flesh or body (for the language shifts from one term to the other), such as the paradoxical contrast between a 'physical' (or 'psychical', *psychikos*) body and a 'spiritual' (*pneumatikos*) body (vv. 44-49), which emphasize the point that one cannot 'hold on' to the promised future. In distinction from traditional wisdom, which taught how to manage life, this wisdom teaches how to find it by letting to. In that way this rhetoric also deals with an aspect of community, that is, a way of entry into and participation in community. As we shall see, the rhetorical use of wisdom language has important implications for reference.

### The Pattern of Hope

Experience of Christ as risen was the foundational experience that released the power by which the community was enabled to abandon elitist distinctions and become a radically open community, or at least to move in that direction. This experience (or these experiences) was so deeply shaped by expectation that it could be known and shared only in the most powerful language of transformation available—that of apocalyptic renewal. We may put it strongly by saying that if the early Christians who affirmed the resurrection of Christ had not believed that they were going to be raised from the dead, they would not have been able to experience Christ as raised from the dead. But this language was reshaped to bring into the present what had been presented as still to come.

Yet the transforming power had not visibly changed the world; it was accessible only by faith. The complete transformation of reality had to be understood as still to come. This often-discussed pattern of hope produced the tensions that, in the vision of this chapter, required a coming complete transformation if the reality known in faith was to be a genuine reality (15.12-20).

This pattern of transformation of powers that were still exercising influence casts light on what is often taken to be an abrupt shift, at the end of the chapter, from the poetic lines of praise from Isaiah, 'Where, O death, is your victory; Where, O death, is your sting?' to the prose comment, 'The sting of death is sin, and the strength of sin is the law' (vv. 55-56). Some have even regarded this latter prose statement as an interpolation because it so abruptly introduces 'the law', which until that point had not been in view. But if the law is understood in terms of its function in Galatians and Romans as the occasion of a temptation to erect an elitist boundary, the connection with the main pragmatic theme of the chapter is clear, and this prose verse, which looks forward to an existence in which the law will not offer its elitist temptation, makes an effective transition to the concluding practical comment, 'Be steadfast, unmovable, always abounding in the work of the Lord, for in the Lord you know that your labor is not in vain' (v. 58). 'Sin' surely had broad connotations for Paul. But if we consider the pervasive emphasis in 1 Corinthians, grounded in hope in the present chapter, that is, the emphasis on the breaking down of elitist boundaries and the maintaining of a radically open community, then we can see that attention to this cluster of verses supports the widespread reconsideration of 'sin', 'justification' and 'law' in Paul (see especially Sanders 1983 and Boers 1994).

### The Theme of Empowerment

Through the course of Christian history, most readers probably read the imagery of 1 Corinthians 15 with a combination of a fairly simple 'correspondence' understanding of the chapter's reference and some additional appreciation of the poetic, imaginative character of the language, some recognition that not all the images were to be taken literally. Today there is a much wider sense that the language is not literal. But if the language is not to be taken literally, how is it to be taken? My claim is that a literary study of this question moves toward the referential question if it is to do justice to the text.

Abstraction of themes from a dense, imaginative statement always impoverishes that statement, but this is an almost inescapable route as one interprets. Of course, themes are identified in the interplay between the text and the concerns of the interpreter—but that does not mean that they are chosen at will. Thus, the theme of the overcoming of loss and grief is not present in this chapter, even though it does appear in the somewhat parallel passage, 1 Thess. 4.13-18.[2] Even more specific to

2. I first learned this from my mother, Frances Davis Beardslee, who made very

ch. 15 is the absence of the explicit theme of judgment, which is so central to many apocalyptic visions. We will elicit two themes from Paul's eschatological vision: empowerment and a continuity between the present and the expected future, which we shall term 'being remembered'. The first theme has already been mentioned by sketching the recurring note of 'not in vain'. The vision of the resurrection gives the community hope that its actions can change the situation. The kind of change that is in view is particularly the enabling and actualization of a radically open community.

Eschatological hope as empowerment has been a major theme in recent discussion. 'The poor cannot live without an eschatology.'[3] Studies of the book of Revelation have explored this theme (e.g. Schüssler Fiorenza 1985). In the analysis of literary form, categories derived from study of the modern literature of the 'fantastic' have attracted attention recently and been used to good effect in reflection about eschatological language (see Aichele and Pippin 1992). One model derived from this area is particularly relevant to the question of reference: a model derived especially from the work of Ernst Bloch (see Zipes 1992; Bloch 1986).

In Bloch's thought, the pattern of hope, empowering people to act for a society without elitist distinctions, has much in common with the hope for a non-elite community that Paul envisaged, though the scale has changed from a small, separated community in Paul to the society as a whole. Of course Bloch worked assiduously to form a naturalistic interpretation of hope and empowerment. Using Bloch's socially-oriented model of hope inescapably leads to reflection about the give-and-take between the text, the reader's experience and the social setting of the reader, that is, to the question of reference. Bloch's aesthetic category of 'anticipatory illumination' (Zipes 1992: 18) requires that the actual society and not only the text be part of the interpretation. This model not only leads to the hearer as challenged to act, but also to the environing structures as both oppressive and as patient of change in response to humanly-oriented actions. Of course Bloch was a vigorous, and, we may say, biblically-oriented, atheist. Nonetheless, his model of interpretation embodies the claim that reality can be responsive to the acts generated by hope. The biblical tradition itself, despite what Bloch saw as its hidden atheism (Bloch 1980), affirmed that these possibilities

clear that she found passages from 1 Corinthians 15 inappropriate at funeral services.

3.     Thomas Hoyt, in a lecture at the School of Theology at Claremont, Spring, 1993.

of transformation were focused in a center of value (God); for Bloch the possibilities are more diffuse, arising from the nature of the interaction between the society and its members.

In other words, the vision of an open society, which we have presented as a 'vision', is a symbolic action, a political effort to change the relations among people. And as Frank Lentriccia remarks, commenting on the work of Kenneth Burke, 'And literature conceived as symbolic action is not only broadly representational. It is at the same time thoroughly pragmatic. It is what Burke calls "equipment for living"' (Lentriccia 1983: 139).[4]

### The Theme of Being Remembered

Our second theme, the theme of being remembered, has been less the focus of recent interest—though it is a serious question whether the theme of empowerment can persist unless it is linked to what we call the theme of being remembered. It is this kind of image that links the two major parts of the chapter, the recollection of the proclamation and the expectation of the resurrection. 'Being remembered' is thoroughly basic to the foundational experience that Paul recounts: 'he appeared also to me...I am...unfit to be called an apostle, because I persecuted the church of God. But by the grace of God I am what I am' (vv. 8b-10a). The narrative speaks of a special kind of remembering: being accepted, remembered without the appropriate consequences being required. The confidence that he (and all) were and would be remembered supplied much of the energy for 'I worked harder than any of them' (v. 10) and for the confidence that with the passage of time, 'all' would not be forgotten, but remembered ('all will be made alive in Christ', v. 22).

The tension between being remembered and being forgotten is an important clue to one of the central affirmations of the chapter: that

---

4. The other major contributor to models of interpretation of the fantastic is T. Todorov's *The Fantastic* (1973). By the nature of his work, Todorov's model will be less useful for reflection about reference. He explicitly brackets this question: 'The literary work does not enter into a referential relation with the "world", as the sentences of everyday speech often do; it is not "representative" of anything but itself' (p. 10). Further, Todorov's understanding of the fantastic as producing a response of hesitation between the marvellous (where supernatural forces act) and the uncanny (where a natural explanation is possible, though the action is unusual) (ch. 2) is not easily applicable to New Testament eschatological texts, which call for a more direct response.

death will be overcome. Death was strongly associated with being forgotten both in the biblical tradition and in the Hellenistic-Roman world. Many of the psalms, for instance, are eloquent expressions of this association; cf. Ps. 88.4-5: 'I am...like those forsaken among the dead... like those whom you remember no more'. In the world to which Paul addressed his message, the quest for 'fame' was a principal way of warding off the forgetting that came with death. Some forms of modern existential anxiety about death were probably quite foreign to Paul's world, but anxiety that one would simply be forgotten was a central preoccupation. The narrative or myth of the death and resurrection of Christ is put to the use of countervailing this anxiety.

To affirm that the fragile acts, springing from relationships and enacted in relationships that constitute human community, are not forgotten, but somehow 'remembered', taken up into the fabric of reality, leads inescapably to the question of reference.

This connection has been narrowed by the history of interpretation. The classic clarification of the issues raised by ch. 15 took place in Barth's *Die Auferstehung der Toten* (1924), and in Bultmann's review of this book in *Theologische Blätter* (1926) (Barth 1933; Bultmann 1958). Both writers aimed to show how remote from control by ordinary notions of reference the substance of the chapter was. They agreed that resurrection must be understood in sharp antithesis to human or cultural conceptions of how there might be a continuity, a 'being remembered' in the face of death; they expressed this by separating 'resurrection' from the culturally-accepted 'immortality of the soul'. Both further differentiated '*Endgeschichte*', or an account of the ultimate, from '*Schlussgeschichte*', or an account of a temporally final sequence of events. Barth nevertheless affirmed that Paul's intention could be communicated only in a rendering of God's action; for Barth ch. 15 was the culmination and focus of the letter. The consequence of Barth's position was well worked out by Hans Frei (1975); we know that 'we are remembered' through a narrative, but the narrative has no reference outside itself. When one stands within it, it could not not be true.

Bultmann, on the contrary, held that all narrative was 'mythological', and that the heart of the matter was the *agapē* already-present to faith, which is the gift and manifestation of acceptance by God. Hence for him ch. 13, not ch. 15, was the center of the letter. For him, though not as sharply as for Barth, the referential dimension of the text reached only to the world it created, even though this was not Bultmann's way of putting it. For him, a stance toward existence can be discerned as something shared by the text and the believer, but this stance derives from, if not the text, then the proclamation that is associated with it. The limitation of reference to a wider world is clear in the distinction he drew between being accepted in love and the structurally very similar existence toward death that Heidegger saw as authentic existence (Bultmann 1960).

To many interpreters it appears that while the theme of empowerment leads naturally to an interaction between the world of the text and the wider experience of the reader, the referential dimension of the theme of being remembered is private to the particular world of the text, as both Barth and Bultmann maintained. Any cognitive dimension of this theme is specific to the life of a particular reader or community of readers.

But this is too narrow a view. I sketch three frameworks within which to incorporate into experience and language the theme of being remembered. First is the model noted above, in which the text is seen to affirm that the reader, or a particular kind of reader, is remembered. The grounds for confidence in this outcome, both as to the present and as to the future, are set forth in a narrative or picture that is so separate and different from the reality otherwise known and experienced that though this is a fundamental reality 'beyond' the text, it is a reality the grounds for which are made evident only in the text and the community life that springs from it. Reference to a 'wider world' is excluded. Such a view has commended itself to many literary critics because it has liberated them from the narrow 'factual' understanding of reference mentioned earlier in this article.

In the history of interpretation, however, it is fair to say that a second model has been more widely used. In this model, the text and the world it creates provide entry into the reality of being remembered, but the same elements that give confidence that this is a real experience are also encountered in the world at large. The link between the biblical text and the wider world is the character of God, who is seen to be active both in the biblical 'story' and in the world of the reader, and active in similar ways. Evidence for the character of God is found in the whole created world, though the focus and entry point is the tradition of the community. However, it is not expected that the range of experience in the world will include instances of the way in which it is expected that being remembered will take place. That is reserved for the future. The renewal of life after death is the usual form in which being remembered is expressed, and this hope is grounded in the character of God as made known in the biblical story and in other ways, but the renewal of life is not supported by parallel experiences in 'ordinary life'.

The third model holds that the whole gamut of experience provides evidence of the reality of being remembered. The world is shot through with unusual experiences, is open to the unusual in such a way that both the character of God and also the occurrence of unusual experiences provide confidence in the reality of being remembered. Such a view is seen in the recent interest in 'near death' experiences and in similar psychic phenomena. Though this model is often dismissed as 'new age', and though it has often not even been considered by scholars, it competes seriously with the first, exclusivist, model and with the second, creation theology model, in the way it speaks to ordinary people. A fine statement from this point of view can be found in Epperly 1992. A major, often overlooked, strength of this model is that it opens possibilities often foreclosed without reflection by the dualistic presuppositions of many of those who reflect about these issues using the first or second models sketched above.

Though the interpretation of Paul in this century has been dominated by the first model, under the powerful influence of Barth and Bultmann, the presence of wisdom rhetoric in ch. 15, and the central role of wisdom rhetoric in ch. 13, show that Paul is better understood in the second model, in which the experience of Christ opens the way to being remembered, but other aspects of experience are understood to confirm and broaden this experience. This is the point of the reflections about 'how' the future will be shaped, with the images of different kinds of bodies or flesh. I hold that a recovery of this model will strengthen both the literary interpretation and the appropriation of such a text as 1 Corinthians 15.

The decline of the second, creation theology model in the present time is a reflection of the decline of confidence in the orderliness of the world. This decline is well-grounded if one expects 'orderliness' to be (1) the linear, natural law orderliness that has dominated modern thought and/or (2) a teleological orderliness that understands all events as moving toward a predetermined end. Most modern interpreters have been strongly shaped by the first of these presuppositions, while the second has dominated traditional religious interpretation and is clearly a part of Paul's imaginative vision.

But the failure of deterministic models, whether focused on linear cause-

and-effect or on a predetermined conclusion, is no ground for abandoning an overarching vision such as that expressed in 1 Corinthians 15. I have discussed this issue at greater length elsewhere and here can only sketch an alternative image to a closed narrative (Beardslee 1990a, 1991). An act of imagination is called for by the interaction between the ancient vision of a triumphant conclusion and our awareness of the disorderliness of life. That act images an open story in which act and person are embedded in an ongoing process, a process of interaction among many 'stories', and the process is truly open. As I put it elsewhere,

> Thus though we cannot go back to finding our place in the biblical story just as it used to be told, this story is still a vital source for shaping our vision of life. If we are able to let its vital insights speak, we shall be able to find an open, improvisatory overarching story, which does not have a predetermined end, and which does not allow us to regard ourselves as specially privileged, but which does set us free to commit ourselves to action and also to thought, in both cases as explorations of the possibilities that are as yet unrealized. Such an open vision may be widely influential both in religious communities committed to the Bible, and among those who resonate to the values of this story though they set it to work outside of the churches, as we work and live together to find a more human world (Beardslee 1991: 236).

## Values and Reference

A closely related shift in imaginative appropriation of the themes of empowerment and being remembered is called for also in respect to reference. Here I can only sketch lines of transformation that will require more space for careful development.

The Marxist tradition to which Ernst Bloch, mentioned above, belonged, held that values were intrinsic to actual social existence. Empowerment to undertake difficult and risky action was motivated by the confidence that reality would eventually respond because the world was ultimately governed by the values espoused. The decline of the Marxist-socialist perspective has contributed enormously to the 'linguistic turn', which denies the possibility of seeing a structure of values in the world itself. For literary criticism to be serious, it is important for it to be once more affiliated with a perspective that affirms that value is intrinsic to the world.

There are signs that the intellectual environment is changing and becoming more open to recognizing intrinsic value. I have touched on this revisioning of the world elsewhere, but here will briefly note a major effort at reframing the issue of reference that has been mounted by Robert Neville (1989). Rather than narrowing the scope of reference to the vision of a particular community, he moves the model of interpretation from 'conversation', with its emphasis on separate minds coming to understanding, to 'experiment', which is a form of action, with interrelated persons participating in it and relating to the whole environment of which culture is a part. Truth is the carryover of value from the reality in which it is achieved to the interpretation of it as qualified by biology, culture, semiotics and purpose (Neville 1989: 70). Crucial to this view is the distinction between interpretation, with its triadic form (object, sign and interpretant) and the dyadic truth relationship ('is, is not'). Such a position is an extension of the pragmatic hermeneutics that looks to the experience of a community to cover all experience of the world.[5]

Such an approach fully recognizes that any interpretation is part of a chain of interpretations, and also recognizes the role of our perception and the forms of our thinking as well as our historically-located perspective in shaping our interpretations. However, by making clear that values are ingredient in the world and pass from it into our perception, this realistic hermeneutic enables us to affirm that our interpretations are (partly) shaped by the given reality of the world. Thus the interpreter has a basis for distinguishing those readings that more adequately represent reality from those that are less adequate. We will always be fallible and limited but we must aim at representing and judging both the world intended by the text and the relation between that imagined world and the larger reality about which it is, directly or indirectly, a comment.

Neville's is one clearly-worked-out way of saying again in the modern and postmodern world that the world and the entities in it have value in their own terms (strongly put, to themselves), and that, though always imperfectly and perspectivally, we can know these values. This is not a new foundationalism—all interpretation is in the midst and in process—but it clears the path to recover again what the older interpretation presupposed—that values are intrinsic to reality. Neville is well aware of the problems in a simple correspondence theory of reference. His view, that the link between what is interpreted and the interpretation is a 'carryover of value', is not entirely different from a correspondence

---

5.  For an introduction to this difficult reshaping of our hermeneutical approach, see my review (abstracted here) of Neville in Beardslee 1990b: 138-40.

theory (since form is an aspect of value, and form is the link between object and interpretation in correspondence theories), but he avoids the problems of simple correspondence theories, which have been criticized, for instance, by Lategan and Vorster (1985).

Looking at the themes that we have discussed from this perspective, one would be able to see the affirmations of the tradition, including the eschatological and apocalyptic forms of 1 Corinthians 15, as testimonies to experiences of value that are also at work in a wide range of experience although mixed (as also in the life of the community to which Paul wrote) with other, conflicting experiences of value.

What we have called a theme in literary terms can also be regarded as a phenomenological reduction. The soaring images of resurrection that express confidence in being renewed to life after death, at one end of the spectrum, and the hope of being remembered in society through reputation or influence, at the other end, as well as the hope of being remembered by God, are all transformations of a more general structure of 'being remembered'. The text with its specific images can be interpreted in the light of this wide range of possible expressions of the theme, in the confidence that these transformations in their various ways all express a response to something real. Further clarification would carry us into full-scale theological and philosophical reflection that is beyond the scope of this paper (see Beardslee 1972: ch. 7).

*Conclusion*

What is it about? Reference is a many-sided network of connections. We have moved from the rhetorical forms of appeal for response by the addressees to theological questions about the affirmations of the text. Both questions about the community and the theological questions are referential questions. The selection of themes for discussion is not intended to prejudge the questions so penetratingly raised by recent studies about power conflicts between Paul and parts of the congregation (Castelli 1991), nor the questions about how fully Paul had appropriated the vision of an open community (Wire 1990). I do believe that Paul's vision of community is profound and searching, and that he was more self-critical than he is sometimes regarded as being. No doubt it is also true that he had learned a great deal from the Corinthians. But his vision was in many ways imperfect and needs the criticism that it is receiving.

Apart from this range of questions, it is my conviction that a fresh attention to reference will invigorate literary inquiries themselves, saving them from the threat of the 'terrible blandness' of much biblical literary criticism of which George Steiner complains (cited in Wilder 1991: 5).[6] Amos Wilder clearly saw how important the claim to refer to truth is:

> The final question as to any representation, phantasy, graph, emblem, rune or utterance is that of *reference*, referentiality, the ground of communication. But this test which older epochs have called 'truth' would set in motion again all the tropisms, all the impulses toward coherence and survival, of the species from the beginning, moral and cognitive as well as imaginative (Wilder 1980: 322).

Literary criticism has been liberating to New Testament studies by opening dimensions of meaning that were obscured by the narrowly historical approach that dominated the discipline for so long. We are called to strengthen this expanded sense of meaning by a bold yet critical recovery of the traditional conviction that the text and its interpretation deal with the truth and reality of a world of value that can, however imperfectly, be known.

## BIBLIOGRAPHY

Abrams, M.H.
    1953        *The Mirror and the Lamp: Romantic Theory and the Critical Tradition*
                (London: Oxford University Press).
Aichele, George and Tina Pippin (eds.)
    1992        *Semeia 60: Fantasy and the Bible.*
Alter, Robert and Frank Kermode (eds.)
    1987        *The Literary Guide to the Bible* (Cambridge, MA: Harvard University
                Press).
Barth, Karl
    1933        *The Resurrection of the Dead* (trans. H.J. Stenning; New York: Revell).
Beardslee, William A.
    1972        *A House for Hope: A Study in Process and Biblical Thought*
                (Philadelphia: Westminster Press).
    1990a       'Stories in the Postmodern World', in David Ray Griffin (ed.), *Sacred
                Interconnections* (Albany: State University of New York Press): 163-
                75.
    1990b       Review of *Recovery of the Measure*, by Robert Neville, *Process Studies*
                19: 138-40.
    1991        'Vital Ruins: Biblical Narrative and the Story Frameworks of our

---

6.    George Steiner was reviewing Alter and Kermode 1987 in *The New Yorker*, January 11, 1988.

Lives', in *Margins of Belonging: Essays on the New Testament and Theology* (Atlanta: Scholars Press): 219-36.

Bloch, Ernst

1980 *Atheism in the Bible: The Religion of Exodus and the Kingdom* (trans. J. Swann; New York: Herder & Herder).

1986 *The Principle of Hope* (trans. Neville Plaice, Stephen Plaice and Paul Knight; 3 vols.; Cambridge, MA: MIT Press).

Boers, Hendrikus

1994 *Justification of the Gentiles: Paul's Letters to the Galatians and to the Romans* (Peabody, MA: Hendrikson).

Bultmann, Rudolf

1958 'Karl Barth: Die Auferstehung der Toten', in *Glauben und Verstehen*, I (Tübingen: Vandenhoek & Ruprecht): 38-64.

1960 'The Historicity of Man and Faith', in *Existence and Faith: Shorter Writings of Rudolf Bultmann* (ed. Schubert M. Ogden; New York: Meridian): 92-110.

Castelli, Elizabeth A.

1991 *Imitating Paul: A Discourse of Power* (Louisville: Westminster Press/John Knox).

Epperly, Bruce G.

1992 *At the Edges of Life: A Holistic Vision of the Human Adventure* (St Louis: Chalice Press).

Frei, Hans

1975 *The Identity of Jesus Christ: The Hermeneutical Bases of Dogmatic Theology* (Philadelphia: Fortress Press).

Kuck, David W.

1992 *Judgment and Community Conflict: Paul's Use of Apocalyptic Judgment Language in 1 Corinthians 3.5–4.5* (NovTSup, 66: Leiden: Brill.

Lategan, Bernard C. and Willem S. Vorster

1985 *Text and Reality: Aspects of Reference in Biblical Texts* (Semeia Studies; Philadelphia: Fortress Press; Atlanta: Scholars Press).

Lentriccia, Frank

1983 *Criticism and Social Change: With a Postscript by Kenneth Burke* (Chicago: University of Chicago Press).

Neville, Robert C.

1989 *Recovery of the Measure: Interpretation and Nature* (Albany: State University of New York Press).

Sanders, E.P.

1983 *Paul, the Law, and the Jewish People* (Philadelphia: Fortress Press).

Schweitzer, Albert

1968 *The Quest of the Historical Jesus: A Critical Study of its Progress from Reimarus to Wrede* (trans. W. Montgomery; introduced by James M. Robinson; New York: Macmillan).

Schüssler Fiorenza, Elisabeth

1985 *The Book of Revelation: Justice and Judgment* (Philadelphia: Fortress Press).

Talbert, Charles H.
    1992        *Reading Corinthians: A Literary and Theological Commentary on
                1 and 2 Corinthians* (New York: Crossroad).
Todorov, Tzvetan
    1973        *The Fantastic: A Structural Approach to a Literary Genre* (Cleveland:
                Case Western Reserve University Press).
Wilder, Amos N.
    1980        'Post-Modern Reality and the Problem of Meaning', *Man and World*
                13: 303-23.
    1991        *The Bible and the Literary Critic* (Minneapolis: Fortress Press).
Wire, Antoinette Clark
    1990        *The Corinthian Women Prophets: A Reconstruction through Paul's
                Rhetoric* (Minneapolis: Fortress Press).
Zipes, Jack
    1992        'The Messianic Power of Fantasy in the Bible', *Semeia* 60: 7-22.

# INDEXES

## INDEX OF REFERENCES

### OLD TESTAMENT

NEW TESTAMENT